The
Advertising
Business

The Advertising Business

Operations
Creativity
Media Planning
Integrated Communications

EDITED BY

JOHN PHILIP JONES

SAGE Publications
International Educational and Professional Publisher
Thousand Oaks   London   New Delhi

For information:

SAGE Publications, Inc.
2455 Teller Road
Thousand Oaks, California 91320
E-mail: order@sagepub.com

SAGE Publications Ltd.
6 Bonhill Street
London EC2A 4PU
United Kingdom

SAGE Publications India Pvt. Ltd.
M-32 Market
Greater Kailash I
New Delhi 110048 India

Printed in the United States of America

Library of Congress Cataloging-in-Publication Data

Main entry under title:

The advertising business: Operations, creativity, media planning, integrated communications /edited by John Philip Jones.
    p. cm.
Includes bibliographical references and index.
ISBN 0-7619-1238-X (acid-free paper)
ISBN 0-7619-1239-8 (pbk.: acid-free paper)
    1. Advertising—United States. 2. Advertising. I. Jones, John Philip.
    HF5813.U6 A635 1999
    659.1—ddc21   98-40120

    00   01   02   03   04   05   8   7   6   5   4   3

Acquiring Editor:	Harry M. Briggs
Production Editor:	Astrid Virding
Typesetter/Designer:	Danielle Dillahunt
Indexer:	Will Ragsdale
Cover Designer:	Ravi Balasuriya

This series of handbooks is dedicated to David Ogilvy.

While you are responsible to your clients for sales results, you are also responsible to consumers for the kind of advertising you bring into their homes.

—David Ogilvy, 1968
(from an internal Ogilvy & Mather document)

Contents

Part II
Creative Aspects

Part III
Media Aspects

Part IV
Sales Promotions and Specialist Media

Part V
Legislation and Ethics

1

Introduction

The Advertising Business

John Philip Jones

This handbook is the second of five separate volumes devoted to best advertising practices.

This book is concerned essentially with the work of advertising agencies, and it is in five parts. The first describes the main operational functions of these organizations. Part II concentrates on the creative process; Part III on the strategy and tactics of media selection. Part IV is devoted to sales promotions and specialist media, and in particular the rapidly expanding field of integrated marketing communications (IMC). The final part comprises two chapters on the legal and ethical aspects of advertising, and is included as a response to the quotation from David Ogilvy that prefaces this work.

1

All of the books in this series are aimed at businesspeople in all countries who are involved with or interested in advertising. Most of these men and women will work for advertising agencies and for advertiser and media organizations. The series is also suited for universities in which instruction concentrates on the realities of contemporary professional practice.

These books are composed of separate contributions written by different people, and all of the chapters are focused in such a way that each volume provides a reasonably comprehensive review of its subject. The authors are specialists in their fields; most are well-known, and a number have worldwide reputations.

This volume is the work of 38 authors: 23 Americans and 15 international authors (most of whom either work or have worked in the United States). Among them, 25 are practitioners and 13 are academics (many with significant experience in the professional world).

As mentioned, this volume is devoted to procedures and operations, which are mainly the concern of advertising agencies. But before I address the size and shape of the agency business in this introduction, I will review briefly the economic scope of the advertising enterprise in general and advertisers in particular—the organizations whose budgets provide the driving force for advertising itself and for the media in which advertising appears.

How Much Money Is Spent on Advertising?

Soundly based estimates of advertising expenditure in the United States are produced every year by Robert Coen of the advertising agency McCann-Erickson. These estimates appear in the weekly journal *Advertising Age,* figures for any given year being published in May of the following year. I shall start with data relating to 1997. The McCann-Erickson estimates began in 1948, so that we can later in this chapter look back over 50 years, a period long enough to reveal trends.

The McCann-Erickson data give details on the five main advertising media as well as a number of other expenditures—advertising in farm publications, Yellow Pages, business papers, direct mail, and also a large miscellaneous category. The analyses that follow concentrate on the most important data for the purposes of this volume: advertising in the main media, which constitutes

TABLE 1.1 U.S. Advertising Volume, 1997 ($ million)

	$	%
Main media	110,956	
Other media etc.	76,573	
Grand total	187,529	
Main media		
Newspapers	41,670	37.6
Magazines	9,821	8.9
Television	44,519	40.1
Radio	13,491	12.1
Outdoor	1,455	1.3
Total	110,956	100.0

SOURCE: Reprinted with permission from the May 18, 1998, issue of *Advertising Age.* Copyright Crain Communications Inc., 1998.

about 60% of McCann-Erickson's totals for each year. Table 1.1 presents the basic data for 1997.

Similar estimates are made by local organizations in most other major countries, but these are in many cases less reliable than the American figures. In round terms, the United States accounts for about 40% of the media advertising expenditure in the world as a whole. This high proportion of world expenditure is underscored by the generally high level of sophistication of American advertising practice. However, in this the United States is not quite in a class of its own. Many European countries also use advanced techniques, some of which were indeed pioneered in Europe.

The years 1995, 1996, and 1997 constituted a period of growth. American advertising reacted positively to the improvement in business conditions after the industry's less happy experience during the early 1990s. However, taking a long view, aggregate advertising expenditure cannot be expected to change very much year by year, as can be seen in Table 1.2, which reviews the whole 50-year period covered by the McCann-Erickson figures. In order to compensate for cost inflation, the main media expenditure for each year is calculated at a percentage of the gross national product (GNP).

Table 1.2 also indicates the state of the economy in each year. *Growth* means an increase of 3% or more in GNP per capita measured in real terms (i.e., corrected for inflation). *Recession* means any decline in real GNP per capita. In the years that have no indication for either growth or recession, the real GNP per capita

TABLE 1.2 Main Media Advertising as Share of GNP

1948	1.15		1973	1.20	growth
1949	1.25	recession	1974	1.17	recession
1950	1.24	growth	1975	1.14	recession
1951	1.18	growth	1976	1.24	growth
1952	1.24		1977	1.26	growth
1953	1.28		1978	1.30	growth
1954	1.34	recession	1979	1.25	
1955	1.39	growth	1980	1.23	recession
1956	1.42		1981	1.24	
1957	1.39	recession	1982	1.30	recession
1958	1.38	recession	1983	1.39	
1959	1.39	growth	1984	1.45	growth
1960	1.41		1985	1.46	
1961	1.34		1986	1.48	
1962	1.33	growth	1987	1.48	
1963	1.32		1988	1.48	
1964	1.35	growth	1989	1.44	
1965	1.35	growth	1990	1.41	
1966	1.35	growth	1991	1.27	recession
1967	1.30		1992	1.24	
1968	1.29	growth	1993	1.24	
1969	1.30		1994	1.27	
1970	1.24	recession	1995	1.31	
1971	1.21		1996	1.33	
1972	1.24	growth	1997	1.37	growth

SOURCE: Data published by *Advertising Age* and U.S. Department of Commerce, Bureau of the Census. Reprinted with permission from *Advertising Age,* various dates. Copyright Crain Communications Inc., 1998.

grew very modestly (i.e., less than 3%). The current level of expenditure on advertising in the United States averages about $400 per capita.

Table 1.2 shows three things. First, *advertising's share of the GNP is pretty stable year by year.* The average share is 1.31%. During 42 of the 50 years, the share in each year was within 10% of the average (i.e., in the range 1.44% to 1.18%). There is no sign of any long-term increase or decrease in advertising when shares are measured in real terms.

Second, *there are cyclical movements, but the cycles are of unequal length.* During each cycle, there is an underlying but not very strong relationship between advertising expenditure and the pace and direction of economic activity. The 50 years we are looking at reveal four cycles:

- *1948-1969* (22 years): The long period of prosperity that followed World War II saw good times for the advertising industry. Advertising's share of the GNP grew gradually from an average of 1.21% during the end of the 1940s, reached 1.41% in 1960, and eventually settled down at 1.30% during the last 3 years, 1967-1969. During this whole span of 22 years, the balance of economic activity was strongly tipped toward growth, with 9 years of strong growth and 9 years of weak growth, with only 4 years of recession.
- *1970-1981* (12 years): This period covered the economically troubled 1970s. Advertising through these 12 years averaged 1.23% (comparable to the level at the beginning of the post-World War II boom). During the 1970-1981 period a third of the years were recessionary.
- *1982-1990* (9 years): These were the years of strongest increase in advertising since World War II, with advertising's share of the GNP averaging 1.38% during 1982-1984 and growing to 1.44% during 1988-1990. During this period of 9 years there was only a single year of recession. The GNP growth was continuous, although not at a particularly high rate.

  There is a mathematical phenomenon that one must bear in mind in interpreting these figures. As any statistical volume increases (in this case income per head, of which advertising represents a part), a single percentage point of growth represents an increasing boost in volume when this is measured in absolute terms; an equal increase in volume will represent a declining percentage increase. In later years absolute increases may be just as great as during earlier periods, yet the increases appear to be growing smaller and smaller in percentage terms. What matters in wealth creation are the absolutes and not the percentages, which means that the 1980s were fairly prosperous. The steady growth in the absolute figures and some catching up from the stagnant 1970s are the forces that drove advertising upward during the 1980s.
- *1991-1997* (7 years): During these 7 years advertising first fell, then rose to its long-term normal level of 1.31% and beyond. As a share of the GNP, the business returned to the level of the 1960s, although the 1995 level of 1.37%, applied to today's large GNP, represents much more advertising expenditure than the same figure applied to the much lower GNP of the period 30 years ago.

The third observation that may be made from Table 1.2 is that *the data suggest that budgetary planning is largely based on historical precedent.* Aggregate figures such as those discussed here are the end products of countless numbers of expenditure decisions made by individual manufacturers. It is remarkable that the ups and downs of such decisions should produce in the end so little change at the macro level when the data are measured in real terms. The most likely reason for this is that the methods of setting individual advertising budgets have become programmed and essentially routine. They are generally calculated as a share of sales value, so that they rise with inflation. In addition, good economic conditions tend to push budgets up a bit, whereas bad economic conditions depress them slightly.

Most advertised brands have histories, sometimes long ones, and their future advertising appropriations are determined to a large degree by what they have been in the past. Advertising is regarded on the whole as a cost of doing business—nothing more and nothing less. A point of particular importance is that since most consumer goods categories show no growth, it is not surprising that advertising expenditure is also stable. Advertisers who use advertising as an opportunistic tool to upset the conditions of the marketplace are extremely rare. However, it is not impossible that the future of the business will lie in the hands of such advertisers. This is a point to which I shall return at the end of this chapter.

Table 1.1 shows how the total media advertising in 1997 was broken down into the five media groups. Table 1.3 demonstrates how these proportions have changed over the past 20 years. What is clear from Table 1.3 is that although the pace of annual change has been gradual, there has been a clear trend toward the audiovisual media (up from 40.9% to 52.2%) and away from the print media (down from 57.5% to 46.5%). Television expenditures surpassed newspaper expenditures—irreversibly—in 1995. This movement, which still continues, is having a predictable impact on the advertising agency business, notably on the volume of creative work developed for television.

Television has fragmented, however. In 1978, television advertising budgets were spent on airtime on the original three networks and in spot advertising on the large number of regional television stations. For 1997, the data cover four networks, as Fox has joined ABC, CBS, and NBC. In addition, cable stations, growing strongly, accounted for $7.6 billion (6.9% of all advertising) and syndication was responsible for $2.4 billion (2.2% of the total) in 1997. (For discussion of these two media vehicles, see Webster, Chapter 29, and Rosen, York, and Ku, Chapter 30, this volume).

Table 1.3 makes no mention of Internet advertising. The best estimate of 1997 advertising expenditure on the Internet shows a figure of about $900 million, a sum too small for inclusion in the national advertising figures. However, there is considerable optimism in advertising circles about the rate of growth and advertising potential of this medium, although it is a potential as yet unrealized (see Briggs, Chapter 34, this volume).

TABLE 1.3 U.S. Main Media Volume (in percentages), Analyzed by Media Groups

	1978	*1997*
Total	100.0	100.0
Newspapers	43.5	37.6
Magazines	14.0	8.9
Television	30.8	40.1
Radio	10.1	12.1
Outdoor	1.6	1.3

SOURCE: Reprinted with permission from *Advertising Age,* various dates. Copyright Crain Communications Inc., 1998.

Advertisers

As common sense would lead us to expect, the range of advertisers' expenditures is extremely wide: from more than $1.5 billion for advertisers at the top end to about $5 million at the bottom end for national names, and with regional or local advertisers, expenditures that dwindle to a few thousand dollars.

The 20 largest names in the field are listed in Table 1.4, which shows the degree to which the advertising business is fragmented. Among the 20 names, only 4 individually account for as much as 1% to 2% of the total spent by all advertisers in the United States. The top 20 together account for only 14%. The relatively small size of even the largest advertisers restricts the degree to which advertisers are able to dominate the media in the sense that individual advertisers can supposedly dictate editorial policy. But advertisers can influence the price of advertising time and space; the practiced negotiators working for certain large advertisers can exercise leverage on individual television stations as well as print publications and receive favorable rates.

The top 20 advertisers include 6 manufacturers of repeat-purchase packaged goods—8 if we include fast food, which can broadly be considered in this category. The total billing of these 8 names is $6.5 billion, or 43% of the aggregate expenditure by the top 20. Packaged goods therefore represents the largest category among the major advertisers. However, during the early 1960s, the proportion was approximately 70%, which means that although the annual change has been slow, the relative decline in packaged goods advertising represents a very real long-term trend. This helps us to understand certain other advertising movements, notably the evolution of creative styles.

TABLE 1.4 Top 20 U.S. Advertisers by Expenditure in Main Media, 1996

Rank	Advertiser	Expenditure ($ million) %	Audiovisual %	Print %	Other %
1	General Motors Corp.	1,739 = 100	64	33	3
2	Procter & Gamble Co.	1,521 = 100	80	20	—[a]
3	Philip Morris Cos.	1,237 = 100	64	30	6
4	Chrysler Corp.	1,109 = 100	68	30	2
5	Ford Motor Co.	915 = 100	59	39	2
6	Johnson & Johnson	842 = 100	79	21	—[a]
7	PepsiCo	774 = 100	96	2	2
8	Walt Disney Co.	773 = 100	72	27	1
9	Time Warner	747 = 100	60	40	—[a]
10	AT&T Corp.	672 = 100	77	21	2
11	Sears, Roebuck & Co.	613 = 100	59	37	4
12	McDonald's Corp.	599 = 100	96	1	3
13	Unilever NV	593 = 100	79	21	—[a]
14	Toyota Motor Corp.	560 = 100	73	27	1
15	Grand Metropolitan	553 = 100	90	9	1
16	Nissan Motor Co.	439 = 100	79	21	—[a]
17	Viacom	426 = 100	74	25	1
18	Sony Corp.	418 = 100	61	39	—[a]
19	Kellogg Co.	410 = 100	98	2	—[a]
20	Federated Dept. Stores	405 = 100	12	88	—[a]

SOURCE: Reprinted with permission from the September 29, 1997, issue of *Advertising Age.* Copyright Crain Communications Inc., 1997.

Another important feature of the top 20 advertisers is that their media deployment is in nearly every case more heavily weighted toward the audiovisual media, in particular television, than is true for advertisers as a whole. This has a direct influence on the structure of large agencies, the ones who in the main handle the business of the top clients. The large agencies have been and continue to be almost exclusively focused on the development and screening of mass-market television advertising. This concentration has been a source of strength, but it has also imposed a rigidity that has hampered large agencies during recent years and opened the way to competition from talented and aggressive newcomers.

Most of the manufacturers and service organizations on the list of the 20 largest advertisers market brands that compete intensively with a limited number of brands from other organizations in the top 20 and also with some brands from smaller companies. This process, which economists describe as *oligopoly,* is a hyperintensive form of competition—hyperintensive because advertisers focus attention not only on their end consumers but also on their competitors. This is a process that tends to keep up the level of advertising expenditure, for a mix of aims: aggressive intentions to take business from competitors, but also defensive objectives, to protect the manufacturers' own brands from loss of business to opportunistic rivals.

Advertising Agencies

Advertising agencies are service businesses whose prosperity is totally determined by the prosperity of their clients, the advertisers. Large advertisers invariably employ a number of agencies, each handling different brands. This makes it relatively easy for advertisers to compare the performance of their agencies, which is one factor that contributes to the highly competitive nature of the advertising agency business.

The 1980s and 1990s saw the founding of a number of agency conglomerates. These groupings were set up with the aim of generating scale economies, to protect agency income from the problems of the marketplace. They were a delayed response to the lack of growth of advertising during the 1970s. Perhaps more important, they were an attempt to generate additional income in response to the downward pressure on agency income per million dollars of billing—a topic discussed by Said in Chapter 10 in this volume.

The major conglomerates are all international; their names and their volumes of business are listed in Table 1.5. The majority of these conglomerates are publicly owned companies. The component agencies within the overall groups are separately managed and thus operate theoretically in competition with one another. However, in all countries except Japan, it is virtually impossible for clients of an agency within a conglomerate group to permit other agencies within that group to handle their competitors' business. This situation is unlikely to change; indeed, it could get worse as conglomerates continue to acquire new agencies and expand their coverage geographically.

In one aspect of the business—media buying, where size of billings can be used as a lever to reduce media rates—the 1990s have seen a move for the various media elements of each conglomerate to be brought together and to operate in each case as a single unit. This movement was essentially a response

TABLE 1.5 Major Agency Conglomerates Ranked by Capitalized Billing, 1997

Rank	Organization	Headquarters	Capitalized Billing ($ billion)
1	Omnicom Group	New York	31.7
2	WPP Group	London	27.8
3	Interpublic Group of Cos.	New York	25.7
4	Dentsu	Tokyo	14.5
5	Young & Rubicam	New York	13.0
6	True North Communications	Chicago	10.8
7	Havas Advertising	Paris	7.8
8	MacManus Group	New York	7.7
9	Grey Advertising	New York	7.6
10	Saatchi & Saatchi	London	7.2

SOURCE: Reprinted with permission from the April 27, 1998, issue of *Advertising Age*. Copyright Crain Communications Inc., 1998.

to the growth of independent media specialists, which have made spectacular progress in many countries, especially in Europe.

The 20 largest individual agencies in the world are listed in Table 1.6. The billing volume shown for each agency represents its business excluding subsidiaries. The agencies listed in this table represent most of the great names in the advertising agency business. Most have strong historical roots, and they have virtually all at some time been led by, or at least strongly associated with, the most important pioneers in the agency business.

These organizations all have strong identities and cultures that they guard jealously. Paradoxically, however, they have more similarities than dissimilarities in their organization, planning procedures, and professional orientations. When, as often happens, agency people jump ship to join rival organizations, they generally have no difficulty at all in making the change from their old to their new agencies.

It is worth pointing out that in addition to the large agencies discussed in this chapter, there are in all countries much larger numbers of small agencies. These often produce work as striking and as effective as that of the large agencies. However, large agencies have greater resources and wider ranges of clients than do small agencies. This is the reason the special emphasis of this volume is on large agencies.

The largest organizations blossomed into full-service agencies during the 1920s and 1930s. However, it was only after World War II that this type of advertising agency became general in the United States. During the two decades following World War II, many of the most successful agencies became very

TABLE 1.6 Largest Individual Agencies Ranked by Worldwide Capitalized Billing, 1997

Rank	Agency	Conglomerate Parent	Capitalized Billing Worldwide ($ billion)	Capitalized Billing U.S. ($ billion)
1	Dentsu	Dentsu	14.5	0.2
2	Young & Rubicam	Young & Rubicam	13.0	5.9
3	McCann-Erickson	Interpublic	12.9	4.7
4	DDB Needham	Omnicom	11.7	6.3
5	BBDO	Omnicom	11.5	5.8
6	Ogilvy & Mather	WPP	8.8	3.1
7	J. Walter Thompson	WPP	8.0	3.1
8	Grey	Grey	7.6	3.6
9	Euro RSCG	Havas	7.1	2.4
10	Saatchi & Saatchi	Saatchi & Saatchi	7.1	3.1
11	D'Arcy Masius Benton & Bowles	MacManus	6.9	3.2
12	Hakuhodo	Hakuhodo	6.5	Below 0.1
13	Ammirati Puris Lintas	Interpublic	6.5	3.1
14	Bates	Cordiant	6.4	2.0
15	Leo Burnett	Leo Burnett	6.0	2.6
16	Foote Cone & Belding	True North	5.7	3.6
17	Publicis	Publicis	4.1	0.4
18	TBWA	Omnicom	4.0	1.9
19	Bozell	True North	3.1	2.3
20	Carlson	Carlson	2.3	1.6

SOURCE: Reprinted with permission from the April 27, 1998, issue of *Advertising Age*. Copyright Crain Communications Inc., 1998.

large, highly profitable, and rather complacent. They also became vulnerable to the competition of more freethinking newcomers. This helps to explain the emergence of two important changes that have taken place during the past 30 years. The first eventually affected virtually all agencies; the second has applied so far only to a small number of influential ones. The first change was a dramatically increased emphasis on the agencies' creative work, a movement that became known as the creative renaissance of the 1960s, pioneered by a cohort of outstanding creative thinkers from then-small agencies—David Ogilvy, William Bernbach, Jack Tinker, Mary Wells, and others. The second change, a phenomenon of the 1990s, has been the emergence of account planning (discussed by Staveley and O'Malley in Chapter 4, this volume).

However, despite the unquestionable importance of the evolution in the ways in which agencies operate, most of the largest organizations of 1997 were also the largest agencies 30 years ago. Their continued dominance of the advertising scene can best be explained by these agencies' strong and durable cultures, which have enabled them to absorb the changes that have taken place and to some extent to reduce the force of those changes.

I have mentioned the main underlying problem facing advertising agencies at present—sluggish growth due to the generally static nature of consumer goods markets, allied to downward pressure on agency income per million dollars of billing. I believe that the driving force to move the business forward must now come from the large agencies, who have the most to gain from a strong revival and the most to lose if the stagnation that has characterized so much recent history continues. The large agencies must demonstrate more dramatically than they have managed to do recently that advertising can indeed have a significant influence on their clients' brands; they must also demonstrate that they can develop systems that will help them achieve better track records, with more successes and fewer failures. Research tools are available to help the agencies in this endeavor. What is lacking, as usual, is leadership. The outstanding characteristic of the pioneers who built the advertising industry was a single-minded focus on *advertising*. This would not be a bad objective for the leaders of the industry today.

From my personal observation, many important clients are extremely anxious to improve the efficiency of their advertising—not surprising, considering the size of their budgets. A powerful rallying cry from the agencies is likely to receive support, both moral and financial, from the leaders of the advertiser community. But the initiative must come from the agencies, which are seen to be the guardians of advertising expertise. The agencies also have the most to gain from an improvement in advertising's fortunes.

A Note on the Measurement of Agency Size

Actual Billing

The size of an advertising agency is traditionally measured by the agency's turnover—the amount of advertising money that passes through its hands. This is the expenditure for which it generates the advertising. It is also in most circumstances the source of the agency's income—another sum used to measure agency size. The specific measure of an agency's advertising turnover is client billing, which is the aggregate expenditure by all of the agency's clients in any one year. In the case of a client that employs more than one agency, an agency includes only those brands whose advertising it handles completely, and ignores media buying done on behalf of other agencies (a system by which the agency operates as "agency of record" for that client).

The method of agency commission that was virtually universal until the 1960s provided agency income of 15% of the gross cost of all expenditures—money spent on advertising space and time, plus the relevant production. (The space/time commission was rebated by the media.) Because this system was standard throughout the industry, comparison of the sizes of different agencies was straightforward. Agency income was uniformly related to agency billing, and there were no anomalies, such as clients with high billings generating low agency income or vice versa. Agencies measured by billings appeared in the same rank order as if they were measured by income.

However, in the 1960s, methods of agency remuneration started to change. With some clients, agencies began to work on the basis of fees to cover time of staff plus profit, and commissions were rebated. With other clients, commissions were reduced below 15%, with some sliding scales. Still other clients began to use a combination of fees and commission. For certain types of ancillary services, such as package design and public relations, agencies had always charged fees, and many agencies had for a long time calculated and reported the capitalized (or equivalent) value of these. The system is now also applied to fee-based advertising work; I describe this in the following subsection.

Capitalized/Equivalent Billing

The amount of money that agencies receive in fees is income, in the same way that commission is income. In order to make a fair comparison between fee-based work and commission-based work, agencies now generally declare their aggregate income, no matter what its source. The fee element is then inflated or "grossed up" to represent what this would mean in advertising volume. Agencies include the actual billing of commission-based expenditure, and they add a multiple of fee income to bring it up to the level of billing this would represent if the fees were commission.

Where the ruling commission level is 15% of the gross cost of space, $15 million represents the commission on a billing of $100 million. Similarly, a fee of $15 million is "grossed up" to represent a capitalized (or equivalent) billing also of $100 million. In the latter case, the actual billing could be higher or lower than $100 million. Indeed, with ancillary services such as public relations, the fee alone often represents virtually the total billing—the client spends almost no additional money.

Standardization of Commission/Fee Levels

In some circumstances, agencies standardize their client billings at the level these would be if all the agency remuneration were at the traditional rate of 15% of gross space cost. They do this by applying varying formulas to the commissions/fees from different clients, depending on the actual commission percentages used by those clients.

This is not a difficult procedure. However, a comparison of the income and billing figures of American agencies shows that such standardization is not normal practice in the 1990s. The reason for this lack of standardization is that, because agencies now generally work with commissions below 15%, the procedure of standardizing billings on a 15% commission rate would cause the standardized billings to be below the actual billings. Thus the size of the business handled by agencies would appear to be reduced, and agencies are of course reluctant to allow such a notional deflation of their size because it would understate their importance in the marketplace.

Part I

How Agencies Operate

Agency Management

Some Secrets

Eric Mower

I began thinking about agency management early in my career. It was 1968, and I had only recently started work in an established but small retail advertising agency, where I replaced someone who left for a better job. There were four of us in all.

Those were the days before videocassette recorders, when television commercials were distributed on 16-millimeter film. Much of our business involved buying time on local television stations, adding local dealer tags to 30-second commercials produced by manufacturers (known as "factory-produced" ads), and running those spots in weekly "flights."

Nearly every business day, I left our office to view the factory-produced films at a local television station. Often I would go with client in tow, because clients, too, wanted to see what the films looked like. If they were acceptable, these local dealers would spend some of their hard-earned dollars on a media schedule partially paid for by "co-op" funds from the manufacturer.

After 8 months on the job, I proposed to my boss, the agency founder and owner, that we purchase a 16-millimeter projector for use in our office. I suggested that it would make me more productive, our clients feel more welcome, and our profitability more satisfying. His answer, one of the great non sequiturs of all time, was, "I never saw a desk make money." Actually, this was a comment he had used just 2 months earlier when I had asked for a conference table and chairs, so that our clients and others could visit our office and meet.

His mixed metaphor aside, I got the point: We were an ad agency, not a television station. Let the television stations spend their money on such things. My boss wanted to make money by maximizing revenue and avoiding expense. This was his view of managing an agency.

Over the next months our business was strong and I was persistent. I got my conference table with eight chairs, my 16-millimeter projector with folding screen, and a bonus slide projector. These early investments proved profitable. Staff time was saved, productivity improved, clients appreciated the convenience, and we looked more professional by holding meetings in our offices. It was, at the time, agency management as I knew it.

Now, 30 years later and with much agency management road behind me, hindsight allows for clarity and charity—clarity in order to recognize and comprehend the essentials of what it's all about and charity in order to embrace the human nature and unpredictability of everyday agency life.

From Survival to Growth

For a start, all businesses share certain commonalities. Among these are what I call the "four oarsmen" of business success: survival, liquidity, profit, and growth.

- Survival speaks for itself. Every living being is faced with issues of survival in routine threats to existence. In business, such threats can be as simple as overextending obligations or failing to fulfill a contract. Agency managers should never take survival for granted. Yet they often do. Many agencies risk their survival by allowing one or two clients to represent a dangerously high percentage of their volume. If those clients are lost, the agency may lose its life.

- Liquidity is the lifeblood of daily operations. It is the ability to meet payroll week in and week out, to pay the rent and the phone bills, reliably, with no duress or urgency. It is the ability to handle payables in a timely fashion so that work may go on. It is the ability to have adequate credit with banks, which expect regular payments on loans. The ability to spend and invest in those things that will improve the agency's service to clients, competitive strength, and grasp of opportunity all depends on liquidity. To be illiquid is to be disabled.

- Profit fertilizes business. Profit is to be shared with employees as reward for accomplishment and contribution. Profit is to be distributed to shareholders in return for investment, risk, and patience. Profit is to be reinvested in people, plant, proactivity. Profit is to be retained for additional cash resources. Profit is to reaffirm that the company's strategy is working and its operations are sound.

- Growth allows for self-renewal: new opportunities, new challenges, new skills, new people, new clients to replace those that are lost. Growth means additional volume to offset spending declines by existing clients; larger scope of work, greater scope of workers; and a way to keep moving forward, to avoid the staleness of being stationary. Growth reconfirms the good that clients already think of the agency. Growth revitalizes agency morale, making the conditions of employment even more promising. Growth provides a means to enlarge the agency portfolio. Finally, growth enhances the probabilities of success.

Management as a Five-Part Harmony

If survival, liquidity, profit, and growth are the essential characteristics of a healthy agency, five key components contribute to the agency's inner workings: strategy, operations, culture, work, and rewards.

Strategy

Strategy is, for ease of discussion, a reflection of what the agency intends to be all about, as well as how it will get to be that. Every business must have a strategy. Every strategy must have its strategists.

Strategy follows from a vision of the future. If an agency's management envisions growth, accomplishment, distinction, recognition, and rewards, all of these may be objectives. Strategy will be the path taken to meet these objectives and fulfill that vision. Strategy is the first tangible expression of what agency management expects to accomplish and how. It is also the earliest indication of management wisdom and competence.

But managing an ad agency or, for that matter, a public relations or sales promotion or direct marketing agency requires much more than vision and strategy. In addition to strategy, there are four other central elements of management reality: operations, culture, work, and rewards.

Operations

Much of everyday agency management pertains to operations, the business of revenues and expenses, cash flow and bank relations, management information systems, facilities and maintenance, equipment purchase and repair, payables and receivables, contracts and purchase orders, FICA and medical insurance, sales tax, employee manuals, payroll and profit-sharing program administration, tax returns, audits, postage meters, office supplies, and all else that has to do with the logistics of doing business, of surviving, of staying liquid, being profitable and growing.

These are the everyday operations in their most essential embodiment. Components of infrastructure and support common to nearly all businesses are only slightly different in the agency business. That is why virtually none of this is of any interest to clients. At best, these aspects of agency operations are of neutral value to clients, who take for granted smooth, competent business operations in the agency. Only when the work is overdue, over budget, or both; or a client audit finds sloppy accounting procedures; or the phone system is down for the third time in a week; or the computer software that supports the media department isn't supporting the media department—only then will a client take notice of how well the agency runs its business.

Just as crucial is the strength or weakness of operations in determining the load-bearing ability of the agency's foundation. The more an agency wishes to grow, the more important are its operations. Common sense suggests that fundamentally sound business operations and ethical business practices are prerequisites of agency success and therefore of successful agency management.

An agency can establish stable relationships with employees, suppliers, and clients only when the agency's well-being is not in doubt. When employees worry about there being adequate funds in the agency's bank account to cover their payroll checks, when suppliers no longer believe the check is in the mail, and when clients are reluctant to entrust their monies to the agency, the business is fundamentally in trouble.

For many agency managers, such basic business capability is not a problem. They have the knowledge, the skills, and the discipline required. Some other managers lack these resources, and they must be provided by someone else within the agency organization. It is imperative that senior agency managers vest the business operations in those who have the operational competence and ethical behavior necessary to execute the functions well. To do otherwise is folly that invites failure.

It is not unusual to see agencies being managed by the wrong people— founders who would be better off delegating, creative people who would be better off creating, account managers whose time would be better spent with clients. Truly effective agency managers are comfortable in their role, and everyone else is comfortable with them. Employees and clients alike validate management actions through renewed commitment and enthusiasm.

The underlying ethics and judgment of agency management are made tangible in the very acts of assigning business responsibilities to individuals. Issues of competence over position, collaboration over authority, fair play and honesty over fast-buck, quick-fix, whatever-it-takes solutions all signal to those observing just what kind of company this is and will be. In agency management, as in most else, character predicts destiny. Employees know fair from foul, smart from stupid. Those who will tolerate foul will never build a great agency. And those who find foul intolerable will leave for something better. As for stupid, the prospects speak for themselves.

If clients are often too forgiving of certain agency operations that fail to perform as they should, there can be no doubt that clients are the least forgiving when agency operations adversely affect the work and service expected and needed. Here clients see much, think more, and judge most. So much rides on agency performance that clients cannot have a passive attitude about the way in which the real work of the agency is delivered. Any disturbance in the development and execution of the work itself is reason for concern on the part of clients and always is. Missed deadlines. Over budget. Out of brief. Off-strategy. Not exciting. Not integrated. Not acceptable. Operations issues? Of course! But caused by mismanagement of the environment in which diverse agency people devote themselves to serving clients' interests.

Culture

I remember reading of an agency in the mid-1970s that had to call in psychologists because of hallway fistfights between account and creative people. That held my attention for a very long time, because my own agency also had some tensions between account and creative people—no physical confrontations, but plenty of anger and angst. I wondered about all this, and that wondering led me to a continuing vigilance and stewardship of corporate culture and all that contributes to it.

Undoubtedly, agency management is about creating effective new business presentations, negotiating favorable agency compensation, maximizing client retention, attaining creative excellence, exploiting new trends in technology, and optimizing billable time, among other things. But these are not the only concerns of management. There is a separate work dimension that is spiritual, cultural, environmental: the need to develop an organization's heart and soul—to foster an environment conducive to professional teamwork and personal accomplishment that can be measured in effective service to clients and an enthusiasm for the joys and sorrows of agency life.

If unsuccessful in creating such an environment, an agency manager will probably have an agency lacking in strong heart and true soul, and thus be facing a business life of unnecessary difficulty. If successful in this dimension, a manager could have an agency routinely renewed by everyday actions. In this dimension exist the real challenges of agency management—managing operations, policies, practices, and people in circumstances where unpredictable client relationships, uncontrollable business events, and uncertain employment ramifications create high levels of ambiguity, anxiety, and conflict.

Indeed, the agency business has become increasingly demanding and stressful as marketplace forces press client companies to expect more from and pay less to their agencies. Even though this increased level of difficulty is not only manageable by competent people but often welcomed as stimulating and beneficial, it still takes an unnecessary toll. Much of the burden borne each day by those working at every level of the agency organization comes as the result of management's inability to deal effectively with forces that buffet people, process, and, ultimately, individual and organizational performance.

What good is it to have some of the very best creative people if their creative energies are drained by never-ending skirmishes with account people over "what 'the client' really needs or wants"? What good is it to have higher levels of business volume each year if the percentage of agency income to volume continually declines and becomes too thin? What good is it to have some of the best account people if their strategic sensibilities are focused on how to keep constantly changing client management from holding another agency review? What good is it to recruit adroitly and aggressively if the agency is going to discourage and displace employees every time it needs to "right-size" in keeping with current business volumes?

In fact, how is it possible to create a culture and a workplace environment when so many people wonder so much of the time, "Where is this place going and why am I here?" In answering such questions, agency management will find answers in perspective. Change does create tension, but it also creates opportunity. Risk creates anxiety, but it also allows rewards. Both change and risk are omnipresent in the agency business and therefore unavoidable. So the trick is to spin gold from steel wool.

If the eternal question in the agency business concerns how to get and keep good clients, then isn't that what the agency manager wants to focus on? Isn't that what management wants to talk about? Isn't that what the agency wants to prepare for, work for, hope for? Isn't that what management should make part of the agency's vision? Its mission? Its reward? The answer to all of the above is yes!

Partnership, Excellence, Change, Integrity, Optimism, Success

An agency must predicate its organizational substance on a culture that provides understanding of and appreciation for the realities and necessities of the agency business. To do so requires open communication, full and reliable information, honest assessment, and management accessibility on a routine basis.

Agency employees need to experience real involvement, in order to feel themselves an important part of the business. Agency employees will gain understanding through information sharing, interpretation, and comprehension. Agency employees will declare commitment to the directions and actions taken by the agency through participation in the process of management, regardless of organizational level.

The degree to which open communications are successful will be influenced by other workplace factors that have long affected the agency business. Agencies survive, grow, and proper in direct relationship to the contributions of people. And those contributions must be made every day in relatively unstructured circumstances where ambiguity and anxiety take their toll.

Agency managers must focus their energies on stabilizing people who work every day in instability. Policies, procedures, and programs all must contribute to countering the negative aspects of the agency business and to optimizing the positive aspects. Failure to do so will result in talent depletion, client dissatisfaction, and business decline.

Unfortunately, all too many agency managers are unable to assemble the proper mix of people and performance to enable their agencies to get and keep good clients. Too many agencies routinely win new business on the strength of their presentations and then lose much of that new business on the weakness of their operations. Their losses result from a failure, in one way or another, to satisfy the needs and expectations of, first, employees and, then, clients on an everyday basis.

There are agencies that historically have been unable to keep their best people from leaving. In so doing, they have destabilized agency/client relations and disrupted agency operations. On both counts, inability to keep people and inability to keep clients, two requirements are at issue: values and competencies. Nearly every aspect of agency management—indeed, agency success—is linked to the values that make for an agency's ethos and the competencies that make for an agency's abilities.

Values and Competencies as Part of Culture

The concept of an agency's having values and competencies is not new. In advertising, in the 1950s, agency values were rooted in social relationships, shared history, school affiliation, homogeneous thinking, compatibility, conformity, and, above all, client comfort. As for competencies, those were the days when real advertising competency was relatively undeveloped. Very few had the skill sets in creative, media, production, sales promotion, direct marketing, public relations, marketing, and research that today we take for granted in any capable practitioner.

Clearly, different times have required and allowed for different types of skills and different levels of performance. Today, an agency's values and competencies are more decisive in its life and its management. And values today are far more demanding and telling. Employees want to see a corporate culture in which merit and fair play are real and tangible; where workplace advancement is predictable, comprehensible, and rational; where professional commitment and accomplishment are recognized and rewarded. Clients want to see a service relationship with an organization built for success from the ground up, where both process and product seek a level of excellence that will help clients to survive and prosper. And all employees and clients want to see an organization that is capable of embracing change in the marketplace, change in technology, and change in society and of turning those changes to advantage.

The Culture of Agency Recruitment

But what of the people, those who are invited to join the agency? Where does agency management come into play here? The answer is in what I call *natural selection* of an agency population and how managers identify the right people to work within their organizations. Certainly, not everyone is suited to the advertising agency business. Increasingly, agencies have become less and less hospitable to the faint of heart. The pace, the pressure, the competition, the uncertainty—all combine to make for an extremely demanding workplace.

Natural selection, or selection of those who by their very personalities are naturally suited to agency life, is key to populating an organization with professionals who haven't lost even before they have begun. In all too many agencies, much attention is paid to résumé and portfolio, with very little attention given to determining whether or not the prospective employee and the agency culture will make a good match—or, for that matter, whether the job candidate is really well suited to the advertising industry.

An agency must be true to its own self, and agency management must make that self uppermost in the consciousness of those who recruit and select new agency employees. If an organization prides itself on integrated communications services, why would it want to hire an award-winning art director who only wants to do television? No matter how many awards might be won, is it worth stultifying the culture by allowing for a creative caste system? And if an organization takes issues of harassment very seriously, why would it want to hire someone whose initial demeanor during the interviews was eyebrow-raising? No matter how much new business this prospect may attract, what is the signal being sent to every other employee? If an organization has prospered by satisfying client needs even under the most demanding of circumstances, why would it want to invite in someone who believes that great work is not done expeditiously? He or she may be right, but not for that cultural reality.

Natural selection is the logical pursuit of particular individuals by an agency management that has established competent business operations, ethical standards and practices, and an adaptive workplace environment and wants to populate that environment with professionals who will thrive in a common culture.

Work

And when those professionals thrive, so will their work. If, from an environmental perspective, the conditions for excellence of work and individual productivity are in direct relationship to agency culture and intelligent recruiting, what needs to be said about the work itself? Actually, many things could be said about the work: the role of research in determining advertising strategy and setting creative direction, the decision-making process in apportioning budget dollars for campaign expenditures, executional components for developing a complete campaign, the team process in uniting account, creative, production, and media in the overall work process. The list could be quite long, but there is one essential work-related topic that must be included in this too-brief chapter on agency management: integrated communications.

Integrated Communications

No matter what the type of agency—advertising, public relations, sales promotion, direct marketing, or collateral—the responsibility of agency management is undeniable when integrated communications are a goal. And they should be.

Historically, most agencies have caused the work process to skew decidedly toward advertising, with "below-the-line" services like public relations, direct marketing, sales promotion, and supporting/collateral material bringing up the rear. The reason for this advertising dominance is economic in origin and nature. Advertising agencies understand advertising best. It is what they do. It is also the least labor-intensive among the various communications services included in an integrated plan. Therefore it is the most profitable. Combine relatively low levels of labor with generous rates of income derived from media commission, and the result is a very favorable profit margin. This is a very tempting reason for agency management to focus on advertising to the exclusion of other communications modes.

This focus, however, is not in the best interests of clients, who correctly believe that integrated communications enhance their ability to compete in the marketplace. Clients also believe that most agencies are not committed to the effective provision of integrated services offerings. As a result, they choose to do the integrating themselves by working with a number of different providers.

Coincidentally, heightened recognition by agency managers of what their clients want comes at the same time that agencies are moving from commission-based to fee-based compensation. As media budgets have declined and client service expectations have not, agencies increasingly embrace service fees where compensation is based on total numbers of hours of work provided. As a result, many agencies are now rushing to offer integrated services, whereas in the past they were indifferent or resistant. This is both good and bad—good because clients may now be able to obtain from their agencies what they have wanted and needed for some time, and bad because the level of agency management commitment is often lacking to the point where implicit and explicit management attitude will sabotage the integration process.

Integrated communications offerings from an agency will succeed only when all the professional providers within the agency feel as though they are equals. Successful integration requires a collaborative—even collegial—workplace, where no single mode of communication is considered to be more desirable than another. Too often, advertising agencies do not accomplish this collegiality, even though they add other services, such as public relations or direct marketing, to their client offerings. For integrated communications to become a viable service capability, agency management must be committed in word and deed to such integration regardless of personal bent, economic considerations, or professional rivalries. (These issues are also discussed later in this volume by Said, Chapter 10; Schultz, Chapter 32; and Deighton, Chapter 33.)

Rewards

The fifth element in the formula that begins with strategy, operations, culture, and work relates to compensation: a reward system that captures the essence of the agency workplace and satisfies the needs and desires of the agency worker.

There are no easy answers here, but there are simple rules for those who wish to create an organizational culture in which compensation is a positive force. They must start with a salary system that is reasonably structured, with levels, ranges, job specifications, job descriptions, performance reviews, salary reviews, and honest application for all employees. There must be no special deals, no secret handshakes, no discrimination, no favoritism, no unfairness.

The same goes for benefits. Management must not create a caste system within the agency—no favoring television over print, no favoring advertising over direct marketing, and no giving "special perks" to "special people." Not today, not in this world. And the profits should be shared generously, but based on a balance of individual performance and group results. Management should recognize and reward extraordinary contributions by some while also recognizing and rewarding organizational success by all.

The best way to develop a beneficial compensation format is to make the process inclusive rather than exclusive. Depending upon the size of an agency, its management should recognize that the more people who are involved in establishing a reward system, the more who will be understanding and committed. No matter what, management should avoid unilateral, vest-pocket, authoritarian compensation setting. It won't be any more successful than unilateral, vest-pocket, authoritarian agency management.

The Five Secrets Summarized

Early in this chapter I indicated that there are five central elements of agency management: strategy, operations, culture, work, and rewards. No one of them is simple. No one of them is easy. But they are comprehensible, and they are always identifiable.

Those agencies that excel and succeed are the ones that have attended to their business through a routine—but highly competent—application of these basic principles. Factoring in hard work, common sense, persistence, honesty, and some good luck, successful agency management can be understood and described. But understanding and description are one thing—implementation is something else. Agency managers have to respond—perhaps more than executives in other organizations—to their day-to-day pressures and many conflicting priorities. Therefore the successful practice of my five central principles, with all the focus and disciplined diligence necessary, is not accomplished as easily as outside observers might think.

The Account Executive in an Advertising Agency

Jay Quinn

They go by many names: management supervisor, account manager, account supervisor, account director, account executive. But don't let the titles confuse you. Account service people, regardless of their titles, the sizes of their agencies, or their levels of responsibility, are expected by both their agencies and their clients to provide a consistent level of proactive, intuitive, high-quality account management.

This chapter covers how clients and agency heads define excellent account management and what it takes to be a successful account executive (AE). I approach this topic from the perspective of a well-established midsize agency.

In its simplest terms, the role of an account executive is to manage all advertising agency services conducted on behalf of a client. For an individual to do an effective job as an account manager, it is crucial that he or she recognize the inherent dual reality of the job. This duality is best illustrated by the well-worn axiom, "A good account person is the client's representative at the agency and the agency's representative at the client."

The Account Executive's Role— Within the Agency

Much like the conductor of an orchestra, an account executive must ensure that a large group of specialists are all playing the same music—on key, on time, in harmony, and with feeling.

Advertisers need advertising agencies for creativity and ideas, but if these "right brain" contributions aren't delivered on time, on budget, and on strategy (in classic "left brain" fashion), clients will quickly look for a new agency. Both clients and agency management look to account management staff to bring order and responsibility to agency work.

A successful account executive needs to master both the content and management style necessary to manage an effective team process. We will look at content issues first and management style issues second.

Understand the Situation, Isolate the Problem, Solve It

First and foremost, the account executive needs to be expert in understanding the marketing situation of the client. Using the familiar marketing tool of the "Four Ps," a good account person should have a well-rounded understanding of the client's business:

- *Product:* The AE should know the entire line as well as the discriminating benefits and selling niches of each individual product.
- *Price:* The AE should understand the client's pricing strategy and where the product or service fits in the price continuum of the marketplace. The AE should also be knowledgeable about the relative elasticity of pricing and sales in the category.
- *Promotion:* The AE should understand the advertising and promotional history of the brand as well as its successes and failures, and should be up-to-date on all competitive product positionings and their relevance to the marketplace.

- *Place (i.e., distribution):* The AE should be familiar with which channels (e.g., supermarket, drug, mass merchant, warehouse club, hardware store) are most successful at selling the product. What new delivery areas make sense? Catalog? Interactive? Is the geographic reach appropriate?

An understanding of these marketing concepts, as well as a full understanding of the target market, is crucial for the account executive. Current consumer knowledge probably gives the most insight. It provides important information an account person can pass on to the team at the agency. For both creative and media people, nothing is more important than an understanding of the attitudes and opinions of the client's customers. How do these customers feel about Brand X? Does it perform well? Is it worth the money? Are its consumers loyal, or are they easily swayed to a competitor? What kinds of lifestyles do they lead? What are their core values? These are all questions that can help the creative team make a connection between the product and its audience.

Generalist Versus Specialist

An account executive, in one view, is a generalist who represents or manages a group of specialists. These specialists include writers, art directors, media planners and buyers, production specialists, broadcast producers, graphic designers, researchers, public relations professionals, direct marketers, and sales promotion specialists. A good account executive is expected to have a working knowledge of all of these areas—not necessarily to be proficient at media buying or copywriting, for example, but to be able to distinguish among good, better, and great work.

Once an account executive can identify a strategy for solving a client's problem, he or she must be able to decide which members of the team and which disciplines would be best used to create solutions. Advertising is not always the best method for solving a marketing communication problem. It is the account executive's responsibility to determine whether or not sales promotion, direct marketing, or public relations would be better suited than advertising for a strategic solution. And if a mix of marketing inputs is preferable, a good account person will be able to create synergy from this combination.

The Briefing:
The Account Executive in High Profile

From a content standpoint, the most critical responsibility of an account person in the advertising process is to conduct the briefing. Simply put, bad briefings cause bad advertising and, ultimately, bad client relationships.

The briefing is the AE's opportunity to synthesize all the knowledge gained about the client's pricing, promotion, products, and distribution and create an effective advertising strategy. Following are the most important elements that any good briefing will contain:

1. *Product description:* What is the product being advertised and what makes it special? Why do consumers use the product and what causes them to make the purchase decision in the first place?

2. *Target audience analysis:* Who buys the product? Do they buy it for themselves or others? Is it a luxury or a necessity? A complete demographic and psychographic analysis of who makes up the target audience is important, not only for the creative team but for the media team as well.

3. *Budget:* This should include both a production budget and a media budget. The AE should be able to provide a responsible viewpoint on production budgets and media budgets and their comparative size.

4. *Time frame:* A critical path of key dates for initial internal presentations, client presentations, and media deadlines for materials should be spelled out at the outset.

5. *Advertising strategy:* In plain, unadorned language, the AE describes the distilled essentials of what must be communicated to a specific target audience. It is here that the account person can contribute most to a successful end product. (For more on advertising strategy, see Jones, Chapter 13, this volume.)

The Ideal Skill Set for Account Service

Many of us have taken various tests of personality and job aptitude in our lives, tests that tell us what our personal strengths and weaknesses are. In my experience, successful account executives exhibit the following skills:

- *Motivation:* In any group process, motivation is the key ingredient to energize and mobilize action. A good AE must have the ability to motivate team members to high levels of achievement, both qualitatively and quantitatively.

- *Communication:* Advertising is a communication business. An AE must be able to write and speak clearly. Persuasive presentations, clear briefings, and positive communications are all integral to establishing client confidence.
- *Innovation:* Clients don't want agencies simply to regurgitate their instructions. Agencies and their account staffs must consistently "bring something to the party." Whether it be a new service, an unanticipated idea, or a promotional concept that extends an advertising campaign, clients love to be surprised and are delighted by proactive thinking. Account people need to have the ability to spot opportunities and act on them creatively.
- *Organization/planning/control:* When leading a large, diverse group of professionals, strong logistical skills are necessary to make sure the process doesn't get out of control. The AE must be half traffic cop and half air traffic controller, so as to bring order to an often chaotic process.
- *Clear, unbiased thinking and evaluation:* Account people must be able to step back from their day-to-day service mentality to appraise honestly how the agency is doing. They must have the ability to ask themselves if the agency is doing all it can do for the client—Are there areas that can be improved on? Is the work as good as it can be? This ability constantly to "raise the bar" prevents malaise from ever setting in.

The Account Executive's Role— From the Client's Side

The leadership, organizational, and motivational skills that are so important for an account person inside the agency are less important when he or she is dealing with the client. An entirely different set of skills and personal qualities is needed to be successful outside the agency.

Salesmanship: Face Up to It—It's Necessary

It is common to hear account people disdain the notion of salesmanship. "We're professionals! We're consultants! We're advisers! We're not sales-people!" They are wrong. If you are in the business of representing your agency, and your agency sells its services and expertise to clients, then you are a salesperson. The AE must learn to be a good one.

Let's look at the qualities, strategies, and techniques that make for a successful salesperson and apply them to the advertising profession and the role of the account executive in dealing with the client.

- *Listening skills:* Clients hire advertising agencies for specific reasons. Seldom will an account person be given carte blanche to develop an advertising program in a vacuum. Clients have specific needs and wants when it comes to the type of advertising needed—its tone, its target, its content. If AEs practice careful listening skills, they can avoid missteps and miscommunication and bring their clients into the creative process rather than keep them on the outside.

- *Proactivity:* Whenever an agency gets caught in a routine of giving clients exactly what they asked for and nothing more, the countdown to losing the account has begun. One top-10 international agency has instilled a discipline in its account staff to bring one unsolicited new idea to each client at least once a month—a wonderful and valuable practice. Clients devalue order takers and yes-men (and I suppose this includes yes-women). They treasure account people who can avoid the obvious and solve problems ingeniously.

- *Ability to recognize opportunity:* A good salesperson, and a good AE, for that matter, can spot an opportunity for a sale. For example, in the advertising business, a typical client assignment might be to develop a consumer advertising campaign for a product. A good opportunistic thinker might suggest a brochure that would merchandise the campaign to the sales force as well as to trade audiences (i.e., retailers and others in the distributional chain). Another spin-off idea would be a publicity effort targeted toward both consumers and the trade to get extra mileage out of the campaign news. In this example, the account executive, in one fell swoop, has added to the effectiveness of the campaign, presented him- or herself as an "idea person," and earned more income for the agency.

- *"When in Rome":* When interacting with client personnel, good account people tend to "become" clients. Agency representatives should never come across as outsiders in front of their clients. They need to be seen as family, as trusted associates who understand the needs, the culture, the politics, and the zeitgeist of life on the client side. The one overarching goal for any account executive is to become a completely indispensable member of the client's marketing operation.

- *Ability to learn the client's business:* Agency representatives should work at their clients' retail locations. Pump their gas. Flip their hamburgers. Spend a day on their customer information hot lines. And by all means, use their products. Nothing shows agency commitment more than this kind of effort. In addition, it's the fastest way possible for the AE to understand the consumers' mind-set and point of view regarding the clients' products.

4

Account Planning

A BRITISH PERSPECTIVE

Nicholas Staveley

A ccount planning is an important advertising agency function that has been carried out in British agencies for more than a quarter century. Its focus is on the initial formation of advertising strategy and thereafter upon campaign development, through a closer understanding of the client's final customers or other target(s). First pioneered in the United Kingdom in the 1960s, it has gradually infiltrated agency practice in other countries, and is now quite widely applied throughout the developed world.

The application of account planning—and its importance relative to other functions—varies considerably from one agency to another. For instance, account planning should not be confused with the established discipline of media planning. Account planners may sometimes replace media planners altogether, but more often the relationship is complementary, and sometimes account planning is seen simply as a creative rather than a media influence.

The planners may be primarily researchers, or else generalists who in turn employ advertising researchers.

Whatever the exact role and status of account planners within an agency, their successful introduction involves radical changes in both the agency's philosophy (its attitudes, role, and client relationships) and its structure. These requirements explain why adoption of the system is not always successful, at least at the outset, and also why it has taken so long to become part of best practice in many present-day agencies.

Agency Philosophy

Conceptually, account planning emphasizes the importance of the target consumers: understanding them, finding advertising strategies that will best fulfill the client's marketing objectives in terms of attitudinal or behavioral response, and then evaluating the advertising developed on this basis, through pre- and post-testing, long-term tracking, and so on. Plainly, this consumer focus has to be shared by everyone in the agency, not just the planners who lead it.

Such a philosophy also marks out a somewhat changed relationship with the client. Instead of simply mirroring the client's marketing strategy and goals (usually expressed in terms of markets, volumes, brand shares, and revenue), the agency provides a complementary expertise—that directed at an intimate knowledge of the target group. This involves conducting a dialogue with consumers to understand better who they are, how advertising directed to them will work best, how they use it, and in which media, and, afterwards, how well it is doing once a campaign is up and running.

Agency Structure

Functionally, the agency must also change—not only in importing the new account planning skills (and absorbing their cost), but in redefining the relationships of everyone else involved in planning, making, and placing advertisements for its clients. Those particularly affected are the account handlers, the creative team, and (as noted above) the media people. Account directors, in particular, can find it hard to accept the apparent loss of their traditional leading role in planning; creative people may similarly distrust a powerful potential critic if they have no experience of the compensating practical help and understanding a good planner can provide.

The most common reasons account planning may fail to take root in a particular agency are (a) that it is arbitrarily added as a sort of "bolt-on" to the existing structure, with no allowance made for an adjustment of existing roles and (b) the recruitment (or internal reshuffle) of people without the skill or sensitivity to make good planners.

How It Began

The origin of account planning (and the use of this term to describe it) occurred at about the same time in the mid-1960s in two leading British advertising agencies, and was in each case the product of a dominant single thinker. The agencies were the J. Walter Thompson Company (JWT) London office and the then new, very small agency Boase Massimi Pollitt (BMP), now BMP DDB Needham, also in London. The two dominant personalities involved were JWT's Stephen King and Stanley Pollitt of BMP.

Apart from a shared emphasis on the consumer, the approaches of these two agencies were very different, representing two distinct ideologies. However, both were remarkably successful, and both have had profound influence on subsequent advertising practice. Inevitably, there has been some dispute about which came first and which was the better.

The important point is that the two events were independent of one another, although they had much in common, and that each led to the production of advertising of extraordinary quality. Nor did either King or Pollitt see the other as rival or copyist. It is therefore interesting to consider each approach separately, to illustrate the very great differences in the way account planning can be applied effectively. Moreover, the ideas then formulated remain vivid and relevant today.

The JWT Approach

In the 1960s, JWT was the largest agency in Britain and had already acquired a formidable reputation both for its creative work and for the intelligence of its people. It was also uniquely admired and trusted by its (typically very large) clients.

Not long before, it had introduced the "Thompson T-Plan," a consumer-oriented strategic planning system. Its points of emphasis were, first, improved definition of target groups and, second, the importance of considering advertising in terms of response, rather than message or input. Thus it identified the three principal classes of consumer responses that could be considered in advertising planning—responses from the senses, the mind, and the feelings.

Apparently simplistic, the T-Plan in fact emphasized the variability in the ways in which advertising works. It was perhaps the first model that recognized that advertising can work in many different ways, and that its success depends on the effects it causes, not on what it says.

King had also for some time been interested in the potential importance of single-source data—powerful new research sources using very large samples. These could combine longitudinal information about individual respondents' media consumption and product behavior as well as demographics and general attitudes. He explored this interest in tandem with the British Market Research Bureau, JWT's market research subsidiary, which later produced the world's first such study: the Target Group Index. British media research studies, notably the National Readership Survey, had already long been providing some product consumption information, to add important marketing insights to advertising agency media recommendations.

For all these reasons, the JWT version of account planning, which the agency introduced in 1967, had a strong media and single-source research flavor, powerfully underpinned by qualitative studies. The organizational methods employed are also of interest. Essentially, the agency created an intimate new three-person managing team for each of its accounts:

1. The *account director* (or other senior account handler), representing the client, the marketing strategy, and any political considerations—and also the administrative implementation of any decisions
2. The *creative group head,* representing both the "ideas factory" and creative implementation, such as TV production and art buying
3. The *account planner,* essentially representing the consumer, or target group, but also responsible for developing strategies, advertising research, and guiding media planning

The account planners replaced JWT's marketing department. Some account planners were recruited from the old marketing department, others from media, and still others from research. Overall, the new alignment seemed to make better sense of the agency's functions. One of the most interesting results was the harmony with which many of the new triumvirates worked, and how often they exchanged roles.

In all of this—the T-Plan, the alliance of media knowledge with marketing objectives, and creativity—King was greatly supported by the senior creative person in the agency, Jeremy Bullmore (author of Chapters 5 and 15 in this volume).

The BMP Approach

From 1965, Stanley Pollitt had been experimenting with similar ideas at an Interpublic agency, Pritchard Wood & Partners. But it was only when he and others launched a new agency of their own in 1968—Boase Massimi Pollitt— that these efforts came into full flower. Openly borrowing the term from JWT, Pollitt, too, called his new troops account planners.

The infant BMP was of course a very different environment from JWT London. It was tiny, British and not American owned, and had no international affiliations. But it also became sharply creative—shortly acquiring a formidable creative reputation thanks to John Webster, a talent recruited from the London Ogilvy agency—and had a burning desire to show that its creativity was both accountable and effective.

For these reasons, the new BMP planners were destined to be very much more advertising researchers and experimentalists, often engaged in conducting their own fieldwork. Pollitt was, moreover, especially exercised by the introduction of proprietary, quantitative pretesting methods, mostly imported from the United States. He saw these as destructive of truly effective advertising. They prescribed one or another single mechanistic view of how advertising works and imposed rigid norms (interest levels, preference shifts) without any proper dialogue with the consumer.

JWT, too, was alert to these problems, but its massive authority and intellectual status made them less of a preoccupation. For Pollitt's small elite, they were an appalling and immediate threat to the excellence he aimed for. Fortunately, an important BMP confectionery client—John Bartle of Cadbury—

shared and supported Pollitt's views, and enabled him to realize his particular vision of account planning.

Later Developments

The success of account planning at JWT and BMP became widely recognized by both clients and competitive agencies in Britain. The latter soon adopted and adapted the idea on a wide scale; by 1970, all major agencies in London had account planning systems in place.

The 1970s and 1980s were years of expansion for the British advertising business, despite a number of setbacks caused by a general economic malaise and by strikes in all industries, including the media. As agencies grew, account planning became an integral part of their being. Account planning was soon seen as an advertising discipline in its own right, and agencies began to recruit account planners fresh from universities (mostly liberal arts graduates) and to train them in-house. Account planners formed an influential association, the Account Planning Group, which was established to improve and otherwise develop professional practice in the field. This organization currently has more than 200 members.

The Institute of Practitioners in Advertising (IPA) encouraged the growth of account planning, and the IPA Advertising Effectiveness Awards are to a large degree based on the evaluation of campaign effectiveness made by account planners in British agencies. The Account Planning Group has published a handbook on the discipline, *How to Plan Advertising,* an anthology of papers written by the most prominent practitioners, describing the best work in the field.[1]

In Britain, account planning is an evolving discipline. The econometric analysis of advertising effects plays an increasingly important role in account planners' work. Many account planners are also engaged in expanding the frontiers of the research used for advertising development, including explorations of fields as wide-ranging as anthropology and symbiotics.

Account Planning

AN AMERICAN PERSPECTIVE

Damian O'Malley

In a 1992 booklet titled *What Every Account Executive Should Know About Account Planning,* the American Association of Advertising Agencies (AAAA) defines the account planner as follows:

> A planner is essentially the account team's primary contact with the outside world; the person who, through personal background, knowledge of all the pertinent information, and overall experience, is able to bring a strong consumer focus to all advertising decisions.[2]

This definition contains four key elements:

- Consumer focus
- Part of team
- All advertising decisions
- Planner not just planning

However, it leaves out how account planners do what they do. The best are great generalists who are able to take a complex mass of disparate information and make it coherent—in other words, they are able to see the forest, not just the trees.

Much of the account planner's information comes from market research, but an account planner is not simply a type of researcher. Researchers are principally concerned with measurement and analysis, whereas planners are more concerned with insight and synthesis. Research is about what has been and what is; account planning is about what will and could be.

Account planning detractors often argue that great advertising was produced before account planning was invented. This illustrates a very important point: The planning process predates the account planning discipline. Bill Bernbach and David Ogilvy, apart from being creative geniuses, were clearly both great "planners." As Ogilvy says in his book *Confessions of an Advertising Man*:

> I started my career with George Gallup at Princeton. When I started Ogilvy & Mather I wore two hats. On Thursdays and Fridays, I was the Research Director. On Mondays, Tuesdays and Wednesdays I was the Creative Director. As far as I know, I am the only creative genius who started his career in research.[3]

Bernbach often expressed the view that "at the heart of an effective creative philosophy is the belief that nothing is so powerful as an insight into human nature, what compulsions drive a man, what instincts dominate his action, even though his language so often camouflages what really motivates him." [4]

Far from being an argument against account planning, this is the strongest argument in favor of planning. Few agencies have access to "genius." The invention of account planning was a deliberate attempt by agencies to help creative people with the difficult task of identifying powerful human insights. The implementation of account planning is an organizational strategy to replace genius with a culture—to create a team with shared values concerning what constitutes good advertising and shared practices about how to make good ads. In fact, account planning is an early example of reengineering.

In the rest of this chapter, I cover the history of account planning in the United States, outline the issues facing account planning today, and end with a short discussion of the significance of account planning in American advertising.

A Short History of Account Planning
in the United States

The account planning discipline was invented in the United Kingdom in the 1960s. Originally there were two "schools" of planning, the Boase Massimi Pollitt (BMP) school and the J. Walter Thompson (JWT) school. JWT stood for brand marketing and quantitative methods, and BMP emphasized qualitative pretesting of rough creative work. The differences, always exaggerated, were once summed up famously and fatuously as "strategists" versus "ad tweakers."

Both agencies did well during the 1960s and 1970s, and their unique way of developing advertising, account planning, soon began to be widely copied. BMP, in particular, begat many new agencies in Britain that either included BMP planners as founders or else employed them to start planning departments, notably Abbott Mead Vickers, Gold Greenlees Trott, and later—the so-called third wave—Howell Henry Chaldecott Lury, Woollams Moira Gaskin O'Malley, and Butterfield Day Devito Hockney. Perhaps the most significant U.K. agency in the late 1980s and early 1990s, Bogle Bartle Hegarty, also included a planner—John Bartle—in its lineup. He was first exposed to account planning while a client of BMP at Cadbury Ltd.

The rise of account planning in the United Kingdom was associated with the flowering of U.K. creativity. For a while in the late 1970s and 1980s, the United Kingdom was unquestionably the world leader in advertising creativity, combining clever strategies and whimsical originality. Many of the campaigns lauded at the leading creative award-giving shows—Designers & Art Directors (D&AD), the One Show, and Cannes—also won medals in the IPA Advertising Effectiveness Awards, the world's most rigorous advertising competition. Over time, these awards have been dominated by BMP and JWT.

The pattern of great creative agencies experimenting with account planning, enjoying great critical and material success, and thus spawning copies that in turn spread the discipline has been repeated in most of its essentials in the United States.

The pioneer agency in the United States was Chiat/Day (now TBWA Chiat/Day, part of the Omnicom network). Jay Chiat was a frequent visitor to the United Kingdom and a great admirer of its advertising. He reflected on why U.K. advertising seemed to be better than U.S. advertising. The only clear difference he could see was account planning. He rightly rejected the idea that

U.K. advertising people were somehow more talented than their U.S. counterparts. With the vision and determination that are his hallmarks, Chiat decided to implement account planning in his agency.

In 1982 he hired Jane Newman to work in his New York office. Newman started her career as a planner at BMP and for the preceding few years had been working as an account executive at Needham Harper & Steers in Chicago. Thus she had a thorough grounding in account planning and an understanding of the workings of the U.S. advertising business. Newman in turn brought over many talented planners from the United Kingdom, including M. T. Rainey, Rob White, Nigel Carr, and Rosemary Ryan.

Chiat/Day was explosively successful in the 1980s. It was named "Agency of the Decade" by *Advertising Age*; created arguably the most influential commercial of all time, "1984," for Apple Computers; gained and lost business with legendary aplomb; and won both more Gold Lions at Cannes and more Grand Effies (advertising effectiveness awards) than any other agency at that time.

Chiat/Day was adored in the advertising industry, particularly by the smaller creative shops. Many copied the account planning innovation, often by hiring Chiat/Day planners or importing their own from the United Kingdom. Such agencies included Fallon McElligott, Wieden & Kennedy, and Goldberg Moser O'Neill (a Chiat/Day breakaway).

Account planning in the United States was given a significant impetus by the 1988 purchase of fledgling agency Goodby Berlin & Silverstein (GBS) by BMP. They are both now parts of Omnicom. Part of the reason GBS agreed to the purchase was the agency's interest in the account planning discipline. Jon Steel soon left BMP to start account planning at GBS, subsequently renamed Goodby Silverstein & Partners (GS&P), where he is now the general manager. GS&P has the largest account planning department for its size of any agency in the United States; in fact, it employs more account planners than account executives. It also has a stellar creative reputation based on work for Sega, Norwegian Cruise Lines, Polaroid, the California Milk Advisory Board, Isuzu, and many others. In 1994 it both dominated the Effie awards competition and was given a retrospective by the One Club for Art & Copy. It is perhaps the most admired American agency today.

These are the influences that have shaped the development of account planning in the United States. What is its current status? Based on my attendance at Account Planning Group conferences in the United States, it is clear that account planning has reached near orthodoxy on the West Coast, where Chiat/Day and GS&P have been most influential. On the East Coast, account planning is strong in many small and medium-sized agencies, such as Messner Vetere, Kirshenbaum and Bond, Mad Dogs, and Angotti Thomas Hedge. There have also been several start-ups in New York that have included account planners as principals, notably Weiss Whitten Stagliano, Merkley Newman Harty, and Berlin Cameron Doyle. In Adam Stagliano's words, "That's the best testament that we're beyond asking whether account planning will survive. . . . It's a given. It took too long, but today it's unquestionably considered a legitimate discipline within ad agencies." [5]

The one agency sector that has not yet fully embraced account planning is the classic, large American agency. I address the reasons for this in the next section.

Issues Facing Account Planning in the United States

In discussing the success of account planning in the United States, one has to be careful to distinguish between the success of the discipline itself and the success of the rhetoric about the discipline. As I have noted, the discipline has been hugely successful in small and medium-sized agencies, but with a few exceptions it has yet to penetrate into large U.S. agencies. The main exceptions are DDB Needham (part of the same network as BMP, TBWA Chiat/Day, and GS&P) and JWT.

The major reason, however, that account planning continues to be so interesting and controversial is that it is the only nontechnical change in the process whereby advertising is produced since Bill Bernbach put art directors and copywriters together as teams. The rhetoric has been so successful that every agency is forced to take a position on account planning. Some, like Saatchi & Saatchi, Bates Worldwide, and Ogilvy & Mather, claim to be implementing partial account planning; others, like McCann and Ammirati Puris Lintas, have their own "version" of planning; still others, like Young & Rubicam, are "assessing" account planning; and a fourth group that includes Leo Burnett and BBDO have argued that account planning has nothing to offer them.

In all these instances, account planning faces the same fundamental issue, that of "scale." The U.S. advertising market is roughly 10 times the size of the

U.K. advertising market. This difference in scale creates a number of important barriers to account planning that are particularly acute in large agencies: more quantitative business culture; large, entrenched, hierarchical, bureaucratic agency and client structures; and a shortage of skilled account planners.

New arrivals from the United Kingdom are always struck by the emphasis placed by U.S. clients and their agencies on quantification. This is most obvious in the continued widespread use of quantitative copy testing, a practice that has all but died out in the United Kingdom. Copy testing survives in the United States despite the logical and empirical arguments often ranged against it.

Some people have argued that the American culture is more quantitative than European culture, or that the differences stem from the different philosophical traditions of the two countries. Both of these observations may be true, but a more obvious distinction is the one of scale. Many U.S. clients are understandably reluctant to authorize or recommend to their superiors the expenditure of sometimes tens of millions of dollars based on, as they would see it, a few focus groups. They require reassurance that seems altogether more rigorous and "scientific." Numbers always give at least the illusion of precision.

Account planning stems from a radically different tradition, one that prizes understanding consumers rather than counting them and favors individualized models of advertising effect drawn from first principles over "black box" copy-testing techniques, no matter how impressive their sales literature. In the context of large clients in large agencies, account planners are often seen as irredeemably "warm and fuzzy."

This cultural barrier is compounded in large agencies by the agencies' sheer size. Nowhere in the world is advertising produced by such bureaucratic organizations as the large U.S. advertising agency (the obvious exception, Dentsu in Japan, is organized on principles very different from those of U.S. agencies). Size makes it very hard for such agencies to embrace change. Often, existing power bases and existing relationships are threatened, and, it is argued, the benefits of change are outweighed by the costs.

Even if the will to change is present, there is a shortage of skilled planners to effect change. This shortage is the key barrier facing the rapid and successful future growth of the discipline. Account planning cannot be sustained in the long term through the importing of U.K. account planners. To be thought of as truly successful, the U.S. advertising industry must create an indigenous planning culture. There are signs that this is happening. Several universities, including Northwestern, Syracuse, North Carolina, and Tennessee, are now aware of account planning and are beginning to incorporate some of its precepts into their courses. The AAAA has set up a training program for middle-ranking planners. The U.S. Account Planning Group incorporated formally in 1995 and, undoubtedly, training will be a major priority.

Much more training is critical if the United States is to avoid a backlash caused by the rhetoric of account planning outrunning the supply of excellent planners. The seeds of just such a backlash are already present. Recently in *One to One,* the bimonthly newsletter of the One Club for Art & Copy in New York, Tim Delaney of U.K. agency Leagas Delaney opined, "Back here in England, where all the trouble started, some of us have grown increasingly skeptical of planning in particular and research in general." He then went on to detail a number of supposed problems with account planning that were all either fallacious or caused by bad planners rather than account planning per se. Of course there are bad apples in all barrels; the challenge in the United States is to ensure that bad or inexperienced planners do not color overall perceptions of the discipline.

The Significance of Account Planning

As I have already noted, and unlike both their clients and suppliers, advertising agencies have not been used to regular reorganization. The instability of agency employment is notorious, but agency structures have remained constant and reassuringly familiar. Now, however, all agencies face what *Business Week* has called the "modern business dilemma—how to do more with less and do it better."

In fact, during the first years of the 1990s agencies faced the same scenario as most of their clients: falling sales, falling margins, and rising redundancies. Yet, with few exceptions, full-service advertising agencies did not take the opportunity to rethink fundamentally how they do business.

But too much has changed for a simple economic upturn to right all that is wrong with the advertising business. Agencies lost more than money in the years before the recent cyclical upturn; they also lost much of the influence, mystique, and prestige that once attached itself to Madison Avenue. Indeed, the two factors, influence and money, go hand in hand. The principles and practices of account planning point to better ways of both satisfying the fundamental needs of clients and reviving agency prestige.

As we move into the "information age," as businesses become "knowledge businesses," there will be an increasing need for synthesizers and generalists. Increased complexity tends to result in increased specialization—witness, for example, the degree of specialization now common in large media departments and independent media buying companies. If increasing information is not to lead to "paralysis by analysis," then we must have a cadre of people skilled at deciding out of all the possible options which is the best one to take. Account planning is the first example of an entire discipline recognizing the need to create this new type of person within advertising.

Account planners pioneer new ways of thinking about brands; for example, they have been a major voice in the debate about brand valuation in the United Kingdom. Their deep interest in brands naturally leads account planners to ponder a client's full portfolio of brands. Portfolio planning is a major contemporary concern, particularly for packaged goods clients. Account planning helps the agency to develop a consumer-driven point of view on how best to manage brand equity.

Account planners think long and hard about how consumers use commercial communication (not how it uses them). They believe that advertising can and does work in many different ways. More sophisticated models of communication will be essential in a future in which interactive media fundamentally challenge the two dominant assumptions of U.S. advertising: passive consumers and mass media.

Account planning brings novel ideas and novel kinds of people into the advertising business. The introduction of the account planning discipline to an agency signals an increased emphasis on understanding and fresh thinking. It communicates a desire by the agency to move on from knowledge, which is available to everyone, to unique insights likely to have demonstrable impacts on a client's business.

Undoubtedly the debate about the relevance of account planning in the United States will continue for some time. But, in truth, the discipline is already successful and well established because it is a better way to produce advertising. This is not to say that account planning is perfect; it is not, and it will change as it accommodates to a different advertising culture and adapts to the demands of greater scale. The real significance of account planning, however, may be that it can serve as a model for the development of the other "noncreative" disciplines within the American advertising agency. Perhaps soon we will have business account planners and media account planners alongside the "consumer" account planners of today.

Notes

Damian O'Malley is grateful for help from many professional colleagues, in particular Jane Newman and Adam Stagliano.

1. Don Cowley (ed.), *How to Plan Advertising* (London: Cassell, 1989).

2. American Association of Advertising Agencies, *What Every Account Executive Should Know About Account Planning* (New York: American Association of Advertising Agencies, 1992).

3. David Ogilvy, *Confessions of an Advertising Man* (New York: Atheneum, 1984).

4. Quoted in Denis Higgins (ed.), *The Art of Writing Advertisements: Conversations with William Bernbach, Leo Burnett, George Gribbin, David Ogilvy, Rosser Reeves* (Chicago: Advertising Publications, 1965).

5. Quoted in *Agency*, Fall 1994.

The Advertising
Creative Process

Jeremy Bullmore

There are a great many advertising and marketing case histories in the public domain, most of them extremely comprehensive. Mainly, they follow a familiar pattern. There is a detailed description of the nature and history of the market, the nature and history of the featured company and its competitors, the social and economic climate prevailing at the time, and the strengths and weaknesses of the brand in question. There is well-documented detail about consumer beliefs and misconceptions and a painstaking description of the thought processes that led to a final advertising brief. What the advertising is required to communicate, and to whom, is clinically identified and articulated. And then, almost without exception, the case history moves into fast-forward mode. It skips in less than a sentence from the brief to the idea, and then to the responses that the idea achieved. It is as if the case history for the legendary 1950s Hathaway shirt campaign had identified the need for the shirts to be seen to be upmarket, well-made, and masculine, to be followed immediately by an account of the success of the "Man in the Hathaway Shirt" advertisements.

What we most want to learn—so that we can do it, too, or do it more often—is how the idea happened. Yet how the idea happened is what we never get. It isn't quite coitus interruptus; it's more like the final chapter of a detective story in which the intuitive hero identifies the murderer as the bishop but declines to tell us how he worked it out. We don't challenge his contention—any more than we challenge the success of the "Man in the Hathaway Shirt" campaign. But it leaves us unsatisfied and no better informed for the future.

So we are faced with a curious fact. The feature that clients find most valuable in advertising agencies is their ability to think of things: new products, brand personalities, brand extensions, advertising ideas, new ways to reach people, new strategies. Yet you can read a million words about advertising agencies and never encounter a single sentence devoted to how they think of things.

You will learn about their processes and their proprietary methodologies and their systems for evaluation and their many successes. You will learn what they did *before* they had an idea, and you will learn what they did *after* they had an idea. But the one thing you will never learn is *how* they had an idea.

It will probably never be possible to retrieve and record just what happened in one person's mind at one point in time when an idea occurred. Even the mind itself may not know, and by the time the idea has been relayed, challenged, modified, and justified, the precise process of its generation will have gone forever. But this seems no reason to despair, to resign ourselves to an acceptance of magic moments, forever mysterious and never to be consciously replicated. There must be some value in the examination of the creative process, of the circumstances and contexts from which relevant ideas seem to emerge most frequently. There must be some help we can call upon from a world elsewhere.

The word *creative* is a dodgy one. It deflects the mind dangerously toward the fine arts—and advertising has nothing to do with the fine arts. It is true that some advertisements may be pleasing enough to be appreciated as art is appreciated. But that is rare, almost certainly accidental, and probably happens much later in the advertisement's life and has nothing to do with advertising's purpose.

It is the fact that advertising has a purpose in a way that art does not that makes references to the arts so foolish—and any expectation of relevant insight from them so futile. A far more useful source of help is the study of scientific methodology—and the processes, deliberate or accidental, that have led to scientific discovery; and there are few more instructive starting points than the familiar but little understood story of Archimedes and his bath.

The story, accurate I believe in essential fact but told with a degree of poetic latitude, goes like this. In 250 B.C. there lived a man called Hiero II, who was the Tyrant of Syracuse. His resident sage, problem solver, and creative consultant was called Archimedes.[1] One day, Hiero received an extravagant gift from a neighboring Tyrant, a man of whom Hiero had good reason to be suspicious. The gift in question was a crown of great and intricate beauty, purportedly made of the finest, purest gold. Hiero, however, had his doubts, so he called in his sage. He said to Archimedes: "This crown may indeed be pure gold or then again it might be—as I strongly suspect—an alloy. You have until a week from Wednesday to tell me which."

In the creation of a work of art, there is no problem to be solved (though creation may be inspired by the existence of a problem). In scientific thought and in the creation of advertising, there always is—either a problem to be solved or a task to be undertaken. The brief that Archimedes took would be familiar enough to advertising agency people, as would the existence of a deadline.

To fulfill that brief, Archimedes needed two pieces of information, two numbers: He needed to know the weight of the crown and he needed to know its volume. Establishing its weight presented no difficulty; the specific weight of pure gold was known fact. Establishing its volume was a different matter altogether. The only objects whose volume could be determined accurately were those whose dimensions were strictly geometrical. Hiero's crown was complicated, it was asymmetrical and intricately wrought. It defied conventional measurement completely.

There was, of course, an obvious solution available. Had Archimedes simply melted down the crown in a crucible of measurable dimensions, the precise volume of metal could have been established as soon as it cooled. It is likely, however, that Archimedes was quick to spot the snag: "Excuse me, Hiero. Good news, I'm happy to say. It is gold. Or to put it another way, it was gold. Had to boil it up, I'm afraid. Still, I cracked it."

He would have spent several sleepless nights. The problem never left him. It preoccupied him.

The days passed. Hiero would not have bothered to conceal his impatience. It is possible that Archimedes' contract was due for renewal. There was much talk of a new and younger sage in whom Hiero was rumored to have expressed interest. The deadline loomed. And then it was that Archimedes got into his bath.

Now, it is inconceivable that this was the first bath that Archimedes had ever taken. He must have taken many, perhaps one every day—probably as many as thousands in the course of his lifetime. So he must have noticed many, many times that when he lowered himself into a bath, the water level rose, and that when he got out again, the water level sank.

But this time, he not only noticed this phenomenon, he made an instant connection between the behavior of the water level and the problem that continued to occupy his mind. And that is when—and why—he cried, "Eureka!" He'd made an instant, intuitive, hypothetical connection between the phenomenon of the bathwater and the problem of the crown. And at once, he would have felt the need to test this instinct against hard logic.

I do not know how long this process took, but his sequence of thought must have gone something like this:

> My body, like Hiero's crown, is a complicated solid and I do not know its volume. But when I put it into water, the water level goes up, and the more of it I put in, the higher the level goes. There must, therefore, be a relationship between the volume of my body and the amount of water it replaces. If I could measure the water levels both before and after my total immersion, I would have measured the precise equivalent of my own volume. But I can't because my bath is not geometrical in shape, although there's no reason why it shouldn't be. So if I took a vessel of geometrical dimensions, half filled it with water, marked the level, totally submerged that bloody crown, marked the new level, and then calculated the cubic difference—then I would have determined the volume of the crown itself. And kept both my job and my self-respect.

No wonder he cried "Eureka!" It must have been a wonderful moment.

With only a little license, that is the true story of Archimedes. And, though the parallel is of course imperfect, it is instructive in a great many ways for those of us engaged in the rather more prosaic problem of trying to think up a new advertising campaign for, as it might be, canned pineapples.

Perhaps most important, it reminds us of the relationship of *problem* to *observation*. There was once a view that the purest form of observation was that conducted with an absolutely empty mind, one that was uncontaminated by prejudice or initial hypothesis. Indeed, there is the story of the well-educated person of the 19th century who recorded everything he observed, every day, during the full course of his adult life. And on his death, he left these observations to the British Museum, where they reside to this day. But they are of no value to anyone because they have no shape, were based on no hypotheses, and so made no new connections. Today, it is generally recognized that observation in the absence of hypothesis is likely to be valueless.

The hypothesis does not have to be sharply focused; it can exist in the form of a preoccupation or obsession. It means that all observation is colored by the occupying belief that everything observed, however randomly, is potentially relevant.

Preoccupation of this kind can come from many sources. There is a certain kind of driven, scientific mind that seems to provide its own obsessive stimulus. When Sir Isaac Newton was asked how he came upon his great discoveries, he replied, "I keep the subject constantly before me, till the first dawnings open slowly, little by little, into the full and clear light." But most of us will be more like Archimedes: We need some external stimulus, such as fear, greed, vanity, or open competition, to "keep the subject constantly before" us. We need a client and a deadline.

From the moment that Hiero set his challenge and imposed his deadline, Archimedes must have considered everything he observed at some level of consciousness for potential relevance. The phenomenon of the rising bathwater was not the only observation he made, nor was it a new one. It just happened to be the one that connected. Arthur Koestler calls this kind of collision "bisociation."

In essence, this process of invention is a kind of improvisation. If you want to feed birds in the winter and keep them safe from predatory cats, you might look in your attic to see if you've got a bird table. But if you set out to look for a bird table, you will look narrowly, screening out everything that isn't a bird table—and you may fail to find one. Yet if you look not for a bird table, but for something (or for some things) from which a bird feeder could be improvised, you will see a dozen possibilities. You will see and evaluate everything in your attic as you never have before—not for what it is, but for what, quite specifically, it might be. That is how Archimedes saw his bathwater.

I do not know how David Ogilvy and his team settled on an elegant man in a black eye patch for the Hathaway shirt campaign, but I would be prepared to bet that the process was not dissimilar to that of Archimedes. They had, rationally and sequentially, decided on the desired positioning: upmarket, male, well made. They then needed to find some (preferably nonverbal) stimulus that would evoke such responses in the minds of their audience. From that moment on, they would have subconsciously assessed everything they saw—in life and in the media—against this need. When they saw a man in an eye patch, it would not have been the first time they had ever seen a man in an eye patch; it was simply the first time they had seen one since they had been preoccupied by the problem.

Creative people in advertising agencies sometimes yearn for greater freedom, for release from what they see as the tyranny of the brief. But it is, of course, precisely this tyranny that provides the stimulus for invention—painful as it may seem at the time.[2] Ask a writer of fiction simply to write a story, and he may not know how to begin. Ask the same writer to write a story about (at random) an international terrorist and a tube of toothpaste, and he'll soon get started. (It may not be a very good story, but ideas do not have to be good to qualify as ideas.)

So the function of the brief is not just to ensure relevance; it is also to encourage original thinking. As Edward de Bono points out, unfettered minds tend to drift into familiar patterns of thought, as water will follow its own previous patterns through the sand. Only by building the equivalent of a dam will a new course be attempted. Indeed, one of the techniques for creative thinking that de Bono recommends is what he calls the *intermediate impossible*. For instance, you may be required to think of ways of maximizing returns on expensive commercial aircraft; the intermediate impossible is that the aircraft must never leave the ground. By consciously and artificially rejecting the obvious, at least initially, the mind is forced to explore original possibilities: the use of a Boeing 747 as an upmarket restaurant or launch venue for a new product, for example.

The next critical lesson from the story of Archimedes is the importance of distinguishing between the act of discovery and the act of justification. We still seem to believe that it is somehow not respectable to admit that an idea may materialize apparently spontaneously, and can be seen to hold good, to withstand analytic challenge, only in retrospect. Disparagingly, this process is called postrationalization, and we are taught that it is used only by people with little intellectual integrity.

But the truth of the matter is that the thought processes that lead to the first possibility of the discovery of an idea and the thought processes that then test its validity are almost totally different. The first is fast, intuitive, almost certainly in part subconscious, whereas the second is rational, rigorous, disciplined, and may be extremely slow. Once an idea has materialized, by whatever means, we then have to ask ourselves: Could I, theoretically, have arrived at this answer logically and sequentially? In the words of Edward de Bono, "It is sometimes necessary to get to the top of the mountain in order to discover the shortest way up."

Arguments between those who claim that the creative process is all about intuition and those who claim that it's all about deduction and hard slog are barren arguments. The creative process demands both, and we need to recognize and honor both. But marketing case histories, like scientific papers, seldom concede this truth. Because of the superstition that the only respectable scientific methodology is one that is relentlessly deductive and sequential, case histories and scientific papers consistently cheat. As the Nobel Prize winner Sir Peter Medawar has written, "Scientific papers in the form in which they are communicated to learned journals are notorious for misrepresenting the processes of thought that led to whatever discoveries they describe."

Advertising agencies and marketing directors should be just as notorious for exactly the same reason: The conclusions they reach may well be demonstrably valid, but they consistently misrepresent the processes of thought that led to them. It is as if Archimedes, restored to favor by Hiero and with the threat of early retirement lifted, had chosen to write up his discovery in the following manner:

> The task of ascertaining the volume of complicated solids has perplexed scientists for centuries. We approached the problem logically, objectively, and deductively. We reasoned that a solid object was no more nor less than the temporary formation of a liquid, as ice is to water. Theoretically, therefore, all that was required was a methodology allowing a solid to become a notional liquid for the purposes of measurement. Because volume by definition implies space occupied, it followed that space occupied within a liquid allowed for the measurement of the volume of liquid both before and after the total immersion of the object in question. The difference between the two, which for the purposes of this paper we shall denominate "displacement," therefore equaled the volume of the solid immersed. The only requirement thereafter was the choice of a vessel of the requisite size, and of a shape that was readily susceptible to conventional linear measurement.

Here, as in so many papers and case histories, the process of discovery has been totally falsified. In the interests of respectable rationality, the process of discovery has been tortured to match the process of justification.

There are those who think this doesn't matter. Why should it, as long as the discovery is valid, as long as the solution can be replicated and stands up to challenge? But of course it matters a great deal, because, in advertising as in science, the ambition is to be more inventive more often. To believe that the processes of discovery and the processes of justification are identical is to approach your next problem in a manner that makes it less likely to be solved. We need to remember all the time: That which leads us to form an opinion is only rarely that which justifies our holding it.

Within an advertising agency, the implications of all this for organization and leadership should be fairly self-evident. There is first the need to be clear about the precise function that the new advertising campaign is expected to perform, the equivalent of the need to measure the volume of a complicated solid. But by that I do not mean, "This advertising campaign is expected to increase sales." There should always be an intermediary stage on which the strategy is based, and the intermediary stage will itself be a hypothesis.

"It is our belief that if more people knew that this product exists/felt that this product is modern/realized that you can use this product for making cakes/learned that this airline goes to Bali, then more people would buy or buy more often." It is against this intermediary stage that the advertising will initially be judged. And it is this intermediary objective that must be clear and fixed in the minds of the creative group.

It is *not* the direct function of the advertising to increase sales. It is the direct function of the advertising to achieve changes in attitude or behavior— which, it is hypothesized, will then increase sales.

The task of thinking of the idea—of creating the stimuli—to effect such changes is usually then allocated to the creative people: the writers, art directors, and television specialists. And it is sometimes believed that the most efficient and thoughtful way of effecting the handover from strategy (What do we want to communicate?) to execution (How are we going to communicate it?) is the one-line brief. It is as if the creative mind is too tender and too intuitive to be burdened with information or engaged in deduction.

This is almost always a mistake. Even the best of briefs will be no more than an informed stab at something. It is often only in the search for a solution that the true nature of a problem will be revealed. And the chances of a brief being fully understood and accepted will be greatly enhanced if those left with the responsibility of meeting it have themselves been involved in its formulation.

Now is the time to go into nonrational mode. The objective is reasonably clear and has been accepted. The need has been articulated and transferred to the subconscious. Now add external stimuli, which must include a deadline, because only when external stimuli are applied will the creative people's awareness of the need become so obsessive that they will assess everything they observe or experience against it. The process of improvisation has begun.

Random exercises should be encouraged; logic-based objections to putative ideas should not. There will be muddle and confusion and despair and absurdity—but everything will have become potentially relevant.

And there will be many false starts, many nearly Eureka moments, because at this stage in the process, an important difference from the scientific process becomes evident. Whereas there may be more than one way to measure the volume of a complicated solid, and there may be many nontoxic antibacterial agents to be discovered, in the search for a new advertising campaign there is no limit at all to the number of potentially successful solutions. For this reason, Eureka moments in advertising lack the instant sharp certainty that so delighted Archimedes.

Archimedes, having tested his hypothesis and found it solid, could be satisfied that his responsibilities had been discharged. In advertising, when an idea materializes and withstands the subsequent beady scrutiny (Could we have arrived at this idea logically and sequentially?), the doubt remains: It may be a relevant idea, it may be a good idea, but is there a better idea? In the assessment of an advertising idea, there can be no fine certainties.

But it must, of course, be tested. By *tested,* I do not mean that it should be subjected to some mechanical black-box procedure, but that it should be probed and prodded. This is not a popular stage with the idea's parents. They do not like to see their fragile, newborn concept being challenged so brutally. But an advertising idea is not a work of art; it should be as functional as a forklift and robust enough to survive the most exacting of interrogations.

And here it can be helpful to remember Sir Karl Popper's parable of the swans and why, even in science, it is seldom possible to validate a hypothesis completely. Validation and invalidation, says Popper, are not symmetrical opposites; they are different in kind. For example, you may make an assumption that all swans are white. And you may spend the rest of your life observing swans, and every one of them may be white, but you can never say that you have validated your hypothesis. The best you can say is that with every white swan observed, you can entertain your hypothesis with a slightly higher level of confidence.

However, you have only to observe one black swan, and your hypothesis is dead. Unlike validation, invalidation is cruel, clean, unarguable, and immediate. There can be no argument about it.

As tempting as it undoubtedly is to persuade your client that your idea has been thoroughly validated, in truth it can't be. You can say only that the most conscientious attempts to invalidate it have so far failed and that the client can therefore entertain its adoption with increasing confidence. And in answer to the question "Are you sure there isn't an even better idea?" you can only say no, you never can be.

This whole process is known as the hypothetico-deductive method of scientific thought. In encapsulated form, what it says is this:

- We must make a clear distinction between discovery (or believed discovery) and proof or justification. The elementary act is having an idea, which must begin with a hypothesis. Techniques and pressures and preoccupation can help—but the process of having an idea is neither logical nor illogical; it is alogical. It is outside logic and cannot be made the subject of logical rules. For all that, the process is respectable, necessary, and part of demonstrable scientific methodology.

- Having been generated, ideas must be criticized and tested; we now switch back to logical, deductive mode. If we can invalidate in the light of observable phenomena (a black swan), we feed back, modify, or start again, but at the very least with a greater body of knowledge. The failure to invalidate does not imply validation.

In creating advertising, we need to be intuitive, instinctive, scared, and lucky. *And* we need to be rigorous, disciplined, logical, and deductive. Both kinds of mind and thought are required; the trick is to recognize which kind we need and when we need it.

Notes

1. The story of Archimedes and how it relates to the generation of advertising ideas was first told in Jeremy Bullmore, *Behind the Scenes in Advertising* (Henley-on-Thames, UK: NTC Publications, 1991), 141-152.

2. This point is also raised by an analyst with a marketing background in John Philip Jones, *How Much Is Enough? Getting the Most From Your Advertising Dollar* (New York: Simon & Schuster-Lexington, 1992), 126-127.

6

The Art Director

John L. Sellers

Ａll advertising agencies have one or more art directors; large agencies have substantial numbers. The primary responsibility of the art director (AD) is the planning and execution of the visual appearance of each element in an advertising campaign, print or television. Before ADs begin any creative work, they make sure they thoroughly understand the product or service being advertised, the objective of the advertising effort, and the target audience. This information usually comes from the research department, the account planning department, an account executive, or a creative director, depending on the size and structure of the agency. Good ADs intuitively understand what to do with that information.

An AD normally works with a copywriter, as a team, first to develop rough sketches of ideas (roughs), being careful to assure that the verbal and visual concepts complement each other, and that the mood and design of each sketch make the intent of the advertisement or commercial instantly apparent and intriguing to the reader or viewer who is the target audience. When the best sketches have been chosen, the AD develops more finished, full-size layouts and selects the headline and body typefaces, the illustrative medium (type, photography, illustration), colors, and so on. He or she then executes comprehensive drawings (comps) or storyboards, usually with felt-tip markers, but increasingly with computer-generated graphics, to approximate closely the look wanted in the finished pieces. When one or more of the comps have been approved by the creative director and the client, the AD chooses and hires either the photographers or illustrators he or she believes can most competently produce the image planned for a printed piece or the director who can best produce the mood and image desired in a commercial. The AD then supervises the execution of the image, usually participating in the selection of models or actors (talent) who will appear. In the choice of outside talent, the copywriter with whom the art director works also contributes an informed opinion. Many agencies also employ television producers who relieve the AD of the supervision of the film production.

Once the images are created, the AD supervises the assembly of the print advertisements, making sure each is the right dimensions, and that the agency intentions are accurately expressed in television productions. The actual assembly of print advertisements may be completed by an assistant art director, by the production department of the agency, or by the AD. For a commercial, the assembly is done by a television production house. Often, a particular print advertisement will appear in several publications of different sizes, formats, or proportions, and with different mechanical requirements. The same visual image may be destined for several different media, such as magazine ads, newspaper ads, billboards, television commercials, displays, and packages, and adjustments must be made to ensure that each piece is the precise size and proportion needed for the intended medium.

When the images are finally designed and assembled, and finally approved by the client (and often researched), the finished ads and commercials are turned over to the traffic department of the agency for distribution to the appropriate media. The traffic department works closely with the account executives and "polices" the work that goes through the agency.

An AD and a copywriter usually work as a team on specific accounts. This team is sometimes referred to as a marriage, because the AD and the copywriter are so dependent upon one another. If the image produced by the AD fails to attract the eye of the intended viewer, or if the copy is designed so that it is difficult to read, the copy, no matter how superb, will not be read. By the same token, a spectacularly attractive ad may suffer if the copy doesn't live up to the promise of the visual. A team that works well together will create a concept that is visually attractive, verbally compelling, persuasive, and memorable. The team's objective is to create a campaign that will leave the consumer saying, "I need that, now," by convincingly pointing out the brand's advantages or by using other techniques, such as humor or emotion.

Senior ADs in larger agencies often supervise several assistant ADs and normally report directly to an associate creative director. In smaller agencies, senior ADs report to the creative director (CD), who is responsible for the overall creative efforts for the agency's clients. When an AD has mastered the craft, he or she is ready to be promoted to senior AD. If the AD also becomes an excellent copywriter or critic of copy—and in particular demonstrates conceptual skills—he or she may be ready to be promoted to associate creative director and assume responsibilities for total campaign ideas.

A good AD is an artist with type and images. There are literally thousands of styles of lettering and typefaces available, for instance, each of which projects a slightly different mood or feeling. A good AD will develop an instinctive and automatic appreciation for the characteristics of each of those typefaces and an expertise in selecting the right one for each purpose intended.

Here is a parable that originated some time ago at J. Walter Thompson, London. The reader is invited to think of the appropriateness of type or lettering style for two different signs. One offers a service (flying lessons); the other offers a product (fresh eggs). A viewer would be likely to believe that the "fresh eggs" offered on a hand-scrawled sign, on perishable corrugated cardboard, with wet paint still running, would indeed be fresh. The "flying lessons" offered in Helvetica (a "no-nonsense" and precise type face) would probably be considered safe and trustworthy. Reverse the typefaces, however, and the consumer's response will change, with disastrous consequences. The egg sign would certainly look less believable—less fresh—when lettered in Helvetica. And it would be a desperate person indeed who would respond positively to a hand-scrawled sign on cardboard offering flying lessons.

This example is extreme, but it is true that different typefaces influence viewers in slightly varying ways. Some typefaces are more or less warm, honest, and friendly, whereas others are more or less cold, technical, and precise. Each has its perfect use, and one of the AD's jobs is to specify the typeface that will elicit the desired response from the consumer with whom the advertisement is trying to communicate.

The same holds true for the selection of photographic or illustrative styles. An outstanding AD, like an outstanding painter, seems to select the appropriate visual imagery for every audience and purpose effortlessly, whereas an inept or heavy-handed one invariably produces images that leave the viewer vaguely uncomfortable, unmoved, or unconvinced. An outstanding AD consistently produces visual images that leave the intended viewer with an overwhelmingly positive attitude about the ad—and the product or service being advertised.

Although most effective advertising is the result of team effort, some campaigns are identified as art director's campaigns, whereas some are identified as copywriter's campaigns. An outstanding current, yet long-running example of one identified as an art director's campaign is that for Absolut Vodka, produced by the TBWA agency (now TBWA Chiat/Day). This is described at the end of this chapter.

Whereas in the past many advertising ADs achieved prominence with little or no formal advertising education, most advertising ADs now receive their education at art schools such as Pratt, Parsons, the Art Center School, and the School of Visual Arts or at universities such as Syracuse University or the University of Texas, where advertising design education is supplemented with broad liberal arts studies and also computer instruction, and where the objective is to educate students to be potential CDs. Part of the overall trend toward specialization is the result of advertising agencies' increasing need for young art directors who require little or no additional training in the use of computers. Whereas a few years ago excellent conceptual ability alone was enough to ensure a job for a recent graduate, agencies now recruit assistant ADs who are technically proficient as well. This trend will probably continue until the current senior ADs become computer proficient and no longer need technicians to execute their concepts.

Just as the widespread development of commercial television in the early 1950s changed the traditional role of the print-oriented art director, the phenomenal development in computer and communications hardware and software in the past decade has dramatically changed the working habits of art directors in the 1990s. In the early 1980s, not one advertising AD in a thousand used a computer for design or execution, but by the late 1990s, most

ADs use computers on a daily basis, and young designers without computer literacy are virtually unhirable.

Powerful computers with user-friendly graphical interface, such as the Macintosh, and software such as Aldus PageMaker and QuarkXPress give art directors the capability of rapidly trying out and testing an almost limitless number of design and type variations. Color printers enable them to execute a number of those variations with little need for time-consuming handwork. Similarly, time-based software programs enable proficient ADs to operate inexpensively to produce and present animatics—"roughs" of television commercials—complete with motion and sound. As hardware and software continue to improve, it is anticipated that art directors will become deeply involved in designing and producing interactive videos for their clients, which will be played back by consumers on CD-ROMs, VCRs, and home computers, in addition to the traditional advertising media.

These watershed technical developments are reducing the numbers of persons needed to produce advertisements, requiring fewer assistants, production people, and outside suppliers, but the creative role of the versatile art director is becoming ever more important. As consumers read less and watch more, the artistic ability to conceive and produce powerful and persuasive visual communications and images will inevitably become an even more necessary and valuable commodity. Furthermore, the current trend toward global advertising, where a commercial, poster, or other image is expected to work equally well in countries where different languages are spoken, makes the old adage "A picture is worth a thousand words" take on new meaning. Art directors will be called upon to create ever-more-important transcendent and universal visual images.

EDITOR'S NOTE ON THE ABSOLUT VODKA CAMPAIGN

John Philip Jones

In Chapter 4 of this volume, Damian O'Malley describes how Chiat/Day (which in 1995 became TBWA/Chiat Day) pioneered the concept of account planning in the United States. The Absolut vodka campaign, illustrated here by 8 examples from its long series of advertisements, was conceived and first exposed by TBWA before its merger with Chiat/Day. Whether or not the Absolut campaign was developed with the use of account planning, the Absolut advertisements illustrate well some of the characteristics of the account planning discipline.

In the first place, the advertisements are well targeted. They reflect the psychographics of the target audience. At an explicit level, they show special types of lifestyle activities—for example, private swimming pools, ski slopes (plus innumerable examples from other advertisements in the campaign). But, implicitly, the response is also targeted—the advertisements are aimed at magazine readers who are subtle, smart, and sophisticated—in the same way that Absolut drinkers are seen to be subtle, smart, and sophisticated. Advertising medium, audience, and brand are brought into harmony. The element of the advertisements that drives this response is their visual presentation, which is the specific contribution of the art director.

The second point about the campaign is that it confronts a product category, vodka, in which the functional differentiation between brands is minimal, and it constructs a unique identity. Absolut speaks an advertising language that no other vodka can use. This is again a strategic imperative that is normally articulated by the agency's account planners. The expression of this identity is predominately visual, although contributions of the writers—the important captions in the advertisements—underscore the visual communication with their own wit and style.

The campaign was conceived for color magazines for the obvious reason that advertising for hard liquor is not allowed on television. Looking at the campaign as a totality, it is difficult to conceive how it could have achieved such a focused impact if the regulations had permitted television to be used. For one thing, magazines are able to target the demographics and psychographics of the target audience more efficiently than advertising on network or spot television. But more important, the advertising itself is intrinsically very powerful because it exploits its medium so well.

The campaign was first run in 1981, when the brand was a small one with U.S. sales of approximately 20,000 cases. The campaign made an early impact on both the liquor trade and the consumer. Indeed, people with the psychographics targeted by the brand soon began collecting the individual advertisements. This has now become a cult—Absolut is one of a small handful of advertising campaigns that have an intrinsic appeal in their own right. Absolut soon because TBWA's flagship campaign, unquestionably elevating the profile of this high quality but (at that time) small agency. The account director of the Absolut business at TBWA/Chiat Day, Richard W. Lewis, has edited a 270-page volume of Absolut advertisements, which came out in 1996. This collection demonstrates engagingly and forcefully the overall impact of the campaign.[1]

Although, as mentioned, the Absolut advertisements all have a distinctive art director's "feel" to them, the individual subjects in the campaign were and are developed as a team effort—with a synergy that operates both within the agency account group and between the agency and the client. The unmistakable impression made by the campaign is that it is the end-product of imagination and enthusiasm.[2]

During the 15 years between 1981 and 1996, more than 500 advertisements were exposed. The production values of the campaign are high, which means that the individual advertisements were expensive in mechanical production costs. This is normally a price worth paying.

The campaign has had a remarkable impact in the marketplace. Sales of the brand grew from 20,000 cases in 1981 to 3,000,000 cases in the mid-1990s.[3] This represents a 150-fold increase. Absolut had done much to drive the total product category, and Absolut has become the number-one brand of vodka in the United States.

The campaign has another unusual feature. The advertisements are not subjected to pre-testing, since the agency has always felt that most types of pre-testing are too insensitive to detect the ways in which the Absolut campaign stimulates its responses from its target consumers.[4] There is thought to be an ever-present danger that pre-testing could kill creativity.

It should be no surprise to readers that the campaign has won hundreds of advertising awards over the years. Such awards are an expression of peer esteem within the advertising agency business rather than marketplace effectiveness. However, in 1992 the brand was awarded charter membership in the American Marketing Association's Marketing Hall of Fame. The other two brands inducted at the same time were Coca-Cola and Nike, both of which employ television predominately for their campaigns.[5] The Absolut advertisements represent magazine advertising at its most original. Regrettably, most larger agencies are too fixated on television to give full attention to the potential of print media—a point made with great force during the early 1980s by David Ogilvy.[6]

Notes

1. Richard W. Lewis, *Absolut Book: The Absolut Vodka Advertising Story* (Boston: Journey Editions, 1996).

2. Ibid., xii.

3. Ibid., xi.

4. Ibid., xiii

5. Ibid., xi.

6. David Ogilvy, "Wanted: A Renaissance in Print Advertising," in *Ogilvy on Advertising* (New York: Crown, 1983), 70-102.

CREDIT: A. Arlow and P. Lubalin, Creative Directors; Geoff Hayes, Art Director; and Graham Turner, Copywriter. "Absolut Perfection," August 1982.

CREDIT: A. Arlow and P. Lubalin, Creative Directors; Michael Roux, Art Director; and Michael Roux, Copywriter. "Absolut Warhol," June 1986.

CREDIT: A. Arlow and P. Lubalin, Creative Directors; Geoff Hayes, Art Director; and Graham Turner, Copywriter. "Absolut Attraction," August 1986.

CREDIT: A. Arlow and P. Lubalin, Creative Directors; Tom McManus, Art Director; and David Warren, Copywriter. "Absolut L.A.," February, 1988.

CREDIT: A. Arlow and P. Lubalin, Creative Directors; Tom McManus, Art Director; and David Warren, Copywriter. "Absolut Fax," October, 1990.

CREDIT: A. Arlow and P. Lubalin, Creative Directors; Steve Feldman, Art Director; and Harry Woods, Copywriter. "Absolut Peak," December, 1990.

CREDIT: A. Arlow and P. Lubalin, Creative Directors; Brennan Dailey, Art Director; and David Oakley, Copywriter. "Absolut Evidence," October, 1991.

CREDIT: A. Arlow and P. Lubalin, Creative Directors; Alix Botwin, Art Director; and Lou Graham and David Oakley, Copywriters. "Absolut Magnetism," April, 1994.

Budgeting for Advertising and the Advertising-Intensiveness Curve

John Philip Jones

How Advertising Budgets Are Set

Manufacturers can make or break an advertising campaign in a number of ways. To do its job, a campaign must advertise a brand that is functionally effective, competitively priced, and in good retail distribution—all matters under the direct control of the client. The client also determines the weight put behind a campaign by setting the advertising budget.

In all countries, the advertising budgets for most brands are derived from the brands' sales volume. The majority of manufacturers use the "case-rate system" or one of the large number of its variants.[1] The case-rate system ties a brand's advertising budget to its sales by allocating a certain number of advertising cents or dollars to each case of the brand sold. As a result, sales and advertising move directly in step. Despite its popularity, this procedure raises two important and surprisingly obvious questions.

First, what does this system tell us about whether a brand's actual advertising budget is the right sum for generating optimum sales and maximum profit? The answer to this question must be "nothing," because the procedure is directed inward to the brand's costs and not outward to the market, the place where the brand's sales are determined. The system determines what the brand can afford; it does not tell us whether the amount the brand is able to afford will be operationally effective. Like most rules of thumb, the case-rate system is easier to use than educated judgment. It is, however, far less efficient.

The second question is, Are advertisers fully aware that the advertising budget has a double influence on profit? We are generally used to thinking about the long-term influence on profit of the extra sales generated by advertising. But because advertising and profit are both residual expenses, there is also the immediate and direct influence of budget changes on immediate profit. When the advertising budget goes up, profit is immediately reduced. On the other hand, any advertising cutback goes straight to the bottom line (hence the prevalence of fourth-quarter advertising cancellations to counter the effect of anticipated shortfalls in sales). And how many advertisers realize that the short-term influence of advertising on profit is often a geared effect? If the brand's net earnings ratio is smaller than its advertising-to-sales ratio, an increase or decrease in advertising will have a greater proportional effect on profit.

Are there any realistic options available to most advertisers other than overspending or underspending on advertising? These two unappealing alternatives generally represent our sole choices until better budgetary methods are developed, believed in, and used. The sums of money involved underline the importance of this. The average major advertiser spends tens of millions of dollars on advertising above the line for each of its individual brands, and often hundreds of millions on all brands combined. Therefore, marginal improvements in productivity are likely to provide very significant payback when measured in terms of absolute dollars.

What this all amounts to is an enormous need for more efficient advertising budgeting, and this means that some new tools are badly needed. However, if they are to be of the faintest practical use to those people who actually manage brands, such tools must be relatively simple in all respects. There must be no confusion about how they are constructed or how they can be used to tackle specific brand situations. And they must also be more than theoretical "constructs"; they must be recognizably derived from the experiences of brands in the real world. There is no shortage of magic formulas, but the problem is that practitioners are unable to accept (or sometimes even to comprehend) the contents of most of them.

Advertising Works Harder for Bigger Brands

Case-by-case information that I have collected during my professional career has always suggested that large brands are less advertising-intensive than small brands—that per dollar of sales value there is less advertising spent on larger brands than on smaller ones. Another way of expressing this point is to say that a given number of advertising dollars spent on large brands produces more sales than a similar number spent on small brands.

If this hypothesis could be proved, it would obviously tell us something of operational value for the budgetary strategy for large brands. It might also throw some light on the very opaque problem of *quantifying* the intrinsic value of strong brands in comparison with weak ones.

An investigation was carried out by J. Walter Thompson in the fall of 1987. The agency's offices around the world were sent a questionnaire calling for a limited amount of clearly defined and solidly based factual data. A total of 242 completed questionnaires came back to New York, each referring to a single product category in a single country. Data were sent in from 23 countries around the world. The investigation was relatively simple. Nevertheless, no inquiry covering the same ground had ever been carried out anywhere before.[2]

Basic information was collected relating to a total of 1,096 advertised brands. This number of readings represents an excellent gross sample size, as long as it is not broken down into too many subsamples for the examination of special groups based on product types, brand sizes, or blocs of countries. In this chapter, when I present data in percentages based on total subsamples of fewer than 100, I show the percentages in parentheses.

Most of the brands covered—although certainly not all of them—were repeat-purchase packaged goods. The markets for such goods are almost invariably oligopolistic, and they are generally mature and stable in countries outside the Third World. Sales and advertising expenditures for individual brands also tend to remain fairly constant. The advertising-to-sales ratios of such brands are normally in the range of 4% to 8%.

The best way to examine advertising intensity is to estimate the advertising-to-sales ratio fairly precisely on a brand-by-brand basis. This approach needs reliable estimates of both the brand's advertising expenditure and its sales value. Although it is not difficult to arrive at an estimate of advertising expenditure, it is virtually impossible to make a tight estimate of sales on the basis of the retail audit/scanner or consumer panel data on which we have to rely if we want to examine a broad spectrum of brands. It is therefore necessary to find an alternative system of evaluating the importance of advertising in relation to sales.

Fortunately, there is an alternative method of calculating advertising intensity, and this was the method used in this investigation: It is simply to compare a brand's *share of market* (on a volume or value basis, volume being used here) with its *share of voice* (the brand's share of the total value of the main media advertising in the product category).

The rationale for this method of calculating advertising intensity is that the cost structure of one brand in a category tends to be similar to that of any other. The manufacturers of competitive brands are also conscious of one another's advertising expenditures; this is a characteristic of oligopolistic competition. The result is that brands of similar size tend to spend similar amounts on advertising, and a brand that is twice the size of another tends to spend twice as much on advertising as the smaller brand.

The comparison of brands of different sizes introduces the concept of a normal approximate similarity between a brand's share of market and its share of voice. There are obviously some erratic exceptions, and nothing can be done to allow for these. But there are also consistent exceptions that relate to brands of different sizes. The purpose of this study was to examine these consistent exceptions.

The first step was to break down the data into two categories:

- *Profit-taking brands (or underspenders):* those whose share of voice is the same as or below their share of market
- *Investment brands (or overspenders):* those whose share of voice is clearly above their share of market

TABLE 7.1 Analysis of Profit-Taking and Investment Brands

| | All Brands | | Profit-Taking Brands[a] | Investment Brands[b] |
	no.	%	%	%
Total	1,096	100	44	56
Share of market				
1-3%	224	100	27	73
4-6%	218	100	37	63
7-9%	153	100	41	59
10-12%	112	100	45	55
13-15%	(77)	(100)	(56)	(44)
16% and over	312	100	59	41

a. Share of voice equal to or smaller than share of market.
b. Share of voice larger than share of market.

In Table 7.1, all the brands have been put into groups covering 3 percentage points of market share (1% to 3%, 4% to 6%, and so on). The reason is that the sample could not be reliably broken down to allow an analysis based on single percentage points of share. The analysis is confined to advertised brands; unadvertised ones are excluded. As can be seen in this table, profit-taking brands are in a minority among those with small market shares, but the proportion increases consistently as the brands get larger. The trend is uninterrupted: from a ratio of 27:73 for brands with a 1% to 3% share of market to a ratio of 59:41 for those with a share of 16% or more.

The picture is remarkably clear, and there are three forces at work that are responsible for it. The first is that new and burgeoning brands (which are of course nearly always small) normally receive advertising investments deliberately calculated to exceed their market share percentages. Indeed, A. C. Nielsen has long recommended this budgetary policy on the basis of an extensive empirical study of successful and unsuccessful new brands. This factor accounts for many small-share brands having relatively high shares of voice.

The second factor is the all-too-common practice of "milking" older and often quite large brands. This is a tempting strategy for manufacturers, because significantly reducing advertising and promotional support can bring about a sometimes dramatic increase in a brand's earnings in the short run (although sales will almost certainly be adversely affected—an outcome that will eventually lead to the demise of the goose that lays the golden eggs). Manufacturers are sometimes persuaded to adopt this strategy because of a belief in brand life-cycle theory. This belief is essentially self-fulfilling, because the very act of cutting down support when a brand's sales are turning down, in the expectation that such a downturn is inevitable, will actually drive the downturn further.

The third factor causing a consistent disparity between shares of market and shares of voice is the most interesting and possibly the most important of the forces at work. Many large brands flourish in the marketplace with shares of voice consistently below their shares of market. This means that for such brands, advertising works harder, dollar for dollar, than it does for most smaller brands. This creates a clear advertising-related economy of scale for such large brands. This scale economy can be expressed for any brand using a dollar value calculated from the difference between its appropriation with a parity of share of market and share of voice and the smaller dollar amount actually spent on it. This is one of the real strengths of the branding phenomenon.

The cause and operating mechanism of this scale economy are not known with certainty, but they are thought to be related to a characteristic of consumer purchasing behavior: a tendency for large brands to benefit from above-average purchase and repurchase frequency. I have used the phrase *penetration supercharge* to describe this phenomenon.

Average Share of Voice:
A Budgetary Planning Tool

These findings provided satisfactory confirmation of the original hypothesis that large brands are less advertising-intensive than small ones. The next step in the investigation—the calculation of average shares of voice for brands of different market shares—provided a practical budgetary tool.

Table 7.2 concentrates exclusively on typical packaged goods categories that are reasonably balanced competitively (i.e., not excessively polarized, with one or two brands with massive market shares). These categories provide data with the maximum of internal consistency and that give relatively clear results. There were 666 brands that could be classified in this way, and these were again grouped into families covering 3 percentage points of market

TABLE 7.2 Share of Market Compared With Share of Voice (666 brands in 117 balanced packaged goods categories)

Share of Market	Share of Voice Minus Share of Market (percentage points)
1-3%	+5
4-6%	+4
7-9%	+2
10-12%	+4
13-15%	+1
16-18%	+2
19-21%	no difference
22-24%	−3
25-27%	−5
28-30%	−5

share. For each brand, the difference between share of voice and share of market was calculated, and these differences were averaged within each family of brands. The differences vary according to the sizes of the brands. Again, there is a fairly consistent picture. Brands in the 1-3% range overinvest in advertising by an average of 5 percentage points, and brands in the 28-30% range underinvest by an average of 5 percentage points. The size brackets in between follow an approximate continuum, but with some discontinuities.

These data can be set out diagrammatically (see Figure 7.1), and although the trend line is not a perfect fit, there is a reasonable-looking curve, which descends in a convex path. This convexity provides a hint that the gap between share of voice and share of market tends to increase as share of market grows. Figure 7.1 illustrates the *advertising-intensiveness curve* (AIC).

The AIC can be used for operational purposes. The advertising appropriation for any brand in a balanced packaged goods category can be tested according to the averages embodied in this curve. The brand's market share can be located on the curve, and the advertising share of voice for all brands of that same size can be read off. This figure can be converted without much trouble into an advertising expenditure calculated in dollars or any other currency. And such a money estimate will provide a normal expenditure level with which the brand's actual expenditure can be compared, and from which operational conclusions can be drawn.

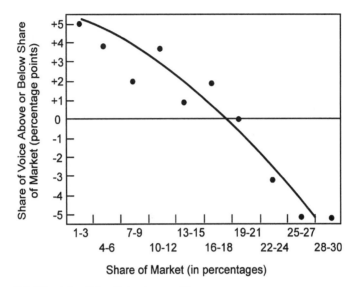

Figure 7.1. The Advertising-Intensiveness Curve

Table 7.3 is captioned "Average Advertising Intensity Ready-Reckoner" because one can apply its data simply by looking up one set of numbers and reading off a second. For a brand of a given market share (in the first column), the table gives in the third column the appropriate advertising intensity, calculated from broad averages and expressed as the percentage points of share of voice per percentage point of market share.

The Practical Value of the Budgetary Planning Tool

The AIC has two important features. First, it gives a measure—that is, a useful objective comparison between a brand's advertising expenditure in its own marketplace and the expenditures of many other brands of a comparable size in different marketplaces. Second, it provides a change of viewpoint, a shift away from the usual inward-directed system based on the brand's case rate. We move outward to the market, where the brand's sales are made. As a result,

TABLE 7.3 Average Advertising Intensity Ready-Reckoner

Share of Market (%)	Share of Voice Above (+) or Below (−) Share of Market (% points)	Advertising Intensity[a] (% points)
1	+5	6.0
2	+5	3.5
3	+5	2.7
4	+4	2.0
5	+4	1.8
6	+4	1.7
7	+2	1.3
8	+2	1.2
9	+2	1.2
10	+4	1.2
11	+4	1.2
12	+4	1.2
13	+1	1.1
14	+1	1.1
15	+1	1.1
16	+2	1.1
17	+2	1.1
18	+2	1.1
19	=	1.0
20	=	1.0
21	=	1.0
22	−3	0.9
23	−3	0.9
24	−3	0.9
25	−5	0.8
26	−5	0.8
27	−5	0.8
28	−5	0.8
29	−5	0.8
30	−5	0.8

a. Recommended share of voice per percentage point of market share.

it becomes psychologically easier for us to accommodate other market-based criteria. A single rule of thumb will give way to a sensible use of judgment in weighing facts from different sources. None of these facts is good enough on its own, but each brings something important. The different inputs enable us to strike a balance. Let us look at four such inputs, beginning with the AIC.

Average Share of Voice

The AIC is generally useful in determining the overall expenditure bracket for a brand of any size, as it has been averaged from a broad range of brands of a similar size. The particular value of the AIC is to help determine the specific level of underinvestment that may be acceptable for larger brands, subject to area testing. Underinvestment in this context means controlled programs of low expenditure that are well short of milking the brand. AIC calculations have been made for specific product categories, and these are sometimes more helpful than the overall curve covering all categories.

Marketplace Trends

The advertiser should evaluate trends in category sales, trends in the brand's sales, the competitive situation, trends in total category advertising, the current level of the brand's advertising, and trends in the advertising budgets of specific competitors. Although these pieces of information are all important, major changes in any year tend to be the exception and not the rule; most packaged goods markets are reasonably stable in most respects. The value of studying stable markets is to determine normal levels of the main marketing variables, including advertising budgets. But the existence of normal levels does not imply immovable stasis; indeed, gradual changes are always possible and over long periods often take place.

The Brand's Response
to Advertising Pressure

Many long-established brands have built useful track records of experience of varying levels of advertising pressure. In a substantial minority of cases, econometric studies have produced a specific advertising elasticity—an esti-mate of the marginal increase in sales that will follow a 1% increase in the advertising pressure put behind the brand. This is an input of extraordinary value and importance, and it should also be emphasized that experimental marketplace testing of different levels of advertising pressure to determine such a coefficient, despite the fact that it is still a relatively uncommon procedure, is something that is likely to increase in importance in the future.

The Cost Structure of the Brand

The cost structure of the brand tells the advertiser what level of advertising is affordable while a given level of profit is maintained. If the first three factors add up to a higher expenditure than does this last factor, the advertiser is in an obviously difficult position and must rethink the short-term profit objective for the brand and decide whether it will make sense to accept reduced (or zero or negative) profit for a finite period, in the expectation that the brand will pay out and recoup the investment at a targeted future date. This is a worst-case scenario, but it is a less unattractive option than spending what the brand can afford in the strong likelihood that it will be too little to have any effect.

It is possible, however, that the first three factors will suggest a smaller expenditure than will the fourth. In this case, there is a good reason now to conduct some carefully evaluated area testing of advertising downweighting.

The evaluation should measure the effects of any advertising reduction on the brand's sales volume. From this, the loss of profit can be computed. Anything more than a marginal loss of sales may endanger the brand's "critical mass," with its ability to generate scale economies. However, this is by no means a certain outcome. If competitive brands also follow the path of budget reduction, the eventual outcome will probably be no loss of aggregate sales in the market and reasonable stability in the shares of the individual brands. Even if our brand goes it alone, there may be no serious reduction in its overall sales because advertising elasticities are generally low. But the important point is that area testing can help us evaluate in advance the likely extent of a sales reduction and how far the loss of profit on any fall in sales will offset the (normally substantial) amount of money saved by the advertising cutback.

Some advertisers may fear that advertising cutbacks on their part may be met by opportunistic advertising increases on the part of their competitors. This is a possibility, but the consequences need not be much feared. As I have indicated, the advertising elasticity for most brands tends to be low, so that the sales response to additional advertising pressure is very limited. The result is that our brand is unlikely to lose much share, and may be making significant savings in advertising expenditure.

Notes

1. Andre J. San Augustine and William F. Foley, "How Large Advertisers Set Budgets," *Journal of Advertising Research*, October 1975, 11-16; Steven E. Permut, "How European Managers Set Advertising Budgets," *Journal of Advertising Research*, October 1977, 75-79.

2. John Philip Jones, "Ad Spending: Maintaining Market Share," *Harvard Business Review*, January/February 1990, 38-42.

Advertising Media

A Changing Marketplace

Carla V. Lloyd

A Rapidly Expanding Media Environment

We are in the midst of an advertising media boom. Anything that can hold, carry, or display an ad can be called an advertising medium—that is, as long as it delivers the ad message for the brand squarely in front of the eyeballs of the consumers we are trying to engage, and as long as it delivers this message to consumers when they are predisposed toward thinking about or purchasing the brand. And, of course, it should deliver the ad message clearly, efficiently, and cost-effectively.

This broadened view of advertising media has given us advertising messages that are visible everywhere and on everything, creating a media environment that industry experts describe as cluttered and unpredictable. Currently, ads hound us underfoot, pelt us at eye level, and linger overhead. Look around: Ads are on fruit, eggs, Barbie dolls, gasoline pumps, parking meters, grocery carts, airport baggage carousels, turnstiles at sports arenas, goal posts, ski lifts, and the bottoms of golf hole cups. They've recently cropped up in such unlikely places as bathroom walls, urinal stalls, stadium roofs, tops of bus shelters, theater tickets, and grocery store receipts. Advertising space can even be had on the arms that sweep away toppled bowling pins.

Today, almost every space is a commercial space. In school, there's Channel One; the New York City school system sells space on the sides of its school buses, and college campuses allow company-sponsored videos in their cafeterias. At work, commuters ride on buses painted with advertising messages that go from headlight to taillight. Herds of cows decked out in sandwich-board advertisements and grazing along busy train routes capture the attention of rail commuters. Arm Guard is a plastic sleeve printed with ads and worn on the arms of car drivers traveling daily on heavily trafficked Los Angeles highways. Paid, participating drivers are asked to hang their Arm Guards out of their car windows to reach captive commuters stuck in rush-hour traffic.

Few venues nowadays are commercial-free zones. In the airport, there are news networks and kiosks; in the airplanes themselves, ads make their way onto airsickness bags. In London, Fox Broadcasting recently had a Boeing 737 painted bright yellow with characters from *The Simpsons* all over it to advertise the network's popular animated series. At the movies, we see product placement, commercials before the films, and ads on popcorn bags. Ads cover the shower curtains at health clubs and blare on the video screens in front of the Stairmasters. Ads are played on ATM screens and telephones while on hold, lie on grocery store floors, appear in digital display units in taxis, grace the sides and tops of 18-wheelers, and appear at the doctor's office, on the front pages of some daily newspapers, and on hats and T-shirts. Ads are sent to fax machines, e-mail addresses, and active Web sites; stuck inside catalogs and monthly bill statements; printed on the back of ATM transaction receipts; slapped on serving trays as liners at fast-food restaurants; and run for nearly 5 minutes before the feature film begins on rental videos. A half a million coupon machines presently cling to 27,000 grocery and drugstore shelves, according to *News America Marketing*.

Ads are even making their way onto the packaging of other brands. According to the London-based *Independent,* " 'Help Ad' is a new program designed by the Red Cross that enables brands to sell space on their packaging to other brands and then donate the proceeds to charity." [1] And advertising is quite literally out of this world, with advertising space for the European-built Maxus II rocket turning into a bidding war in which one 26-square-meter poster sold for more than $1 million.

All of these—from cows to shower curtains, from kiosks to kiwi fruit—constitute what we now call advertising media. Today's advertising media are wide-ranging, sometimes far-flung, if not unorthodox, and can be defined broadly as any opportunity that allows advertisers to deliver persuasive messages to consumers on behalf of the brand. Not so long ago, advertisers had a more traditional, less-expansive view of what advertising media were and were not. Ad media were seen predominantly as traditional "channels of communication" that could carry advertising messages to consumers—channels such as newspapers, magazines, television, radio, and outdoor. These are all still considered the primary major advertising media, and they are where the bulk of advertising revenues are invested today. In 1997, advertising expenditure in the United States totaled $188 billion, with $111 billion spent in the major media alone. *Business Week* reporters Mary Kuntz, Joseph Weber, and Heidi Dawley, in an article titled "The New Hucksterism," assert that "the new ad permutations aren't replacing the traditional television, magazine, and billboard messages. Rather, advertisers are adding new weapons to their arsenals because the traditional venues are packed full." [2] The traditional media have become too cluttered, too fragmented, too expensive for some advertisers, forcing them to find new, innovative ways to reach their prime prospects. Faced with declining viewership brought on by the popularity of cable TV, the traditional broadcast networks have added even more 30-second commercials. In the first 10 weeks of the 1997-1998 TV season, ABC's prime-time commercial volume was up 11.8%, with NBC at 6.1% and CBS at 4.8%, according to SFM Media Corp. [3] Only 1% of network commercials are 60 seconds long, according to an SRI Imagery Transfer Study. Shorter commercials translate to more clutter on broadcast TV, where 64% of commercials are 30-second spots, 32% are 15-second spots, and 4% are other lengths.

The media marketplace is saturated with traditional electronic and print advertisements. As Kuntz et al. point out, "Consumers are bombarded with hundreds of ads and thousands of billboards, packages, and other logo sightings every day." [4] Research shows that every American consumer is confronted with 3,000 advertising messages every day. City dwellers are really blitzed, with one recent study showing that urban Americans are bombarded with 13,000 ads, logos, and corporate plugs per day. The old venues "are packed to the point of impenetrability as more and more sales messages are jammed in." [5] There are now 10,625 magazines, with 933 new publications bowing during 1996 alone, according to the Magazine Publishers Association. Some 50% of each of these magazines is devoted to advertising. New spin-off magazines, with such titles as *Teen People* and *Time for Kids,* are splintering audiences into even smaller segments and cranking up the clutter even more. American highways are sprinkled with 400,000-odd billboards, and of the 60,000 buses that transport commuters to and from work, school, and play, 37,000 are plastered with billboard-sized ads.[6]

Cable-television households—now more than 65% of all U.S. homes—receive an average of more than 50 channels. And ad clutter on cable TV is even worse than on broadcast television. Network broadcast TV generally carries 24 commercials per hour, whereas cable often carries as many as 28 per hour. The Internet is congested with 320,000 Web sites, and *Wired* magazine reports that thousands of new sites are added daily. Supermarkets carry 30,000 different packages, up from 17,500 just a decade ago, according to the Food Marketing Institute.[7] Product packaging has become bolder and more important as brand loyalty has diminished, and with more than two-thirds of all consumer decisions about purchasing one brand over another made right at the store shelf. "Networks air 6,000 commercials a week, up 50% since 1983," according to Pretesting Co.[8] Each hour, prime-time TV carries more than 10 minutes of paid advertising, about a minute more than was carried 10 years ago. And when the network promotions are added into this commercial mix, we wind up with nearly 15 minutes of every prime-time hour devoted to ads alone. Consumers are hit with 38,000 TV commercials per year. No wonder they are grabbing their remotes to zap the ads.

Media clutter has created a sort of a feeding frenzy among advertising strategists, whose job it is to break through this babble by startling, surprising, and shocking consumers. Audacious advertising has to be backed up with equally daring media placement; as one media strategist has observed, "It ain't what you do, it's the place that you put it." [9] As a result, advertising is everywhere, and it has made some consumers inured and, worse yet, perturbed. For advertisers, it's a battle royal to find a place that is free from competitive noise and clutter. Mark Whelan, an account director at Duckworth Finn Grubb Waters in London, explains what today's advertisers are up against: "You're fighting for a share of voice among the clutter. Television is expensive. Using unconventional media can be a good a way of getting better value for money." [10] Deciding where and when to place ads has become increasingly more important as the media marketplace has gotten more complicated.

The Increasing Complexity of Media Planning

Media planning, the strategic decision-making process of selecting and scheduling media, has become increasingly involved, creative, and complex. Dealing with this saturated, erratic, and fragmented media environment requires media strategists to put more emphasis on the consumer and on creativity, flexibility, and total communications programs.

Today's consumers are advertising weary—they've been blasted with too many ads, logos, promotional offers, and corporate sponsorships. A computer saleswoman who had bought an apple that bore a *Liar Liar* video sticker told *New York Times* reporter Carol Marie Cropper: "It just really annoyed me. I don't want my apple defiled with advertisements. I get frustrated with all the ads everywhere you look." [11] Procter & Gamble's Bob Wehling, speaking about agency compensation at the 1998 meeting of the American Association of Advertising Agencies, said, "The idea is to reach consumers in the most effective way possible." And this involves not merely selecting media that will cause the biggest effect for the client's investment, but carefully selecting media and marketing communications forces that will readily blend together to speak in concert with one another to engage consumers. Wehling recommends that media planners "surround the consumer by blending the various media into a harmonious mix." [12] It all starts with a focus on the consumer.

The technology explosion has changed all the rules, for advertisers and consumers alike. Technology is erasing the lines that once separated different forms of media. Neat boundaries have given way to convergence, where TV becomes more like a retail store thanks to the success of home shopping networks. Computers are direct marketers. Newspapers, radio, and magazines have meshed with the Internet to find new voices and methods of distribution. Some industry experts believe that the Internet has changed the face of media in general, making "all media an interactive experience." *Adweek*'s John

Markman speculates that in 5 years "the various media are likely to meld together so seamlessly that accessing information and entertainment . . . will be almost as simple as turning on a light." [13] And what's on the drawing board? A few scientists are busy working on developing an electronic "nose" that will transmit smells through personal computers. Convergence indeed.

WPP Group's chief executive, Martin Sorrell, has asked today's advertisers to get out of their rut of thinking exclusively in terms of 30-second network TV and start thinking more creatively in order to meet the challenges of the technologically intensified marketplace: "For 40 years in the United Kingdom and even longer in the U.S., agency skills, agency reputations and agency profits have been centered round . . . the conception and production of 30-second spots for network TV. But there are vast and irreversible changes taking place in the world of communications, and not one of these changes will favor network TV." Sorrell strongly believes that the future of brand advertising rests on the advertising world's ability to "increase its breadth of creativity it can provide for its clients." He asserts that agencies must develop "a much wider understanding of the meaning and nature of creativity than we commonly hold today." [14]

In an overly cluttered, technologically charged media world, media planning should not be isolated from the creative. Already media planning, with its quantitative focus on research, costs, and audience delivery, has more or less been divorced from the creative department. Some argue that the quantitative disciplines of the media department and the qualitative disciplines of the creative department should be more unified. Typically, media planners have planned and scheduled the media, supporting their strategic decisions with ample research—all of which has helped to bolster the overall strength of the advertising process. And many times, the media planner's work has stopped there. Some think that it should not.

Media-savvy clients, intense media competition, the technological boom, and budgetary shifts have created major changes in media buying. Beginning in the late 1980s, the recession caused widespread belt-tightening among advertisers. Media dollars shifted from above-the-line (brand advertising) to below-the-line (promotional) spending (see Jones, Chapter 31, this volume). Media rates escalated, just when audiences were being blown apart—fragmented by the rise of niche media. *Accountability* became the mantra of advertisers and media buyers alike. And the role of media took a giant leap forward in the minds of advertisers, where they viewed it as an important part of the promotional mix. Media clutter became a nuisance that all—from consumers to clients, from planners to buyers—would have to live with. The upshot of all this activity was a media marketplace that was forever changed— a marketplace that was more complicated, more intense, more competitive; a marketplace that redefined how media would be bought and sold. And out of this groundswell of change came some new ways of buying and selling media that persist today.

For instance, print media are negotiable. Big deal making, involving multimillion-dollar investments and often with cross-media sponsorship, is popular. Big media dollars have become important venture capital for the media business. Media buying has been unbundled from advertising agencies, and has led to the birth of independent buying services. But perhaps the most significant development on the media-buying front in recent years is the consolidation of billion-dollar media assignments to one or two media buying outfits. Media buying is now a consolidated activity. Clients such as Campbell's, Chrysler Corporation, General Motors, and Procter & Gamble consolidate their media buying instead of spreading it across their numerous advertising agencies. This gives these advertising giants, with their billion-dollar budgets, significant clout, allowing them to buy their media cheaper.

This trend climaxed in 1997, when packaged goods giant Procter & Gamble made history by handing out nearly $1.2 billion for television planning and buying to New York-based Televest and centralizing about $180 million in print media planning and buying with Leo Burnett. Prior to this landmark move, P&G had its nine brand agencies managing media planning for each brand, using an agency of record for print buying only. The complexity of the media is fueling this change, making advertisers seek out companies like Televest that specialize in media buying and employ specialists with particular talents and skills to figure out how media dollars can be spent to achieve maximum effect for the lowest cost.

But to today's consumers it is all advertising, because they do not see the content of an ad separate from the media that deliver it. They react to the overall impression that the ad creates. Because of this, some professionals suggest that the media and creative departments should work more closely together. This union of quantitative and qualitative minds would help create more forceful communication that is based on a keener identification of and understanding of how to reach and engage today's consumer—a person who receives an overload of communications.

Recommendations

At no other time have advertising media multiplied at such breakneck speed. The traditional media have answered the rallying call, sprinting fast to snare their fair share of a media audience that is splintered and ad dollars that are being reshuffled. The newcomers, like the Internet, are still getting their footing when it comes to advertising, but have made the race for ad revenue and audience share unusually heated. Competitive noise has amplified. Consumers are ready to throw in the towel. And with more innovation waiting at the gate, the race appears to have just begun.

Communications strategists, left to deal with the traditional media's ongoing metamorphosis and new media's unpredictable surge, have had to change the way they do business. How media planning has been done in the past does not entirely hold sway anymore. Strategists who want to cut through the din and clutter to grab the waning attention of consumers can do so by considering the five following recommendations.

1. *Begin all media planning with an intimate understanding of the brand.* Kirshenbaum & Bond's headline-grabbing and exceptionally sharp media director, Steve Klein, who has been the brains behind such memorable and inventive media plans as those for Bamboo lingerie, Hennessey cognac, and Snapple, says that today's media planners must be seen "as the keepers for how the brand speaks." [15] Each brand, in Klein's mind, has a "voice." It is up to the media planner, working along with other members of the account team, to discover each brand's voice. Once this is accomplished, the media planner must decide what level of "volume" suits the brand's voice. In other words, if the brand has a "loud volume"—like Candies Shoes—its voice can be cranked up to equally loud volume in brash media such as MTV. If the brand has a "soft volume"—like Mont Blanc pens—it must be treated with respect and advertised in "low-volume, soft-spoken" media vehicles, such as the *New Yorker.* Thinking of a brand in this conceptual way allows the media planner to create a plan that speaks appropriately for the brand and reaches consumers in ways that conventional media planning may have never thought of.

2. *Develop a complete knowledge of and respect for the consumers and their lifestyles.* In this way, media planners can find ways to intersect with consumers at the precise moment when they are most predisposed and

receptive to hearing the brand's message. DDB Needham has developed a comprehensive system—the "personal media network"—for determining when it is most beneficial to reach consumers with a brand's message. This is just part of an elaborate research process. DDB Needham strategists begin their work by plotting a day in the life of one of the brand's prototypical prospects. From the moment the prospect clicks the alarm clock off until his or her head hits the pillow, DDB Needham media professionals plot the prospect's every activity, especially media usage. Once this comprehensive log is complete, media planners have a better idea of when it is most advantageous to schedule advertising messages to get maximum effect from the brand's prospects. They find the precise moment when the consumer may benefit from what the brand has to offer and when the brand might make his or her life easier.

Computer technology allows advertisers to track consumers as never before. The amount of information that advertisers have amassed about consumers is, as *Advertising Age*'s Bob Garfield says, "frightening." [16] If advertisers act responsibly on this information, this will guarantee that consumers are not inundated with advertising at times when advertising is not welcome.

3. *Attain fluency in all the many voices that can speak on behalf of the brand as well as fluency on when to use them.* Media strategists must be fluent in all the various ways that a brand can reach consumers. These include all types of advertising plus sales promotion, direct marketing, and public relations. Media directors must function as generalists and surround themselves with specialists who understand how each of these various disciplines functions and how each can be used to maximum effect for the brand. This is how advertising agency BBDO's media department is structured. Burt Manning, former head of J. Walter Thompson, notes that "today's complicated marketplace calls for someone who understands how all of the promotional communications operate." [17] The industry currently needs professionals who know when it is most profitable to use one promotional tool over another, given the brand's current marketing situation, explains Manning. Kirshenbaum & Bond's Steve Klein says that it is the job of media strategists to keep up on everything, from the obscure stuff to the more salient, because, as he explains, "you never know when you will be able to use this media opportunity for a client." [18] This means that today's media planners are active learners who must stay abreast of a vast number of growing media options.

4. *Keep a focus on accountability.* Some media directors strongly believe that their clients should not be in the business of providing revenue to test new media. New media make sense only when the money is spent efficiently and effectively to help achieve the marketing objectives. With so many media sales representatives vying for a finite number of media dollars, the media strategist must place even more emphasis on trying to get the biggest bang for the client's buck.

5. *Gain a much wider understanding of the meaning and nature of creativity.* Breaking through the clutter to make sense of a radically changed media landscape requires ingenuity and imagination.

Getting messages to consumers who have clashed with too many ads is a challenging process. Now that advertising media are being expanded to include any opportunity to speak on behalf of a brand, and technology is giving media the means to do so, media planners are finding that their job is fast becoming more important, more formidable, and certainly more creative than it has ever been.

Notes

1. Jim Davies, "It's Not What You Do, It's the Place That You Do It: You Can Run But You Can't Hide From Advertising 'Terrorists,' " *Independent,* March 5, 1996, Media sec., 20ff.

2. Mary Kuntz, Joseph Weber, and Heidi Dawley, "The New Hucksterism," *Business Week,* July 1, 1996, 77-78.

3. Cited in Chuck Ross, "NBC Mulls Fewer, Longer Ad Breaks," *Advertising Age,* April 13, 1998, 4.

4. Kuntz et al., "The New Hucksterism," 77.

5. Ibid.

6. Brad Edmondson, "In the Driver's Seat," *American Demographics,* March 1998, 47.

7. Cited in Kuntz et al., "The New Hucksterism," 77.

8. Cited in ibid.

9. Quoted in Davies, "It's Not What You Do."

10. Quoted in ibid.

11. Quoted in Carol Marie Cropper, "Fruit to Walls to Floor, Ads Are on the March," *New York Times,* February 26, 1988, A1.

12. Quoted in Rance Crain, "It Was a Good 4A's Meeting—for Trial Balloons and Intrigue," *Advertising Age,* April 13, 1998, 21.

13. John Markman, in "Media Outlook '98," *Adweek,* September 8, 1997.

14. "Agencies Face New Battlegrounds: Sorrell" (excerpts from WPP Group Chief Executive Martin Sorrell's speech to the annual meeting of the American Association of Advertising Agencies, April 1998), *Advertising Age,* April 13, 1998, 22.

15. Steve Klein, personal interview conducted at Kirshenbaum & Bond advertising agency, New York, February 12, 1992.

16. Bob Garfield, interview on *Morning Edition,* National Public Radio, April 1998.

17. Burt Manning, speech delivered to the student body at the S. I. Newhouse School of Public Communications, Syracuse University, February 27, 1998.

18. Klein, personal interview.

9

The Media Buyer in the Advertising Agency

Debra L. Merskin

The job of media buying is central to the functioning and success of the advertising agency. In the economically troublesome times of the early 1990s, accountability became key—the advertising message had to reach the right people at the right time for the least amount of money. In light of an increasingly competitive and complicated media environment, the burden of accountability continues to fall on the shoulders of the advertising agency media buyer.

Historically, media buying has been known by other names. These include time buying and, in prebroadcast days, space buying. Media buyers traditionally have been women, as the tasks of costing out and purchasing time and space have been thought of as primarily clerical skills. Typically, the buyer was simply handed a list of cities in which space was to be purchased, along with the space requirements, and instructed to make a buy. Interestingly, space buying was the basic function of the first advertising agencies. Regardless of

101

the name, the function of the department has remained largely the same—procuring space or time from those who own it for those who wish to be displayed in or on it. The media buyer works as an agent between client and medium.

Depending upon the size of the advertising agency, a few or a large number of individuals may work in the media department, which is responsible for deciding the best places for advertising messages to run (such as on television or in newspapers) and for purchasing the time or space for these sales messages. The chief functions of the media department are to plan, review, recommend, select, and buy individual media, or combinations of media, that will produce for the client, the advertiser, the most precise reach of the prospects for a product or service at the most affordable price.

Media buying is complicated and time-consuming, requiring very specialized skills. It is the job of the media buyer to put into action the plans for a product's advertising. A media buyer may be defined as *the individual in an advertising agency who is responsible for reviewing, recommending, negotiating, and buying media time and space that will support the brand's positioning.* The buyer is responsible for executing the ideas of the planner, turning thought into action. This activity requires considerable expertise and creativity because of the constantly changing nature of the media environment.

Today's media buyers are faced not only with the ever-increasing challenge of buying media at rising prices, but also with keeping track of all the different places where an ad may be run. There are two classifications of media: traditional and nontraditional. Traditional media comprise more than 1,500 television stations, 9,000 commercial radio stations, 11,000 cable systems, 1,600 daily and 7,500 weekly newspapers, as well as more than 12,000 magazine titles.[1] These media include increasingly narrowly targeted forms that are geared to particular cultural or social interests, such as African American, Spanish, or gay readers. Nontraditional media comprise a growing group that includes opportunities to place advertising on parking meters, in grocery carts, on the Airport Channel, and in the sky, using skywriting. Buyers can now purchase advertising space on ski slopes, on clouds, on computer billboards, in phone booths, and even in urinals.

As marketing research techniques have grown more sophisticated and the media options have grown more complicated, buyers' skills have had to extend far beyond the calculation of costs and circulations. At one time, advertising choices were limited to print media, such as newspapers and magazines; then the broadcast media followed. With more than $104 billion spent on main-media advertising in 1996, 200-plus markets in the United States, and more than 200 forms of media to choose from, maintaining a working knowledge of pricing structures and media availabilities has gone beyond a clerical function.

A very important job of the media buyer is to use his or her knowledge of the media available in a particular area to develop a pricing structure that is equitable for the client and the station or publication. Prices for most forms of media are not fixed; rather, they must be negotiated. The media buyer participates in making specific media recommendations and negotiates prices for the media time (e.g., 30 seconds during *Friends*) or space (e.g., a full page in *Time*). The media buyer also serves as agency and client representative to the media, responsible not only for the management of millions of dollars of client money, but also for the client's and the agency's reputations in the business community.

The Media Buying Process

Whether the advertising schedule (the buy) involves millions or hundreds of dollars, the same general process occurs. In large agencies, many individuals are involved in a hierarchical management relationship: media director, media planner, media buyer.

The media director fills a management position; he or she oversees the activities of the media department and interacts with the account service people. Typically, media planners are assigned to a specific account or group of accounts and are responsible for formulating the media plan. The media plan, a written document, is an extension of the overall marketing plan and is constructed for three levels of decision making that set the tone for the actions that follow. These actions are executed by the media buyer. The three levels, in descending order of specificity, are as follows:

- *Media objectives:* These are statements of goals that are most likely to achieve the objectives of the marketing plan, such as determining who is most likely to buy a product or service (the target group), how many of these individuals are out there, and when advertising should occur. For example, if the advertiser is a specialty chocolate manufacturer and the event is Mother's Day, the logical prospects are men 18 years old and older who are likely to buy the product for their wives, girlfriends, and mothers.
- *Media strategies:* These develop out of the objectives. Strategies define actions, which result in specific decisions and answers to questions. For example, if men

are the target audience, what media would most effectively and efficiently reach them? When should the advertisements be scheduled? What size should they be? How many are needed? And in what position (e.g., inside the front cover of a magazine) should the ads run? Essentially, strategies help set the goals the media buyer will be shooting for in terms of reach (how many target audience members need to be exposed to the message) and frequency (how often this is necessary) within the available budget.

- *Media tactics:* These are the steps taken in the actual implementation of the media plan. This is where the activities of the media buyer are critical. Once the planner has made recommendations in written form—after the who, what, when, where, and why of the media plan have been articulated and approved—the media buyer is responsible for identifying the precise vehicles that can best accomplish the advertising goals. These vehicles include specific television stations and dayparts, radio stations and dayparts, magazines, and newspapers.

Media buyers use a combination of mathematical skills, research tools, and common sense to come up with the forms of media that will best attract the audiences desired by the advertiser, all within a specified budget. Returning to the chocolate example: If the goal is to reach married men and sons with advertisements promoting gourmet chocolate as an ideal Mother's Day gift, ads placed in the business or sports sections of the local newspaper might directly target this group. Media buying is not an exact science; rather, buyers must rely on a combination of quantitative measures—statistical descriptions and analyses of the population—as well as on their own experience in the market and their relationships with representatives of the media.

To illustrate better what a media buyer does, I offer below an example that follows the process of a media buy, from initiation by the planner to execution by the buyer, using an imaginary product, Bunting Baby Blankets.

How Does a Buy Happen?

Typically, a media buy is said to "happen" when the actual order for a buy arrives on the media buyer's desk. This is a document that identifies the client who wishes to advertise, the media to be advertised in or on (such as magazines or radio), how much the buyer has to spend (budget), and the goals for the buy. The goals of the media buy are stated in very specific mathematical figures that indicate how many individuals in the audience need to be reached by the message, and how often, to implement the strategy behind the media plan. In this case, for Bunting Baby Blankets, the target audience is expectant and new mothers ages 25-49 who live in the Florida cities of Tampa, Orlando, Jacksonville, and Miami. The media to be included are television, radio, outdoor, and newspapers. The budget is $4 million and is divided equally among the four media. The campaign is to run for 8 weeks.

The media buyer is given a goal sheet for each medium that shows the rating points to be achieved. Rating points indicate the percentage of individuals (or homes) exposed to a particular radio or television program.[2] Ratings are also used to calculate the effectiveness of outdoor, newspapers, and magazines. These statistics give the buyer a sense of how many individuals are likely to be in the audience for an advertisement. In the case of Bunting, the company distributes the product only in Florida. As only four markets are included in this buy, the buyer will make what is referred to as a "spot" buy as opposed to a national or network buy, which would cover the entire country.

Techniques in Media Buying

The media buyer pays attention to the programs in which the commercials are to run and to the times of day the programs air, to ensure that there is a logical match with the interests of the target. For example, expectant mothers might be in the audience for daytime television if they are at home, and for evening prime-time programming if they are at work all day.

Radio

The kind of programming or music format a radio station plays—talk, rock, oldies, polka—is important. It is not likely that many new mothers are 24-hour Led Zeppelin listeners, but they might enjoy Top 40 hits or oldies. A ratings book from a syndicated rating service such as Arbitron or Nielsen helps the buyer calculate the number of rating points needed to achieve his or her goals on the appropriate stations. The buyer then calculates how much money can be spent on each station by estimating a cost per rating point. Radio commercials are typically purchased in 60-second units (although other lengths are available), and spots are normally bought in quantities (known as packages).

Television

Program type is also an important factor in TV buys. In the case of Bunting Baby Blankets, *Live With Regis and Kathie Lee* and *Touched by an Angel* might be good choices. Sometimes stations will have unsold inventory available and may offer time on top-quality programming at reduced prices ("fire sales"). Television time is typically sold in units of 30 seconds; prices vary from as low as $50 in small-market late night to as much as $500,000 for a national spot during a top-rated prime-time situation comedy (such as *Seinfeld* in the mid-1990s). Television is considered to be a "reach" medium, as it reaches many more people at one time than does radio, which is considered to be a "frequency" medium—one on which it is affordable to run many commercials during an hour of programming time.

Outdoor

Billboards are also the responsibility of the media buyer, who must "ride the market." This means the buyer must physically go to a community and drive past all the outdoor boards available for rental. This time-consuming task is important, because many times billboards are not located in ideal places. For example, a tree might be growing directly in front of a board, obscuring the view of drivers and pedestrians. Or a board might be located adjacent to a business or a church, which could make it inappropriate for use in advertising a social cause or a state lottery respectively.

Outdoor advertising is purchased either in painted boards or in poster panels. As the name implies, boards are painted in a plant and are more permanent, whereas panels are smaller, less expensive, and more mobile. Painted boards are typically purchased on an individual basis; posters are purchased en masse in what is referred to as a showing.

Newspapers

Newspapers are the fourth form of media in the hypothetical Bunting buy, and the prices (column inch rate) are fixed. Unlike radio, television, outdoor, and, to some extent, magazines, newspaper advertising prices are nonnegotiable. In most communities there is one daily newspaper, and the price is *the* price. The buyer calculates the size of the ad to be run in terms of columns wide and inches long and the price for each inch of that space. Then the buyer selects the preferred day of the week. In most cities, Monday is an important shopping day, and Sunday has the largest overall circulation. Frequently, newspapers run special editions for sports, back to school, wedding planning, and other activities of wide interest. The buyer in this case might work with the newspaper advertising representative to locate such a feature appropriate for Bunting.

Making the Buy

Because many forms of the chosen media are negotiable in terms of price, individuals who serve as salespersons or representatives (reps) of these media compete with one another for a share of the client's budget. It is the job of the media buyer to corral all this interest by meeting with reps on a regular basis. It is interesting, however, that reps often hear of a potential buy long before any formal announcement is made to the media community and start pressing the buyer, claiming to be "just dropping by," bringing small gifts and offers of lunch, concert tickets, and trips if only the buyer will keep the reps' stations in mind. As a result, buyers begin talking with these media reps about prices and opportunities for good buys, any programming or format changes, and editorial opportunities that might be available. Most of the deals are actually made over lunch. The more money the buyer has to spend, and has spent in the past, the better the price (and the meal) is likely to be. Thus there is a distinct advantage to clients who go with bigger agencies who have clients with bigger budgets. Being readily available also serves the rep.

There is considerable negotiation back and forth in terms of what the media buyer is willing to pay for a particular media offering and what the rep feels he or she has to get for it. Although each television and radio station publishes a "rate card," the rates shown are only the starting point for negotiations for most buyers.

A media buyer is considered to be good at the job if he or she has a reputation for being "tough." Women who under any other circumstances might be referred to in derogatory terms for their shrewdness in negotiation, knowledge, and firmness when doing business are considered to be nobody's fools as media buyers. Knowing the numbers, the prices, and how much negotiation room the media rep has, are all critical to the buyer's getting the best price available—meaning equal to or lower than what any other agency is paying for the same time or space.

Postbuy Work

Once the media buyer has met with all the necessary individuals, either in person or over the telephone, a price is agreed upon and the buy is placed. The media buyer double-checks to see that everything is in order in terms of goals and budget and then orders the time or space. The media outlet responds by sending a contract listing the time ordered, or, if the buy is for a print medium, such as newspaper, the buyer sends in an insertion order. This document is an official form describing the size of the ad ordered and the date it is to run. In the meantime, the buyer notifies the department in the agency that handles getting videotapes of commercials or mechanicals of print advertisements to the media—the traffic department.

Once the dates of the advertising schedule have passed, the buyer waits for one of two things to happen—either the television or radio station calls to say that one of the commercials in the schedule did not run and for what reason (usually the station then offers to run the commercial at an equivalent or better time on another date; this is known as a "make good") or the invoice arrives. The buyer always checks the invoice to be certain that the commercials ran as ordered. There are laws that require broadcast stations to keep logs of the airing of commercials, and these logs can be checked. The buyer also conducts a postbuy analysis—a check to see if the programs purchased achieved the rating points the buyer and rep agreed on. If not, the stations typically make up the points by offering free commercials at another time at no charge.

Skills of the Media Buyer

The skills required by the media buyer are of two types. The first set of skills has to do with knowledge; the second involves the buyer's mind-set.

Knowledge-Based Skills

- *Comprehensive knowledge of markets:* Before the buyer can begin looking at the media, he or she must first look at the consumer or potential consumer of the product or service. The buyer does this by conducting target market research—learning all there is to know about the people who buy the product. Typically, media buyers are assigned to particular communities or regions of the country in which they do all the buying for a client or collection of clients. Buyers need to know about the characteristics of the populations that reside in their markets. This includes information on income, sex, race, age, and occupation (demographics) as well as lifestyle characteristics such as how these people spend their leisure time and how willing they are to try new products (psychographics).

- *Knowledge of media:* The media buyer also spends considerable time researching the overall characteristics and costs of different forms of media, to be able to match the advertising message and medium most efficiently with the target. In addition, it is important that the buyer know that different consumers use different media. Buyers also should have a sense of what media should cost in particular communities. Based on the size of the population and the demographics, buyers should be able to estimate what prices to expect. Only hands-on experience, however, can give buyers the information they need to understand adequately the makeup of particular markets.

- *Comprehensive knowledge of the product or service:* Once the media buyer is faced with making an actual buy, he or she must be familiar with the characteristics of the product or service: its price, promotions, and where the product is distributed.

- *Familiarity with the advertising plan:* The media buyer should be familiar with the overall advertising plan, not just the media portion of it. This includes promotions, public relations, and creative strategies. It is critically important for the buyer to know about the creative message and its component parts in order to place the messages and assure campaign continuity.

- *An accurate picture of the advertiser's market:* Knowing what the competition is and has been up to is an important part of media buying. It might be advantageous for a buyer to imitate the competition's advertising plan if it seems to be working, or it might be strategically wise to come at the prospect from another direction. In addition, it is important that the buyer know what media the client has used before and what was paid for the time or space; this can save the buyer a great deal of start-up time and help him or her to avoid mistakes.

Mind-Set

In 1932, John C. Esty, who then worked at J. Walter Thompson, stated that the degree of importance of the media department in an agency rests upon the ability of the space buyer.[3] Esty noted seven qualifications necessary for this type of work, and these still apply today. The media buyer must be all of the following:

- *Analytical:* The buyer must be mathematically inclined, able to use the research tools available, and able to probe beyond the obvious to make deductions.
- *A clear thinker:* The ability to notice weakness or error in the strategy of one's competition is a prized skill. For the buyer, the ability to discern flawed reasoning or the omission of important information is critical.
- *Fair and open-minded:* The media buyer should get all the facts before coming to a decision and should recognize that the media rep has to make a living too.
- *Insatiably curious:* The buyer must be curious about people and their lives, the work they do, and the things that interest them and that they aspire to.
- *Able to get along with people:* The media buyer is the contact person for individuals at television, radio, and cable stations as well as editors and publishers. It is important that the buyer not antagonize these people, but come to a point of mutual respect with them, as each has a job to do. In addition, the media buyer must work within his or her own cohort of agency peers. This requires team effort and spirit to accomplish the demanding work of advertising.
- *A salesperson:* Often the media buyer is asked to represent the media department, along with the media director, to the agency and often to the client. It is important for the buyer to know how a buy happened and be able to present it enthusiastically and realistically.
- *In touch with changing interests:* The buyer should be in touch with the interests of viewers and readers as well as with changing editorial policies or orientations of the media. The buyer should participate generally in the social and cultural environments of the people to whom he or she is trying to sell.

In the last analysis, the media buyer can make a significant difference to the cost-efficiency of a client's advertising campaign. In some cases this can represent cost savings of hundreds of thousands of dollars. (For more on advertising media, see Lloyd, Chapter 8, this volume.)

Notes

1. See Craig Gugel (ed.), "Bates USA," *Technology Watch,* vol. 1, no. 2, Summer 1994.
2. Jim Surmanek, *Advertising Media Planning* (Chicago: Crain, 1982).
3. John C. Esty, *Careers in Advertising and the Jobs Behind Them,* Alden James (ed.) (New York: Macmillan, 1932).

Advertising Agency Compensation Systems

Rana S. Said

I t is virtually impossible to discuss the advertising industry as it exists today
without tracing the issue of agency remuneration back to its historical roots.
No other aspect of the advertising industry serves as such a strong reminder
of its earliest days. This chapter delineates the history of agency compensation, focusing in particular on the commission system, changes and developments in the system, and the different methods of agency payment that exist
today.

History

In the mid-1800s, the earliest advertising man was one who worked on behalf
of newspaper publishers. Although his role was to sell space to advertisers, he
was not in fact a "wholesaler of space" as some accounts have suggested.

Working on behalf of the publishers of newspapers, the advertising agent brought advertisements from several clients in return for a commission on the cost of the space. The historical development of the commission system and the advertising agency evolved in four major phases, which are described in turn below.

The Publisher's Direct Agent

Volney Palmer, described by most accounts as the first advertising man, started an advertising agency in Philadelphia in 1841 to represent newspapers looking to sell their space. He provided a place where (a) the seller of space could find a buyer and, conversely, a buyer could find a seller; and (b) the price to be paid could be discussed between both parties. Palmer worked specifically for newspaper publishers, and by 1846 he had achieved such credibility that the *Boston Chronotype* wrote about him, "You have only to step into his office with the notice which you wish to have given the whole people of the United States and it is done." [1]

Palmer demanded "recognition" that he was a particular publisher's agent, and in some instances he would go so far as to demand the publisher's recognition of him as sole agent. In his capacity as the publisher's direct agent, Palmer would make contracts on behalf of the buyer and seller of space in addition to collecting the payment. As a fee for this service, Palmer earned a commission of 25% of the gross cost of the space from the publisher. This amount was accepted by the publishers as a small amount to pay for the increase in business brought in by Palmer and later on by other agents following his lucrative path. Publishers today may find that rate of commission excessive, but later it rose to 40%.

The chief stock-in-trade of the agent was the list of newspapers and the advertising rates for those accepting advertising. These lists did not even exist before Palmer appeared on the scene. Palmer's success encouraged competition. His first competitors were managers of offices he had himself set up in other major cities, such as Boston, New York, and Baltimore, and before long, competition came from other agents. The effect of this increase in competition among agents was a lowering of the advertising rates the publishers put on their rate cards. It was not until the late 1860s that the competition among agents began to influence the commission level, which was then reduced to a standard 15%.

Agent as Broker

Volney Palmer was essentially a mediator, in the sense that he brought buyer and seller together. This initial role of the agent that Palmer made famous began to change due to developments in the business itself, such as the fluctuation of publishers' rates and the increase in manufacturing and advertising in general.

The name most associated with the second phase in the history of the advertising agency is George P. Rowell, eventual founder of the trade magazine *Printer's Ink*. In 1865, Rowell had the idea, driven by the increased competition among both agents and publishers, of setting up a plan or "contract" with newspapers. The plan was simple: Newspapers would sell to Rowell a column of space each week for a year. Rowell, in turn, would sell the space—which he had bought in bulk—to advertisers in 1-inch units. At such a rate, the advertiser was offered an inch of space per month in a hundred newspapers for a hundred dollars. While Rowell made a healthy profit with this system, he was also able to compete with other agents by underbidding their rates for the same space. This era is often referred to as the "wholesaling" phase of advertising. Although Palmer was the creator of the commission system, Rowell modified the system by adding two new elements now common in most agency-media relationships: (a) a guarantee of payment whether the advertiser paid or not and (b) a 3% discount for cash payment within 30 days.

As the commission system became more elaborate, so did the lists used by the agents. Unlike Palmer's relatively basic list, by 1869 Rowell's list covered several sections of the United States and listed 5,411 newspapers. Rowell thus set the stage for other agencies such as N. W. Ayer (in 1868) and (in 1864) Carlton & Smith (later to become J. Walter Thompson) to establish their own lists of publications. Typically, these lists were mostly compilations of popular religious papers and farm journals of the time; the agencies simply assumed the management of the publications on their lists.

The Open Contract Phase

In 1875, N. W. Ayer changed the rules with his "open contract" system and his description as "special" agent. Ayer gave advertisers access to the true rates charged by the newspapers and religious journals. He acted at all times as the *advertiser's* agent.[2] The move from "general" to "special" agent marked the differentiating point between the agent as salesman of space and the agent as buyer of space for the advertiser. Some agents, particularly from other regions of the country, such as the Midwest, took this as an opportunity to continue working for the publishers rather than the advertisers. However, as exemplified by Ayer, the role of the agent now was to buy space for the advertiser and to give the advertiser the lowest rate for this space, then billing the advertiser for this net rate plus 17.65% (representing 15% of the gross cost of the space).

Agent to Agency

From the publisher's point of view, the emergence of the special agent was expected to coincide with the departure from the scene of the general agent. The "expert" agent during that time was considered the one who could obtain "good" rates. The role of the agent was far from being perceived as one of strategic and creative consultant. The ability to secure reasonable and competitive rates was seen as more important. By the early 1900s, with lists no longer the sole property of agents, any agency in effect had access to these lists, making the role of the agent as buyer no longer sufficient to justify the commission being paid. Agencies therefore began to expand their areas of expertise to include creative consultation, preparation of advertisements, and other services common today.

Since the development of the commission system, the actual parties involved have not changed: advertiser, agent, and the media. Initially, the commission was paid by the publisher of a newspaper to the agent. N. W. Ayer engineered the change whereby the advertising client in effect paid the agency commission.

This saw the beginning of the stabilized commission rate at 15% of the actual cost of space. By 1901, the same guidelines were devised for magazines. The rate paid by the magazines was traditionally set at 10%. Later, under pressure from the American Association of Advertising Agencies, magazine publishers would increase their rate to 13% and then to 15%, with an additional 2% discount for prompt payment.

It was the newspaper trade association, the American Newspaper Publishers' Association, that in 1893 adopted a resolution stating that a commission was to be paid only to agencies, and that no similar price reduction was to be granted to direct advertisers.

Criticisms of the Commission System

At different times and for different reasons, the commission system has come under attack from advertisers, agencies, and the media. In fact, it has been accompanied by criticism during almost all the years it has been in existence. As early as 1912, during a trade meeting, supporters of the fee system of remuneration blatantly attacked the commission system. In response, *Editor & Publisher* magazine wrote an editorial supporting the commission system.

Recent critics of the traditional 15% system have described what they see as reasons for the failure of the system. These opinions are diverse, but *Adweek* in 1993 reported an opinion that summarizes the majority. At a panel discussion of top advertising executives, Andrew Parsons stated:

> The advertising commission system is damaging the integrity of brand advertising. Going forward, I could see much smaller advertising business volume, certainly in the packaged-goods area. But it would be a much higher margin business because advertising agencies will be regarded as professional and rewarded for the quality of their professional counsel as opposed to the volume of their efforts.

Parsons's comments highlight the basic problem with such a compensation system: It is tied to expenditure of advertising in main media rather than to the performance or effectiveness of this advertising.

In the background are clients' feelings that agencies make too much money. The move toward public ownership of agencies during the 1960s and 1970s disclosed large profit figures, and a number of prominent practitioners made significant capital gains by selling their holdings of agency stock.

The basic discontent with the commission system on the part of advertisers has to do with the scale economies that accompany the system. Scale economies work to favor large advertising agencies—those that have large billings and large, profitable commissions that clients feel they should share. Clients therefore legitimately feel that although the scale economies are a result of their large expenditures, the advertisers themselves lose the benefit. (On the other hand, small advertisers like the commission system because they have to pay their agencies so little.)

Criticism of the commission system is not an artifact of recent changes burgeoning in the industry, although arguably it may have played a secondary role in driving some of these changes. For example, an early criticism of the commission system—and one that still applies today—is that it induces agencies to recommend commissionable media rather than untraditional (non-commissionable) media. Criticism of the commission system, therefore, comes from both the advertisers and the media.

In an attempt to address this weakness, innovative clients and agencies have experimented with other methods of compensation. For example, in the early 1990s, Procter & Gamble announced that it was changing its compensation system by paying agencies 15% commission on advertising in all media, both traditional and nontraditional, such as shopping carts. This was not the first time that an advertiser paid a negotiated "commission" on expenditure for nontraditional media buys.

Another criticism of the commission system of compensation is that it makes it very difficult for agencies to predict their income, because they cannot forecast how much advertisers will spend.

However, even as more criticism surfaces, the traditional 15% commission system still has its supporters. Their argument tends to be fairly straightforward: Of the current choices, the traditional commission system is the best, and it would be unwise to abandon it without the availability of a better alternative. A British opinion compares it to the House of Lords: "It is obviously wrong, but it seems to work."

Current Compensation Systems

Today there are three main methods of compensation for advertising: the traditional 15% commission system, commission at lower rates, and the labor-based fee system. The Association of National Advertisers (ANA), founded in 1912, attempts to track the methods of compensation used by advertisers through repeated surveys of advertisers' practices.[3] Under the research system set up by William Weilbacher, the ANA surveys advertisers on the methods of compensation they use. The relative importance of these systems is displayed in Table 10.1.

The Traditional Commission System

The traditional 15% commission system applies to all media with the exception of outdoor advertising, which uses $16\frac{2}{3}$%. To illustrate the mechan-

TABLE 10.1 Trends in Methods of Agency Compensation (in percentages)

Year	Traditional 15%	Commission Not 15%	Labor-Based Fee	Other Systems
1986	43	24	30	3
1989	35	29	24	12
1992	33	26	32	9
1994	14	45	35	7
1997	9	26	53	12

SOURCE: Data from the Association of National Advertisers.

ics of the 15% system using the example of television, if a television spot costs $100,000, the agency bills its client $100,000 but will pay the television station only $85,000. The $15,000 is kept by the advertising agency as its commission.

As can be seen in Table 10.1, the actual rate of 15% has been dwindling under pressure from advertisers. Rates are often as low as 12%, and even, in rare cases, down to 5%. These trends indicate a continual decline in the traditional 15% media commission as a form of agency compensation. This decline reflects both a substantial use of commissions less than 15% and an even more important movement to a labor-based fee structure.

It is not uncommon for the agency and the advertiser to agree on an unusually low rate of commission as a stipulation for new business. Other agencies and clients operate on a sliding scale system depending on the size of the billings (in the language of advertising, *billings* refers to the total amount of its clients' money that an agency spends). This is usually the case with very large advertisers. For example, 15% might be the commission on billings of up to $10 million, but the commission may fall to 10% for billings of more than $25 million. Some categories of advertisers tend to favor certain types of compensation, such as cigarette companies, which often pay a commission of 10%.

Fees: Time of Staff and Retainers

In a system modeled after the fee system used by lawyers and accountants, the client and agency agree on a reasonable hourly fee or charge, which is calculated by taking all the expenses incurred and translating these into an hourly rate, usually based on the agency's estimates of cost accounting for salary (time of staff), rent, telephone, postage, travel, any other attributable expenses, plus agreed profit. Often the agency writes in a basic monthly minimum, called a retainer, which is exceeded when the work builds up. All agency people working on a particular client's work keep close track of the time spent.

There are advantages in the fee system for both advertiser and agency. For the advertiser, the amount paid to the agency covers just the services needed. Furthermore, a cut in an advertiser's budget does not need to be accompanied by a reduction of agency staff. On the other hand, one of the reasons that some resist the fee system is that it takes a lot more time and effort on the part of the agency, which must be specific in terms of costs for labor, overhead, and other expenses. In fact, there is a very heavy markup for both direct and indirect overhead, generally well over 100%.

Reasons for changes in the compensation system include other trends as well, such as media inflation, advertisers becoming more cost-conscious and therefore tougher in negotiating commission rates, and advertising agencies' willingness to do more nonmedia work. Certain categories of advertisers, such as those in the business-to-business field, and those advertisers requiring a great amount of below-the-line activity and print collateral material (services such as hotels and banks) tend to favor the fee system.

Some agencies use a combination of methods. For example, Unilever uses the fee system with new product development, and commission with established products. Unilever has also established a base commission, but with incentives for superior work. This introduces an important new argument: a demand for increased accountability from the advertising agency in terms of the development and performance of the advertising that it generates. I shall return to this point later in this chapter.

In addition, television and print production has traditionally been billed to the advertiser with a markup, usually 17.65% of the net cost paid by the agency to its outside supplier. However, in recent years, as labor-based compensation has become more popular, production costs are being charged net to an increasing degree.

David Ogilvy has provided an extremely succinct summary of the advantages of the fee system:[4]

1. The agency can be more objective in its recommendations; or so many clients
   believe.

2. The agency has adequate incentive to provide noncommissionable services if needed.
3. The agency's income is stabilized. Unforeseen cuts in advertising expenditure do not result in red figures or temporary personnel layoffs.
4. The fee enables the agency to make a fair profit on services rendered. The advertiser, in turn, pays for what he gets—no more, no less.
5. Every fee account pays its own way. Unprofitable accounts do not ride on the coattails of profitable accounts.

However, Ogilvy has also concluded that the business is not yet ready for the fee system: Client resistance is a real impediment to its universal adoption.

Accountability

In tandem with other industry trends is a move toward more accountability in the business in general. The traditional commission system, among other things, is under scrutiny from advertisers who want to measure accurately the effects of their advertising dollars. Proactive clients and agencies alike are taking action. Clients such as Campbell's are adapting to it by grading their agencies based on performance. Research-intensive agencies such as DDB Needham have created a system in which compensation is tied to the performance of their clients' brands. If the clients are demanding more from their agencies in terms of accountability and negotiating for different and lower levels of commission, the agencies are in turn demanding compensation for services once provided free, such as the development of the strategy, the foundation for all advertising.

In 1997, 30% of advertisers were paying their agencies according to some "incentive" or "accountability" formula. This turbulent debate regarding agency remuneration often resurfaces, in particular around the times of trade conferences and professional association meetings. The debate ebbs and flows. In recent years, it has flowed increasingly often.

The issues surrounding the compensation system in advertising are not unique to the United States. The situation varies from one country to another, but the issues surrounding it remain the same. The Incorporated Society of British Advertisers has proposed that agencies should be paid according to a sliding scale of commissions that would be lower than the established 15%. Among Canadian advertising agencies, the traditional 15% is now being used by fewer agencies. Many informed observers feel that if changes in compensation structure would serve as the impetus for advertisers and advertising agencies to operate closely together in developing and working toward specific objectives, then the changes would be worthwhile.

As this book was going to press, two important pieces of news were announced regarding agency compensation systems in the United States.

First, Procter & Gamble stated that it planned to implement, from early 1999, an incentive-based agency compensation scheme for seven of its brands: a change that could mean the end of this advertiser's use of media commission "within a year."[5] Second, General Motors announced its intention to scrap agency commissions totally, in favor of fee-based compensation, with effect also from January 1999. General Motors was joining a long list of clients renumerating their agencies by fees for whole or part of their accounts: a list that includes Mercedes-Benz of North America, BMW America, MasterCard International, American Express Co., IBM Corp., Unilever, Colgate-Palmolive Co., Kmart Corp., Levi Strauss & Co., Procter & Gamble Co., and Ford Motor Co.[6]

Notes

1. Quoted in James Webb Young, *Advertising Agency Compensation* (Chicago: University of Chicago Press, 1933).

2. Martin Mayer, *Madison Avenue, U.S.A.* (New York: Harper & Brothers, 1958), 17.

3. Association of National Advertisers, *Current Advertiser Practices in Compensating Their Advertising Agencies* (New York: Association of National Advertisers, various years). The most recent data appear in Judann Pollack, "ANA Survey: Under 50% Pay Agency Commissions," *Advertising Age,* June 15, 1998, 18.

4. David Ogilvy, *The Unpublished David Ogilvy* (New York: Ogilvy Group, 1986), 128.

5. Sally Beatty, "P&G Will Test Payment Scheme for Ads," *Wall Street Journal,* November 10, 1998.

6. Jean Halliday, "GM Will Scrap Agency Commissions," *Advertising Age,* November 16, 1998.

New Business Activity

Account Reviews

Randall Rothenberg

Don Peppers, a likable schemer who headed the business development efforts at, sequentially, the Levine, Huntley, Schmidt & Beaver, Lintas, and Chiat/Day advertising agencies in New York before becoming a consultant and best-selling author, uses a terse maxim to describe the essence of agency business: "Life's a pitch." [1]

Few activities in advertising—indeed, in all of American industry—capture so fully the fervor, the excesses, the heartaches, and, most of all, the euphoria that drive capitalism than the pitch, known more formally as the advertising account review. Requiring the rapid mobilization of personnel and money, cunning and creativity, these contests among ad agencies to win or retain clients' business are, in no small way, a central force in the shaping of consumer culture.

NOTE: Copyright held by Randall Rothenberg.

"Look at what excites people in other fields," says Jim Dale, the former president of the W. B. Doner agency in Baltimore. "They are instances where ideas change circumstances. In science, someone is searching for an idea to extend our life expectancies. The novelist is taking an idea out of the air. We get to take a particular business we're not in and change its destiny."

Although the recession of the late 1980s and early 1990s gave rise to the belief that clients were switching agencies with increasing alacrity, little statistical evidence exists to support this. Neither *Advertising Age* nor *Adweek,* the industry's two leading trade publications, maintains comprehensive statistics on account switching. The closest the American Association of Advertising Agencies (AAAA), the industry's main trade association, comes to keeping tabs is a once-a-decade survey of account tenure. The AAAA's 1985 survey showed an account's average length of stay at an average agency to be 7.2 years, with the largest agencies maintaining their client relationships for 14 years. Those figures indicate little change from 27 years earlier, when Martin Mayer, in his book *Madison Avenue, U.S.A.,* found reports showing that the average large account at the average large agency stayed for 4, 7, or 10 years, "depending on which of three studies you believe." [2]

Certainly, however, there have been striking—and expensive—changes in the way business is pursued in advertising. Some have been impelled by new research and production technologies that allow for the more rapid study of consumers' desires and the creation of near-finished print and video executions. For the most part, however, the reorganization and spiraling costs of account reviews stem from agencies' desperate efforts to maintain themselves in an era of advertising-weary consumers and ever-shrinking margins.[3]

The existence of "rainmakers" like Don Peppers, frequently well-compensated executives charged solely with the task of trolling for prospects, is one such change. Before the 1980s, this responsibility was generally held by an agency's chairman and president, who pursued new accounts largely through social contacts made via club memberships, artfully managed "chance" meetings, and lavish entertainments. Once, in Lancaster, Pennsylvania, to chase the Armstrong Cork Company account, David Ogilvy even arranged to deliver a speech at the church he knew the company's president, a Scottish American, attended. With eloquence, Ogilvy lauded the Scots Presbyterian role in the nation's history, linking together Patrick Henry, John Paul Jones, 35 justices of the U.S. Supreme Court, and the president of Armstrong Cork. Needless to say, Ogilvy & Mather got the account.

"There's no question that everybody tried to get as close to a prospect as possible," Bart Cummings, the late chairman of the Compton agency, said in 1989. "Many of us were given opportunities to present ourselves because we got close to some important people."

The slowdown in advertising spending that accompanied the last recession spelled the end of old-boy networking. As Bert Metter, then chairman of J. Walter Thompson U.S.A., said during the depth of the last economic downturn: "It's become so competitive in the past five or six years that it became apparent you can't have a huge operation with no sales department. Since there has to be a concentrated effort on getting new business, specialists grew up." Many of these rainmakers—by most accounts at least half of them—are women, a phenomenon that ad executives attribute in part to the growing feminization of the industry.[4]

Another change has been the growing importance of creative work in securing new accounts. In contrast to decades past, rare today is the account review that does not rest in large part on the perceived quality of the speculative advertising shown. Cummings has noted that in the late 1930s, when he was at Benton & Bowles, any agency that prepared material for a prospective client "was looked down upon." According to Cummings, "Everyone thought that was in bad taste, and ethically not right."

Although agencies began using speculative creative work after World War II, clients' and agencies' reliance on it is a contemporary phenomenon. Marketing and agency executives attribute this in part to the agencies' abandonment of quantitative research, until recently a primary agency function but now a role performed by third-party, syndicated services. Some marketing scholars point to studies showing "likability," which is almost purely a function of creativity, to be a more accurate gauge of advertising effectiveness than recall, persuasiveness, or other, more conventional measures. Whatever the reason, "the emphasis has shifted from a preoccupation with substance," says William Weilbacher, a leading marketing consultant who has assisted such giant advertisers as Prudential Insurance and Burger King with their account reviews. "A lot more time and money is being spent on what the finished product looks like."

For all the changes, ad executives old and young appear to agree that the account review is the most emotionally and intellectually satisfying part of their business. "It's one of the joys," says Michael Moore, an agency marketing researcher. "I get tired of refining the same solution [for existing clients]." Jack Taylor, a consultant and former partner in the New York agency Jordan,

McGrath, Case & Taylor, says that "aside from the agony and the risk involved, the review is probably the most fun there is. After you get the account, there's baggage and politics."

Politics, however, is never far from the review process. Whereas stagnating sales and market share pressures often motivate advertisers to reexamine their agency relationships, as often as not other, more personal reasons drive a client to throw its account open to competition. A new senior marketing executive may want to consolidate his power; firing the existing ad agency and dismantling its support network within the client company can facilitate this. A chief executive officer trying to force an unpalatable distribution strategy on her salespeople may decide to sacrifice her ad agency to soothe the fractious minions.

For such reasons do corporate executives, who are otherwise steeped in the details of marketing science as taught in business schools, look to other, more ephemeral qualities in agencies when they embark on account reviews. "It is not just like a regular vendor relationship, it is almost a marriage," said Mark Dunn, then the advertising manager of Subaru of America, when the car company began an account review in 1991. "And you've got to like these people as individuals, and respect them as individuals, and like the same things they do, to understand it."

For the marketer, there are no easy steps in selecting an agency. Even coming up with a manageable list of agencies capable of handling the business and free from account conflicts is complicated by the sheer numbers of agencies in the United States. Altogether, the U.S. Department of Commerce estimates that there are some 20,000 companies in the United States that deserve to be called advertising agencies. The *Standard Directory of Advertising Agencies,* a thick guide known in the industry as the Red Book, lists more than 5,000 advertising agencies. Weilbacher, the consultant, recommends in his authoritative handbook, *Choosing and Working With Your Advertising Agency,* that marketers looking for an agency limit themselves to the narrower list of *"bona fide* advertising agencies" published annually in *Advertising Age.* But even this more selective catalog still numbers 533 companies.[5] Thus it is not uncommon for marketers today to employ search consultants to help them wend their way through the thicket of names, organize reviews, and arrange contracts and compensation.

The rise of search consultants and the pressures on agency performance and profitability date from 1986, when a Napoleonic 5-foot, 4-inch ad executive from New Jersey named Robert Jacoby sold his agency for $500 million, netting a personal profit of $112 million. Clients, unsurprisingly, began thinking that maybe they were paying their agencies a tad too generously.

To the broad public, Jacoby's agency, Ted Bates Worldwide, represented everything that was most annoying about American advertising. Bates was the agency that had promoted the Unique Selling Proposition (USP)—the theory that claimed that the endless echoing of a single slogan or product benefit would sell that product—forever! (Jones describes this technique in Chapter 23, this volume.) Few outside the agency understood how immensely profitable the USP was to Bates. As sales by Bates's clients ballooned during the boom years of the 1950s and 1960s, the agency used the USP to argue its clients into ever-increasing ad spending. Those ads, per the USP, rarely changed a whit. (Once, Rosser Reeves, the father of the USP, and a client were sailing in the Caribbean, and the client, as a tease, asked the ad man, "You have 700 people in that office of yours, and you've been running the same ad for me for the last 11 years. What I want to know is, what are those 700 people supposed to be doing?" According to Martin Mayer, Reeves responded, "They're keeping your advertising department from changing your ad.") Under the fixed-commission system, every additional dollar Bates's clients spent on advertising was almost pure profit to the agency.

So it was that, thanks to the USP, Bates accrued a vast treasure—the largest share of which went to Bob Jacoby, the third chairman-owner in Bates's history, when he decided to cash out in 1986 by selling the agency to the British conglomerate Saatchi & Saatchi. Jacoby's personal windfall might have gone unnoticed had Saatchi, the British advertising empire that was then gobbling up every available agency in sight, not taken out double-page advertisements in the *Wall Street Journal* and the *New York Times* touting its impressive profitability—profitability that, its clients noted, was built on their own advertising expenditures!

Jacoby's fortune and Saatchi's crowing were acutely embarrassing to the agency business, and the repercussions were swift. Giant consumer-products companies fired longtime agencies, publicly complaining about client conflicts in the merged conglomerates but privately grumbling about excessive agency compensation. And to find new agencies, marketers large and small began turning to advertising search consultants. The consultants' role was not only to manage account reviews, but also to negotiate the victorious agency's compensation down to a reasonable level—*reasonable* being defined as something that would not make the client look like a patsy if its agency got sold and the account executives retired to Gstaad at age 35.

Ad agency compensation, to be sure, had always been a bone of contention between marketers and their agencies. The Association of National Advertisers, the trade organization that represents the marketing departments of consumer-product and service companies, was founded in 1912 specifically to destroy the fixed-commission system of agency pay. This effort came to naught. In 1956, the U.S. Department of Justice accused the American Association of Advertising Agencies of price fixing for enforcing the system and persuaded the trade group to sign a consent decree and abandon the practice. By that time, however, the fixed 15% commission was engraved in clients' minds. As late as the mid-1980s, 43% of all clients gave their agencies the full 15% commission, rarely questioning the logic behind the catechisms (see Said, Chapter 10, this volume).

By the late 1980s, however, the "megamerger" boom (as the period of agency consolidation was called) and the subsequent disclosures of agency wealth pushed clients over the edge. Consultants and compensation negotiation became de rigueur in account reviews. Their presence created anguish in agency executive suites. In 1987, several ad agencies pursuing the $150 million Nissan automobile account disclosed that the Japanese car company's search consultant was offering agencies compensation equaling 8% of billings—little more than half the age-old standard commission. Ogilvy & Mather angrily withdrew from the competition at the last minute, its U.S. chairman telling the car company's advertising director, "If you pay peanuts, you get monkeys."

In May 1988, Leonard S. Matthews, president of the AAAA, publicly attacked Nissan's consultant, a former marketing research executive at J. Walter Thompson and Grey named Alvin Achenbaum, calling him a "quisling." "Why are we letting the consultants of this world tell our clients we can get by just fine—and will happily do so—on less?" complained Matthews. He failed to remind his audience of agency executives that their own greed had inspired the consultants' rise. His well-publicized tirade served only to highlight the compensation issue and to attract marketers to the consultants.

The consultant's first job, generally, is to arrange the would-be client's "credentials visits." These are tours of and presentations by a select group of agencies to the client's senior executives. Agencies are usually asked to expound on their corporate philosophies, present case studies of brand positionings or turnarounds, and run through reels of creative product. Astute agencies will use the credentials visit to advertise their expertise in the visitor's line of business, and even to take a stab at analyzing the prospect's marketing problem. From the credentials visits, the client selects a list of finalist agencies to pitch its account.

Marketers are not alone in turning to outsiders for help in account reviews. Increasingly, finalist agencies, too, look to external expertise in organizing a pitch. Commonly, an agency will hire a consultant with knowledge of the prospect's industry—a former marketing executive, for example, or a former agency executive with analogous account experience—to organize the review. This expert analyzes the research; coordinates the creative teams; meets with the prospect's executives, suppliers, and dealers; and participates in proprietary qualitative studies.

"You have to understand how the distribution system works—how dealers and manufacturers go together," says C. Ray Freeman, who has been a senior manager at the Lord, Geller, Federico, Einstein; Lord Einstein O'Neill & Partners; and Dentsu Corporation of America agencies, as well as at IBM. "You need to know the structure that supports the product, which is complex."

The prospective client is usually told that the consultant is in the employ of the agency; in fact, he or she frequently works on a contingency contract, under which the consultant will accept employment only if the account is awarded to the agency.

Freelance copywriters, art directors, and producers also are brought in to develop strategies and speculative creative work for a pitch. Some call these seasoned creatives, who can charge as much as $1,000 a day, "creative Hessians," because prospective clients are not told that the strategies and mock ads they are seeing are the work of outsiders.[6] Ron Travisano, a commercial director and cofounder of the agency once known as Della Femina, Travisano & Partners, has said: "To bring somebody from the outside to pitch an account is living a lie."

Executives and freelancers say the primary reason outsiders are used for new-business presentations is the reduction in the size of agencies' staffs. By the late 1980s, average ad agency employment had fallen well below two people for each $1 million of capitalized billings, down from 3.57 people a decade earlier, according to the AAAA.

Whether they hire outsiders or not, agencies accepted into the finals of an account review will usually organize their personnel in similar ways. The pitch director (usually the outside consultant, the head of new business development, or the account executive who is slated to head the account) will serve as a sort of cerebrum, joined in a "central brain" setup by the agency's research director (the cerebellum) and the media director (the medulla oblongata).

Together, they will draw in all the available knowledge about the client company, its problems, its politics, its markets and competitive difficulties, and its consumers and the way to reach them. Syndicated market research firms, media planners, and qualitative research suppliers will provide stimuli—from hard data to soft impressions—to this brain, which will translate the information into a plan of action for the agency's creative teams. This plan of action, called the *brief,* is usually a one-sentence (hence the name) assertion of how the prospect should position itself in the marketplace.

The wide availability of syndicated research has forced ad agencies pitching an account to rely more and more on their own qualitative research; it is the only way for them to put a signature "spin" on the data and justify their strategies and creative product. Wilder Baker, the head of the Warwick, Baker & Fiore agency, has explained his shop's use of research in the 1991 Subaru review:

What they [Subaru] have is a lot of knowledge—segmentation studies, research—but when we looked through it we didn't see in it an understanding, from their research, why they were losing business. They've got to find out who their target audience is and broaden their appeal to the next concentric circle. We started with one-on-one interviews in Chicago and Philadelphia. We employed a research technique that borders on such intense concentration it could almost be hypnotic. They're one-hour, two-hour interviews with Subaru owners. Really intensive. We wanted to understand them. Then we went and talked to others we thought would be like them. Then we started doing lines and concepts and ideas with our creative people.

Many agencies involved in a major account review will set up several competing creative teams, all sharing the same information and addressing the same brief, but working separately to develop speculative print ads, television commercials, direct-mail pieces, and point-of-purchase displays. Almost without exception, these teams try first to devise a new slogan for the prospect, the slogan having established itself—for reasons probably best left to anthropologists to describe—as the sine qua non of American advertising. "Creative people want an anthem, a banner, to create to," says Ray Freeman, explaining the importance of the slogan. "It's a neat summation of what the advertising leads you to expect. And clients expect it."

Although they deny it, clients also expect gorgeously rendered speculative creative work, too. For this reason, agencies engaged in pitching an account will spend much time and money on beautifully painted storyboards and print ad mock-ups, and on mock television commercials. The TV spots are often composed of footage spliced together from existing commercials, hence their name, *ripomatics,* their material "ripped off" from others' work. The prevalence of ripomatics (which, in the pitch, are often backed by existing popular music tracks) helps explain the look-alike/sound-alike quality of so much contemporary advertising.

The final element required of an agency pitching an account is a compensation proposal. Although the AAAA has decried the pressure on agency compensation and railed against consultants' involvement in negotiating fees, it is nonetheless true that agencies are increasingly willing to bargain over payment and accept far less than the once-standard 15% commission on media billings. And clients frequently base their agency selections, at least in part, on cost.

The range of compensation offers is well illustrated by the six finalists in the 1991 Subaru review.[7] Jordan, McGrath, Case & Taylor was the highest. Where most agencies rationalized their compensation recommendations with a few paragraphs of analysis, this agency's proposal went on for 11 full pages of detail that, in the end, miraculously added up to a first-year commission of exactly 15%, or a fee of $13 million, based on presumed ad spending of $79 million to $100 million.

Wieden & Kennedy of Portland, Oregon, asked for a 13% commission, which, on $70 million of ad spending, would have come out to a monthly fee of $760,000. Warwick, Baker & Fiore requested a 12.1% commission, or a $7.3 million annual fee. Levine, Huntley, Vick & Beaver, the incumbent, which had been receiving a 12.1% commission for the account, said that it would drop down to an 11% commission, which the agency said would allow it to break even but not earn a profit. W. B. Doner of Baltimore, basing its calculations on an annual ad budget of $55 million, requested compensation of 11.25%, or $6.19 million—exclusive of fees for media buying and public relations. Doner said it would handle media buying for a separate 1.5% commission.

DCA, the New York affiliate of Japan's Dentsu, proffered the lowest arrangement of all. It said it would work at cost for the first 24 months. The agency figured its cost at a far lower rate than any of the other agencies, calculating it as the salaries of the 42 people it planned to devote to the account plus 95% of their salaries to cover indirect labor, overhead, benefits, and taxes. All told, DCA said it would accept an 8.5% commission, or an annual fee of only $4.7 million.

Wieden & Kennedy, with the second-highest proposal, won the account, but accepted lower compensation. In bypassing Jordan, McGrath, an agency they also liked, the Subaru executives pointedly noted in their discussions the size of its compensation package.

Needless to say, the costs of pitching an account can be enormous.[8] Agency executives say that they routinely spend from $100,000 to as much as $250,000 to pursue an account worth $50 million or more in annual billings (which, under the standard 15% commission and conventional profitability calculations, would yield approximately $1.5 million in annual profits, but only after first-year start-up costs are absorbed). "The things that generally cost the most are music tracks and ripomatics," says Philip B. Dusenberry, the chairman of BBDO New York. "Editing, if you want it done right, you go outside your agency to an editing house. It means poring through hundreds and hundreds of movies and commercials to make that spot work. It's very time-intensive and labor-intensive." A single ripomatic, he says, can cost from $20,000 to $50,000.

Research, too, contributes to the expense. Bob Bloom, the head of the Bloom FCA agency, says that $100,000 of the agency's $250,000 out-of-pocket cost in pitching the Nissan Infiniti account in the late 1980s was spent on syndicated and qualitative research. Bloom did not get the account.

Total costs can be nothing short of astronomical. Chiat/Day claimed to have spent $1 million out-of-pocket in its successful pursuit of the Nissan auto account in 1987. "We had an unlimited budget," agency founder Jay Chiat said at the time, "and we exceeded it."

The time, effort, and money come together in a final pitch, which, depending on the number of finalists in the review (two to five is not uncommon), usually takes place over the course of 1 to 5 days. Although agencies strive throughout the review process to differentiate themselves from others, the fact is that they structure their presentations in numbingly similar ways.

The typical presentation will open with the agency chairman or president introducing his staff and promising to accomplish magic for the ailing client. He then introduces the account director, who sometimes is the outside consultant acting under subterfuge, who proceeds to restate the prospect's current marketing position and problem. The research director then takes over and walks the client through the data that led the agency to its conclusion about repositioning, which is then unveiled in the form of the brief. At that point, the agency's creative director takes the reins and, after some teasing, drives the presentation toward the orchestrated revelation of the new slogan. The speculative creative work is then revealed; storyboards are acted out dramatically by agency personnel. Media strategy is almost always relegated to an abbreviated coda. The whole affair is as ritualistic as High Mass.

Such attention to detail, and the expenditures behind it, only hint, however, at what lies at the heart of an account review: politics. In a business built upon relationships, the difference between victory and defeat for an ad agency may come down to contrivance and nuance. When asked whether agencies pitching accounts concentrate on what is necessary to win or on what is required to improve the client's business, experienced researcher Michael Moore answered, "The two are rarely the same."

Hence the focus on glitz, on showmanship. According to BBDO's Dusenberry:

> The trick is to position the brand strategically and have that overlay of creative that socks it home. Every agency is trying to get an edge. The agency is afraid to take the chance to only come in with strategic thinking and bare-bones creative, because they're afraid that the prospect will be swayed by the emotional impact of the work. A finished ripomatic with sound effects and an announcer will leap to life in a far more impactful way than something sitting on a storyboard. Prospects are human. If they hear a song or see a piece of film that touches them in some way, it gives you an edge.

The efforts of senior agency executives and their outside consultants preparatory to a final pitch often revolve around this search for a personal edge. The visits to senior client executives, the tours of sales floors, the dinners with distributors are aimed as much at charming the prospect as at eliciting useful data. Jack Taylor, formerly of Jordan, McGrath, calls such exercises "heroic actions." He notes, "In the end, [an agency] may get better credit for this if [its] strategic recommendations are not that different from the others."

But the construction of a pitch is not solely a cynical appeal to a client's emotions. The consultant on the 1991 Subaru pitch explained the point of account reviews succinctly. "We're looking for an agency that can sell itself," he said. "Because if it can't sell itself, how can it sell Subaru?"

Notes

1. Randall Rothenberg, "Advertising: Chiat Gets 'Rainmaker' From Lintas," *New York Times,* March 1, 1990, D23.

2. Martin Mayer, *Madison Avenue, U.S.A.* (New York: Harper & Brothers Publishers, 1958).

3. Leo Bogart, *Strategy in Advertising: Matching Media and Messages to Markets and Motivations,* 2nd ed. (Lincolnwood, IL: NTC Business Books, 1990).

4. Randall Rothenberg, "Advertising: Women Gain Foothold in Drive for Accounts," *New York Times,* July 25, 1989, D1.

5. William Weilbacher, *Choosing and Working With Your Advertising Agency* (Lincolnwood, IL: NTC Business Books, 1990).

6. See Randall Rothenberg, "Advertising: The 'Creative Hessians' Are Coming," *New York Times,* February 16, 1990, D17.

7. Randall Rothenberg, *Where the Suckers Moon: An Advertising Story* (New York: Alfred A. Knopf, 1994).

8. Randall Rothenberg, "For Ad Agencies, a Costly Hard Sell," *New York Times,* February 4, 1991, D1.

12

The Culture of
an Advertising Agency

John Philip Jones

Sir David Orr, a businessman of great distinction who made his early reputation in marketing and was chairman of Unilever for 8 years, once emphasized something that is not immediately obvious to businesspeople who know manufacturing and trading organizations but are less familiar with advertising agencies. The agency, when compared with other types of organizations, especially the manufacturing companies that are its clients, "thrives on a very different culture. . . . the product company, whether in goods or services, is always more structured and hierarchical. . . . [It] will also be steeped in its product, whereas the agency is more sensitive to wider trends in the market." [1]

It is generally (and I think correctly) recognized that there are advantages in advertisers and agencies being separate organizations with no overlap of ownership, for the very reason that the corporate culture of the agency is or should be different from that of its clients. This is a topic worth exploring, and this chapter is devoted to a formal, although subjective, examination of the meaning of an agency's culture. In my opinion, an agency's culture has important influence on its stability and productivity, matters obviously relevant to the ways we can reduce waste in the advertising system.

First, a definition and some amplification: The notion of *corporate culture* is widely discussed in business circles, and at least one book has been devoted to describing and illustrating it.[2] The authors provide details of the elements that contribute to a corporate culture, but in rather abstract fashion, and the points they raise do not in my judgment help us to understand what happens in an advertising agency. A corporate culture may be most succinctly described as, in the words of a management consultant, "the way we do things around here."[3]

On a recent visit to Wolff-Olins, an outstandingly successful British company that specializes in design and especially corporate identification, I was struck by the firm's way of defining and using this concept of corporate culture. A design organization is different from an advertising agency, but what the large players in both fields have in common is that they work directly for major manufacturing and service organizations by writing and agreeing on a communications strategy for each client and developing creative ideas in response to that strategy.

Design organizations and advertising agencies often establish their own communications strategies (i.e., defining how they in turn should be perceived by existing and potential clients). Wolff-Olins does this neatly, in the way described in Figure 12.1. The figure suggests how the culture of the Wolff-Olins organization is a "soft" expression of that organization's core competencies and also an internal expression of its image as this is presented to the outside world. But not only is the culture derived from the organization's core competencies and image, it is also an expression of a robust quality: the organization's competitive advantages in the marketplace. Its carefully nurtured corporate culture ensures that the imaginative and talented people who make up the workforce will march to the same drumbeat, and in their everyday endeavors generate synergies.

The Wolff-Olins model therefore defines the forces that are brought together to enable the organization to tackle most efficiently its professional challenges. From my own experience of advertising agencies, the culture itself (irrespective of the external and internal influences on it) has two separate dimensions: The type of people an agency recruits (the *social culture*) and the

External Audience	Competitive Advantages	Image
Internal Audience	Core Competencies	Culture
	"Hard" Communication	"Soft" Communication

Figure 12.1. Wolff-Olins's Four Boxes

agency's attitude toward the advertising enterprise (the *philosophical culture*). These things are not always articulated, although they have been in well-known individual cases.

The social culture defines the agency's style, sense of values, ethical principles, atmosphere, and standing in the business community, as well as the (stated or unstated) norms of behavior that an agency expects of its employees. These include the agency's definition of *client service,* an important aspect of which is whether or not the agency is prepared on occasion to give unpalatable objective advice.

The agency's philosophical culture defines its belief in advertising, its understanding of the role of advertising and how advertising works, and—most important—its own distinctive approach to the creation of effective advertising.[4] These beliefs and attitudes are intellectually based, but they all contain or have developed an overtone that can truthfully be said to transcend rationality. Indeed, a distinguished advertising researcher has detected a close analogy between competing agency philosophies and competing religions.[5] The reason that agency philosophies have developed beyond the bounds of rationality is that since the time in the early part of the 20th century when advertising evaluation ceased being an exclusive matter of direct-response pulling power, the industry has had no tough and universally recognized criteria of effectiveness. Theories (of varying quality and usefulness) gradually took the place of objectively verifiable performance, and these theories became associated with particular agencies.

Over and beyond these matters of belief and attitude, an agency culture also covers much simpler matters: how the agency should be organized to produce effective advertising and how this can be done efficiently and profitably. Most of the larger agencies are organized on a "matrix" system, with strong lateral lines of control and weak vertical lines on the organizational chart. This can be a formula for chaos, but the disciplines of the other parts of the agency's culture often manage to provide a cement to maintain cohesion. A culture can, in other words, substitute for a rigid hierarchy.

The culture of an agency can arise spontaneously as part of a process in which mutually compatible people learn to work together, but far more often it is imposed from above. How this actually happens is that younger people consciously or half-consciously model their own work on that of their seniors, whom they respect professionally. This is obviously a lengthy and complicated procedure, but it is unlikely to happen unless an agency management wants it to happen. As Denis Lanigan has noted, the process "cannot be delegated and it cannot be created by osmosis because, though the soil may be fertile, it is up to the management to enrich the soil. I see management's main job in an agency as establishing the sympathetic climate in which creative talent can flourish." [6] It is also important for the management of an agency to establish and reinforce both the social culture and the philosophical culture. The former naturally embraces recruitment and training.

One very obvious aspect of an agency's culture is the extent to which the agency is account driven (dominated by the account executives) or creative driven (dominated by the creative department). As I argue in this chapter, agency cultures do not change much in their character, although they can fade or grow stronger over time. The agency's account or creative orientation is the most immutable feature of all.[7]

The presence of a strong agency culture brings advantages. An agency with a strong culture makes the best use of the most talented people, and this use leads to synergy. A strong culture can also result in improved morale and can make it easier to select new staff. And a strong culture provides continuity—a heritage—in a business marked by volatility as both clients and employees come and go. It cements loyalty on the part of the agency staff. Rather importantly, clients expect an agency to have a recognizable culture. The wiser ones recognize the value to them of what the agency has perhaps unconsciously absorbed from its wider professional experience, which often covers many product fields—experience that has contributed to its culture in important ways. And most client executives who work directly with advertising agencies have backgrounds in sales and expect their advertising to be sold to them; this can be done most convincingly by an agency with depth and special expertise, elements that again contribute to this culture.

The tone of what I have said so far commends the general notion of an agency culture, but this approval amounts to only a partial truth, because there is a downside. In this chapter I will examine both sides of the case in the context of a single prominent agency, one in which I spent most of my professional career.

"Aunty Knows Best"

I worked at J. Walter Thompson, London, for three separate periods: 1953-1955, 1957-1965, and 1972-1980. It is difficult to imagine an advertising agency that has a stronger corporate culture. The agency has never been shy about exercising its judgment and expressing strong opinions, a process described by an elderly client on whose business I worked in the early 1960s with the use of the nursery phrase, familiar to an older generation of Englishmen and -women, "Aunty knows best."

The culture of J. Walter Thompson (JWT) was originally developed in New York and stemmed from the personalities of Stanley Resor and the cluster of outstanding people who, in effect, created the J. Walter Thompson company in its modern incarnation in the 1920s. The culture spread out from New York and involved the increasing number of overseas offices that the company opened. It was only in the 1960s that some important overseas offices—London in particular—became significantly different from the New York office in their culture.

The key to understanding the company's culture as it was created by Resor and his colleagues was the process of analyzing problems through a comprehensive and longitudinal evaluation of brands; JWT was the first agency to be interested in the shape and composition of markets. Following the stage of analysis, the advertising generated by the agency was invariably studied, rational, and soundly based. The culture of the company, as it was explained to me when I was a young man, called for "taking problems apart" [8] and developing well-considered creative recommendations. This was before the time when an agency's creative product (rather than its powers of analysis) had become the most critical competitive discriminator between itself and other agencies. Most of the advertisements produced by JWT appeared in print media until about the mid-1950s in the United States and the early 1960s in Britain, as newspapers and magazines were the dominant media for national advertisers before these dates. The advertisements themselves were composed with a literary rather than an artistic orientation. They tended to be "copy-heavy." The agency was strongly account driven—and it has continued to be so, despite the evolutions that have taken place in its culture.

JWT's culture in the United States and abroad embraced both the elements I have described: the social and the philosophical. The classic expression of the former was (and is) the "Thompson man." He was given this name before the era of feminism, although a few of the most important figures in the company's history have in fact been women. This phrase describes the combination of brains, sophistication, good breeding, and good manners that characterizes most (although not all) of the account executives, creative people, account planners, media people, and researchers who work for the agency. One of the most delightful bons mots attributed to Stanley Resor is the following: "What we have discovered is that we can turn a gentleman into an advertising man, but we have been unable to educate an advertising man to be a gentleman; this is something his mother should have done a long time ago." [9] At J. Walter Thompson there is very little shouting in the corridors, and creative temperaments are in general carefully controlled. There has always been great emphasis on agreeable personal relationships and a friendly and participative atmosphere, although this is not to imply a lack of political undercurrents flowing through the agency, or an absence of relentless, although carefully veiled, competition between personable and pleasant but also tough and ambitious opportunists.

These observations are intended not as criticisms, but merely as a reminder that, despite the common assumption that the "Thompson man" is different, the people at J. Walter Thompson actually have more similarities to than dissimilarities from people in other advertising agencies—something to be expected in a business as competitive as advertising. Perhaps this is another way of saying that, in comparisons of the social and philosophical cultures, the philosophical culture is, in the last analysis, the more important discriminator between one agency and another.

The early 1960s saw an important new trend in advertising: a strong revival of emphasis on the agency's raison d'être, its creative product. This trend coincided with (and was possibly influenced by) a slowing in the growth of aggregate advertising expenditure in the United States beginning in the mid-1960s.[10] It was spearheaded and exploited by the principals of a number of thrusting agencies in New York, notably David Ogilvy, Bill Bernbach, Jack Tinker, and Mary Wells. After some delay, the movement reached London. At that time (and still today) the strongest operations in the J. Walter Thompson firmament were those in the United States and the United Kingdom. However, the ways in which the two responded to the changing conditions of the market allow an instructive comparison.

In the United States, and in the "flagship" New York office in particular, the company seemed unable to come to grips with the change in the advertising business, partly because the agency was so account driven, partly because there was much flux at the top, and partly because there were at the time important changes in its management priorities (the agency was moving toward public ownership). As a result, the management gradually allowed the traditional social and philosophical culture of the agency to fade; it was something just not fully understood by the people running the company at the time. Even today the culture has not entirely disappeared, but there is very little doubt that it was a little weaker in 1970 than it had been in 1960, and that at the end of the 1990s it is very much weaker still.

I have debated with former colleagues whether there was a difference between the philosophical culture of JWT New York and JWT London during the long years when Stanley Resor ruled the company. Both agencies took a seriously inquiring approach, but it is probable that the British put more emphasis on the theoretical underpinning of advertising than the Americans did. This emphasis was essentially a result of the British educational system. The Americans, on the other hand, were always more anxious to produce advertising solutions to problems and to see how such advertising performed in the marketplace. The American approach was more pragmatic and commercial.

By the mid-1960s, however, the London agency's philosophical culture had faded, just as New York's had. JWT London's social culture remained as strong as ever (and it began to be eroded only in the 1970s). But by the end of the 1960s, a major change had taken place at JWT London. The agency's philosophical culture had become significantly and consciously strengthened. This strengthening occurred partly in response to client pressures, but more important, it happened because the management of the company—in particular the young and energetic managing director Tom Sutton—saw a reinforcement of the corporate culture as one of its key objectives.

The revitalized philosophical culture was formalized in a number of stages and described in documents, films, videotapes, presentations, and training programs. The main emphasis was placed on five interconnected disciplines:

1. A redefinition of JWT's old concept of added values to differentiate a brand from an unadvertised product
2. A careful analysis (based on psychological principles) of how advertising works on the consumer's mind
3. The development of qualitative research techniques to help generate and evaluate creative ideas
4. The construction of a new formula for drawing up advertising strategy

5. The transformation of the old agency marketing department into a cadre of "account planners" who were to be the main developers and custodians of brand strategy, adding a further task in the 1980s: the scientific evaluation of the sales effects of advertising, using and developing innovative statistical techniques (see also Staveley's and O'Malley's contributions to Chapter 4, this volume)

The agency remained in essence account driven, and these disciplines were entirely compatible with the historical elements of the agency's culture already described. But the new disciplines represented a development and sharpening of the old. It should also be added, however, that the strengthened philosophy imposed a new restrictiveness and rigidity.

The five changes just described represented a substantial menu. Their formulation and implementation were the combined effort of an oligarchy of executives who also played a substantial part in running the company. Perhaps because of the position of these people, the culture soon became even more all-embracing, entering all parts of the agency's psyche. Very soon there was a (substantially implicit) doctrine covering media planning and budget deployment and—a development with serious implications—a distinctive creative style based on building nonrational, emotionally based discriminators for the brands advertised. These were best expressed in television advertising, something that goes a long way toward explaining the agency's particular bias toward television. This extremely broad dissemination of the culture within the organization may well have been unintended, but my own careful observation suggests that it most certainly took place, and it exists to this day.

When one looks back on the JWT offices in New York and London during the 1960s and their contributions to the destiny of the company, there is no doubt that JWT London, with its strengthened culture, responded much better to a changing marketplace than did JWT New York, with its weakened culture and constant management changes. But the story is more complicated. Up to about 1960, JWT in the United States and JWT London had similar market positions. They were not only market leaders but were also commonly acknowledged to occupy their own special niches. As agencies, they were different in kind from the competition, and what set them apart from the others was largely their corporate culture.

Today each of the two agencies, in its market, is one of a number of evenly balanced competitors, some of which have and some of which do not have strong cultures of their own. Neither of the JWT agencies is the market leader, although JWT London is much closer than is the U.S. agency.

It is also true that Don Johnston, the chief executive of J. Walter Thompson appointed in 1976, was acutely conscious of the way in which the culture of JWT New York had eroded during the previous decade and more. His efforts to rejuvenate the culture, mainly by introducing methods that had originated in London, deserve to be described in greater length than I am able to do here. However, for the purposes of this chapter, it is enough to note that these efforts were mainly unsuccessful, for reasons not connected to Johnston's own drive.

The new ideas simply did not "take" in New York. But they certainly did in London. And there is little doubt that the success achieved by J. Walter Thompson, London, was strongly influenced by the agency's corporate culture. I also believe that its success, great though it has been, brought disappointment in that the agency lost the position of supremacy it had occupied in the 1950s and 1960s. I am convinced that the reason is that its culture, to some extent, held it back. In particular, there have been components of the culture that have narrowed the agency's thinking and made it vulnerable to the assaults of aggressive and more freethinking competitors.

This point could be illustrated with many specific examples, but although these examples are anything but trivial, dwelling on them would inevitably communicate something that is not intended: that the disadvantages of the culture of JWT London greatly outweigh its advantages. However, I do introduce some examples in the next section, where I use them to underpin some general arguments about cultures, and in particular about what readers may already be beginning to conclude: that cultures need to be rather carefully *balanced* if they are to be maximally effective. This balance is an art and not a science, and there is no research available to help us.

Too Little Culture—or Too Much?

One thing that we must continually bear in mind when we think about advertising agencies is that an exceptionally high proportion of their staff—about 60%—is in the professional mainstream. These people are expected to bring their imaginations and intellects with them to the office in the morning. As a result, agencies are not in the least similar to the manufacturing companies that are their clients, although they have some resemblance to the firms of attorneys and accountants that also provide professional counsel to those clients.

Although the proportion of an agency's staff that is in what might be called the officer class is exceptionally high, the talents of this class are—strangely enough—in short supply. This is particularly true of first-class creative talent. The result is that wise managements, as part of the corporate cultures they breed, cherish their staff. Without the most able employees, there would be no business at all. Staff members do not remain with an agency because they have anything resembling academic tenure. They are there because they enjoy it, and the most talented people know their value in a wider marketplace. If they are unhappy where they are, they can change jobs without much trouble. Again, this is especially true of the best creative people.

It follows that it is a delicate task to impose a corporate culture from above. As I have already explained, cultures must be encouraged to grow from below, as mutually compatible people learn to work together. The leadership of the agency principals must be exercised through these people's working closely with the employees, leading, coaxing, and using the employees' own contributions. This approach was not difficult for Leo Burnett, David Ogilvy, or Rosser Reeves because of the great professional respect they received inside (and also outside) their organizations. These men make very good exemplars, and it would be useful now to consider briefly the corporate cultures stimulated by these three notable figures.

The most interesting corporate culture to be found in any agency anywhere seems to me to be that associated with Leo Burnett. It grew out of the challenging notion that the agency should pursue relentlessly the "inherent drama" in the product. High aspiration is an important part of the doctrine. In addition, there are some other important aspects of the culture: It embraces research (Leo Burnett was one of the agencies that pioneered the use of small-scale qualitative research in campaign development, and Burnett today has the largest research department of any agency); its overall management policy is to concentrate the agency's efforts on a small number of very substantial and like-minded clients; and—something whose importance became recognized only in the 1980s—the agency's stock continues to be privately owned.

The culture of Leo Burnett is strongly creative driven; the thrust of the agency's efforts has been unwaveringly to improve its advertising. It is therefore surprising that Leo Burnett is not as strongly associated with the creative revival of the 1960s as are Ogilvy, Bernbach, Tinker, and Wells. The reasons are that the agency is based in Chicago, and its clients (unlike Ogilvy's and Bernbach's in their early days) are mostly manufacturers of mainstream packaged goods. These have always been considered important but inherently unglamorous types of clients, although if we look at the work that the agency does, for instance, for Procter & Gamble and Kellogg's brands, few people would use the word *unglamorous* to describe it.

The culture of Ogilvy & Mather resembles a coin. The obverse describes the ways in which the agency believes that advertising, particularly press advertising, should be written. The reverse demonstrates that all the Ogilvy rules are based on research covering a wide methodological spectrum (although it is not stated that some parts of this research are in fact much less reliable than others). Ogilvy & Mather is one of the few agencies that makes (or at least once made) a major effort to catalog what it knows, and to use operationally the lessons derived. This alone is enough to make the agency noteworthy.

Like that of Leo Burnett, Ogilvy & Mather's culture is concentrated essentially on its creative work. But because the agency tells people how to do things, its culture has been criticized for its rigidity. David Ogilvy has answered this criticism trenchantly, although not in my opinion entirely convincingly.[11]

The culture on which Ted Bates was founded is laid out for our inspection in Rosser Reeves's best-selling book.[12] The most important element is the much misunderstood concept of the Unique Selling Proposition (USP). Bates once found this an enormously useful device, although one of the related concepts, usage-pull, is based on a use of research that has been demonstrated to be fallacious.[13] (See also Jones, Chapter 23, this volume.) The USP is of course concerned almost exclusively with the agency's creative product. Its main weakness is its complete concentration on a rational brand discriminator, ignoring nonrational, emotional arguments for using a brand—an especially important matter when the advertiser wishes to mirror the psychographics of a brand's existing users.

A related criticism of the Unique Selling Proposition is the way in which it concentrates on change and conversion. It is entirely concerned with persuading nonusers of a brand to become users—by no means a universal strategy of marketers in the real world. And an extension of this strategy, which readers can easily take out of Reeves's book, is that it is concerned with turning nonusers of a brand into exclusive users—something that is only very rarely successful in the field of repeat-purchase goods.

The Bates philosophy is concerned with a method or technique of writing advertisements. But because this is a formula approach, the agency's culture is essentially account driven, even though the USP is a creative device and Rosser Reeves was a creative leader.

Of the three cultures I have briefly reviewed, it seems to me that Leo Burnett's has best withstood the test of time. Rosser Reeves's has been subject to the greatest criticism, although it was used by the agency for a number of years in its original or in an amended form.

My own observation of the cultures of Leo Burnett, Ogilvy & Mather, and Ted Bates leads me to think that they have not actually permeated their companies quite as pervasively as the culture of JWT London. One reason is that they have been more concentrated on one aspect of the business: the agency's creative work. The culture of JWT London has become virtually complete in its dominance of the agency's professional endeavors, a point I shall shortly illustrate.

On the other hand, the way in which the culture of JWT London impinges specifically on the creative product seems to me to offer a great benefit. The planning procedures of the agency are response oriented. The agency sets an advertising strategy not as an advertising stimulus (as did Ogilvy and Reeves) but in terms of a desired response. As a result, the JWT approach does not confine people too much; creative people in the agency have, prima facie, great operational freedom.

Why is it, then, that there is, as I have suggested, a recognizable style of advertising from JWT London? This is not an easy question to answer. But in my judgment it has nothing at all to do with what the agency says about creative strategy. It is a clear but indirect result of the all-embracing nature of the agency's culture.

What I have in mind are at least five features of the agency's operational procedures and the subtle influence of the agency's corporate culture on each:

1. The agency's media planning, with an instinctive concentration on television, with its bias toward emotional messages.
2. The general policy of high media concentration, with most emphasis on repetition rather than on the immediate impact of a single advertisement exposure— reliance on repetition encourages gentle, emotional selling.
3. How the agency's thinking about one brand in a market can condition its thinking about a second brand from the same manufacturer, and thus inhibit the latter—the agency tends to think instinctively in motivating rather than discriminating terms.
4. How the agency's work seems much better attuned to market leaders than to smaller brands. Again, there is an emphasis on motivators: Advertisements for

market leaders tend to rely on motivating arguments; those for smaller brands, on harder, brand-specific discriminating arguments.

5. How the agency exclusively uses small-scale qualitative research for creative planning. Technically, this is not uniformly excellent, and it also provides an implicit bias toward emotional advertising; this bias again influences the style of advertising, in particular by softening the edges and giving the advertising a generic rather than a competitive orientation.

What all this leads to is an extraordinary policy of contradiction. The agency first liberates its creative people from the iron shackles that some other agencies apply, but it then ties their wrists with strong but silken bonds. The result is pretty much the same as the end product of the rules of less subtle agencies.

Twelve Practical Lessons

I am going to make 12 brief points. Although these partly summarize what I have been saying throughout this chapter, I am adding some additional arguments. The overall emphasis is on the practical lessons that the analysis can provide for agency management.

1. An agency culture may encompass operational methods, but it is essentially something that transcends these. It is a quality that enters the minds of highly intelligent people and influences their thinking. The procedures and ways of looking at things that form the foundation of an effective agency culture must be relevant, substantial, arresting, and durable. An agency culture that has any real influence cannot be built on platitudes and generalities.

2. An agency culture comprises a social culture and a philosophical culture. These are related to one another and work synergistically. However, the philosophical culture is ultimately the more important in distinguishing agencies from one another. When an agency management is planning how to create a culture, this is the aspect that needs the greater attention, although it is the more difficult one to plan.

3. The trait that most obviously distinguishes the culture of one agency from that of another is whether the agency is account driven or creative driven. An agency culture does not change much over time (although it is capable of becoming weaker or stronger), and the part that changes even less than the other parts is the agency's account of creative orientation.

4. It may be thought that an agency culture can arise spontaneously as the result of continuous cooperative work between mutually compatible people who share a common outlook. Far more often, it is actively stimulated and encouraged by the personal example of the principal(s) of an agency. This can be done successfully only if the staff who are going to be imbued with the culture are receptive to it. The soil must be fertile.

5. An agency culture can bring advantages to an agency: the benefits of cooperative work, particularly as it relates to the widest use of the top talent; improvement in morale; easier recruitment; and strong continuity resulting from staff loyalty. As a result, the agency is also likely to become stronger in a competitive marketplace, something that brings it great advantages. These advantages can have a financial payoff in the elimination of waste, more efficient working, and sharper focus. The agency will drill fewer dry holes. Some of these advantages can be passed on to the agency's clients (see point 6 below).

6. Theoretically, clients can gain from their agency's having an effective culture, and broader social benefits can follow. The main objective of an agency culture is to enable the agency to produce better advertising for its clients more efficiently (i.e., with less waste). Better advertising is unquestionably in the interest of the clients, and is also—theoretically again—in the interest of the public as a whole, because it represents a more efficient use of resources.

During the past decade, there has been a strong move in the United States toward clients' paying agencies reduced commissions (see Said, Chapter 10, this volume).[14] Many agencies manage to make a profit on large accounts that pay as little as 9% on the gross cost of space. This profit has become possible only because of considerable cost savings, in particular through reduction in the size of agency staff per million dollars of billing. It is at least possible that the cost savings yielded by the agency culture may have provided modest economies that have contributed to the reduction in overall agency expenses.

This is, however, an extremely complicated matter. I can think of more than one agency that downsized to meet reductions in its income by firing its gurus—its most important thinkers and the inventors of its planning procedures, and the very people who were doing the most to develop the philosophical culture. When times are tough, agencies and their clients have a more urgent need for objectivity and depth than for responsiveness and fast footwork. Hard business conditions stimulate tactical rather than strategic thinking—an undesirable reversal of priorities.

7. I believe that the most impressive and effective agency cultures (e.g., Leo Burnett) are oriented virtually exclusively toward the advertising the agency produces for its clients. Burnett is one of the large agencies that has maintained its strength (despite temporary setbacks) over a period of decades.

8. An extension of the preceding point is that effective agency cultures grow most commonly in agencies headed by creative leaders, such as Burnett, David Ogilvy, Rosser Reeves, Jack Tinker, Bill Bernbach, Raymond Rubicam, and Mary Wells. Each of these agencies was the "lengthened shadow of one man" (*pace* Ms. Wells). An effective culture enables this shadow to be transformed from something evanescent into something permanent.

9. A real danger is that an agency's culture may permeate too many aspects of the operation. The agency's thinking may become narrowed. Its flexibility may be reduced. Even more seriously, talented people may become impatient with what they see as their intellectual confinement, and they will quit.

Advertising is a very fertile industry, and consumers in the marketplace continue to be bombarded with huge numbers of advertisements in many media, the vast majority of which are "screened out" by consumers' own selective perception. For advertising to make any impression on consumers, there is a great premium on unorthodoxy. There is therefore a heavy downside to an agency culture if it results in uniform solutions to heterogeneous problems—in particular, if the agency leaves too strong a thumbprint on its creative products (see point 10).

10. A plausible way of defining good advertising is that it enables consumers to penetrate into the meaning of a brand without calling too much

attention to itself. Brands are extremely variegated, and this fact strongly suggests that advertisements should be equally variegated. Here lies the subtle benefit of the device used by JWT London to define an advertising strategy in terms of the desired responses of consumers to the brand. This approach contrasts with the common notion that a strategy should dictate what elements should be built into the advertising argument. But as I have suggested in this chapter, there are other elements in the culture of JWT London that tend to negate the creative freedom that the agency initially provides.

11. Unfortunately, research is of little help to us in evaluating whether an agency culture is right or wrong, too strong or too weak, effective or ineffective. There is a lag in the system. A culture takes a period to develop and mature. When it has taken hold and the time comes to weigh its results, it may be too difficult to change. Like a brand, an agency culture is slow to build, slow to run down, and virtually impossible to alter.

12. There is a disgracefully large number of things about how advertising works that are totally unknown, only partially known, or completely misunderstood. It is notable how few agencies devote attention to the weak state of our knowledge. David Ogilvy is viewed by most of the advertising profession, first of all, as a creative innovator. A handful of people (myself included) think of him primarily as a man preoccupied, almost obsessed, with the need to answer fundamental questions about how advertising operates. And he was one of the few agency proprietors who spent the agency's money in trying to find out more and to inoculate a spirit of inquiry into the agency's bloodstream. That is why this series of advertising handbooks is dedicated to him.

Notes

1. Sir David Orr, "Foreword," in John Philip Jones, *Does It Pay to Advertise? Cases Illustrating Successful Brand Advertising* (New York: Simon & Schuster-Lexington, 1989), xxi.

2. Terence E. Deal and Allan A. Kennedy, *Corporate Cultures: The Rites and Rituals of Corporate Life* (Reading, MA: Addison-Wesley, 1982). Cynthia G. Swank of the Inlook Group (P.O. Box 405, Portsmouth, NH 03802-0405) has assembled a helpful bibliography of books and articles that discuss corporate culture.

3. Marvin Bower, former managing director of McKinsey & Company, quoted in Deal and Kennedy, *Corporate Cultures,* 4.

4. Denis Lanigan, former vice chairman of J. Walter Thompson, personal communication, August 1989. I am grateful to him for this and a number of other important contributions to the argument in this chapter.

5. Simon Broadbent, vice chairman of Leo Burnett, London, personal communication, August 1989.

6. Lanigan, personal communication.

7. This distinction has been strongly emphasized to me by William M. Weilbacher, who has extensive experience of both account-driven and creative-driven agencies in the United States.

8. This is a favorite expression of Bill Hinks, who was managing director of the London office of J. Walter Thompson in the 1950s and chairman in the early 1960s.

9. This charming quotation was retailed by my friend Harold F. Clark, Jr., who has also made a number of other important contributions to this chapter.

10. John Philip Jones, "Cure the Industry With More Creativity," *New York Times,* September 10, 1989, sec. 3, p. 3.

11. David Ogilvy, *Confessions of an Advertising Man* (New York: Atheneum, 1984), 89-90.

12. Rosser Reeves, *Reality in Advertising* (New York: Alfred A. Knopf, 1961).

13. Kim B. Rotzoll, "The Starch and Ted Bates Correlative Measures of Advertising Effectiveness," *Journal of Advertising Research,* March 1964, 22-24.

14. Data on compensation systems are released on a regular basis by the Association of National Advertisers.

Part II

Creative Aspects

13

Strategy in Advertising

John Philip Jones

The Advertising Planning Cycle

The easiest and most helpful way to study how advertising campaigns are developed is to use a simple model called the planning cycle, which was devised by Stephen King, formerly of J. Walter Thompson, London, and has been used in many offices of that agency for more than two decades.[1] The planning cycle helps to isolate the roles of the research and creative processes during each of five phases. These phases are framed by five simple questions, as shown in Figure 13.1.

The questions in the planning cycle are intended to help advertisers and agencies guide a brand through the stages of planning, writing, exposing, and evaluating an advertising campaign. For most brands, the cycle is used as an annual procedure; for some brands it is used more frequently, and for others, less often.

The first two questions—Where are we? and Why are we there?—are research based, and are answered from quantitative and qualitative research

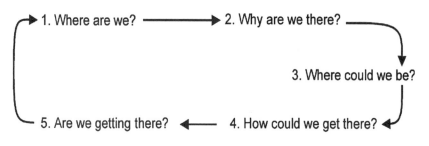

Figure 13.1. The Advertising Planning Cycle

data, some being collected once only and some of it longitudinally (i.e., on a continuous basis). In particular, there is a need to determine how the brand is perceived by consumers in functional and nonfunctional terms (relative to its competition), what is known about these consumers, and what trends are at work in the sales of the brand and in the segment and category in which it is positioned. The reason these questions must be answered is that it is important to understand fully the brand's position in the market and in the consumer's mind before it is possible to draw up the brand's advertising strategy. This is done in response to the third question: Where could we be?

It is at this stage that the strategy is written and approved, and work begins on creative expressions of this strategy. There is also a role for research. The purposes of this research are, first, to help generate and enrich ideas and, second, to screen in the most promising ideas and screen out the less promising ones. The research is carried out essentially to help the agency's creative people.

The type of research most commonly employed is qualitative. Focus groups, which encourage interaction among participants, can lead in promising directions by sparking ideas not only among the members of the groups, but also in the minds of the creative people when they are confronted with the research findings. The agency creative people often view focus groups in action from the other side of a two-way mirror, which is generally a feature of the rooms in which focus group discussions take place. Participants are invariably told that they are being watched, but this does not usually trouble them.

Focus groups are also useful for uncovering reactions to advertising ideas, although a positive reaction can never guarantee that the advertisement will be effective in the marketplace. However, focus groups are good for isolating problems, and are therefore used as a filter to detect seriously deficient ideas, so that these can be discarded.

Focus groups are of no use for assessing the important matter of advertising communication, because the interaction among participants gives the game away—once one member of the group sees the point of the advertisement, they all will. Communication of advertising ideas is generally assessed through the expensive process of individual depth interviews ("one-on-ones").

The fourth question in the planning cycle—How could we get there?—is concerned mostly with the creative process of planning and generating campaign ideas. But research is also involved; it is needed to help evaluate, screen, and refine ideas. At this stage, the advertisements to be researched are in finished or semifinished form. The purpose of the research now becomes final "quality control," to help justify the media investment. The real reason the research is carried out is to support the management decision to spend an often significant media budget. This generally means providing evidence to underpin the recommendations of the brand manager when these are submitted to higher levels of the management hierarchy.

The research is in effect being used to predict marketplace success, and this degree of reliance often raises methodological doubts among advertising practitioners. European researchers are particularly sensitive to these doubts, with the result that such research is not used very extensively in Europe. However, in the United States such research is widely used despite the controversy surrounding it, mainly because of the large size of the media budgets and the risk involved in making wrong decisions.

The research technique most commonly employed is quantitative. Television commercials are screened either in a theater or on the air in a small number of localities. With some types of research, consumers are asked questions about their recall of the copy claims and what the commercials communicate. With other systems, indirect questions (e.g., brand-based lotteries before and after screening the commercial) attempt to determine the persuasive power of the advertising. Some research techniques cover both recall and persuasion; others assess likability and the image attributes of the brand as these are presented in the advertising. The most reliable systems employ theater tests that measure persuasion. For press advertising, individual interviews are generally carried out with shoppers who are intercepted in malls.

The fifth question—Are we getting there?—involves evaluating the effects of the campaign in the marketplace in order to improve its productivity in the future or to provide guidance for new campaigns. This stage is essentially research based. For tracking the effectiveness of a campaign among consumers, quantitative research is normally employed. This takes two forms, and sophisticated advertisers use both techniques. The first type is the continuous measurement of consumer sales, the data being collected by scanners either in stores or in the home. In the second type of research, information is collected (at relatively infrequent intervals) on consumers' brand knowledge, perceptions of brand attributes, and awareness of the advertising. These data are collected both for the brand observed and for its competitors in the category.

An important feature of the planning cycle is that the questions follow a sequence and are in a loop, which tells us that when we get to question 5, it is time to start at the beginning again. This is an admirable reminder that the relationship between everybody concerned with a brand's advertising and the brand itself is a continuous one. It does not stop when the advertising has been exposed to the public. There is also some feedback in the process, through which the answers to one question sometimes cause the agency to reconsider the answers to the preceding one.

The Advertising Strategy

As I have indicated, the advertising strategy is written and used at the beginning of the answer to the third question in the planning cycle: Where could we be? The advertising strategy sets out the underlying plan and objectives for an advertisement or an advertising campaign, and it is related to all the other elements in a manufacturer's blueprint for its brand. To write an effective strategy, one must determine a brand's position in a competitive environment and work out the best way to protect and improve this position. Although the analysis of facts is an essential background activity, the actual development of an advertising strategy is an exercise in judgment.

Writing a strategy is a rational process and calls for the evaluation of data and the ability to make logical deductions. When one proceeds to develop advertisements from the strategy, the actual writing of the advertisements is an exercise in applied imagination and craft. The difference between the mental qualities required for writing the strategy and those required for writing the campaign is an important matter, and it means that the two jobs are almost always done by different people. The strategy and the campaign are, however, intimately linked, because the strategy is the device that points imagination and intuition in the right direction.

Strategy is like a diving board over a swimming pool. It should be strongly constructed and built over the deep end of the pool, so as to give the diver the best possible chance of making a safe and elegant dive. However, the dive itself depends on the skill of the person on the diving board. The diver in this case is the creative man or woman who will be writing the advertisement.

The word *strategy* comes from military science and is most simply defined as generalship, or the art of war. Much more has been written about military strategy than about business strategy, the "art of business." Both are slightly complicated and are made up of a number of layers, or subsidiary strategies. In a business organization, these are the company plan, the brand marketing strategy, and the brand advertising strategy. Because military strategy has many helpful affinities with business strategy, it is worth making a short digression to discuss the art of war, because this will help to illustrate some of the subtleties of the art of business.

The first and most important point about military strategy is that it concerns armies in conflict. It is therefore centrally concerned with one's relationship to one's opponents. There is an obvious analogy with business strategy, insofar as this is embedded in a competitive environment. Indeed, much of the language of marketing and advertising is derived (perhaps unconsciously) from military thinking. The adjectives *offensive, defensive,* and *aggressive* are in everyday use. Manufacturers often conduct *marketing warfare* and aim to *seize a market* and *drive out competitors,* who are then forced to *hoist the white flag.* Advertisements are planned to work as a *campaign,* and to have an *impact* on the consumer. In planning media exposure, advertisers plan *strikes* or *hits.*

The second point about military strategy is that it is planned at more than one level. The highest level, grand strategy, represents the plan of the nation in arms. There is an analogy here with the company plan. Below the level of the nation in arms is a range of military formations of descending size, which are guided by pure strategy, which embraces all phases of military planning that fall short of actual contact with the enemy. When this contact takes place, strategy becomes tactics. The relationship between military strategy and tactics is such that a good strategy saves much bloodshed and effort in its tactical execution. Ideally, the enemy will be maneuvered into such an impossible position that he will see no alternative but to surrender. We can never quite see such perfect use of strategy in business, but there is nevertheless an analogy, in that in business a well-planned strategy enables the resources deployed in its execution to be used more economically and effectively, and waste to be reduced.

It is often difficult to draw a clear line to define where military strategy ends and tactics begin. The same is true in business. However, it is always worth making the effort to draw such a line, for the reason just given: The more one concentrates on the strategy, and the stronger the strategy is, the less effort will be needed to execute it well.

The third characteristic of military strategy is that it is multidimensional. It embraces logistics (deployment of resources), psychology (exploitation of one's own strengths and, no less important, the enemy's weaknesses), and time (the goals have to be accomplished within a finite period). Business strategy also has these constituents. In advertising, media investments are pumped into campaigns, which represent the execution of strategy. The advertising arguments themselves are almost invariably written with some knowledge of psychology. And the execution of the strategy is accomplished within a defined period, during which its effects are monitored. Another point is that effective logistical and psychological planning depends on good knowledge— or intelligence, in military jargon. Again there is an obvious affinity with the use of market research in business.

In the same way that a nation has a grand strategy, a firm has a company business plan. This sketches the role that the company plans to play in the market or markets in which it operates (including those it intends to enter in the near future). The plan details how the company will use its resources (capital, labor, know-how, and goodwill) to the best effect. And it often, although not invariably, maps out how the firm will be perceived by its customers, economic partners, and the public as a whole in a broad business and social context. The plan sets objectives and proposes in general terms how these will be met.

Below the level of the company plan are the plans for the individual divisions of the corporation (in the case of diversified firms). And below these are the plans for the individual brands in the company's portfolio. Many firms have a number of brands in each category, and these must be handled separately. But they must conform overall to the company plan, otherwise there will be a risk that brands will cannibalize one another. The marketing strategy for an individual brand (together with the advertising strategy, which stems from it) aims to establish the brand's place in the competitive scene. The importance of the competitive situation cannot be emphasized too strongly, and most of the elements of the marketing strategy should be explicitly framed in competitive terms. A brand marketing strategy consists of four elements (sometimes called the Four Ps):

- *Product:* Product includes, first, the functional characteristics of the brand in comparison with its competitors, and specifically how its functional strengths and weaknesses are perceived by consumers. Second, it includes a description of the market segment in which the brand is positioned as well as the demographic and psychographic (lifestyle) characteristics of the users of brands in this segment and the users of our brand in particular. Third, it describes the brand's nonfunctional added values. Advertising is an important element here because added values are created substantially by advertising. The brand's positioning is also influenced by advertising to a considerable degree. These elements of the marketing strategy must therefore be closely linked to the brand advertising strategy.
- *Price:* Again, the price must be seen alongside the prices of competitive brands. There are two important points that need emphasis. First, this part of the strategy covers the brand's prices both to the trade and to the consumer. The difference between the two represents the brand's distributive margin, and advertising is often able to reduce the size of this. Second, price is rarely fixed, even for short periods. Trade and consumer promotions are mostly price related. Indeed, nearly all trade promotions, because they are discounts of various types, effectively reduce the trade price—that is, the price charged to the wholesaler and retailer. And the majority of consumer promotions (money-off packs, coupons, banded packs, and so on) also operate on price, but on consumer price this time.
- *Retail distribution* (sometimes called *place,* to maintain the consistency of the Four Ps): This describes the extent of the brand's geographic distribution, the types of retail outlets that handle it, and a measure of the present and targeted levels of effective distribution (i.e., distribution taking into account the size of the stores carrying the brand). Distribution is related to the brand's trade and consumer promotional programs because it is impossible to get a brand into distribution (and extremely difficult to maintain it on display in the stores) without competitive levels of promotion.
- *Promotion:* This embraces plans for advertising (above-the-line activities) and also for promotions (below-the-line activities). Publicity and public relations are included among the below-the-line activities. The brand advertising strategy is the foundation for the brand's above-the-line program.

The marketing strategy should of course be reviewed regularly. However, it should very rarely be changed or even modified, and then only when the competitive position of the brand has altered. Many clients tend to tinker with marketing strategies if their brands falter in the marketplace.

Below the level of the brand marketing strategy, and deriving from it, is the brand advertising strategy (and, on occasion, a number of parallel strategies dealing with publicity, merchandising, and direct marketing). The brand advertising strategy involves the setting of objectives for an advertising campaign.

I will describe these elements shortly, but it is worth pointing out immediately that the term *advertising strategy* has very different meanings depending on who uses it. Different advertising agencies—organizations that often pride themselves on the comprehensiveness and efficiency of their working procedures—use a variety of different formulas, some much fuller and more helpful than others. Many cross over the line between strategy and tactics.

How can it be that an indifferent strategy can lead to an effective advertisement? We can press the point and ask a second question: Is a strategy really necessary?

The answer to the first of these two questions is that an effective advertisement can sometimes be produced serendipitously, but that is something one cannot rely on. There is a real danger of wasting effort, time, and resources in following blind alleys. The answer to the second question is yes, a strategy is indispensable if one is to conduct advertising on a businesslike basis—as something better than a hit-or-miss affair. To reduce some of the inevitable waste in the process of developing advertising, one must plan the strategy as soundly as possible before beginning to generate ideas. It is important to make sure that all the ideas generated—both good and bad—are at least relevant. Developing a good but irrelevant idea is totally wasteful and extremely frustrating.

The advertising strategy, like the marketing strategy, is only rarely modified. A well-planned advertising strategy ensures that things will not be forgotten. It reduces the risk of creative people drilling dry holes and wasting their time and their talent, something that is in short supply and that always needs to be nurtured and protected. Good creative people, for reasons that are difficult to explain, respond well to tightly written strategies. Creative people need to understand the limits on what they can and cannot say. In many circumstances, the more confined these limits are, the more intense the imaginative and intuitive effort that is stimulated, and the more arresting the creative solution that emerges in response to the strategy.

The most important reason for an advertising strategy is nevertheless the one described earlier. It is a component of a company's business plan and is therefore a tool of management—a method of setting priorities—that is already in place. Its purpose is to help guide decision making. Also, and rather important, the objectives that form part of the advertising strategy provide a series of targets. With targets established, one is able to measure how closely the advertising comes to hitting them. This measurement in turn helps in the setting of realistic future targets. This point holds good for all advertisers who are in business to make a profit.

Although the advertising strategy is essentially a device to point creative people in the right direction, it also provides a valuable service to the account executives, who normally work closely with the agency account planners and researchers. A good strategy makes it easier to explain advertising proposals convincingly to a client. This is especially true on those (only too rare) occasions when the client is faced with a genuinely unorthodox creative idea. In these circumstances, the best weapon available to convince the client of the advertising's relevance and likely effectiveness is research evidence that the advertising seems to do its job in meeting the objectives explicitly stated in the strategy.

The advertising strategy should not be a lengthy document; it should generally be a page long and should never exceed two pages. If it is longer, creative people will not use it. Although brief, it should, however, be the end product of much thought—more explicitly, it should be derived from an analysis of facts, reflection on their meaning, and judgment in their interpretation. A useful advertising strategy is the end product of serious intellectual mastication, and the way it is written should not be laid down too rigidly; the elements need varying amounts of emphasis for different brands.

The strategy is normally produced by the advertising agency's account executives (in cooperation with a number of agency colleagues). The client provides the basic brief and input when the strategy is drafted. It must of course also be accepted by the client in its final form before creative work is begun. This means that it acts as a discipline for the client as well as for the agency.

In a small but probably increasing number of cases, the client goes further and determines all aspects of the strategy, owing to disenchantment on the part of some American clients with the ability of their agencies to carry out sound strategic thinking. This is less true in London, where account planning encourages agencies to dig relentlessly into the competitive strengths and weaknesses of brands, and specifically into consumer perceptions.

It is important to remember that an advertising strategy is a selective document. An advertisement cannot work effectively if it is expected to do too many jobs. The strategy should concentrate on what matters most, but there is an opportunity cost, because we pay for what we include by the sacrifice of what we omit. This price must be paid, but naturally we must choose what to include (and therefore what to leave out) with scrupulous care.

Strategies are occasionally criticized for being rather dull documents. But it should be stressed that the main quality a strategy should possess is logical soundness. On the other hand, it is extremely important that the advertising that is derived from the strategy not be dull, otherwise it will not do its first job of attracting and engaging its audience.

Ten Steps to an Effective Strategy

In harmony with the point I have made about the brevity of the ideal advertising strategy, I shall now describe the elements of an advertising strategy as succinctly as I can.

General Points

- An effective strategy reduces waste in the process of developing advertisements because it helps to prevent the misuse of expensive and scarce creative resources. The strategic process is separate from the creative process, but the former provides direction for the latter.
- A strategy should be written with knowledge of a brand's competitive position. The brand's situation within its market substantially governs its target group and proposition, as well as the role of its advertising.
- For manufacturers who have a number of brands in a category, strategic differentiation is vital to avoid cannibalization.
- A strategy is always verbal and rational, and it normally contains many words. This does not mean that the ensuing advertising should be densely verbal or exclusively rational. Many points in the strategy can be communicated in the most effective way by pictures, and by music and sound.

Target Group

1. Determine your target group in terms of your planned source(s) of business:
   a. from new users entering a growing product category

    b. from new users entering a growing market segment from a different segment (Which different segment?)

    c. from attracting users from other brands within your market segment (Which other brands?)

    d. from increased purchase frequency from your own users

    e. (if the brand is under pressure) from retaining existing users and maintaining their purchase frequency

2. With the use of Mediamark Research Inc. or Simmons Market Research Bureau data, define your target group demographically.

3. Using qualitative research (or, if this is not available, using judgment based on an extrapolation of demographic data), define your target group psychographically.

Proposition

4. Study the functional characteristics of your brand and its competitors; if possible, use research on consumer perceptions of the brand's functionality. Determine the functional features that should be demonstrated in your advertising. In the main, these will be *motivators* (i.e., rather generic).

5. Determine the extent to which functional features *differentiate* your brand from its competitors. Do not give up easily. If there are no important functional discriminators, find out whether it is possible to create one. Alternatively, is it possible to preempt a general functional discriminator? Major functional differentiation, although reasonably common, does not apply to the majority of brands, and the proportion to which it applies is declining as categories get more crowded.

6. Using qualitative research, determine the nonfunctional qualities—the personality—of your brand. This is a big and important step, and more than one psychological technique should be used. Plot the market on a series of perceptual maps.

7. Your brand's personality will be (by definition) unique. Determine the source of this uniqueness. This is what should be communicated in your advertising, and it normally represents your most important discriminator. This is at the heart of your brand.

8. Consider all questions of *balance,* in particular the balance of motivators and discriminators in your advertising. As a general rule, larger, older brands rely more on motivators than do smaller, newer brands. But all advertising should be a mix of both motivators and discriminators, and this mix strongly influences the tone of voice of the advertising. This tone should be unique to the brand and should be defined as far as possible in the strategy. There is also the balance of the rational and the emotional. A strategy does not have to be exclusively

rational or exclusively emotional. Indeed, emotional signals can provide a powerful reinforcement of the rational elements in the strategy.

Ways in Which the Campaign Should Work

9. What is the role of the advertising? How directly should it work? At one extreme, should it prompt direct action from new users? Or at the other extreme, is the advertising simply to reinforce the favorable attitudes of existing users? If it is not planned to operate at either of these extremes, where on the continuum between them should it operate?

10. Include additional points about the communications gestalt, in particular, how media and promotions should work in conjunction with the creative content of the campaign. The last procedure of all should be a careful review of the strategy as a whole, to make sure that it does not contain any internal dissonances.

Note

1. See John Philip Jones, *How Much Is Enough? Getting the Most From Your Advertising Dollar* (New York: Simon & Schuster-Lexington, 1992), chaps. 7, 8, 9.

Television Advertising

Learning Without Involvement

Herbert E. Krugman

A mong the wonders of the 20th century has been the ability of the mass media repeatedly to expose audiences numbered in millions to campaigns of coordinated messages. In the post-World War II years it was assumed that exposure equaled persuasion and that media content therefore was the all-important object of study or censure. Now we believe that the powers of the mass media are limited. No one has done more to bring about a counterbalancing perspective than former president of the American Association for Public Opinion Research (AAPOR) Joseph Klapper, with his well-known

NOTE: An earlier version of this chapter appeared as "The Impact of Television Advertising: Learning Without Involvement," *Public Opinion Quarterly,* vol. 29, Fall 1965, 349-356. Used by permission of the University of Chicago Press and by Herbert E. Krugman.

book *The Effects of Mass Media,* and another AAPOR president, Raymond Bauer, with such articles as "The Limits of Persuasion." [1]

It has been acknowledged, however, that this more carefully delimited view of mass-media influence is based upon analysis of largely noncommercial cases and data. We have all wondered how many of these limitations apply also to the world of commerce, specifically advertising. I will discuss these limitations here as they apply to television advertising only, because the other media include stimuli and responses of a different psychological nature, which play a perhaps different role in the steps leading to a purchasing decision.

The tendency is to say that the accepted limitations of mass media do apply, that advertising's use of the television medium has limited impact. We tend to feel this way, I think, because (a) we rarely feel converted or greatly persuaded by a particular television campaign, and (b) so much of TV advertising content is trivial. Nevertheless, even trivia have their own special qualities, and some of these may be important to our understanding of the commercial or the noncommercial use and impact of mass media.

To begin, let us go back to Neil Borden's classic Harvard Business School evaluation of the economic effects of advertising, published in 1942.[2] Borden concluded that advertising (a) accelerates growing demand or retards falling demand (that is, it quickens the pulse of the market) and (b) encourages price rigidity but increases quality and choice of products. He warned, however, that companies had been led to overlook price strategies and the elasticity of consumer demand. This was borne out after World War II by the rise of the discounters.

The end of World War II also brought mass television and an increased barrage of advertising messages. How much could the public take? Not only were early TV commercials often irritating, but one wondered whether all the competition would not end in a great big buzzing confusion. Apparently not! Trend studies of advertising penetration have shown that the public is able to "hold in memory," as we would say of a computer, a very large number of TV campaign themes correctly related to brands. The fact that huge sums and energies have been expended to achieve retention of these many little bits of information should not deter us from acknowledging the success of the overall effort.

It is true that in some categories of products the sharpness of brand differentiation is slipping, as advertising themes and appeals grow more similar. Here the data look, as one colleague puts it, "mushy." In such categories the product is well on its way toward becoming a commodity; even while brand advertising continues, the real competition is more and more one of price and distribution. But prices, too, are advertised—although in different media—and recalled.

What is lacking in the required "evaluation" of TV advertising is any significant body of research specifically relating advertising to attitudes, and these in turn to purchasing behavior or sales. That is, we have had in mind a model of the correct and effective influence process that has not yet been verified. This is the bugaboo that has been the hope and the despair of research people within the industry. Always there looms that famous pie in the sky: If the client will put up enough money; if the client will be understanding enough to cooperate in blacking out certain cities or areas to permit a controlled experiment; if the cities or areas under study can be correctly matched; if the panels of consumers to be studied do not melt away in later not-at-homes, refusals, or changes of residence; if the sales data are "clean" enough to serve as adequate criteria—then surely one can truly assess the impact of a particular ad campaign! Some advertisers, too, are learning to ask about this type of evaluation, whereas the advertising agencies are ambivalent and unsure of their strength.

This seems to be where we are today. The economic impact of TV advertising is substantial and documented. Its messages have been learned by the public. Only the lack of specific case histories relating advertising to attitudes and to sales keeps researchers from concluding that the commercial use of the medium is a success. We are faced, then, with the odd situation of knowing that advertising works but being unable to say much about why.

Perhaps our model of the influence process is wrong. Perhaps the process is incompletely understood. Back in 1959, Herbert Zielske, in "The Remembering and Forgetting of Advertising," demonstrated that viewers will quickly forget advertising if not continuously exposed.[3] Why such need for constant reinforcement? Why so easy in and easy out of short-term memory? One answer is that much of advertising content is learned as meaningless nonsense material. Therefore, let us ask about the nature of such learning.

An important distinction between the learning of sense and nonsense was laid down by Ebbinghaus in 1902 when he identified the greater effects of order of presentation of stimuli on the learning of nonsense material. He demonstrated a U curve of recall, with first and last items in a series best remembered, thus giving rise also to the principles of primacy and recency.[4]

Many years later, in 1957, Carl Hovland reported that in studying persuasion he found the effects of primacy and recency greater when dealing with material of lesser ego involvement. He wrote, "Order of presentation is a more significant factor in influencing opinions for subjects with relatively weak desires for understanding, than for those with high 'cognitive' needs." [5] It seems, therefore, that the nonsensical à la Ebbinghaus and the unimportant à la Hovland work alike.

At the 1962 AAPOR meetings, I presented a paper on some applications of learning theory to copy testing. I reported that the spontaneous recall of TV commercials presented four in a row formed a distinct U curve. In the same study, I found that a reanalysis of increment scores of 57 commercials tested in a three-position series by the Schwerin television testing method also showed a distinct U curve, despite the earlier contentions of the Schwerin organization. In these 57 cases, the learning was similar to the learning of the nonsensical or the unimportant.[6]

What is common to the learning of the nonsensical and the unimportant is lack of involvement. We seem to be saying, then, that much of the impact of television advertising is in the form of learning without involvement, or what Hartley calls "unanchored learning." [7] If this is so, is it a source of weakness or of strength to the advertising industry? Is it good or bad for our society? What are the implications for research on advertising effectiveness?

Let us consider some qualities of sensory perception with and without involvement. Along with Ray Bauer, Elihu Katz, and Nat Maccoby, I once participated in a Gould House seminar sponsored by the Foundation for Research on Human Behavior. Maccoby reported some studies conducted with Leon Festinger in which fraternity members learned a TV message better when hearing the audio and watching unrelated video than when they watched the speaker giving them the message directly—that is, video and audio together.[8] Apparently, the distraction of watching something unrelated to the audio message lowered whatever resistance there might have been to the message.

As Nat Maccoby put it, "Comprehension equals persuasion": Any disagreement ("Oh no! That can't be true!") with any message must come after some real interval, however minute. Ray Bauer asked Maccoby if he would accept a statement of this point as "Perception precedes perceptual defense," and the latter agreed. The initial development of this view goes back before World War II to the psychologist E. R. Guthrie.[9] It receives support from British research on perception and communication, specifically that of D. E. Broadbent, who has noted the usefulness of defining perception as "immediate memory." [10]

The historical importance of the Maccoby view, however, is that it takes us almost all the way back to our older view of the potent propaganda content of World War II, that exposure to mass-media content is persuasive per se! What is implied here is that in cases of involvement with mass-media content perceptual defense is very briefly postponed, whereas in cases of noninvolvement perceptual defense may be absent.

Does this suggest that if television bombards us with enough trivia about a product we may be persuaded to believe it? On the contrary, it suggests that persuasion as such—that is, overcoming a resistant attitude—is not involved at all, and that it is a mistake to look for it in our personal lives as a test of television's advertising impact. Instead, as trivia are repeatedly learned and repeatedly forgotten and then repeatedly learned a little more, it is probable that two things will happen: (a) more simply, so-called overlearning will move some information out of short-term and into long-term memory systems; and (b) in a more complex fashion, we will permit significant alterations in the structure of our perception of a brand or product, but in ways that may fall short of persuasion or of attitude change. One way we may do this is by shifting the relative salience of attributes suggested to us by advertising as we organize our perceptions of brands and products.

Thanks to Sherif, we have long used the term *frame of reference,* and Osgood in particular has impressed us with the fact that the meaning of an object may be perceived along many separate dimensions. Let us say that a number of frames of reference are available as the primary anchor for the percept in question. We may then alter the psychological salience of these frames or dimensions and shift a product seen primarily as "reliable" to one seen primarily as "modern." [11] The product is still seen as reliable and perhaps no less reliable than before, but this quality no longer provides the primary perceptual emphasis. Similarly, the product was perhaps previously seen as modern, and perhaps no more modern now—yet exposure to new or repeated messages may give modernity the primary role in the organization of the percept.

There is no reason to believe that such shifts are completely limited to trivia. In fact, when Hartley first introduced the concept of psychological salience, he illustrated it with a suggestion that Hitler did not so much increase anti-Semitic attitudes in Germany as bring already existing anti-Semitic attitudes in Germany into more prominent use for defining the everyday world. [12] This, of course, increased the probability of anti-Semitic behavior. Although the shift in salience does not tell the whole story, it seems to be one of the dynamics operating in response to massive repetition. Although a rather simple dynamic, it may be a major one when there is no cause for resistance, or when uninvolved consumers do not provide their own perceptual emphases or anchors.

It may be painful to reject as incomplete a model of the influence process of television advertising that requires changes in attitude *prior to* changes in behavior. It may be difficult to see how the viewer of television can go from perceptual impact directly to behavioral impact, unless the full perceptual impact is delayed. This would not mean going into unexplored areas. Sociologists have met "sleeper effects" before, and some psychologists have long asserted that the effects of "latent" learning are only, or most, noticeable at the point of reward. In this case, it would be at the behavioral level involved in product purchases rather than at some intervening point along the way. That is, the purchase situation is the catalyst that reassembles or brings out all the potentials for shifts in salience that have accumulated up to that point. The product or package is then suddenly seen in a new, "somehow different" light, although nothing verbalizable may have changed up to that point. What we ordinarily call *change of attitude* may then occur after some real interval, however minute. Such change of attitude after product purchase is not, as has sometimes been said, in "rationalization" of the purchase; rather, it is an emergent response aspect of the previously changed perception. We would perhaps see it more often if products always lived up to expectations and did not sometimes create negative interference with the emerging response.

I have tried to say that the public lets down its guard to the repetitive commercial use of the television medium and that it easily changes its ways of perceiving products and brands and its purchasing behavior without thinking very much about it at the time of TV exposure or at any time prior to purchase, and without up to then changing verbalized attitudes. This adds up, I think, to an understandable success story for advertising's use of the television medium. Furthermore, this success seems to be based on a left-handed kind of public trust that sees no great importance in the matter.

But now I wonder about those so-called limits of effectiveness of the noncommercial use of the mass media. I wonder if we were not overusing attitudes and attitude changes as our primary criterion of effectiveness. In looking for behavioral changes, did we sometimes despair too soon simply because we did not find earlier attitude changes? I wonder if we projected our own attitudes and values too much onto the audiences studied and assumed that they, too, would treat information about such matters as the United

Nations as serious and involving. I wonder also how many of those public-spirited campaigns ever asked their audiences to do something, that is, asked for the kind of concrete behavior that at some point triggers whatever real potentials may have developed for an attitude change to begin or perhaps to complete its work.

I would like to suggest, therefore, that the distinction between the commercial and the noncommercial use of the mass media, as well as the distinction between "commercial" and "academic" research, has blinded us to the existence of *two entirely different ways of experiencing and being influenced by mass media.* One way is characterized by lack of personal involvement, which, although perhaps more common in response to commercial subject matter, is by no means limited to it. The second is characterized by a high degree of personal involvement. By this I do not mean attention, interest, or excitement, but the number of conscious "bridging experiences," connections, or personal references per minute that the viewer makes between his or her own life and the stimulus. This may vary from none to many.

The significance of conditions of low or high involvement is not that one is better than the other, but that the processes of communication impact are different. That is, there is a difference in the change processes that are at work. Thus with low involvement one might look for gradual shifts in perceptual structure, aided by repetition, activated by behavioral-choice situations, and *followed* at some time by attitude change. With high involvement one would look for the classic, more dramatic, and more familiar conflict of ideas at the level of conscious opinion and attitude that precedes changes in overt behavior.

I think now we can appreciate again why Madison Avenue may be of little use in a cold war or even in a medium-hot presidential campaign. The more common skills of Madison Avenue concern the change processes associated with low involvement, whereas the very different skills required for high-involvement campaigns are usually found elsewhere. However, although Madison Avenue generally seems to know its limitations, advertising researchers tend to be less clear about theirs. For example, from New York to Los Angeles, researchers in television advertising are daily exacting "attitude change" or "persuasion" scores from captive audiences, these scores based on questionnaires and methods that, though plausible, have no demonstrated predictive validity.

The plausibility of these methods rests on the presence of a more or less explicit model of communication effectiveness. Unfortunately, the model in use is the familiar one that assumes high involvement. Perhaps it is the questionnaires and the research procedures themselves that are responsible for creating what high involvement is present, which would not otherwise exist. The wiser or more cautious researchers meanwhile retreat to the possibilities of impersonal exactness in controlled field experiments and behavioral criteria. What has been left out, unfortunately, is the development of a low-involvement model and the pretest measures based on such a model. The further development of this model is an important next step, not only for the perhaps trivial world of television advertising but for the better understanding of all those areas of public opinion and education that, socially important as they may be, may simply not be very involving to significant segments of the audience.

In time we may come to understand the effectiveness of mass media primarily in terms of the *consistency* with which a given campaign, commercial or noncommercial, employs talent and research sensitively attuned to the real level of audience involvement. In time, also, we may come to understand that behavior—that is, verbal behavior and overt behavior—is always consistent provided we do not impose premature and narrowly conceived rules as to which must precede or where, when, and how it must be measured.[13]

Notes

1. Joseph Klapper, *The Effects of Mass Media* (Glencoe, IL: Free Press, 1960); Raymond Bauer, "The Limits of Persuasion," *Harvard Business Review,* September/October 1958, 105-110.

2. Neil Borden, *The Economic Effects of Advertising* (Chicago: Irwin, 1942).

3. Herbert A. Zielske, "The Remembering and Forgetting of Advertising," *Journal of Marketing,* January 1959, 239-243.

4. H. Ebbinghaus, *Grundzuge der Psychologie* (Leipzig, Germany: Veit, 1902).

5. Carl T. Hovland, *The Order of Presentation in Persuasion* (New Haven, CT: Yale University Press, 1957), 136.

6. Herbert E. Krugman, "An Application of Learning Theory to TV Copy Testing," *Public Opinion Quarterly,* vol. 26, 1962, 626-634.

7. This is the title of a working manuscript distributed privately by E. L. Hartley in 1964, which concerned his experimentation with new methods of health education in the Philippines.

8. Leon Festinger and Nat Maccoby, "On Resistance to Persuasive Communications," *Journal of Abnormal and Social Psychology,* vol. 68, no. 4, 1964, 359-366.

9. E. R. Guthrie, *The Psychology of Learning* (Magnolia, MA: Peter Smith, 1952), 26.

10. D. E. Broadbent, *Perception and Communication* (London: Pergamon, 1958), chap. 9.

11. E. L. Hartley, *Problems in Prejudice* (New York: Kings Crown, 1946), 107-115.

12. Ibid., 97.

13. The consistency of verbal and overt behavior has also been reasserted by Hovland, who attributes pseudodifferences to those research designs that carelessly compare results of laboratory

experiments with results of field surveys (Carl I. Hovland, "Reconciling Conflicting Results Derived From Experimental and Survey Studies of Attitude Change," *American Psychologist,* vol. 14, 1959, 8-17); by Campbell, who attributes pseudodifferences to the fact that verbal and overt behaviors have different situational thresholds (D. T. Campbell, "Social Attitudes and Other Acquired Behavioral Dispositions," in S. Kock [ed.], *Psychology: A Study of a Science,* vol. 6 [New York: McGraw-Hill, 1963], 94-172); and by Rokeach, who attributes pseudodifferences to the fact that overt behavior is the result of interaction between two sets of attitudes, one toward the object and one toward the situation, and that most research leaves one of the two attitudes unstudied (M. Rokeach, "Attitude Change and Behavior Change," paper presented at the annual conference of the World Association for Public Opinion Research, Dublin, Ireland, September 9, 1965).

15

Humor in Television Advertising

A Practitioner's View

Jeremy Bullmore

The question, Does humor sell? belongs to that fine family of advertising questions none of which is likely to be answered definitively but all of which continue indefinitely to be asked. Other favorites include these: What is the optimum level of advertising expenditure? How many times should a commercial be shown? Is a 30-second commercial better than a half page in the *Daily Mirror*? What about nudity, then?

NOTE: This chapter is adapted, with permission, from Jeremy Bullmore, "If You Make 'em Laugh," in *Behind the Scenes in Advertising,* published by Admap Publications in the United Kingdom (1991).

It is, however, both sensible and respectable to persist in asking these questions, so long as both questioner and questioned resist the temptation to establish or accept glib and all-embracing dogma.

With luck, and hedged about by inevitable questions such as What is humor? and What is advertising? it should be possible to begin to say how, in certain circumstances, certain kinds of humor may fruitfully be used in the advertising of certain products—at least for the time being. People who think that too inconclusive, hypothetical, and unsatisfactory an objective should perhaps choose to earn their living in some simpler and more measurable occupation.

Humor can be kind or cruel, broad or subtle, largely visual or totally dependent on a collision of words. It can be trivial and facetious or deadly serious in its undertones. Between the poles of satire and slapstick lie an almost infinite number of levels and variations of humor. And, as with every kind of communication, each form of humor will be understood and enjoyed only if the listener (or looker) is capable of making that final and necessary act of completion.

A joke that nobody sees is not a joke. A joke that 1 person in a 100 sees is not a joke to the 99. If the concept of irony is alien to the receiver, he may accept the irony at face value, and so not only miss the point, but interpret the message in a way diametrically opposite from the way the sender of that message had intended. (It would be interesting to know, for example, what proportion of the loyal viewers of *All in the Family* would have accepted the reactionary figure of Archie Bunker as the long-awaited spokesman for all that was right and shrewd and sensible. And equally interesting to speculate just how much bigger that proportion might have been in the absence of studio laughter.)

Humor, then, has no universal and objective values. It will always be judged individually and subjectively. A man in a top hat slipping on a banana skin may strike almost everybody as fairly funny, but even that primitive incident relies for its humor on some prior knowledge, some prior attitudes, and some ability to contribute on the part of its observers. Unless the top hat is known to symbolize the upper classes, and unless the observer is already against the upper classes, and unless the observer is capable, however subconsciously, of seeing the undignified upending of a single figure as a comment on the fallibility of privilege, then not only will the incident fail to amuse but indeed it is likely to arouse sympathy and concern. (Few people are likely to be amused by the sight of a frail old lady slipping on a banana skin; but it's just possible that her best friend, slightly older but for years made to feel inferior, might.)

However, there is one characteristic that all forms of humor seem to share (and indeed without which they would fail to be humorous), and that is their *ability to reveal.* Humor, when it works, makes people think; it makes them see the familiar from an unfamiliar point of view. And it makes people think not only painlessly but pleasurably. This pleasure comes not just from the revelation itself, but from the self-congratulation that derives from a contribution made. Just as a joke will fail if it asks too much of a recipient, so it will fail if it asks nothing. If the point is explained, the recipient is denied the chance to participate, and there is no flash moment of perception and pleasure.

So all humor, however broad and however universally understood, is implicit rather than explicit: An explicit joke is either not explicit or not a joke. All good comedians, all good storytellers, all good makers of advertisements entice their receivers into willing and constructive collaboration. It is a skillful, delicate, and difficult thing to do—particularly in advertising, where the pressures of committees and costs tend to favor the explicit, the unambiguous, and the message that just can't fail to be understood.

But the measure of a good joke is much the same as the measure of a good advertisement (judging it now purely in terms of its communications effectiveness). Has it asked enough, but not too much, of its selected audience? Has it allowed that audience to see something for itself? (Whether, in the case of the advertisement, what the audience comes to see is the most persuasive and relevant thing is clearly another question.)

So the principles of humor and the principles of commercial persuasion are very close. Many years ago, the Ford Motor Company wanted to tell American motorists that the company sold more convertibles than did any other automobile manufacturer. Ford could perfectly well have said, "America's best-selling convertible." Instead, the company ran an ad with a headline that read, "The only convertible that outsells Ford." And the picture was of a baby carriage.

That is a kind of humor, and it is almost a joke. It certainly depends entirely on a contribution from its audience for the communication to be complete. But the contribution is a small and pleasurable one, well within the capacity of anyone in the market for a car. And what could have been a piece of self-congratulatory manufacturer's "so what" became engaging evidence of confident leadership. The point had been seen.

In pursuit of better advertisements, there is probably more to be learned from a study of the anatomy of humor than from any other subject. This is a point made with great force in Arthur Koestler's difficult but revealing book *The Act of Creation.*[1]

When we come to look at the deliberate use of humor in advertising, we would be wise to remember this basic similarity of principle. Advertising humor becomes discredited largely because of its misuse, mainly in connection with two great advertising misconceptions:

1. Television is an entertainment medium, therefore commercials must entertain.

This is not true, of course. First, television is not an entertainment medium. It is a medium, just as the telephone system is a medium, and twice as versatile. It is no more an entertainment medium than newsprint is a news medium. It can be used to educate, to carry news, to tell stories. Second, even if a high proportion of television time is devoted to what sets out to be entertainment, it clearly does not follow that all commercials for all products addressed to all people should also seek to divert—involve, yes; reward, ideally; entertain, not necessarily.

2. This is a low-interest product. Unless we do something funny, they'll go and put the kettle on or switch channels.

Any product good enough to be bought, and bought again, is of interest to the people who buy it. (It may, however, be of low interest to the creative people, in which case they should be trained or fired.) This attitude leads to blind headlines ("Let's intrigue them so they just have to read the copy"), mindless use of borrowed interest ("Why don't we get Mick Jagger?"), and animated spokespersons with funny voices mouthing otherwise conventional copy points. Such advertising may not bore, but neither will it persuade.

One of the most important and difficult functions of advertising is to show the familiar and the relatively mundane in a new light. Anyone in advertising who backs away from this inconvenient fact and relies instead on irrelevant and dissociated excitement is abdicating one of his or her more important responsibilities.

If humor is to be used relevantly and effectively, a distinction should first be made between products bought from housekeeping money and those bought from pocket money. Most women buying products from limited housekeeping budgets like to feel they have bought prudently and well. For them, shopping is part of their profession—possibly enjoyable, sometimes sociable, but serious.

There are certain kinds of humor—the clever-clever, the superficial, the transient, the slick, the overly sophisticated—that will, simply through association, begin to make the products themselves seem superficial and cheap. A repeat-purchase product, bought out of housekeeping money, runs a considerable risk of losing its reputation for substance and quality if it is consistently promoted in a jokey manner.

This is still more true of proprietary medicines, even those bought for relatively trivial complaints. There can be a kind of seesaw in people's minds: When the fun end goes up, the effectiveness end goes down. That celebrated series of entertaining commercials for Alka-Seltzer in the United States, having successfully jolted the product into the 20th century, sooner or later had to run the risk of sapping the product of its medicinal magic. And when the magic goes, so will the effectiveness of the product.

But there is another kind of humor that, significantly, we tend to call good humor. Far from being superficial, it can manifest a deep understanding of, and affection for, humanity. People are seen to be real people, with frailties and fallibilities and vanities and perversities. This kind of humor has practically universal appeal. It has permanence and substance and warmth. It reaches the heart as well as the head, evokes a smile rather than a laugh. This kind of humor is perfectly in keeping with the nature and function of everyday, housekeeping products.

Some products, however, are bought not from housekeeping money but from pocket money. The purchasers are more likely to be men than women—presumably because women aren't as easily able to give themselves pocket money. And pocket-money spending is an altogether different affair: freer, less regular, less responsible, more impulsive, more fun. Schweppes soda and mixers, presumably, are pocket-money products—bought if not by, then at least at the behest of, men. And the style and the wit with which Schweppes presents itself to the public again seems true to the nature of the product and the circumstances of its consumption. Humor here, far from debasing the value of the product, is enhancing it, giving it an extrinsic value that must make life very difficult for its competitors.

If you examine very closely all those very funny American commercials we British view with such envy and respect, you will find that a very high proportion of them are for products bought by or for men, from pocket money. Alternatively, they are for products aimed at a small minority of people. It is tempting, but ill-advised, to try to apply a style of wit and humor that is right and relevant for a pocket-money, minority-audience product to a mass-consumption, housekeeping-money product.

Much more could be written on this subject, but perhaps the main points to summarize are these:

1. The principles of humor and the principles of making good advertisements are similar: Both should "reveal."
2. Communication is most successful when the recipient makes the final contribution. Creative skill is needed to ensure that the recipient cannot fail to arrive at the desired conclusion.
3. Economy is not just brevity but implicitness. And for the recipient to contribute, a degree of implicitness is essential.
4. Humor will always be assessed individually and subjectively. What is funny to you may be incomprehensible to members of your target audience, and they are the only ones who matter.
5. Humor, when used, should spring naturally from the product, or from the need the product is there to satisfy.
6. Consistent use of irrelevant and superficial humor can call into question the intrinsic worth and quality of a product.
7. Good humor can be affectionate and kind, and can be evidence of a human and understanding advertiser.
8. Expensive products are not necessarily serious, nor are cheap ones frivolous. It is more important to consider the kind of money with which they are bought: Does the money come from a restricted weekly housekeeping budget or from discretionary pocket money?
9. Wit, irony, understatement, and allusion may be understood and appreciated by a minority of people. For products designed for those people, such humor can add appreciably to their extrinsic value.
10. The nature of the humor used must always be true to the nature of the product (or its desired nature) and to the nature of its present and potential users.

Note

1. Arthur Koestler, *The Act of Creation* (New York: Viking Penguin, 1990).

16

Humor in Television Advertising

A Researcher's View

Paula Pierce

I have found in the course of a large experience that common people are
more easily informed through a medium of a broad and humorous
illustration than in any other way.

Abraham Lincoln

Does Funny Make Money? Dissenting Points of View

Humor is a highly visible and much-talked-about executional technique in
television advertising. Comic advertising is widely considered "highly creative." Invariably, funny commercials are abundantly evident in the advertising
industry's annual creative awards and "best commercial" lists.

"Any selling message is going to work better if it is entertaining, rather
than just boring people into the shops. It would never occur to me that humor

would be opposed." Thus has spoken Tim Bell, a former executive at London's Saatchi & Saatchi, a world-renowned advertising agency. Indeed, in the United Kingdom there is no debate surrounding the value of amusing advertising. Probably 50% to 75% of British commercials are aimed at the funny bone. Playful commercials also are used generously throughout Europe, Japan, and many other corners of the globe, where they represent approximately half of all commercials on TV.

John Noble, an executive at Doyle Dane Bernbach (now DDB Needham), an agency that pioneered humorous advertising in the United States, has defended the value of humorous advertising: "People watch commercials not only to be informed, but to be entertained. There are enough terribly serious things going on in the world without putting them in commercials. Why be ponderous about selling a pound of butter?"

Yet most American advertisers are uncomfortable with the lighthearted sell. In the United States, humorous commercials account for only about 25-30% of all commercials on television.

"Appeal for money in a lightsome way, and you never get it. People do not buy from clowns," said Claude Hopkins, the American "father of modern advertising." Hopkins said that in 1927, but his attitude has had an enduring effect. David Ogilvy, the legendary elder statesman of the trade, continued to oppose funny advertising well into the 1980s: "Housewives don't buy a new detergent because the manufacturer told a joke on television last night. They buy the new detergent because it promises a benefit." The sage Leo Burnett answered questions about the value of humorous advertising with this ambivalent response: "Fun without sell gets nowhere, but sell without fun tends to become obnoxious."

Perhaps one of the most commonsensical philosophies of advertising humor has come from Roy Grace of Doyle Dane Bernbach: "I like to use humor if humor is relevant to the product and especially if the product is associated with pleasure. I don't believe in using humor to advertise a product whose nature is serious, such as a painkiller."

The Real Issue: Does Humor Achieve Advertising Objectives?

In fact, amusing and entertaining advertising has proliferated on a global scale. The real issue, however, is this: Does the humorous approach achieve advertising objectives? Do funny commercials get attention, generate brand awareness, and communicate relevant sales points? Do funny commercials alter consumer attitudes about brands? Do they, in truth, successfully persuade consumers to purchase products and services? Additionally, how does this device work? Under what circumstances is playful advertising sales productive?

These are the questions that McCollum Spielman Worldwide (MSW) set out to answer in a review of hundreds of humorous commercials that have been copy tested in the company's 25-year history. The data presented in this chapter are all derived from MSW studies.

Study Methods and Measures

The MSW review focused on commercial performance on basic AD*VANTAGE/ACT copy-testing measurements. These are measures of *recall* ("Clutter Awareness") and *persuasion.*

Individual commercial scores were indexed against appropriate category norms, grouped, and compared with similarly indexed groupings of nonhumorous commercials: (a) celebrity commercials, (b) mood/image commercials, (c) "real people" testimonials (testimonials from authentic, satisfied consumers, as opposed to "presenter commercials," which use professional performers to tell about the product or service), (d) monadic demonstrations (i.e., demonstrations of the brand in isolation from other brands), (e) comparative demonstrations (i.e., one brand against another), and (f) presenter commercials.

Does Humor Attract Attention?

Humor emerged as the most powerful executional device for obtaining visibility for advertisers' brands and services. In the sample reviewed, 42% of humorous commercials achieved above-average Clutter Awareness scores. Clearly, the AD*VANTAGE/ACT data demonstrated that humor gets attention.

However, two other devices, the celebrity and the mood/image appeals, were almost equally strong for attracting attention. In these two categories,

TABLE 16.1 Recall Performance (ability to get attention): Humor Versus Other Execution Types

	Percentage of Commercials Scoring Above Norm
Humorous commercials	42
Celebrity commercials	41
Mood/image commercials (soft sell)	40
"Real people" commercials (hard sell)	36
Comparative demonstrations (hard sell)	31
Presenter commercials (hard sell)	29
Monadic demonstrations (hard sell)	25

41% and 40% of the commercials tested achieved better-than-average Clutter Awareness scores.

The four remaining executional formats—"real people," comparative demonstration, presenter, and monadic demonstration—all fairly traditional "hard-sell" styles, proved significantly inferior in their ability to achieve awareness (see Table 16.1).

Commercial memorability is an extremely important factor. The worldwide TV clutter makes it imperative for advertisers to create commercials that are highly visible. In 1986, 64% of consumers were able to recall a commercial seen in the past 4 weeks. By 1990, that figure had declined to 48%.[1]

How Persuasive Is Humor?

Recall (Clutter Awareness) is a critical component in the mental, emotional, and psychological process that culminates in persuasion of the consumer. Many people believe that recall opens the door to persuasion; that is, persuasion cannot take place without recall.

However, recall is not a commercial's only measure of effectiveness. MSW's analytic studies demonstrate that Clutter Awareness is strongly influenced by executional elements and does not necessarily alter attitudes or behavior.

MSW's AD*VANTAGE/ACT system employs a pre-post measure of Persuasion/Attitude Shift that has been extensively validated in the United States

TABLE 16.2 Persuasion Performance: Humor Versus Other Execution Types

	Percentage of Commercials Scoring Above Norm
Comparative demonstrations (hard sell)	44
Monadic demonstrations (hard sell)	41
Celebrity commercials	41
"Real people" commercials (hard sell)	36
Presenter commercials (hard sell)	32
Mood/image commercials (soft sell)	31
Humorous commercials	31

and Europe using micromarket scanner technology and complete control of all variables. The validation studies conclusively demonstrate that Persuasion/Attitude Shift is the measure that shows the highest level of correlation to marketplace behavior (sales).

On Persuasion/Attitude Shift, humor was the bottom-ranking device. Only 31% of humorous commercials attained better-than-average persuasion scores, compared with 44% of comparative demonstrations, 41% of monadic demonstrations, and 41% of celebrity sells. Equaling humor's effectiveness (or relative lack of it) was emotion/imagery (31% were above norm).

Two "hard-sell" formats were also relatively low in the ranking: presenter and "real people" testimonials, with respective above-average score shares of 32% and 36%. Thus it would appear that advertising that is funny or emotional (two indirect or "soft-sell" formats) is less persuasive than celebrity-driven advertising or "hard-sell" product demonstrations (comparative or monadic) (see Table 16.2).

Does Humorous Treatment Affect Communications?

Ultimately, it is the *relevance* of the message that determines whether a commercial is persuasive or not. An irrelevant message remains irrelevant, no matter how entertainingly or touchingly it is presented. No amount of exposure can change this. A recent MSW tracking analysis of one brand's 62 highest-scoring persuaders over a 20-year period clearly illustrated the impact of message relevance. Persuasion levels reached their highest peaks during

TABLE 16.3 The Product Continuum (at the extremes)

Commodity ("me too")	Unique (preemptive)
Execution often "is" concept/strategy (how said).	Product dominates strategy/copy (what said).
Style rules.	Substance rules.
Involvement is low.	Involvement is high.
Model is feel/do (transformational).	Model is think/do (informational).
Stimulus is sensory or psychological.	Stimulus is intellectual.
Repetition can work (buildup effect).	Believability, conviction are essential.

periods in which the brand's communication was at its most relevant. Persuasion levels declined whenever the brand communication became less focused and less relevant.

MSW experience and observation lead to the inescapable conclusion that, in many cases, humorous advertising is tremendously entertaining and arresting, but the communication does not have relevant product purpose. The trap into which many practitioners of humorous advertising fall is that they permit awareness to become the overriding objective, and they overlook the selling message. Hence funny commercials are among the most visible and among the least persuasive.

Is Humor Appropriate for All Products?

The issue of appropriateness, a "good fit," may be critical to the decision regarding the use of humor in a new campaign. The product continuum is a complex entity. If one is fortunate enough to have a unique, preemptive product story, that story should, ideally, rule strategy and copy. It requires no further embellishment. Tell them about it and they will come and buy. The ends of this continuum are shown in Table 16.3.

However, in today's marketplace, the more typical product can be found at the other extreme of the continuum, the commodity or "me too" product. When the product is a commodity, the execution becomes synonymous with the concept. The "how said" is often what distinguishes one highly competitive product from another. In this realm, unorthodox, mold-breaking, and attention-getting executions—if executed with product purpose—can become distinctive product signatures and driving forces that motivate.

Let us assume that you are ready to advertise your brand (which has strong similarities to other brands) in a crowded and highly competitive market with a new and exciting "signature" ad campaign. You develop new storyboards for a humorous campaign. The first question you should ask is, Is humor an appropriate context for presenting my product? How do you know if the humorous approach is compatible with your product? In certain categories, this is self-evident. Some products are inherently humorous. If your product is named Hubba Bubba, Yodels, Doo Dads, Snickers, Butterfingers, or Three Musketeers, the chances are that humor will be appropriate. Fun foods are naturally compatible with a lighthearted approach. More important, they often have high consumption among children and teens—subpopulations that are highly attuned to funny advertising.

MSW's experience also contains many examples of basic foods and condiments with heavy adult consumption that have used playful advertising quite successfully to provide them with distinctive brand personalities in product fields clouded by "sameness." Cat products have carved special niches for themselves by playing on the naturally buffoonish feline character. Noted luggage brands have used apes and athletes to demonstrate product strength and durability through comically exaggerated "torture" tests.

Numerous household products have used light-spirited devices to demonstrate how cleaning is made easier. Detergents have used Pac-Man-type "dirt gobblers" and little persons with scrub brushes to call attention to new ingredients. They have provided merriment in a sea of drudgery. Humor has also proven more tasteful than "live" footage in animated displays of dead insects by insecticide manufacturers. However, in all these product fields, MSW research has shown that humorous commercials have had fairly high success rates because the humor has been used with product purpose and has been appropriate in meaningful product demonstrations.

On the other hand, there are a variety of "serious" products that do not inherently lend themselves to humorous treatment. MSW has found few examples of successful humorous commercials for banks, real estate, insurance, or financial/investment services. Evidently, money, property, and life and death are not laughing matters. Moreover, these kinds of services have complicated (sometimes technical) messages that are hindered by humor (and the time required to set up a joke).

TABLE 16.4   Success Ratio for Humorous Commercials: Established Versus
New Products

	Established Products (%)	New Products (%)
Humorous commercial was successful (acceptable performance on both measures).	59	33
Humorous commercial was a failure (unacceptable performance on both measures).	41	67

High-ticket items—automobiles, entertainment systems, and appliances—
have also seldom been well served by humorous advertising. Apparently,
when that much money is at stake, consumers prefer straight information for
their heads. In addition, drugs and other remedies have generally not been
successful with experiments in humorous advertising. Consumers are more
responsive to pain-relief messages when they are delivered without sugarcoat-
ing. Finally, there are several other product categories—cosmetics, fragrances,
alcoholic beverages, soft drinks, and clothing—in which humor has been used
sparingly because the prevailing approach has been social, image, and status
driven. In these categories, humor is less appropriate than emotional or image
advertising.

MSW has also found that the success ratio for humor declines considerably
if the product is new. With established products, 59% of humorous commercials achieved acceptable (at least average) scores on both basic evaluative
measures. However, only 33% of humorous commercials for new products
met average criteria on both measures. In a deeper analysis, MSW found that
humor can create communication impediments and hinder conviction for a
product or service that does not have momentum or has not had the opportunity to build reputation and image. Generally, humor is not recommended for
new product introductions (see Table 16.4).

Is Humor a Good Approach for Advertisers in Foreign Countries?

Thus far, the data, observations, and conclusions I have presented have sprung
from MSW's American commercial database. However, as mentioned earlier,

TABLE 16.5 Perceptions of Advertising, Europe and United States

	United Kingdom	*France*	*Germany*	*United States*
Advertising is perceived as				
mostly	entertaining, humorous	informative	entertaining, informative	easy to understand
secondarily	informative	humorous, entertaining	humorous, easy to understand	informative
not	believable, easy to understand	believable, easy to understand	believable	believable, entertaining

SOURCE: International AD*VANTAGE/ACT data (GfK and MSW).

American advertisers use humor more sparingly than do advertisers in many other countries. Americans also have a higher rate of unsuccessful experimentation with humor in advertising than do many of their counterparts abroad.

Interestingly, this cultural disparity stems from differences in the historical development of television advertising in the United States and many other nations. In the United States, TV advertising evolved from the philosophy that had been producing hard-sell advertising in print. In the rest of the world, television advertising was preceded by a long tradition of cinema advertising. Cinema advertising was produced for (paying) cinema audiences. If the spots that preceded the motion pictures created negative audience reactions, cinema exhibitors heard about it immediately.

Thus practitioners in other countries developed great skill in creating entertaining advertising for cinema exposure, and audiences accepted entertainment as part and parcel of advertising. When advertising moved to TV, Europe (and particularly Great Britain) already had an entrenched tradition of funny advertising.

Are Americans just out of the loop? Is humor truly the more universal approach to advertising, as practiced in so many other countries? Inasmuch as AD*VANTAGE/ACT tests are conducted in more than 28 countries on five continents, MSW has developed an international normative database, with the opportunity to access a global spectrum of TV tests.

A major study conducted by the Nuremberg-based GfK, MSW's AD*VANTAGE/ACT affiliate in Europe, measured perceptions of advertising in three

European countries. The European data are compared with data from the United States in Table 16.5. Interestingly, Europeans think of commercials as entertainment, with humor an integral ingredient of this entertainment experience. Americans, however, think of advertising as an information tool. Nonetheless, consumers in France, Germany, and the United Kingdom have described their funny and entertaining commercials as hard to understand. In contrast, Americans have no difficulty understanding their "informative" advertising. Perhaps much of the entertaining advertising shown abroad shortchanges or upstages relevant product information. However, Europeans and Americans all appear to agree that their advertising lacks believability, regardless of whether it is humorous or informative.

Is humor universally well received? Is it appropriate for mass audiences? These research findings suggest some problems. At the very least, there are consumer complaints about the lack of information found in entertaining commercials.

Guidelines

Humor is a risky device. It presents too many temptations to allow the joke to steer the story. Humor is also hard to write. There are few "comic geniuses," and the art of writing comedy (including for advertising) is not easily learned—if it can be learned. The technique and craft that go into writing and producing a humorous commercial must be superb. The result has to be sharp, taut—timing and pacing are of the essence. Superb casting and precise delivery are mandatory.

Furthermore, humor is highly personal. What plays in Dallas can be deadly in Düsseldorf; what's hilarious in Helsinki can be obnoxious in Oslo. Today's global culture is extremely diversified. It is extremely difficult to find a style of humor that would give pleasure to all people.

MSW has identified a number of humorous executional styles and devices that can be very risky:

- Children and animals used for humorous effect often upstage the product or message. In some cases, "cute" children are unable to carry the message because they are difficult to understand. Sometimes they are inappropriately used. Although it may be charming to use children for humorous effect, children are often not credible or authoritative product users.

- The lower and broader the humor, the more likely it is to offend someone or to be perceived as just plain idiotic and thus cast a negative light on the product. Broad, farcical humor is also likely to upstage the product.
- Exaggerated and stock types (such as the "dumb housewife") are guaranteed to offend someone and can create unwanted public relations crises for an advertiser. Regional and ethnic stereotypes can be extremely troublesome.

Clearly, however, there are many effective uses of humor. Assuming that one has followed the first two rules (made sure that the humor is compatible with or appropriate for the product and that it uses humor with product purpose), MSW's research indicates some very effective uses of humor:

- More subtle and true-to-life situations give the consumer the opportunity to laugh with the advertiser, not at the advertiser. Amusing, exaggerated situation, slice-of-life, predicament and problem are good setups for a purposeful product benefit.
- Lighthearted mood, emotional, or image appeals can be very effective.
- Parody or spoof tends to be a good kind of humorous execution because it "borrows" familiarity from something that is already well-known and well liked. Less time is needed for setup.
- Light-spirited music and jingles often enhance the impact of a humorous presentation and heighten its memorability.
- Whimsy and animation provide unlimited possibilities for creative experimentation, often with wide-appeal campaign longevity.

Finally, it must be remembered that humor is serious business. Accounts are lost by advertising that reflects an agency's cuteness, insider jokes, or pure entertainment that is not connected to the brand's driving, strategic message.

Note

1. Reported in *Business Week,* September 23, 1991.

17

Celebrities in Advertising

Abhilasha Mehta

Advertisers pay millions of dollars to celebrities, hoping that the stars will bring their magic to the products and services they endorse and make them more appealing and successful. Are the dollars well spent? Not always. Although actress Candice Bergen's "Dime Lady" portrayal for long-distance phone carrier Sprint was highly successful, and Jaclyn Smith moved millions to buy her clothing line at Kmart, Cybill Shepherd and James Garner were discontinued as spokespersons for the Beef Industry Council. And a Pepsi commercial featuring pop diva Madonna that cost megamillions to produce was aired only once in the United States before being pulled off the air. Why? Why did entertainer Bill Cosby fail as an endorser for E. F. Hutton despite his success for Jell-O and Kodak? And what impact did boxing champion Mike Tyson's rape conviction and the allegations of child molestation and drug addiction against pop singer Michael Jackson have on Pepsi, for which both were spokesmen?

These are not only interesting questions, but questions that marketers and advertisers need answers to as they plan their advertising and make decisions

TABLE 17.1 Awareness of Celebrity Advertising

	Print	Television
Mean Awareness Index[a]	134	135
Ads with following Awareness Index[a] (%)		
Low (less than 80)	16	21
Average (80-120)	30	29
High (121 and above)	54	50
Number of ads in sample	248	488

SOURCE: Data from Gallup & Robinson, Inc.
a. Indexed to each appropriate product category norm (= 100).

about whether or not to use celebrity endorsers—and, if so, how. This chapter explores the impact of celebrity advertising and examines the perceptions, persuasion, and processing of advertising that uses celebrity endorsers, mainly entertainment and sports stars. Specifically, I attempt to answer the following questions:

- Is celebrity advertising more attention getting and memorable than other kinds of advertising?
- How are celebrities in ads perceived?
- Is celebrity advertising more persuasive than other kinds of advertising?
- How does celebrity advertising work?

Awareness and Celebrity Performance

Successful advertising must start by being able to break through today's highly cluttered media environment and catch the reader's or viewer's attention. It must also make an impact on the consumer such that the product or service advertised can be remembered. Do celebrity ads do this better than noncelebrity ads?

There is strong evidence that suggests celebrity advertising delivers a premium in terms of impact and memorability. In an analysis of 248 celebrity print ads studied by Gallup & Robinson, Inc., over the period 1982-1993, celebrity ads show about a 34% higher level of awareness than noncelebrity ads (see Table 17.1). Awareness is measured in terms of recall of the advertised brand the day after advertising exposure. In a similar analysis of 488 commer-

TABLE 17.2 Factors Influencing Celebrity Advertising Awareness in Print Ads

	Popularity of Celebrity[a]		Ease of Celebrity Recognition in Ad[a]	
	Less Popular	Popular	Less Easy to Recognize	Easy to Recognize
Awareness Index[b] (%)				
Low (less than 80)	19	8	22	11
Average (80-120)	31	28	37	25
High (121 and above)	50	64	41	64
Number of ads in sample	190	58	106	142

SOURCE: Data from Gallup & Robinson, Inc.
a. Significantly different within groups at 95% confidence level.
b. Indexed to each appropriate product category norm (= 100).

cials over a 3-year period, Rockey and Green found a 35% premium related to the use of celebrities.[1]

The use of a celebrity in the advertising, however, is no guarantee of awareness. As is also shown in Table 17.1, and for obvious mathematical reasons, not every celebrity ad or commercial performs above average. More than one in five commercials and one in six print ads fall 20% or more below the category norm in terms of recall. The obvious question of interest is, Why?

The two most important factors that seem to influence attention getting and memorability in the print advertising analysis are the popularity of the celebrity used and the ease with which the star is recognized in the ads. As shown in Table 17.2, significantly more ads using popular, well-known celebrities and celebrities who could be easily identified in the ads had above-average awareness levels than had average and below-average levels. Similar results were reported in the analysis of celebrity commercials.

Consumers like gazing at stars. The success of magazines like *People* and tabloids like the *National Enquirer* clearly shows that people in general are interested in celebrities' professional as well as private lives. Consumers read and listen to what is said about celebrities. Familiarity with star endorsers encourages consumers to pay attention to the advertising in which they appear. Better-known stars, therefore, perform better in terms of awareness. When celebrities in advertising are hard to recognize because of the way they are used in the ads, this premium is minimized or lost. When Telly Savalas wore a hat to endorse Gillette Twinjector, the ad performed only at norm. But when he took the hat off to show his famous bald pate, the awareness level was almost twice as high.

Perceptions and Celebrity Characteristics

It is, of course, not enough that advertising breaks through the clutter and is attended to. To be fully effective, advertising must persuade the viewer or reader to feel more positive toward the advertised product or service. Buying intentions and usage of product or service should also be favorably influenced.

Before getting into a discussion about whether celebrity advertising is more persuasive than other kinds of advertising, I would like to address the issue of how consumers perceive celebrities when they endorse products and services in ads. One would expect that these perceptions would influence how effective particular celebrities might be in persuading consumers. Are celebrities perceived as being trustworthy and endorsing brands out of real interest, or are they perceived to be doing it just because they are being paid?

In a nationwide survey of 661 magazine readers, only about 1 in 4 (24%) respondents indicated agreement with a statement that celebrities appear in ads because they are genuinely interested in the products they endorse; 57% disagreed with the statement. An overwhelming majority (90%) of these respondents felt that financial and publicity reasons were very important to celebrities who appear in advertising. These perceptions are not surprising, considering news reports such as those about Cybill Shepherd, then spokeswoman for the Beef Industry Council, having admitted that she avoids red meat whenever possible, and about Pepsi spokesman Michael J. Fox having been seen sipping Coke. When James "Buster" Douglas became a boxing champion in February 1990, his aides were quoted as saying that marketers and media were "coming out of the woodwork" in the days after the title fight, and that "about the only endorsements the new champ won't be doing are alcohol and tobacco. But, other than that, we will do what the market will bear." [2] Clearly, such news stories are not conducive to building consumer trust in celebrity advertising.

However, when confronted with real celebrity advertising, consumers often tend to rate celebrities quite highly on a variety of characteristics—indeed, significantly higher than noncelebrity endorsers in identical or very similar advertising. Research studies have shown this to be true again and again. For example, young adult college women rated Jaclyn Smith in a Kmart commercial for her clothing line as significantly more believable, trustworthy, attractive, and likable than an unknown but young and attractive professional model in a very similar commercial.[3] In the same study, Victoria Principal in a

Jhirmack hair-care products commercial was also rated more believable, trustworthy, and physically attractive, although not more likable, than a noncelebrity endorser in an identical commercial.

Similarly, Friedman, Termini, and Washington found higher levels of believability among their respondents for an ad for a fictitious brand of sangria wine when it was endorsed by actor Al Pacino than when it was endorsed by a professional expert, a company president, or a typical consumer.[4] Atkin and Block studied three pairs of celebrity-noncelebrity ads featuring Telly Savalas, Happy Hairston, or Cheryl Tiegs for alcoholic drinks and consistently found higher ratings on trustworthiness, competence, and attractiveness—although not for believability—for the celebrity endorsers.[5]

There is a halo effect. Celebrities enjoy higher source ratings because they are stars. In another interesting study, college women rated celebrities Jaclyn Smith and Victoria Principal significantly higher in physical attractiveness than two other unknown, attractive professional models only when the respondents recognized the celebrities as actresses. Those viewers who were not familiar with the stars rated the unknown models equally or significantly more attractive than the celebrities.[6]

What impacts do these favorable perceptions of celebrity endorsers have on the overall effects of the advertising? Is celebrity advertising more persuasive than noncelebrity advertising?

Persuasion and Celebrity Influence

Celebrities have often, though not always, been found to be more persuasive in advertising than other endorsers. In most instances, the attitude toward the product is more favorable when the product is associated with a celebrity. Results are mixed, however, for the variables of overall ad effectiveness and purchase intentions.

It has been found, for example, that endorsements attributed to celebrities produce higher intention to buy, and significantly more positive scores have been found for brand attitude and purchase intentions for a celebrity ad compared with its noncelebrity counterpart.[7] Other research, however, has found no difference in buying intention as a function of the endorser's celebrity status. Petty, Cacioppo, and Schumann found that the product was liked better when it was endorsed by sports stars, but intention to buy did not differ.[8] It should be noted that most of this research has investigated the effects of celebrity advertising on fictitious brands, and thus the consumer participants in these studies have had no prior knowledge of or attitudes regarding these brands. The results, therefore, are most applicable to new brand introductions.

Advertisers pull in new celebrities to endorse existing brands all the time. Some have done well in these situations. A study of an Amoco Oil campaign using celebrity Johnny Cash found not only increased awareness of the advertising, even in periods of lower media weight, but also a positive change in company image, especially among users.[9] Unilever's beauty bar Lux is sold in more than 70 countries and is a leader in many of them. The company's strategy all over the world for more than six decades has been to use current leading national and international film actresses as endorsers. Stars can persuade consumers to buy. Kmart has had huge success in tying in with Jaclyn Smith; it has been estimated that 30 million American women owned items from the Jaclyn Smith collection shortly after the launch.[10]

All celebrity advertising, however, does not persuade. In an analysis of print celebrity ads, "Persuasion" (among recallers using the measure "Favorable Buying Attitudes" on a 5-point scale) showed a figure 20% higher than its product category norm for only about one in three ads (see Table 17.3). The mean for all celebrity ads was only at the norm. In fact, one in five ads fell at least 20% below norm. In a similar study of celebrity commercials, Rockey and Greene report a mean somewhat higher at 110; and whereas one-third of the celebrity commercials performed above norm, one in four fell 20% below.[11]

One of the most important variables that seems to influence how persuasive a celebrity will be in any advertising is the appropriateness of the celebrity for endorsing a particular brand and product. This appropriateness may be defined as the natural linkage between personality and product category, regardless of how the celebrity is actually used in the ad. As shown in Table 17.4, significantly more ads and commercials using appropriate celebrities have high Persuasion Indexes than those that use less appropriate celebrities (or inappropriate ones).

The selection of the appropriate celebrity thus becomes a very important decision for the advertiser. Researchers have studied celebrity-product appropriateness under a variety of names, including the *matchup hypothesis* and *product-brand congruence*.[12] To understand this selection process fully and implement it successfully, it is important to understand how celebrity adver-

TABLE 17.3 Persuasion in Celebrity Advertising

	Print	*Television*
Mean Persuasion Index[a]	104	110
Ads with following Favorable Buying Attitudes Index[a] (%)		
Low (less than 80)	19	24
Average (80-120)	50	40
High (121 and above)	31	36
Number of ads in sample	123	189

SOURCE: Data from Gallup & Robinson, Inc.
a. Indexed to each appropriate product category norm (= 100).

tising works. Why is matchup or celebrity appropriateness important? What are the dynamics of the celebrity advertising process?

Processing and Celebrity Dynamics

Source Model

Early attempts at understanding the influence of any source in the persuasive context suggested that an attractive, trustworthy, likable, or credible source facilitates the message-learning and acceptance process.[13] Results, however, have been mixed in celebrity advertising. Highly desirable sources have been effective under some, but not all, conditions. Further, although in one study respondents rated a product for beauty (razors) higher when a physically attractive celebrity endorsed it compared with an unattractive celebrity, in other analyses for fashion and cosmetic products—namely, jeans and perfume—the celebrities' expertise, rather than attractiveness or trustworthiness, influenced intentions to buy.[14] Even highly credible sources have not been found to be universally influential. These mixed results have been explained on the basis of the interacting influence of consumer involvement.

Cognitive Response Model

It has been suggested that involvement levels may influence to what extent a celebrity or any other source is successful in being persuasive. The elabora-

TABLE 17.4 Celebrity-Product Appropriateness and Persuasion

| | Celebrity Appropriateness | | | |
| | Print | | Television | |
	Less Appropriate	Appropriate	Less Appropriate	Appropriate
Persuasion Index[a] (%)				
Low (less than 80)	19	20	34	18
Average (80-120)	56	42	36	37
High (121 and above)	25	38	30	45
Number of ads in sample	68	55	67	122

SOURCE: Data from Gallup & Robinson, Inc.
a. Indexed to each appropriate product category (= 100).

respondents use the source (celebrity) in the message as a peripheral cue to help them accept or reject the message (peripheral route processing).[15] However, under conditions of high involvement, the influence of the source is minimal and respondents "elaborate" on the message itself (central-route processing) and diligently consider the information provided. Peripheral and central-route processing can be monitored by means of capturing the thoughts and feelings—cognitive responses—respondents generate during advertising exposure. The more favorable these responses, the more the likelihood of persuasion in the desired direction.

Although simultaneous processing of the peripheral and central routes has generally been found to occur in most cases, celebrity advertising was found to dominate through the peripheral process in the study of Kmart clothing with Jaclyn Smith. As viewers watched the Kmart commercials (either featuring celebrity Jaclyn Smith or an attractive professional, noncelebrity source), the thoughts and feelings generated during the exposure were measured by means of thought lists. These lists were categorized as related to (a) the product or brand, (b) the source (celebrity or noncelebrity), or (c) ad execution. Although all viewers generated all types of thoughts, the celebrity advertising viewers had significantly higher numbers of source-related thoughts than did the noncelebrity commercial viewers. Further, structural equation modeling showed that it was clear that the persuasive process had been different for the two groups. As shown in Figure 17.1, for the celebrity ad, source-related thoughts significantly influenced commercial attitude, which influenced brand attitude and intention to buy. With the noncelebrity ad (Figure 17.2), neither source-related thoughts nor commercial attitude had any influence on the brand attitude or buying intentions.

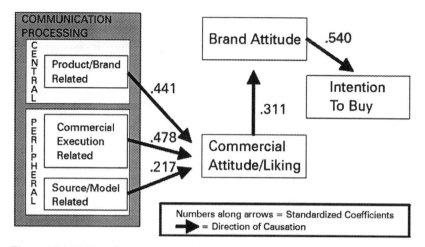

Figure 17.1. K-Mart Celebrity Commercial—Jaclyn Smith
SOURCE: Abhilasha Mehta, "How Advertising Response Modeling (ARM) Can Increase Ad Effectiveness," *Journal of Advertising Research,* May/June 1994, 62-74.

The implications of these findings are important to advertisers. The finding that celebrity-related thoughts influence the persuasive process suggests, first, that it is important that the celebrity herself, and her use in the commercial, generate positive thoughts so that persuasion is in the desired direction. Second, because product-related thoughts are few in connection with the celebrity herself, and do not influence overall attitude and buying intentions directly, it is important that the use of the celebrity in the advertising is able also to bring some focus on the product. Often the advertising is remembered, the celebrity in the advertising is remembered, but the brand name is lost. Clearly, that kind of vampire creativity is not beneficial to the advertiser. Also, under conditions where peripheral cues are important, as is the case here for the celebrity advertising, the celebrity-product/brand associations need to be reinforced strongly to establish a stable association. Often, the impact of the peripheral cue is lost when cues are no longer present—unless strong associations are built.

The Matchup Hypothesis and Balance Theory

Recognizing the need for a celebrity to influence the endorsed product positively, it is well established that the message conveyed by the image of

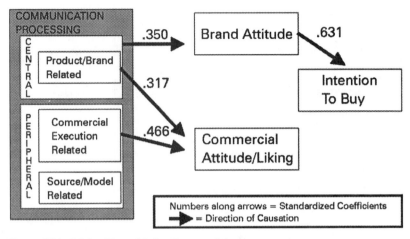

Figure 17.2. K-Mart Noncelebrity Commercial
OURCE: Abhilasha Mehta, "How Advertising Response Modeling (ARM) Can Increase Ad Effectiveness," *Journal of Advertising Research,* May/June 1994, 62-74.

the celebrity and the message about the product ought to converge in effective ads. The matchup or congruence between the two is important because it allows for meaningful processing and makes it more possible for the brand name to be effectively linked and associated with the celebrity.

From an advertiser's perspective, whether the celebrity is brought in to endorse a new brand or an existing one is an important consideration. It is easier to create a new attitude than to change an existing one; thus it should be less difficult to associate the meanings of a celebrity with a product lacking an existing meaning than to change the existing meaning of a brand by adding new associations. Change should be particularly difficult when there is a discrepancy between the existing meaning and the proposed new meaning, or when there is a perception of product-endorser incongruence.

When the celebrity's image or attributes do not coincide with the known attributes of the brand, product, or service, incongruence results. This incongruence produces tension and generates forces in the reader or viewer to restore balance.[16] This can be achieved either through a change in perceptions of the celebrity or through a change in attitudes about the product or service. As a result, a positively viewed celebrity could improve a not-so-positively viewed brand or, alternatively, suffer negative perceptions her- or himself if the brand perceptions are highly negative. Thus the perceived strength and nature of a celebrity's attributes as well as the perceived image of a known brand interact to produce the final outcome, which may or may not be a successful celebrity endorsement process.

Cultural Meaning Transfer

Research has focused on explaining how this celebrity endorsement process may be better understood, proposing a "meaning transfer" perspective. According to the model hypothesized by Grant McCracken, celebrities' effectiveness as endorsers stems from the cultural meanings with which they are endowed. A celebrity, possessing a unique, "individualized and complex bundle of cultural meaning," may transfer that meaning to the product, and from the product, it may transfer to the consumer.[17] The research suggests that celebrities are effective endorsers to the degree that they are able to bring clear and unambiguous meanings to the products they endorse.

From this perspective, then, Candice Bergen was effective in the Sprint commercials because her portrayal in the advertising used the same wit that made her character on *Murphy Brown* a hit. Her savvy, smart, and humorous attitude in the campaign easily transferred to Sprint as she simplified and explained to consumers the complexities of long-distance calling plans, setting the carrier apart from its overly serious-minded competitors, AT&T and MCI.

It is also easy to see how Bill Cosby's image of a fun-loving, good-humored father figure transferred successfully to Jell-O and Kodak but not to E. F. Hutton, and why Elizabeth Taylor was a successful spokeswoman for the fragrances Passion, White Diamonds, and Fragrant Jewels, as were Joan Collins for Scoundrel and Cher for Uninhibited; the perfect image transfers, indeed, in all three cases. In a Gallup & Robinson test of these fragrance brands' ads, scores were extremely high for intrusiveness—more than 60% higher than the norm for Elizabeth Taylor's Passion and more than twice the norm for Joan Collins's Scoundrel. Uninhibited by Cher scored more than two and a half times the norm. On the other hand, when John Wayne, wearing a tuxedo, endorsed Datril pain-relief medication, it just did not work. The ad tested below average. It was hard to believe that this icon of macho would ever get a headache, much less take a pill for it!

It is very important for the advertiser to measure what the cultural meaning of a particular celebrity is. Whereas early attempts were made to measure celebrities on source characteristics such as trustworthiness, credibility, attractiveness, and likability, McCracken proposes that these are not enough. It is possible that two or more celebrities may be rated similarly on these scales, but that this "sameness masks profound and thoroughgoing differences."[18] It is not enough to know the degrees of attractiveness or credibility—the *kinds* of attractiveness and credibility must also be measured, and how these meanings serve the endorsement process must be better understood. For example, although Jodie Foster and Madonna are both seen as physically attractive, there are clear differences in perceptions of the two women. In a study with a college student sample, Jodie Foster's beauty was perceived to be of the "sophisticated and elegant" kind, whereas Madonna's was seen as being the "sexy and slutty" type.[19] Some researchers have expanded the list to measure as many as 25 different image traits in attempts to capture "unique cultural meanings," but it may be useful to employ other methods that do not limit respondents' reactions.[20]

Qualitative procedures were used in one study to allow consumers to free-associate about celebrities' images, and meaningful image profiles were drawn up by means of multidimensional concept mapping.[21] This method allowed for the quantifying and relating of celebrities' unique meanings to congruent products.[22] Results revealed multiple, though related, facets of Madonna's persona; she was mostly seen as "daring/outspoken" (58%), "slut" (42%), "sexy" (33%), and "talented/artist" (32%). These perceptions influenced her possible congruence with particular products and services. Whereas the "daring/outspoken" Madonna was seen as appropriate for endorsing lingerie and underwear, her "attractive and powerful" image was considered congruent with fragrance and cosmetics; the "slut" persona was seen as right for condoms, and "obnoxious and sexy" Madonna was perceived as suitable for selling "sex products." She was not seen as an appropriate endorser of the "vote in the election" message—a campaign in which she appeared.

Dynamic and Ever-Changing Celebrity Personas

An important consideration in the use of celebrities in advertising is the dynamic nature of their cultural meanings. Celebrities embody their personal and professional achievements. As these change, their cultural meanings also change. Sometimes, they change to become incongruent with brands they are endorsing. For example, James Garner could not continue to be an effective spokesman for the Beef Industry Council after he reportedly suffered heart trouble. With embarrassing reports of celebrities testing HIV-positive, or being accused and even arrested on drug and sex charges, advertisers need to worry about who they choose for endorsements. Some are even reaching for celebrities guaranteed never to offend—dead celebrities! Diet Coke, Hershey, and Levi Strauss have used Humphrey Bogart, Marilyn Monroe, and James Dean. The Gap's well-received print campaign for its khaki trousers featured stars such as Orson Welles, Rock Hudson, Humphrey Bogart, Sammy Davis, Jr., and Marilyn Monroe.

The changes in celebrity personas over time can sometimes be expensive for advertisers, as Pepsi can testify. After spending large sums to have pop star Madonna featured in a 60-second commercial, the commercial was taken off the air after one exposure due to the controversy surrounding her then-new video and album release. Another celebrity endorser Pepsi used was Mike Tyson, who has served time in prison for rape. As if the then-recent allegations of drug addiction and child molestation were not enough, when Michael Jackson canceled his 1993 Pepsi-sponsored summer tour in Thailand because of dehydration, Coca-Cola found a special competitive advantage and came up with an ad in the newspapers reading, "Dehydrated? There's always Coke."

Social Validity Hypothesis

Although cognitive response theory, balance theory, and the cultural meaning transfer hypothesis provide theoretical frameworks to explain the celebrity endorsement process, there are situations in which more is needed. For example, what is the mechanism that operates when a celebrity endorses a pain-relief medication or a fruit yogurt—or even a financial service or bank? Can there really be a meaningful transfer of image when celebrities endorse such products? It appears that when a celebrity endorses a product for which "image" is not critical, and performance or taste of the product is the key to product acceptance, the celebrity may serve as a source of social validity. In consumers' minds, a celebrity can typically have anything he or she wants; if a celebrity chooses this particular brand, it must be a good brand. In other words, if this brand is good enough for a successful star (given, of course, that I believe the celebrity uses the brand), then it is good enough for me, a regular customer. This is the mechanism that allows the celebrity to be successful, and celebrities who are well liked and respected can serve as influential social validators.

Audience Characteristics
and Celebrity Influence

Audience characteristics also moderate the extent to which celebrities may be effective. Some studies have shown that younger adults may be more influenced by celebrities than are other groups. Users of a brand have also been found to be more influenced by celebrity advertising than have nonusers of the brand.

Inherent personality variables may also influence how effective celebrity advertising will be. The influence of one such variable, cognitive style, has been studied.[23] *Cognitive style* refers to an inclination to be more (or less) likely to differentiate various kinds of messages, environments, and so on. Respondents with low differentiation, referred to as *field dependent,* are less likely to be cognitively, perceptually, and socially inclined to analyze the environment than are respondents who are *field independent,* who tend to be highly analytic. As expected, field-dependent consumers rated the product (clothing) significantly higher and had slightly higher buying intentions when the product was endorsed by a celebrity than when it was endorsed by a noncelebrity, and the ratings were also higher than for field-independent consumers watching a celebrity commercial. More such research involving different product categories and a variety of celebrities is needed, because the marketing implications of these findings are very large indeed. Further, from a marketing perspective, it is important to identify demographics and other usable characteristics of field-independent and field-dependent respondents. There is some indication that higher education may be concomitant with cognitive style.

Conclusions and Recommendations

Clearly, all that celebrity glitter is not gold, but it can be. If appropriately used, celebrity advertising has a payoff. The strategy of using celebrity testimonials has endured over time. From 1903 to 1905, Coca-Cola was endorsed by Lillian Nordica, the then-reigning American queen of Wagnerian opera. Other opera stars, such as Adelina Patti, and stage actress Lillie Langtry recommended Pears soap as far back as 1888.

Celebrity advertising does deliver a premium in terms of impact and memorability. There is also a positive influence on persuasion, though less strong. As discussed above, the success of the celebrity endorsement process depends on many factors. Using a celebrity in advertising is no panacea, and many such uses have failed. There is evidence that well-known celebrities do better, and it is important that advertisers facilitate the recognition in ads of any celebrities they use. Further, it is also clear that consumers must see the celebrity as congruent to the advertised brand, and the message must be believable. It is less clear, however, how advertisers can establish this congruency. Advertisers need to study, on a case-by-case basis, the various aspects of the brand and celebrity in question as they develop the strategy and executions of any advertising. Equally important are the characteristics of target audience members and their perceptions of both the brand and the celebrity.

It is not enough that the celebrity in the advertising be remembered; more important, the brand must be. In using celebrities as endorsers, advertisers need to understand not only how to choose celebrities, but also how to use them in the advertising. The strategy and creative execution should reinforce strongly and consistently the celebrity-brand association. And the celebrity should not only evoke positive reactions, but help focus attention on the brand in the advertising. Thus the product will be made more desirable because of its association with the star.

Notes

1. Ernest A. Rockey and William F. Greene, "Celebrities in TV Commercials: Do They Pay Their Way?" in Gallup & Robinson, Inc., *New York: ARF 25th Annual Conference* (Princeton, NJ: Gallup & Robinson, 1979).

2. Steven W. Colford, "Sign Me, Buster," *Advertising Age,* February 19, 1990, 1.

3. Abhilasha Mehta, *Celebrity Advertising: A Cognitive Response Approach* (Ann Arbor: University of Michigan Dissertation Service, 1990).

4. Hershey Friedman, S. Termini, and R. Washington, "Effectiveness of Advertisements Utilizing Four Types of Endorsers," *Journal of Advertising,* vol. 6, 1976, 22-24.

5. Charles Atkin and Martin Block, "Effectiveness of Celebrity Endorsers," *Journal of Advertising Research,* vol. 23, 1983, 57-61.

6. Abhilasha Mehta, unpublished manuscript, S. I. Newhouse School of Public Communications, Syracuse University, Syracuse, NY, 1991.

7. Friedman et al., "Effectiveness of Advertisements"; Michael Kamins, "Celebrity and Noncelebrity Advertising in a Two-Sided Context," *Journal of Advertising Research,* June/July 1989, 34-41.

8. Atkin and Block, "Effectiveness of Celebrity Endorsers"; Richard E. Petty, John T. Cacioppo, and David Schumann, "Central and Peripheral Routes to Advertising Effectiveness: The Moderating Role of Involvement," *Journal of Consumer Research,* vol. 10, 1983, 135-146.

9. Joseph Kamen, Abdul C. Azhari, and Judith R. Kragh, "What a Spokesman Does for a Sponsor," *Journal of Advertising Research,* vol. 16, no. 2, 1975, 17-24.

10. John P. Cortez, "Shaping Kmart's New Style," *Advertising Age,* December 7, 1992, 20.

11. Rockey and Greene, "Celebrities in TV Commercials."

12. Lynn R. Kahle and Pamela M. Homer, "Physical Attractiveness of the Celebrity Endorser: A Social Adaptation Perspective," *Journal of Consumer Research,* vol. 11, 1984, 954-961.

13. Carl I. Hovland, Irving K. Janis, and Harold H. Kelley, *Communication and Persuasion* (New Haven, CT: Yale University Press, 1953). See also Martin Fishbein and Icek Ajzen, *Belief, Attitude, Intention, and Behavior: An Introduction to Theory and Research* (Reading, MA: Addison-Wesley, 1975).

14. Kahle and Homer, "Physical Attractiveness of the Celebrity Endorser." See also Roobina Ohanian, "The Impact of Celebrity Spokespersons' Perceived Image on Consumer's Intention to Purchase," *Journal of Advertising Research,* February/March 1991, 46-54.

15. Richard E. Petty and John T. Cacioppo, "The Elaboration Likelihood Model of Persuasion," *Advances in Experimental Social Psychology,* vol. 19, 1986, 123-205.

16. Fritz Heider, *The Psychology of Interpersonal Relationships* (New York: John Wiley, 1958).

17. Grant McCracken, "Who Is the Celebrity Endorser? Cultural Foundations of the Endorsement Process," *Journal of Consumer Research,* vol. 16, 1989, 320.

18. Ibid., 312.

19. Fiona Chew and Abhilasha Mehta, "Can 'Material Girl' Get Out the Young Vote? An Analysis of Celebrity Attributes Congruent With Political Participation," paper presented at the annual meeting of the Midwest Association for Public Opinion Research, Chicago, November 20-21, 1992.

20. Lynn Langmeyer and Mary Walker, "Assessing the Effects of Celebrity Endorsers: Preliminary Findings," in Rebecca Holman (ed.), *Proceedings of the 1991 Conference of the American Academy of Advertising* (New York: American Academy of Advertising, 1992), 32-42.

21. Fiona Chew, Abhilasha Mehta, and Alice Oldfather, "A Reexamination of the Source-Message Effectiveness Model: Analyzing the Pieces of the Celebrity Endorsement Puzzle via Source Models, Cultural Meaning Transfer and Concept Mapping," paper presented to the Theory and Methodology Division at the annual meeting of the Association for Education in Journalism and Mass Communication, Kansas City, MO, August 10-15, 1993.

22. M. Mark Miller, *User's Guide to VBPro* (1991). (Available on-line: http://excellent.com. utk.edu/~mmmiller)

23. Mehta, *Celebrity Advertising.*

Emotion and Advertising

Esther Thorson

The role of emotion in advertising processes has been a popular topic in academic and practitioner circles since the early 1980s, but as long ago as the 1920s, Walter Dill Scott, an early student of advertising, pointed out that it is important for advertising to create emotional responses in people:

> Anything will be remembered which awakens our emotions, whether the thing be ugly or beautiful, whether it causes us to smile or to sympathize with the sorrows of others. That which excites an emotion is not easily forgotten, and hence is a good form of advertising, if it can convince the reason at the same time that it stimulates the feelings.[1]

Interestingly, Scott was also arguing that advertising should influence both thinking and emotional responses. Whether advertising should indeed target both processes remains an important question in advertising today.

In the early 1980s, practitioners began to suggest that ads that emphasize "feelings" over arguments might be disfavored by what, at that time, was one of the most popular copy-testing procedures—day-after recall.[2] Researchers and practitioners alike became interested in how to test "feeling" ads in a way that is fair and appropriate to the different kinds of impacts they were thought to have. It was perhaps this search for an evaluation strategy that led to the spate of research into "emotion and advertising."

What is emotion, and what role does it play in the advertising process? This chapter looks closely at the major aspects of what we know about these questions from research that has included at least several hundred scientific articles and scores of books on psychology, advertising, marketing, and consumer behavior. Because the area has proved complex and often contra- dictory, we will use a current psychological model of emotion as our guide to and organizer of the literature. We look first at that model, and then proceed to a summary of what is known about advertising and emotion.

What Is Emotion?

From an intuitive point of view, *emotion* refers to a subjective feeling state that we can name, such as fear, anger, happiness, or joy. We experience emotion differently from mood, which is generally defined as a mild but long-lasting affective response, often not directly connected with any causative event.

Psychologists have shown recently, however, that emotion is much more than what we experience consciously. Emotion involves expressive activities, such as smiling or crying; physiological responses, such as shallow breathing or quickened heart rate; and overt behaviors, such as approaching a positive stimulus (e.g., food) or avoiding a negative stimulus (e.g., flight from a wild animal). In fact, it is now believed that much of emotional responding is not available to our consciousness.[3]

A good example of unconscious emotional activity is the "mere exposure effect."[4] When people are shown pictures or shapes at such short time durations that they cannot report having seen anything, they still prefer previously seen stimuli to those not previously seen. Thus affect is created by exposure to a stimulus, even when there is no consciousness of that exposure.

How Is Emotion Created?

To explain both conscious and unconscious emotional processes in simple terms, let us assume that the human brain has an area (called the amygdala) that receives input from other areas of the brain that register sensory input—things seen, heard, felt, and so on. The amygdala then itself sends output to both the brain system that controls automatic (unconscious) and motor responses (things like running, crying, laughing) and the brain system that controls conscious processes (such as experiencing fear, sadness, or happiness). The unconscious area is much more basic; it responds faster and is automatized—that is, it does not require the individual to do conscious voluntary responding. It is in this automatic system where many of the basics of "unconscious emotion" occur.

The other brain system involves the kinds of emotion that we humans can talk about and "know" we are experiencing. As will be seen, advertising is thought to operate on both the conscious and the unconscious systems.

What Components of Ads Create Emotion?

Although practitioners and academics alike seem to know an ad that causes emotion when they see one, there has been at least some effort to understand what features of ads create emotion.[5] The earliest study of these features identified seven general categories of emotional cues that could appear in ads. These features included actors, actor relationships, scenes/stories, announcers, music, cinematography (camera angle, film speed, focal subject, sound effects, special visual effects), and product references (role of the product, attributes, benefits, number of times the brand name is mentioned). Although they were not looking specifically at stimuli that cause emotion, Percy and Rossiter added some further ad features that had been shown to create emotion in consumers.[6] These included sexual content, challenges to the consumer's self-esteem, language style, visual and verbal interactions, commercial length, and commercial "rhythm" (the pattern of information in the ad—where it is dense and less dense).

Nonconscious Emotional Processes in Advertising

We look first at the more basic and primitive nonconscious system and its connection with advertising. One of the first guesses that both practitioners and academics made about how emotion produced by advertising works was that it was "conditioned"—that is, learned automatically by the simple associating of emotional response and the brand name or its attributes. In "affective conditioning," some aspect of the ad (often a nonverbal one, such as music or pictures of people's faces expressing emotion) is paired with a brand. A common result of this pairing is that people begin to feel good about the brand and even prefer it to competitors. There is clear evidence that people often are not consciously aware of how their liking for a brand developed. This kind of process likely underlies the success of ad campaigns in which no real arguments are made about the brand. The brand is simply connected with objects or events that create emotion (e.g., beautiful hair, sexual scenes, well-liked music). One of the best-known examples of advertising built on this theory of emotion is that of Coca-Cola, which for years has simply tried to bring us advertising that makes us feel good about Coca-Cola.

A second area of nonconscious emotional effects has been called *mood or emotion induction.* In this process, a mood (a transient feeling state that is pervasive, but which gently colors and directs thoughts and actions) or an emotion is created either by some event preceding the ad (such as its programming context) or by the ad itself. Information about the brand is then presented. Research clearly indicates that the mood or emotion affects liking for the brand, intention to purchase it, and actual selection of the brand when the opportunity is presented. Again, however, it does not seem necessary for people to be consciously aware of the mood or the emotion, and certainly not of the connection between the emotion and the brand.

Conscious Processes of Emotion and Advertising

Much of the research on emotion and advertising has focused on conscious emotional processes. A central concern has been people's ability and willingness to report the emotions they experience in response to advertising. There are about 10 to 15 different systems for both measuring and talking about those responses. Here we look at the most common systems for talking about emotional response to advertising.

In one of the earliest approaches, it was argued that self-reported emotional responses by viewers of ads could take one of three forms.[7] In the *descriptive* mode, the viewer could report that the people in the ad were experiencing an emotion. For example, in a coffee ad, people were perceived as in love, and enjoying their time together. In the *empathic* mode, the viewer would jointly experience the happiness, love, and enjoyment along with the actors in the ad. In the *experiential* mode, the viewer might experience a different emotion entirely from that depicted in the ad, perhaps feeling sad that she and her husband never have such enjoyable times together. Interestingly, no matter which mode of emotional response people had to ads, experiencing a given mode of response produced more persuasion toward the brands than did not experiencing that mode. For example, those who had emotional responses in the experiential mode liked the ads better, liked the brands better, and remembered the brands better than those who did not have an experiential response.[8] This approach then provided an early indication that people's conscious emotional responses to ads could be categorized and would predict more effective persuasion.

Another popular approach to looking at conscious emotional responses to ads has been concerned with labeling different kinds of emotions. One approach has used Plutchik's eight emotional categories: joy, acceptance, fear, surprise, sadness, disgust, anger and anticipation.[9] Generally, these emotions are used as basic measures of which kinds of emotions are being experienced by viewers.

Another approach has employed a three-dimensional emotional system introduced by Osgood, Suci, and Tannenbaum and developed by other analysts.[10] This system includes the dimensions of pleasure/displeasure, arousal/ nonarousal, and domination/dominance. It was also found that all three of these emotional dimensions could be used to predict people's liking for ads and their liking for the advertised brands.[11]

A fourth approach employed three feelings scales: upbeat, negative, and warm.[12] Again, it was found that all three kinds of feelings that people experienced in response to ads were predictive of how they evaluated ads, how much they liked ads, what beliefs they had about the brands, and their attitudes toward the brands.

A fifth model of labeling emotions was developed by Izard, who suggests 10 primary emotions: interest, joy, surprise, sadness, anger, disgust, contempt, fear, shame, and guilt.[13] Allen and his associates have been the most active users of Izard's system, and have reported that the types of emotions most commonly created by advertising are joy, interest, surprise, and disgust.[14]

A sixth approach to measuring conscious emotional responses to ads has involved monitors of emotional responses during the ad's exposure. With this approach, the analyst can observe the comings and goings of the intensity of an emotional response, and can observe whether the viewer is feeling positive or negative. One such system uses a "warmth monitor"; the viewer simply draws a line while watching an ad, moving it upward as she feels more "warmth" and moving it downward as she feels less.[15] In a more high-tech version, the viewer turns a dial from zero to 100 to indicate positive emotional experience (and its intensity as indicated by the distance upward from zero) and from zero to –100 to indicate negative emotional experience.[16] Both examples of these continuous measures of experienced emotion have been shown to predict liking for ads, liking for brands, and memory for both ads and their brands.

A seventh and highly technical approach to measuring emotional response has used psychophysiological responses. For example, heart rate has been used to measure positive and negative feelings; brain waves have also been used, and so has galvanic skin response. Again, although complicated and expensive to use, these measures have all been shown to relate to more common measures of advertising effectiveness. There are, in fact, advertising research companies that routinely offer psychophysiological measures as diagnostics to the effectiveness of ads. For example, Jack Shimell and Jim Fletcher are principals in a company called Inner Response, Inc., which uses skin conductance to measure the occurrence and patterns of emotional responses to ads as an indication of their effectiveness.[17]

Finally, a small number of measurement systems for looking at emotional responses to advertising have been developed by advertising agencies themselves. The best-known example is BBDO Worldwide's use of card-sorting techniques. For instance, the ad agency shows a consumer a commercial, and then asks him or her to go through a photo deck that consists of a series of 53 photos of actors expressing emotions ranging from happy/playful to disgusted/revolted. The consumer is asked to choose those faces that reflect how he or she feels after having viewed the commercial. This approach is used primarily to test whether an ad has generated the emotion that the creators intended.[18]

The Connection of Rational and Conscious Processing of Ads With the Influence of Emotion

In keeping with the early theorizing of Walter Dill Scott, a conscious, rational model of how people respond to advertising has dominated the study of emotion and advertising. It has been assumed that people are convinced by strong, logical arguments that a brand is preferable to others or is at least worth trying.

There are many rational models of how advertising works, thus it is not surprising that much of the research on emotion and advertising has attempted to understand how emotion operates at the same time the rational processing is occurring. We turn now to some of the models that combine rational and emotional processing of advertising.

One of the most influential models of how advertising works has also come to include some discussion of the role of emotion. Petty and Cacioppo suggest, in their elaboration likelihood model (ELM), that processing of persuasive messages of any kind, but certainly including ads, occurs via one of two routes.[19] In the central route, people carefully study and evaluate the logic of the arguments used about the issue or brand. They then base their responses on those arguments. In the peripheral route, however, there is less or no attention to arguments. Instead, people in a mentally lazy mode, a mode more precisely described as "low involvement," depend upon "cues," such as the credibility of the source of the arguments or the "emotional" impact of the message, to respond.

Traditionally, the ELM represented emotion as predominantly a cue that could be used in lieu of argument strength to determine whether people were persuaded by a message. It was eventually also suggested, however, that emotional response could be used as an "argument" about what is the right response to the message. For example, the image of beautiful hair, which creates a feeling of happiness, might become an argument for using a particular brand of shampoo. Whether a person does peripheral or central processing has been shown to depend upon three other variables: the person's motivation to make an informed (i.e., argument-influenced) decision, the person's ability to use (understand) the argument information, and the person's opportunity to use it.

A second model of how advertising works that has incorporated the effects of emotional responses has been the attitude-toward-the-ad model.[20] An attitude, in contrast to an emotion, is defined as an evaluative response to a stimulus object (e.g., "Brand X is good" is an attitude statement). Somewhat to the surprise of researchers, it became clear in the early 1980s that a person's attitude toward an ad (rather than toward the brand) is itself an important predictor of the person's liking the brand, intending to buy it, and even of actual purchase. A family of closely linked models of how attitude toward the ad, attitude toward the brand, thoughts about the brand, and how emotional responses relate to each other soon sprang up. There has come to be fairly clear evidence that emotional response influences attitude toward the ad and sometimes directly affects liking for the brand. This outcome seems more likely to occur when the individual is not motivated to process closely the arguments made in the ad (thus linking this theory with the ELM). However, it has also been shown a number of times that emotional processing seems to occur regardless of which route, central or peripheral, is taken. But the decision making tends to be influenced more by arguments when central processing is dominant.[21]

Differences in Affective and Nonaffective or "Cognitive" Judgments

A final area of interest concerning emotion and advertising has involved the relative impacts of emotional and cognitive responses to advertising. Here, the dominant finding has been that when people make judgments that are dominated by emotion, these judgments tend to be automatic, primary, and holistic. Emotion-based judgments occur without effort. Cognitive judgments, on the other hand, tend to be deliberate, secondary, and specific. They involve more effort, and they are more likely to occur when people are motivated to seek information about advertised products. It has also been argued that emotion-based judgments are less long-lived than those based on rational, cognitive processing.[22]

In general, emotional responses to advertising clearly constitute an important persuasive process. It has been argued that as more and more brands appear within a single product category, and as those brands are more and more alike, the more it is necessary for advertisers to turn to emotion as the main way to motivate people to purchase their brands.

Notes

1. Walter Dill Scott, *The Psychology of Advertising* (New York: Dodd, Mead, 1921).

2. Hubert A. Zielske, "Does Day-After Recall Penalize 'Feelings' Ads?" *Journal of Advertising Research,* vol. 22, no. 1, 1982, 19-23.

3. Joseph A. LeDoux, "Emotion as Memory: Anatomical Systems Underlying Indelible Neutral Traces," in Sven-Ake Christianson (ed.), *The Handbook of Emotion and Memory: Research and Theory* (Hillsdale, NJ: Lawrence Erlbaum, 1992). See also Betsy A. Tobias, John F. Kihlstrom, and Daniel L. Schacter, "Emotion and Implicit Memory," in the same volume.

4. Robert B. Zajonc and Hazel Markus, "Affective and Cognitive Factors in Preferences," *Journal of Consumer Research,* vol. 9, September 1982, 123-131.

5. Deborah J. MacInnis and Robert A. Westbrook, *The Relationship Between Executional Cues and Emotional Response to Advertising,* working paper (Tucson: University of Arizona, Department of Marketing, 1987).

6. Larry Percy and John R. Rossiter, "Advertising Stimulus Effects: A Review," *Journal of Current Issues and Research in Advertising,* vol. 14, no. 1, 1992, 75-90.

7. Patricia A. Stout and John D. Leckenby, "Measuring Emotional Response to Advertising," *Journal of Advertising,* vol. 15, no. 4, 1986, 35-42.

8. Patricia A. Stout and John D. Leckenby, "The Nature of Emotional Response to Advertising: A Further Examination," *Journal of Advertising,* vol. 17, no. 4, 1988, 53-57.

9. Robert Plutchik, *Emotion: A Psychoevolutionary Synthesis* (New York: Harper & Row, 1980).

10. Charles E. Osgood, G. J. Suci, and Percy H. Tannenbaum, *The Measurement of Meaning* (Urbana: University of Illinois Press, 1957); see also Albert Mehrabian and James A. Russell, *An Approach to Environmental Psychology* (Cambridge: MIT Press, 1974).

11. Rajeev Batra and Morris B. Holbrook, "Developing a Typology of Affective Responses to Advertising," *Psychology & Marketing,* vol. 7, no. 1, 1990, 11-25.

12. Julie A. Edell and Marian C. Burke, "The Power of Feelings in Understanding Advertising Effects," *Journal of Consumer Research,* vol. 14, December 1987, 421-433.

13. Carroll E. Izard, *Human Emotions* (New York: Plenum, 1977).

14. See, for example, Chris T. Allen, Karen A. Machleit, and Susan S. Marine, "On Assessing the Emotionality of Advertising via Izard's Differential Emotional Scale," *Advances in Consumer Research,* vol. 15, 1988, 226-231.

15. David A. Aaker, Douglas M. Stayman, and Michael R. Hagerty, "Warmth in Advertising: Measurement, Impact and Sequence Effects," *Journal of Consumer Research,* vol. 12, March 1987, 365-381.

16. Marian Friestad and Esther Thorson, "Remembering Ads: The Effects of Encoding Strategies, Retrieval Cues, and Emotional Response," *Journal of Consumer Psychology,* vol. 2, no. 1, 1993, 1-24.

17. See Jim Fletcher and Jack Shimell, "The Role of Skin Conductance Measures in Evaluating Television Advertising," in William D. Wells and Thomas Jones (eds.), *Measuring Advertising Effectiveness* (Hillsdale, NJ: Lawrence Erlbaum, 1994).

18. Gary Levin, "Emotion Guides BBDO's Ad Tests," *Advertising Age,* January 29, 1990, 12.

19. Richard E. Petty and John T. Cacioppo, *Communication and Persuasion: Central and Peripheral Routes to Attitude Change* (New York: Springer-Verlag, 1986).

20. Richard J. Lutz, "Affect and Cognitive Antecedents of Attitude Toward the Ad: A Conceptual Framework," in Linda F. Alwitt and Andrew A. Mitchell (eds.), *Psychological Processes and Advertising Effects: Theory, Research and Application* (Hillsdale, NJ: Lawrence Erlbaum, 1985), 45-63. See also Andrew A. Mitchell, "The Effect of Verbal and Visual Components of Advertising on Brand Attitudes and Attitude Toward Advertisement," *Journal of Consumer Research,* vol. 13, 1986, 12-25; Terrence A. Shimp, "Attitude Toward the Ad as a Mediator of Consumer Brand Choice," *Journal of Advertising,* vol. 19, no. 2, 1981, 9-15.

21. Rajeev Batra and Debra Stephens, "Attitudinal Effects of Ad-Evoked Moods and Emotions: The Moderating Role of Motivation," *Psychology & Marketing,* vol. 11, no. 3, 1994, 199-216.

22. Petty and Cacioppo, *Communication and Persuasion.*

19

Hierarchies of Effect

Advertising Theories

John Philip Jones

Theories of advertising communication, especially those that analyze the stages of psychological processing, have been widely studied, particularly in schools of journalism and communications in American universities. In my opinion, the relevance of these theories to professional practice is not quite as great as many academic commentators believe. This is because the effects hypothesized, despite their potential interest to practitioners and students of advertising, suffer from the disadvantage that they cannot be studied empirically from large samples of consumers, although some small laboratory experiments have been carried out and reported.

I confine discussion in this chapter to two extreme ways in which advertising effects are believed to make themselves felt: (a) as a logical sequential process (the *learning hierarchy*) and (b) as a process that encompasses fluidity and feedback (the *low-involvement hierarchy*). The learning hierarchy is often associated with certain types of print advertising, notably direct response. The low-involvement hierarchy was developed and proposed to explain how television advertising influences the psyche and the behavior of buyers of repeat-purchase packaged goods.

Advertising can work only if it is received, comprehended, and responded to in some way. Response is a matter partly of psychology (learning and attitudes) and partly—but most important—of behavior. In consumer goods marketing, behavior generally means buying—for the first time, more frequently than before, or as frequently as before.

Learning, attitudes, and behavior are all influenced in some way by advertising, but to understand how advertising works, we need to know the order of events. If we learn this, then we might be able to write better strategy, and we might also be able to employ research to help us progress from stage to stage.

The Learning Hierarchy

The earliest theory of advertising was based on a simple chain of causality, described by Charles Ramond in 1976 as "learn–feel–do." [1] According to this theory, people receive factual knowledge about a brand. As a result, their attitudes toward the brand change and they develop a preference for it. Then they buy it. There is one-way traffic as people are gradually moved toward the brand. The phrase *hierarchy of effects* has been coined to describe the sequence; it has also been called the *learning hierarchy.* The notion is an old one, the germ of which can be found in Daniel Starch's writings in the 1920s. Over the years it has been presented in at least 16 different forms. The best known of them is familiar from the acronym used to describe it, AIDA (Awareness–Interest–Desire–Action).

The theory has been disputed constantly, for a variety of reasons, the most serious being the following three:

1. There is substantial evidence that communication also works in the reverse direction. Behavior influences attitudes as people strive to reduce cognitive dissonance. Indeed, the greatest single influence on attitudes toward a brand is people's use of it. Behavior also influences learning, as a result of selective perception. In particular, users of a brand are normally those most conscious of the advertising for it (see Brown, Hanc, and Pangsapa, Chapter 20, this volume).

2. The theory concentrates exclusively on change (increase in learning, improvement in attitudes, first purchase) and gives no attention to stable patterns of consumer behavior connected with repeat purchasing—the normal situation in real markets.

3. The theory fails to enlighten us about certain well-established phenomena in the real world, such as the high failure rate of new brands and the continued existence of minor brands with small market shares and advertising budgets. Small brands are always outspent in advertising, yet their market shares are generally protected. And if change is so simple and sequential, why does it not happen more often?

Perhaps most serious is that there have been only limited attempts to validate the theory empirically, with results falling far short of conclusive. In the opinion of Michael Ray, who has been responsible for almost all the experimental work in this complex field, the learning hierarchy may possibly operate in cases in which "the audience is involved in the topic of the campaign and when there are clear differences between alternatives."[2] It is likely that this hierarchy operates more with print than with television advertising, and especially with direct-response advertising, which, when it works at all, does so as a complete stimulus. A direct-response ad works on its own on a one-exposure basis to convert nonusers into users; it must therefore embrace change in knowledge and attitudes.

The Low-Involvement Hierarchy

A more subtle and pregnant theory than the learning hierarchy is the low-involvement hierarchy, first propounded in the mid-1960s by Herbert E. Krugman and described by Ramond as "learn–do–feel." The notion hinges on the concept of low involvement as it applies to people's relationships to products, brands, and media—relationships that might be described as lacking emotional commitment because of the relative unimportance of purchase decisions to the consumer.

Krugman sees television commercials as received and responded to by consumers as simple descriptions of brand attributes. Decisions about buying are made as a result of consumers' being subjected to a rearrangement of the relative salience of such attributes. "Thus with low involvement one might look for gradual shifts in perceptual structure, aided by repetition, activated by behavioral-choice situations, and followed at some time by attitude change."[3]

An extension of Krugman's hypothesis is the notion that the two hemi-spheres of the brain store different impressions and carry out different mental functions. The right hemisphere is supposedly concerned with pictorial impressions. The change in the salience of attributes that is characteristic of low-involvement learning, as described by Krugman, is essentially a right-brain function. On the other hand, verbal processes, including reading and speaking, are supposedly the function of the left brain; high involvement is a function of the left brain.

Whether these two types of mental processes have different physical locations has not been established with absolute certainty, but this aspect of the problem is not of material importance. However, at least one practical attempt has been made (by Sidney Weinstein and his colleagues Valentine Appel and Curt Weinstein) to establish levels of brain-wave activity for magazine and television advertising.[4] Their work provides at least directional evidence that magazine advertising generates more brain-wave activity than does television advertising and that magazine advertising tends to generate more left-brain activity.

In contrast to the learning hierarchy, which (if it operates at all) works with an involved consumer and clear differences between brands, the low-involve-ment hierarchy works with uninvolved consumers and few obvious differ-ences between the brand alternatives. But what of the cases where the functional differences between brands are of less importance than those based on added values that were built by time and advertising? In these cases, which represent the majority of brands in real marketplaces, the low-involvement hierarchy does not tell the whole story. But it does lead to a modification of the concept developed by the British mathematician Andrew Ehrenberg.[5]

The central idea in Ehrenberg's theory is trial and reinforcement: advertis-ing addressed to existing users of a brand and aimed at reinforcing their preference for it, so that it will remain at least in its present position in their repertoire, and perhaps be upgraded from minor to major brand (and in exceptional cases from major to sole brand). As the theory might have been described by Ramond, it is "do–feel–do," or an interaction of the behavioral and attitudinal processes in existing users of a brand. A word borrowed from natural science, *resonance,* is an evocative way of expressing this continuous interaction of behavior and feelings. In Krugman's terms, this process might encompass the use of advertising to increase the degree of consumer involve-ment in a brand.

This theory is the only one of those considered that explains the way advertising operates as a contribution to the maintenance of stable patterns of consumer behavior for repeat-purchase packaged goods. Krugman's original low-involvement hierarchy emphasizes changing patterns of learning, behavior, and attitudes and explains new brands, sharply growing brands, and sharply declining brands. It is Ehrenberg's extension of the theory that explains the more common situation of ongoing brands.[6]

Notes

1. Charles Ramond, *Advertising Research: The State of the Art* (New York: Association of National Advertisers, 1976).

2. Michael L. Ray, Alan G. Sawyer, Michael L. Rothschild, Roger M. Heeler, Edward C. Strong, and Jerome B. Reed, "Marketing Communication and the Hierarchy of Effects," in Peter Clarke (ed.), *New Models for Mass Communication Research* (Beverly Hills, CA: Sage, 1973), 158-164.

3. Herbert E. Krugman, Chapter 14, this volume.

4. Sidney Weinstein, Valentine Appel, and Curt Weinstein, "Brain Activity Responses to Magazine and Television Advertising," *Journal of Advertising Research,* June 1980, 57-63.

5. A. S. C. Ehrenberg, "Repetitive Advertising and the Consumer," *Journal of Advertising Research,* April 1974, 25-33.

6. John Philip Jones, *What's in a Name? Advertising and the Concept of Brands* (New York: Simon & Schuster-Lexington, 1986); see chap. 6 for detailed source references.

20

Cognitive Dissonance and Selective Perception

Their Relevance to Advertising

Carri Brown
Betzi-Lynn Hanc
Nujchayada Pangsapa

C lutter is common in the mass media. The advertiser constantly struggles to be heard. Academics and professionals conduct research in an attempt to understand the complexities of consumer behavior. What are the needs of the consumer? What messages are received? What motivates a consumer to purchase a specific brand? Simple answers are not possible, but as research advances in the fields of social psychology and communication, theories emerge that provide a greater understanding of consumer behavior. Two theories that are applicable to advertising are the theory of cognitive dissonance and the theory of selective perception.

Cognitive Dissonance

Psychologist Leon Festinger published the theory of cognitive dissonance in 1957.[1] In general terms, Festinger says that every individual strives for inner consistency, or consonance. Psychological discomfort, or dissonance, results from inconsistency. Cognitive dissonance varies in magnitude and degree depending on the situation and the individual who is experiencing the discomfort. Regardless of the strength of the conflict, the individual will try to reduce the dissonance, eliminate the dissonance, and/or avoid situations and information that increase dissonance.

The presence of dissonance is dependent upon the relationship between two cognitions. A cognition is the knowledge one has of oneself, one's beliefs, and one's surrounding environment. Cognitions vary according to their degree of resistance. For example, a fact such as "The sky is blue" is very resistant to change; however, an opinion such as "Air travel is too expensive" has little resistance to change.

A stimulus is capable of creating either consonance or dissonance. Anything that makes an individual question a self-made decision or choice generates some dissonance. New events in life, receipt of additional information, cultural mores, and logical inconsistencies of information are possible sources of dissonance. New information can cause an individual to experience dissonance, as this new information may be in conflict with an individual's present belief system.

Cognitive dissonance in consumer behavior, according to Festinger and other psychologists, can occur after a purchase decision has been made. Because the decision-making process for any purchaser is usually one that is difficult and frustrating, the degree of compromise involved can leave the consumer in doubt about the choice made. As a result, the feeling of anxiety or dissonance that the individual experiences after a purchase is referred to as *postpurchase dissonance.*

Festinger's theory of cognitive dissonance does not state that dissonance *will be reduced.* Rather, it states that an individual *will be motivated to reduce* dissonance. Dissonance is a motivating factor; the discomfort experienced leads the individual to take action to reduce the dissonance. The method the individual chooses to reduce the dissonance is dependent upon the relative cognitions and their resistance to change.

Newly acquired cognitions are more resistant to change. This can be attributed to the prominence of the newer cognition in the mind of the individual and to the increased presence of dissonance, because changing a newly acquired cognition may imply indecisiveness (and other negative characteristics). In sum, cognitive dissonance is a motivator, because an individual who experiences dissonance will be motivated to reduce or eliminate it.

Selective Perception

When people watch commercials on television or look at ads in a magazine, they have a natural tendency to perceive information that is of interest to them and to screen out what is not. When a person perceives only the headline, photograph, or an attractive model in an ad, he or she is engaging in a process called *selective perception.*

The phenomenon of selective perception has helped advertisers understand why individuals perceive messages differently and what causes them to retain only certain information. Perception is always selective because human beings, by nature, have limitations. Such limitations of the brain and the five senses further narrow what a person retains from any message that is received. It has been demonstrated that we cannot possibly perceive all the stimuli that surround us. According to a study by Bauer and Greyser, the average consumer is exposed to approximately 1,500 ads per day.[2] Because there is such an overwhelming amount of advertising information, the individual automatically filters out a large number of ads. Therefore, a consumer actually perceives only 76 ads in a day. Of this total, only 12 ads at most will produce a response. Moreover, the average rate that consumers are exposed to a brand's advertising, as Jones notes, "can be measured in minutes per year."[3]

According to the theory of selective perception, people consciously and unconsciously filter stimuli as they are received. On a conscious level, people learn to block out certain sounds, colors, motions, and so on. This ability to focus away from certain stimuli can help people who are faced with unwanted distractions on a regular basis. The ability to focus on what is necessary helps us to get tasks done. However, unconscious filtering also occurs—that is, the brain is selective even without any instruction. Studies have shown that certain shapes, colors, and locations within a field of vision have better reception than others.[4]

On a conscious level, selective perception enables an individual to attend to specific stimuli and disregard or filter out unimportant or unsupportive information. Because selective perception involves active participation in the reception and digestion of incoming stimuli and the filtering out of unwanted stimuli, choice is present. In the case of advertising, the concept of selective perception needs to be extended to incorporate the theories of selective exposure and selective attention (see the section below headed "The Concepts Summarized, With Examples").

The stimuli an individual chooses to perceive depend upon both personal factors and characteristics of the stimuli themselves. Personal factors affect perception because what the individual expects or is prepared to see is governed by past experiences, needs, values, desires, beliefs, interests, gender, and self-concept. For example, a male smoker who sees himself as tough and adventurous will be more likely to perceive a Marlboro ad than an ad for Virginia Slims. A person's needs are also determinants of selective perception. An individual who feels thirsty in the summer will more likely focus his or her attention on a Nestea commercial than on one for Folgers coffee, because of the refreshing, ice-cold image Nestea portrays. Moreover, because past experiences from using a certain brand could be either good or bad, product preferences that develop as a result will determine which ads a person will be more likely to perceive in the future.

Relationship Between Cognitive Dissonance and Selective Perception

Cognitive dissonance and selective perception are related theories. The former deals with the conflict that individuals encounter when they make choices; the latter suggests ways in which individuals filter the stimuli they receive. Putting the theories together, selective perception can be viewed as a form of cognitive dissonance reduction. One way to reduce dissonance is to change an action or a group of related actions with the goal of achieving consonance. Another common response is to avoid situations and information that have the potential to increase dissonance. Both responses are aimed at bringing the individual back to a psychological state where knowledge and actions are consistent.

Selectivity is necessary, given that people are presented with far more stimuli each day than they can possibly process. As we have noted, some selection is unconscious (color, shape, field of vision, and so on). However, on a more conscious level, individuals will both avoid stimuli that create cognitive dissonance and seek out information that will support the choices they have made.

It is not uncommon that in everyday life people will actively seek out information. Some information is used to make decisions, but it can also be gathered to reinforce a choice that has been made. When information is sought and is successfully found for reinforcement purposes, cognitive dissonance is reduced. Questions of doubt have been diminished or eliminated.

In an experiment with recent car buyers in 1957, Ehrlich, Guttman, Schonbach, and Mills discovered that advertisements for a car recently purchased were read more often than were ads for the car(s) not chosen. Thus information about the unchosen car(s) was avoided. This supports "the derivation from dissonance theory that persons seek out supporting or consonant information after an important decision, in which they have rejected an alternative having positive attributes." [5]

It has been observed that an increase in the level of difficulty of a choice, through the manipulation of desirability, results in an increase in our selective approach. In other words, in Ehrlich et al.'s study, more advertisements for the chosen product were read. As Festinger puts it, "Analysis of selective exposure indicated that dissonance reduction might best be served by exposure to information consistent with one's commitments." [6]

Festinger's hypothesis of dissonance reduction explains how selective exposure is involved in the approach/avoidance method of information processing. In short, information that has the potential to create or increase dissonance will be avoided, whereas information that has the potential to lower dissonance will be approached. A 1967 experiment conducted by Brock and Balloun exemplifies how individuals select information that reinforces their decisions. The researchers presented two groups of subjects, classified as smokers and nonsmokers, with an auditory message with static; the subjects could press a button to remove the static. A greater number of nonsmokers than smokers pressed the button when the message discussed a causal link between smoking and cancer. The information supported the choice not to smoke, thus nonsmokers approached the information in order to increase consonance and minimize dissonance. Smokers avoided the message in order to minimize dissonance. When the auditory message communicated no causal link between cancer and smoking, a greater number of smokers pressed the button. The information supported the choice to smoke, thus the smokers approached the information to increase consonance and minimize dissonance.

A 1982 study of cognitive dissonance showed that consumers can simply screen out information that is uninteresting and unsupportive, and focus their attention on information of interest.[7] It is also possible to "screen in" information that supports a thought, idea, or decision. A study by Spence and Engel gives further evidence that screening does occur. These researchers showed that brand recognition reflects selectivity, as consumers tend to recognize preferred brands faster than they recognize less preferred brands. Consumers are more attuned to an advertised brand that they are using, because it is one that is familiar and preferred. Therefore consumers, in general, respond better to preferred brands than to ones about which they have less knowledge or with which they are less familiar.

The Relationship of Cognitive Dissonance and Selective Perception to Advertising

The presence of information in an advertisement that contradicts a consumer's present attitudinal belief about the specific brand can cause the consumer to experience cognitive dissonance. According to Jones's "weak theory" of advertising characteristics: "Advertising is not strong enough to convert people whose beliefs are different from what is claimed in the advertising. Advertising is generally not capable of overcoming resistant attitudes." [8]

Moreover, because the brain unconsciously "zaps" more easily than does the button on the television remote control, advertising needs to communicate effectively by appealing to the right audience. Whether it is based on the issue of gender, interest, belief, or need, advertising must engage the audience's attention first in order to generate both brand recognition and recall.

Attention is also dependent upon the marketing stimuli—the nature of the product as well as the nature of the advertisement or commercial. The consumer's perception of a product is determined by its physical attributes, the brand name, and the package design.[9] For example, many marketers who have turned toward the "clear" concept, such as Pepsi (Crystal Clear soda) and Ivory (clear dishwashing liquid soap), have successfully differentiated their products based on physical attributes. Consumers perceive such products to be natural and free of artificial ingredients, and thus more appealing. Because people are brought up with a set of social and environmental influences that shape what and how stimuli are processed, it is crucial for advertisers to understand how different stimuli affect different consumers. Advertisers need to be aware of reception inhibitors when creating their advertising messages. Because individuals are known to exercise selective perception subconsciously, the goal should be to recognize and apply the best strategy in creating the right advertising message that will be received and remembered by the target audience.

The Concepts Summarized, With Examples

Cognitive Dissonance

Dissonance has been used to motivate people to make behavioral modifications. In a field experiment on water conservation, a group of users of a recreational facility were made to feel hypocritical about their showering habits. The desired end result was an increase in water conservation efforts—or, more directly, a reduction in water usage. The subjects of the experiment were reminded of their past behavior and then were urged to make a public commitment to be more conscientious. The dissonance created was enough to motivate the subjects to increase their conservation efforts.[10]

Selective Perception

To investigate the concept of selective perception, Cornell University researchers Neisser and Dube conducted an experiment using a videotape they had made that required selective looking. On the tape, they superimposed two events: Both consisted of three participants playing a game of catch, with the groups differentiated by shirt color. Each experimental subject was required to attend to a specific shirt color group and to press a button every time the ball was caught by a member of the specified group. A portion of the way through the viewing, a woman carrying an umbrella appeared on the screen for approximately 4 seconds. When questioned afterward, only 6 of the 28 subjects remembered having seen the woman with the umbrella. The subjects attended to the desired stimuli only, and thus filtered out irrelevant stimuli.

Personal Factors Affecting Selective Perception

In their work, Levine, Chein, and Murphy have demonstrated how personal factors, such as an individual's needs, can alter message perception. In the first few hours of an experiment conducted by these researchers, subjects were given a set of ambiguous pictures after they had been deprived of food. As they became hungrier, their need for food caused them to perceive more food objects. However, after about 9 hours, their perceptual level decreased, and they began to see fewer food objects because the experience had become too painful. As a result, it became important for them not to see the images of food, so they subconsciously screened out the stimuli.[11] This is referred to as *perceptual defense.*

Self-esteem has also been found to act as a selection screen.[12] Individuals with moderate self-esteem are more easily influenced than individuals at either the upper or the lower extreme. High self-esteem is associated with a tendency not to yield to unwanted influences, whereas individuals with low self-esteem have difficulty receiving the message. Each group would require its own communication process for message sending and receiving.

Gender is another determining factor in perceptual selectivity. One study of influences on judgments of beauty determined that women were more influenced by peer evaluations than were men. This means that women weighed the evaluations of others when forming their own judgments. What makes this interesting is that it seems that the judging of beauty should be subjective. Negative ratings were found to be particularly influential in this study; women were less likely to rate someone as attractive if they knew that other women had rated her differently.[13]

Selective Exposure

Consumers tend to seek out messages that are pleasant or sympathetic with their views and to avoid those that are painful or threatening. Thus consumers selectively expose themselves to advertisements that reassure them of the wisdom of their purchase decisions.

Selective Attention

Consumers have a greater awareness of stimuli that meet their needs or interests and a lesser awareness of those that do not. Thus they are more likely to attend to ads for products that meet their needs and ignore those that are irrelevant to them.

The three related concepts (selective perception, exposure, and attention) exhibit the notion of choice—choice to attend to selected information. Advertisers are interested in understanding these selective processes because they influence whether consumers will perceive an ad, and whether the message is effective enough that they will remember such details as brand name and/or product features.

Notes

1. Leon Festinger, *Theory of Cognitive Dissonance* (Stanford, CA: Stanford University Press, 1957), 1-31.
2. R. A. Bauer & A. A. Greyser, *Advertising in America: The Consumer View* (Cambridge, MA: Harvard Business School, 1968).
3. John Philip Jones, *How Much Is Enough? Getting the Most From Your Advertising Dollar* (New York: Simon & Schuster-Lexington, 1992), 49, 257.
4. See, for example, Martin Heil, Frank Rosler, and Erwin Hennighausen, "Imagery-Perception Interaction Depends on the Shape of the Image: A Reply to Farah," *Journal of Experimental Psychology: Human Perception and Performance,* December 1993, 1313-1321.
5. Ehrlich, Guttman, Schonbach, and Mills, cited in R. A. Wicklund and J. W. Brehm, *Perspectives on Cognitive Dissonance* (Hillsdale, NJ: Lawrence Erlbaum, 1976), 10.
6. Festinger, *Theory of Cognitive Dissonance.*
7. Cited in William Wells, John Burnett, and Sandra Moriarty, *Advertising: Principles and Practice* (Englewood Cliffs, NJ: Prentice Hall, 1992), 154.
8. Jones, *How Much Is Enough?* 49.
9. Leon G. Schiffman and Leslie Lazar Kanuk, *Consumer Behavior* (Englewood Cliffs, NJ: Prentice Hall, 1987), 158.
10. Ruth Thibodeau, Elliot Aronson, Dayna Miller, and Chris Ann Dickerson, "Using Cognitive Dissonance to Encourage Water Conservation," *Journal of Applied Social Psychology,* June 1992, 841-855.
11. R. Levine, I. Chein, and G. Murphy, "The Relation of the Intensity of a Need to the Art of Perceptual Distortion: A Preliminary Report," *Journal of Psychology,* vol. 88, 1954, 129-134.
12. Nancy Rhodes and Wendy Wood, "Self-Esteem and Intelligence Affect Influenceability: The Mediating Role of Message Reception," *Psychological Bulletin,* January 1992, 156-172.
13. William G. Graziano, Lauri A. Jensen-Campbell, Laura J. Shebilske, and Sharon R. Lundgren, "Social Influence, Sex Differences, and Judgments of Beauty: Putting the Interpersonal Back in Interpersonal Attraction," *Journal of Personality and Social Psychology,* September 1993, 522-532.

21

The Creative Characteristics of Successful Television Advertising

John Philip Jones

M any well-known advertising practitioners have given their views in published works and speeches on the characteristics of the most successful campaigns. The points made in this chapter are derived from two sources: (a) the opinions of these advertising gurus and (b) what I have personally learned and observed from the television campaigns of the most successful brands according to the findings of pure single-source research.[1]

This chapter describes three distinct characteristics of successful television campaigns, characteristics about which there is total agreement between the experts and the marketplace evidence. The additional and varied points the experts make in their writings—if unsupported by the evidence I have studied— have no place in this chapter. Experienced practitioners are often right, but not every time.

This chapter is devoted in the main to television advertising. Successful television campaigns (a) are intrinsically likable, (b) are visual rather than verbal, and (c) encourage engagement by communicating their promise in terms relevant to consumers. There is nothing especially original about these points, but to put them in focus, we should appreciate the features that successful campaigns do not possess. Such campaigns are not hard-selling; they do not make strong and direct product claims. There are no "slices of life," no men in white coats making product demonstrations, no happy families—in fact, none of the most widely used—and tiresome—advertising clichés. The campaigns are not didactic and verbal. They are characterized by the relatively small number of words on their sound tracks—well below the normally agreed maximum of 60-70—although this does not detract from the strength of their visual demonstrations.

In general, the campaigns are concerned with what are described in advertising jargon as consumer benefits, rather than with product features. But there is a delicate balance here, which I shall try to describe in this chapter.

Intrinsically Likable

Advertising is totally ineffective unless some people, at least, are prepared to look at it. This is one of the reasons advertising communication is such a difficult art. All viewers, listeners, and readers can recognize what advertising is, and most people turn away from it as an immediate and automatic reaction. The advertising writer's first task is therefore to think of a message compelling enough—or friendly and involving enough—to cause some consumers to pause before they switch off their mental engagement and then to stimulate some of the people who pause to go on further (see Brown, Hanc, and Pangsapa, Chapter 20, this volume).

There is no formula for getting through to the consumer, but it is a striking feature of the most successful campaigns that the advertisers in every case manage to hold viewers' attention by giving a reward for watching. With television campaigns, this is done by making the commercials engaging, entertaining, lighthearted, and amusing to look at. The advertisers address viewers as their equals and do not talk down to them. They respect the public's intelligence.

The commercials are often amusing, but they tend not to employ broad humor (see Bullmore, Chapter 15, and Pierce, Chapter 16, this volume). A striking characteristic of the sound tracks of the commercials is their generally understated tone of voice. This is often slightly ironic, as if the advertisers do not take themselves too seriously. This is appealing to viewers and persuades them to form a bond with the advertisers based on the relevance of the brands and how they are presented. Music also has an important role in many cases.

The ability of a commercial to entertain is occasionally at odds with how strongly it can sell (and vice versa). A commercial is nothing more than a piece of paid-for communication that has a behavioral objective. With the most effective commercials, the entertainment is embedded in the brand. If the entertainment in the commercial generates a warm glow, this is directed toward the brand—with the most successful campaigns, the glow can actually surround the brand.

Visual

The most powerful cultural trend during the past half century has been the development of visual literacy—the growth in communication through images and symbols. This is true of all societies, from the most educated to the least, and it is of course a direct result of the growth of television. The accompanying decline in verbal literacy is an even more important—and totally deplorable—phenomenon, but this is not the place to discuss and lament it.

Television, the main engine driving the growth of visual communication, is also the main medium for packaged goods advertising. Advertisers would be acting against their self-interest if they did not exploit television's potential, in particular its power to demonstrate and its ability to generate mood and emotion. All successful campaigns are models in their effective and variegated use of visual communication.

Communicating Their Promise
in Terms Relevant to Consumers

Consumers buy brands for the benefits those brands give them. But manufacturers should not believe that in a highly competitive world success will result if they only communicate bald functional advantages, even if their brands are the only ones to offer particular advantages. Functional benefits are very important, but advertising claims about these are processed in two ways in the consumer's psyche.

First, a functional advantage is often broadened in the consumer's mind into something much more emotional. This has a stronger effect than functional claims on their own, and the resulting amalgam is unique to the brand. The manufacturer's future business is improved to the extent that this happens. A statement in an advertisement for a food brand that it has no cholesterol or sugar or salt releases a torrent of emotional signals about health and long life. The click of a camera shutter in a commercial can be transformed in the viewer's mind into a highly charged message that this click records—and in effect freezes—the high points in his or her life.

The second way in which claims are processed is that the functional (or the functional-cum-emotional) qualities of a brand are perceived as having value to the consumer solely to the extent that they relate to his or her day-to-day life. Unless a brand has functional features superior to the competition in at least some respects, it will not be bought repeatedly. But these alone are not enough. The consumer must find the brand's functional features more *relevant* than the advantages offered by any competitive brands he or she may be considering at the time.

It follows that unless the consumer is shown a brand's qualities in highly personal and focussed terms, it will have no appeal. Advertisers determine how to do this by studying their buyers. The positioning of their brands—that is, where their brands fit into a competitive marketplace—and the creative ideas are both the direct result of advertisers' knowledge of their consumers.

One rather obvious point is that advertising that shows people is likely to be more successful than advertising that does not. Qualitative research has shown that advertising about products on their own can generate cold, impersonal image associations.

The positioning of the brand in relation to its competitors must be thought out with agonizing precision. This positioning embraces the brand's functional as well as nonfunctional features. A major brand of repeat-purchase packaged goods that became one of the most successful launches of the early 1990s illustrates this point. Its selected positioning was the end product of an extraordinary process of experimentation. This involved the writing and testing of 19 alternative positionings, which were tested in the form of more or less finished films. The cost of this film production was many millions of dollars, and, perhaps more seriously, the procedure took more than 2 years. But the result repaid the cost and trouble, because the brand was and is a triumph in the marketplace.

An even more important point about functional features is that advertising that sells them successfully must be based on an idea. As I have already implied, this idea can be—and generally is—enclosed in an emotional envelope. But if the idea is going to work at all, this envelope must contain something important to the consumer. The commercials should be likable—but the selling message must be unmistakable.

In successful campaigns, the rational features of the brand are almost invariably demonstrated. The purpose of this is partly to provide a rational selling argument. Just as commonly, it is aimed at providing the consumer with a postpurchase rationalization—a justification for a preference that may have been totally nonrational. Psychologists have a name for this curious effect; they call it the *reduction of cognitive dissonance* (see Brown, Hanc, and Pangsapa, Chapter 20, this volume).

Note

1. John Philip Jones, *When Ads Work: New Proof That Advertising Triggers Sales* (New York: Simon & Schuster-Lexington, 1995).

Comparative Advertising

Jan S. Slater

I f you watch television, you've been exposed to it: the war between competitors—the cola wars, the burger wars, the long-distance wars, the credit card wars; Pepsi versus Coca-Cola, Burger King versus McDonald's, MCI versus AT&T, Visa versus American Express. In each case, comparative advertising is being used to grab the consumer's attention, to say, "We're better than the competition." There hasn't always been open warfare. There was a time when good manners curbed advertisers' notions of discrediting their competitors. But in today's competitive marketplace, where everyone wants to be a market leader and where product proliferation jams supermarket shelves with more than 20,000 items, the gloves are off and comparative advertising has infiltrated the media.

Definition

Comparative (or comparison) advertising may be defined as the direct or indirect comparison of a sponsored brand to a competitive brand in an advertisement. The direct claim (explicitly naming the competition) is the type most often referred to, because its use is supported by the Federal Trade Commission (FTC). The indirect claim, however, is more common and is frequently used to promote established brands. This type of comparison does not name the competitor, but the advertised brand is described as being superior on specific attributes or benefits.[1] Comparisons can be verbal or visual, brand or category specific.[2]

Today, several types of comparisons are used:

- Inferiority comparisons: Typically, these are offset by superiority comparisons (e.g., "We're the highest priced computer in the market, but we're worth it").
- Parity comparisons: These are claims of equal functionality or service to the compared brands (e.g., "We're just as good").
- Superiority comparisons: These are claims to be better than the compared brand on one or more attributes or benefits (e.g., "Ours tastes better, works faster, lasts longer").
- Combination comparisons: These use two or more of the previous categories (e.g., "We're just as roomy, but lower priced").[3]

There is much debate between practitioners and academics as to the effectiveness of comparison advertising, even though it has been in widespread use for only a little more than 20 years.

History

Comparison advertising was basically avoided by advertisers until the 1970s. There were, however, a few early exceptions. Pepsi made an obvious but unnamed reference to Coca-Cola in its 1939 slogan: "Twice as much for a nickel, too. Pepsi-Cola is the drink for you." Coke was selling its 6-ounce bottle for a nickel when Pepsi introduced its 12-ounce bottle at the same price.[4] And in 1962, Avis Rent-A-Car launched the "We Try Harder" campaign against the market leader, which was widely recognized at the time as Hertz.[5]

But in general, most advertisers steered clear of comparisons for several reasons. First, there were concerns about the legal issues of using a competitor's trademark or brand name. Second, many advertisers shared the belief that making a reference to a competitor could actually help the competition. And third, there was a sense of "fair play" in the industry that called for avoiding what could be viewed as disparagement of the competition.[6] Furthermore, the advertising industry itself discouraged the practice of comparison ads. The American Association of Advertising Agencies (AAAA) issued official policy statements on the subject that tended to discourage the use of comparisons, and the National Association of Broadcasters' Television and Radio Code opposed its use as well.

By the 1970s, things had changed. The FTC encouraged network television to accept comparison commercials as a means of providing more information to consumers. The FTC believed that explicit comparisons would stimulate comparison shopping, product improvements, and competition in general.[7] Michael Pertchuck, a former FTC chairman, observed, "Comparative advertising that supplies useful price and performance information to consumers can help business carve out better marketplace positions." [8]

The first major advertiser to name its competition was American Motors in 1971. In 1972, the three television networks agreed to run comparison ads, and by 1974 the AAAA reversed its policy and recognized comparative advertising as a "reality." [9] By 1975 the Pepsi Challenge commercials hit the airwaves. The use of comparison ads was on the rise, and since that time the trend has not subsided. In 1973, comparative ads accounted for only 7% of all advertising. In 1977, approximately 5% to 10% of television ads were comparative, and by 1982, 23% of all advertising was reported to be comparative.[10] A 1990 study reported that 80% of television commercials contained direct or indirect comparative claims.[11]

And what of the legality of comparative ads? They are indeed legal insofar as they are truthful. Remember it was the FTC, the primary regulator of advertising, that encouraged the practice. The FTC requires that any comparative claims be substantiated by two scientific tests.[12] Otherwise, an ad making such claims could be perceived as being deceptive and fall under the jurisdiction of the FTC. However, the 1988 Trademark Law Revision Act strengthened the Lanham Trademark Act, which previously had only prohibited false claims about one's own goods.[13] Under the revision, injured parties could sue anyone who "misrepresents another person's goods, services or commercial activities" using false or misleading representation of fact in commercial advertising or promotion. Comparative advertising is challenged under the Lanham Act more often than by the FTC, and of all the false advertising cases tried under the Lanham Act even between 1955 and 1988, 58% involved comparative advertisements.[14]

Advantages and Disadvantages

What determines the use of a comparison ad? There has been much discussion and research conducted on this device. Advertisers and agencies are favorable toward comparative advertising, especially in its direct form. They view it as useful, effective, and informative.[15] Academic research, however, has found little evidence that there are any particular advantages or disadvantages in naming competitors.[16]

Nevertheless, the overwhelming reason cited for the use of comparative advertising is that it provides more information about brands in the marketplace.[17] Recall that this was the FTC's original motivation: Put as much information as possible in the consumer's hands. If that is the case, consumers may be the ones who gain from comparison ads.[18] Second, comparative advertising is noted for being effective in positioning a brand.[19] The format can help a challenger who may have an unknown position in the marketplace to grab a niche close to a well-known and respected brand.[20] More important, if the advertised brand is targeting users of the competitive brand, there is no better way to reach them than to name the competitor.[21] Furthermore, there is evidence that well-executed comparison campaigns can result in more sales. Savin copiers, Pepsi, Care Free, Comtrex, Schick, and Helene Curtis's Suave shampoo all gained significant market share on the strength of such campaigns.[22] Finally, comparisons can reduce confusion among consumers about what product attributes are important.[23] If the brand is superior to its competitors, the most effective means of differentiation is the use of a direct comparative ad, explicitly naming the competitor and stating its inferiority on the featured attribute.[24]

Comparison ads have their disadvantages as well. Many believe that comparisons confuse the consumer.[25] For example, the long-running comparison campaigns used by AT&T and MCI may have a boomerang effect. The consumer is overloaded with information, and the back-and-forth price claims and telephone calling programs make it difficult to remember which brand made what claim. It is not unusual for consumers to ask, Who's advertising what in this commercial?[26]

Others believe that comparisons are a sign of "bad manners," which only annoys or angers consumers. Focus groups made up of women consumers often comment that they don't like to hear their brands criticized, whether or not the claims are true.[27] Again, the comparative format may have a boomerang effect, decreasing the believability of the advertisement and credibility for the advertised brand rather than enhancing it.[28]

Finally, comparisons might be sources of misinformation. Only a few key points can be conveyed in the course of an advertisement. Although a point of superiority may be true, it may not be a significantly important feature of the product. So by focusing on that one point in the advertising, the commercial may inaccurately imply overall product superiority.[29]

Effectiveness

As I noted earlier, there is still much debate on the effectiveness of comparative advertising. A 1989 study summarized the outcomes of academic research on the practice: 17 studies were found to have positive results (comparative advertising worked), 30 studies had negative results (comparative advertising didn't work), and 57 studies showed no difference between comparative and noncomparative ad effectiveness. There is evidence, however, that effectiveness of direct comparative advertising is contingent on the relative market position of the advertised brand.[30]

Established brands with low market shares can benefit from comparative advertising. Direct comparative claims are more effective than indirect comparative ads or noncomparative claims as far as increasing the purchase intentions of buyers of the low-share brand. It has also been shown that direct comparisons attract more attention to the advertised brand, while not increasing awareness of the competition.[31] Perhaps more important, the image of the low-share brand is enhanced by its comparison to the more prestigious high-share brand.[32]

Advertisements for high-share brands have been found to be more effective in increasing purchase intentions where no comparative claim was made.[33] However, direct comparative ads for high-share brands gain more attention. It should be noted that when a high-share brand is compared with a smaller, lesser-known brand, the comparison is more likely to enhance the image and increase awareness of the competitor.[34]

A new brand or a low-share brand may use direct comparison ads to differentiate the brand from the competition. This is often accomplished by promoting a feature that is not usually associated with the compared brand. This can be quite dangerous. The Subaru Legacy used a direct comparative advertisement claiming that it was less expensive than a Mercedes. Although the purpose might have been to enhance Subaru's image compared with that of the more prestigious Mercedes, the comparison was not differentiating because it is well known that Mercedes is much more expensive than Subaru—in fact, it is in a different class. Therefore, the consumer's perception of Subaru was not enhanced because the promoted feature was contradictory to the image of the comparison brand—that is, low price versus luxury.[35]

Finally, there is a case to be made regarding consumer confusion and direct comparative ads. When parity brands are compared directly, research suggests that consumers can misunderstand or forget which brand sponsored the ad.[36] For example, take the AT&T and MCI television commercials. Not only are the services the same, the ads are similar as well. The format adds to the confusion by comparing prices and caller programs. It's the perfect case of "Who was the sponsor of that advertisement?"

Conclusion

There are many pitfalls to comparative advertising. Is there something to compare? Can the comparison be supported? Is it relevant? Is it easily understood? Will the claim withstand the legal system? Advertising agencies appear to believe that comparison ads are effective under certain conditions. Academic research provides some indications that it works under certain conditions as well. But the major problem with the research stems from the lack of case studies of advertisers who use comparative advertising. That would be the real measure of effectiveness.

Nevertheless, comparison advertising is not for every brand. It is not always the best strategy, either offensively or defensively. It could be risky in any situation. The decision to use comparative advertising must be supported by quality research, a well-defined target group, a robust creative strategy, and a differentiation between products that can be scientifically proven and perceptible to consumers. Without these qualities, comparative advertising will benefit only the competitor.

Notes

1. Cornelia Pechmann and David W. Stewart, "The Effects of Comparative Advertising on Attention, Memory, and Purchase Intentions," *Journal of Consumer Research,* vol. 17, September 1990, 180-191.

2. Thomas E. Barry, "Comparative Advertising: What Have We Learned in Two Decades?" *Journal of Advertising Research,* vol. 33, March/April 1993, 19-27.

3. Ibid.

4. Ross D. Petty, *The Impact of Advertising Law on Business and Public Policy* (Westport, CT: Quorum, 1992). See also Stephen A. Greyser, *Cases in Advertising and Communications Management,* 2nd ed. (Englewood Cliffs, NJ: Prentice Hall, 1981).

5. Greyser, *Cases in Advertising.*

6. Ibid.

7. Petty, *The Impact of Advertising Law.*

8. Quoted in John C. Rogers and Terrell G. Williams, "Comparative Advertising Effectiveness: Practitioners' Perceptions Versus Academic Research Findings," *Journal of Advertising Research,* vol. 29, October/November 1989, 22-36.

9. Greyser, *Cases in Advertising.*

10. Rogers and Williams, "Comparative Advertising Effectiveness."

11. Pechmann and Stewart, "The Effects of Comparative Advertising."

12. Bruce Buchanan, "Can You Pass the Comparative Ad Challenge?" *Harvard Business Review,* July/August 1985, 106-113.

13. Bruce Buchanan and Doron Goldman, "Us vs. Them: The Minefield of Comparative Ads," *Harvard Business Review,* May/June 1989, 38-42.

14. Petty, *The Impact of Advertising Law.*

15. Darrel D. Muehling and Jeffrey J. Stoltman, "An Investigation of Factors Underlying Practitioners' Attitudes Toward Comparative Advertising," *International Journal of Advertising,* vol. 11, 1992, 173-183.

16. Pechmann and Stewart, "The Effects of Comparative Advertising." See also Cornelia Pechmann and David W. Stewart, "How Direct Comparative Ads and Market Share Affect Brand Choice," *Journal of Advertising Research,* vol. 31, December 1991, 47-54.

17. Barry, "Comparative Advertising."

18. Meryl Freeman, "Comparative Cautions," *Marketing & Media Decisions,* September 1987, 78-85.

19. Darrel D. Muehling, Donald E. Stem, Jr., and Peter Raven, "Comparative Advertising: Views From Advertisers, Agencies, Media, and Policy Makers," *Journal of Advertising Research,* vol. 29, October/November 1989, 30-48.

20. Barry, "Comparative Advertising."

21. John Philip Jones, *How Much Is Enough? Getting the Most From Your Advertising Dollar* (New York: Simon & Schuster-Lexington, 1992).

22. Rogers and Williams, "Comparative Advertising Effectiveness."

23. Barry, "Comparative Advertising."

24. William L. Wilkie and Paul Farris, "Comparison Advertising: Problems and Potential," *Journal of Marketing,* October 1975, 7-15. See also Cornelia Pechmann and S. Ratneshwar, "The Use of Comparative Advertising for Brand Positioning: Association Versus Differentiation," *Journal of Consumer Research,* September 1991, 145-160.

25. Freeman, "Comparative Cautions"; Rogers and Williams, "Comparative Advertising Effectiveness."

26. Barry, "Comparative Advertising."
27. Freeman, "Comparative Cautions."
28. Barry, "Comparative Advertising."
29. Freeman, "Comparative Cautions."
30. Pechmann and Stewart, "How Direct Comparative Ads."
31. Pechmann and Stewart, "The Effects of Comparative Advertising"; see also ibid.
32. Pechmann and Ratneshwar, "The Use of Comparative Advertising."
33. Pechmann and Stewart, "The Effects of Comparative Advertising."
34. Pechmann and Stewart, "How Direct Comparative Ads."
35. Pechmann and Ratneshwar, "The Use of Comparative Advertising."
36. Ibid.

The Unique Selling
Proposition and Usage-Pull

John Philip Jones

The Unique Selling Proposition (USP) is one of the best-known terms associated with the advertising business. It is used to describe the single most important feature or argument—and a special type of feature or argument—on which an advertisement is based. The concept of the USP was originated in the 1950s in the Ted Bates agency by the agency's senior creative figure, Rosser Reeves. It was described and illustrated by Reeves himself in a book, originally published in 1961, that has reached a large audience of advertising agency people and clients.[1]

The meaning of USP has, however, become debased by its being used rather loosely by journalists and even advertising professionals in describing advertising claims. As the phrase was originally used, it had an explicit and narrowly defined meaning:

- Unique: The advertising claim is and can be used only by the advertised brand, except on the exceptional occasion when one brand manages to preempt a claim that more than one brand is able to use, and therefore takes over as its unique property.

- Selling: The advertising claim must be powerful enough to induce consumers to buy the brand.
- Proposition: The advertising claim is normally (although there are rare exceptions) encapsulated in a single but distinctive phrase or slogan—such as "Wonder Bread helps build strong bodies 12 ways," or "Colgate cleans your breath while it cleans your teeth," or "M&Ms melt in your mouth, not in your hand."

The USP has always been concerned with what consumers take out of an advertisement rather than what a writer puts into it. USPs are researched for their memorability.

The USP has invariably been associated with advertising that is fact based—rational rather than emotional. USP campaigns are based on strong persuasive arguments, and are known in the advertising business as hard-selling. Ted Bates advertising was and is strongly associated with highly competitive brands in substantial categories of repeat-purchase packaged goods.

Related to the concept of the Unique Selling Proposition is the research technique of *usage-pull*. The users of a brand who do not remember its USP are known as the unpenetrated. The higher number of users who do remember the brand's USP are described as the penetrated. The percentage difference between the penetrated and the unpenetrated represents the campaign's usage-pull—the proportion of a brand's users who are persuaded, or brought to the brand, by its advertising.

To people unfamiliar with how advertising works, the USP and usage-pull concepts were (and in some cases still are) a plausible explanation of how advertising operates. The two notions are simple, and they accord well with common sense. They certainly had great appeal to clients of the Bates agency, which experienced strong growth during the 1950s and 1960s, substantially as a result of the agency's use of the USP and usage-pull. These two ideas in effect articulated the philosophy of the agency.

USP has not, however, stood the test of time, for three interconnected reasons:

1. Demonstrable functional differentiation is not always available to a brand, particularly because changes in formulation are easily copied and in most cases are rapidly diffused through a product category. Successful brands rely on a rich web of nonfunctional added values, and a brand's USP does not exploit these. To answer this objection, the Bates agency experimented with broadening the

USP to embrace a brand's "Unique Selling Personality," but this definition had a short life. The USP is now all but forgotten even at Bates, despite occassional attempts to revive it.

2. USP is built on the idea of conversion: persuading nonusers of a brand to become users of it. This marketing objective is relevant only to new brands and (to some extent) to brand restages. In the field of repeat-purchase packaged goods, most advertising is concerned with continuous buying by existing purchasers. There is no conversion involved in most consumer behavior in repeat-purchase categories. Once a brand is established, its main driving force is purchase frequency.

3. There are two major problems with usage-pull. First, the difference between the measures of the penetrated and unpenetrated cannot be taken to indicate causality—that advertising brings about the switch from lack of penetration to penetration. One of the best-known facts about advertising communication is that users of a brand are more familiar with its advertising than nonusers are, because of selective perception. It follows that knowledge of a USP is a signal of existing brand use, rather than that the USP has engineered such brand use in the first place. Second, copy claims of the explicit USP variety are easy to remember without necessarily being able to sell better than more indirect and subtle arguments. This factor biases the findings of usage-pull research in favor of a style of advertising that may not always work well. As a predictive device, usage-pull is a poor research tool for image-oriented campaigns, many of which are demonstrably effective in sales terms.

Readers should note that Reeves uses the word *penetration* in a special sense, in relation to whether or not consumers can remember a brand's advertising campaign. The word is more commonly used to describe the number of a brand's buyers, in particular the proportion of households that buy the brand at least once in a defined period.

Note

1. Rosser Reeves, *Reality in Advertising* (New York: Alfred A. Knopf, 1961).

Truth and Weasels

David Ogilvy

I want to make some points about truth in advertising.

I don't know the precise state of public opinion. Personally, I think that actual truth has become more or less a dead issue. Most advertising nowadays is a great deal more truthful than the public realizes.

Our problem is to make the public believe the true things we say. It's no use telling the truth if people don't believe you. So, how can we copywriters make our ads more believable?

Well, we can start by turning our backs on the weasels. The kind of weasels that still disgrace so much advertising for toothpaste, cigarettes, detergents, and low-calorie beer. The kind of weasels that depreciate the whole currency of copy. *Verbal* weasels and *typographical* weasels. Most of us on the creative side are connoisseurs of the weasel. Far more than the public, we comprehend

NOTE: This chapter first appeared in *The Unpublished David Ogilvy* (New York: The Ogilvy Group, 1986), 72-74. It is based on a speech by David Ogilvy, "What the Creative Man Can Do to Increase Public Acceptance of Advertising," delivered to the Association of National Advertisers in March 1954. Reprinted by permission of Ogilvy & Mather.

the villainies of the weasel merchants. . . . Let's take our tongues out of our cheeks. Let's try and write like human beings.

We hope that the people whom I am addressing—the clients of advertising agencies—will encourage us in this, because most of us are very sensitive to what our clients are thinking.

A Practical Experiment

If any clients have any private qualms about the continued presence of weasels in your own advertising, I want to suggest that you try a novel experiment. When you get back to your office on Monday morning, send for your agency people and address them in these terms:

> Our production people are very proud of their product. They think it's such a damn good product that you ought to be able to advertise it without weaseling.
>
> Our stockholders include a lot of widows and orphans. Sure, they need profits and dividends. But they don't want you to cheat in pursuit of their dividends.
>
> So please take another look at the advertising we have scheduled for next year. Ask yourself if you would feel any compunction about exposing your own children to it.
>
> Ask yourself if any of it could possibly fan the flames of public resentment against advertising.
>
> Ask yourself if any of it could possibly damage our company's reputation in the long run.
>
> And finally, ask yourself if any of it is in conflict with your own private standards of morality and good taste. As the clients of your agency, we have no desire to increase the load of guilt you carry through life.

But one word of warning. This can be an extremely *dangerous* experiment. If you decide to try it, I advise you to make it crystal clear to your agency that you aren't looking for soft, gutless advertising. And that you aren't looking for mere entertainment. Explain that you still want advertising with selling teeth in it. *Honest* teeth, but *biting* teeth.

The effect on your agency may well be electrifying. I can imagine nothing better calculated to stimulate creative people to produce great advertising for you. . . .

Every time you run an advertisement that is genuinely *creative* and *interesting,* you benefit not only your own company, but all your fellow advertisers.

If we in the agency business can create enough interesting campaigns, we can get consumers to drop their resistance.

Don't let's be dull bores. We can't save souls in an empty church.

Television Production Costs

Jan S. Slater

I n the early 1980s, O.J. Simpson dashed through airports, hurtling through luggage and people, before jumping into the seat of his Hertz rental car. The price tag for 30 seconds of O.J.—$500,000.[1] In 1989, Anheuser-Busch gave Americans a second Super Bowl, the Bud Bowl. Created to coincide with the Super Bowl telecast, the stop-action animation depicting Budweiser and Bud Light bottles playing football was said to tally $1 million, and the ad aired only once.[2] By the 1990s, Coca-Cola introduced polar bears gazing at the northern lights while drinking the soft drink that refreshes. The price tag— $600,000 for 30 seconds of computer animation.

Although each of these commercials cost well over the industry average at the time, is it any wonder the advertising community is concerned about the rising costs of producing television commercials in general? There has been much documentation regarding the increase in costs, but little consensus as to its causes and how to control the constant growth.

History of Rising Production Costs

The concern about rising production costs is not a new one. In 1961, the following quote from a production company president appeared in *Back Stage*:

> The waste and the inefficiency in the production of commercials is appalling, and it's the fault of the advertisers, the agencies and the film producers. I'm not saying that the commercial can be less expensive, but I am saying there can be better cost control, that more return for the dollar invested is possible through improving the system that begets the commercial.[3]

In 1983 it was reported that $60,000-$75,000 should cover production costs for most 30-second spots, but instead it was estimated that the range was from $100,000 to $200,000.[4] The Association of National Advertisers (ANA) had reported industry production averages in annual surveys, but it was criticized for basing its findings on small samples of clients and relatively few TV spots. For example, the 1979-1984 ANA report was based on 10 major advertisers, and its 1984-1985 study sampled only 17 advertisers.[5]

In 1984, the American Association of Advertising Agencies (AAAA, also known as the Four A's) undertook the task of tracking television commercial production costs and released its first report for 1984-1986 costs. The AAAA data were based on survey results from 37 of the 100 largest agencies that were members of the association. These included 8 of the top 10 agencies and represented 85% of the dollars spent on commercial production.[6] Already, the sampling method had improved somewhat. However, the averages reported were not exclusively for 30-second spots. The data covered different commercial lengths.

Based on 1,627 ads, the average television commercial in 1984 cost $103,682, with commercials in the automotive category being the most expensive at $145,299. The packaged goods category was the least expensive at $87,658. Other categories included appliances, $131,533; beauty/fashion/cosmetics, $113,708; consumer services/travel/image, $125,983; and fast food/beer/soft drinks, $120,584.

Incredibly, by 1985 production costs had risen 14%, to an average of $117,962. The greatest category increase was in appliances, which rose 19% to $156,958. Although packaged goods remained the least expensive category for production, its average jumped 14% to $99,890. A total of 2,084 ads were included in the AAAA 1985 report.

Good news arrived in 1986—"Spot Production Costs Drop 4%" was the headline in *Advertising Age.*[7] Indeed, the average cost declined to $113,940. The automotive industry cost decreased 20%, bringing its average to $116,495. Only two categories increased their average: beauty/fashion/cosmetics, $138,831 (+10%); and packaged goods, $105,766 (+6%).

The research sample in 1986 was 2,771 ads—a larger sample than before, and some people attributed the lower average cost to the more reliable sample. But more important, industry experts believed that agencies and clients had made a commitment to controlling costs and had succeeded. "The fruits are finally beginning to come to bear after years of discussion and debate," said George Bragg, vice chairman of the AAAA committee that made the study at the time.[8] The jubilation wouldn't last long.

The Situation in 1987

The 1987 AAAA study revealed that production costs had risen almost 28%, bringing the average cost to $145,600. The 2,402 spots again varied in length, but more than 68% were 30-second spots. The fast food/beer/soft drinks category became the most expensive, averaging $241,900. Industry experts expected this because of the competitive and flashy campaigns conducted by Coca-Cola, Pepsi-Cola, McDonald's, Anheuser-Busch, and so on. Dry packaged goods remained the least expensive category at $119,500, still a 13% increase.[9] Other findings were significant:

- The average commercial cost for a *national* advertiser was $156,600 (more than 7% over the norm).
- Regional advertiser costs averaged $102,200 (almost 30% below the overall average).
- Local advertiser costs tallied $56,900 (60% below average).
- Production costs in Los Angeles and New York were much higher than elsewhere, averaging $105,800, in comparison with costs in other cities in the United States and Canada, which averaged just $53,000 (U.S. dollars).
- Although 48% of the commercials in the sample were shot in studios (averaging $64,300 per day), location shots (23% of sample) took longer and averaged a cost of $75,700 per day, a 15% difference.

- More than 60% of the spots in the sample used some type of music, which added an average of $7,200 to a spot. If the music was well-known, it added as much as $19,800 to the total cost, because of the heavy usage fees that had to be paid.
- Approximately 65% of the advertisements sampled were produced at or below the average. Therefore, it was the remaining 35% that cost the most and could have affected the sample enough to skew it disproportionately upward.[10]

The End of the 1980s

Relief was in sight. The 1988 AAAA survey was touted as good news, even though it showed a 12% increase in costs, to $163,072. The primary reason for the relatively small increase was an increase of only 9% in production company costs. The largest increase was in talent costs, which rose 27%.[11]

There was even more to celebrate in 1989. National advertisers' costs were up only 8%, to $190,000, whereas regional spots decreased by 6%.[12] The AAAA hailed the study as proving "the definitive end to the era of runaway production costs." [13] The credit for the stabilization was given to agencies and commercial producers for cooperating in order to control costs, together with a decrease in the producer's standard markup (from 35% to 30%). The use of noncompetitive bidding was also considered a factor in the leveling off. Previously, agencies had required bidding from several production companies, believing it would lead to lower overall costs. In 1989, agencies experimented with using a single source—choosing one production company, planning the job, and then negotiating the costs up front. That not only saved money, it saved time.

The 1990s

The trend of cost stabilization continued into the 1990s. From 1989 to 1992, production costs increased at less than 4% annually, making the average cost of a commercial $196,000 by 1992. Indeed, the industry believed that it had its act together and production costs were under control. Not quite. The 1993 AAAA survey reported an increase of 13%, pushing the average commercial cost to more than $200,000—$222,000, to be exact.[14] This was the first double-digit increase in 5 years, and everyone feared that average production costs could easily go over the quarter-million dollar mark by 1994. Indeed, production costs for 1994 posted an average of $268,000, and by 1996 they again passed the quarter-million dollar mark at $278,000.[15]

The explanations for the increase seemed obvious, according to the survey:

- Production costs rose 13% because production facility costs also rose 13%.
- The jump in facility costs was caused by the fact that commercials were requiring more time to shoot. The number of shooting hours was also up 13%.
- Location shots cost more because they required more shooting hours as well. For the first time in the history of the survey, more commercials were shot on location than in studios.
- Overtime increased a whopping 21%.

The question was why. Why were commercials taking so much longer to produce? While the industry players—commercial producers, advertisers, and agencies—pointed fingers at one another, George Bragg, the former chairman of the AAAA Committee on Broadcast Production, who originally conceived the study, suggested four explanations:

1. Commercial concepts had become more complex and required more time to execute.
2. Production companies were padding the amount of time it took to shoot spots to compensate for smaller profit margins and fewer projects.
3. Agency creative people were employing more extravagant production techniques to cover their bases.
4. Advertisers were increasing demands on agencies and production houses to develop several versions of one spot.[16]

What Bragg did not discuss was the more ambitious nature of commercials. The creative trends made them more complicated than ever before: big-name directors, more technology, more animation, MTV-style effects, all produced more quickly, all costing more money. And everything had to be more perfect: the best broiling burger shot ever, the most perfect lighting, perfect casting, and the most wonderful original music. If the commercial was perfect last time, it would be even more perfect this time. Commercials took longer to shoot and edit to achieve that more perfect perfection, and costs went up.[17]

Obviously, it is important to understand why television production costs have increased almost 114% in just 10 years. But the industry wants more than understanding—it wants to know how to control costs.

What Can Be Done?

Advertisers, agencies, and production companies must stop pointing fingers and all take responsibility for the rising production costs. All, in their own way, have taken certain steps to control costs. Most major advertisers have hired cost consultants to work with the agencies. Production companies have cut their markups and decreased profit margins. Agencies have tried hiring freelancers and using in-house production facilities, and some have promoted fixed bidding. But there is no question that a greater commitment and more discipline on the part of advertisers, agencies, and production companies would go a long way toward reducing or at least stabilizing production costs.

In 1987, the Association of National Advertisers formed a TV Commercial Production Task Group to work with its members in controlling costs. This task force developed a document titled "Considerations on Managing Your Commercial Productions," which was sent to all their members along with a letter. Excerpts of both are worth repeating here. The letter stated:

> While the attachments are not intended to solve all your problems, they are designed to stimulate some conceptual thinking on how your organization is approaching its television commercial production. You need to make your own decisions based upon your own circumstances as you deal with this subject. It is the unanimous opinion of the experts in the business that if you are unhappy with the cost trends in your commercial production projects, then nothing will ever change unless you do something about it.[18]

The cost considerations are detailed by the Association of National Advertisers in the task force document. The arguments are addressed directly to advertisers and agencies:[19]

The Problem

> If there is a problem, it is your problem. It is not the agency's problem. It is not the production company's problem. It is your problem. It is, after all, your money, and if others are spending your money in inappropriate or extravagant ways, then you are the problem.

Cost Control Starts Early

The best time, and perhaps the only time, to exert cost control is before you commission a creative assignment. Advertisers should inform the agency how much they are prepared to spend on a television production before the creative people do their work.

Get Everyone in the Boat

Do not start a creative assignment without clear advertising objectives and creative strategies that are agreed upon with the agency's senior account executive, senior creative person, senior agency producer and the client executive who ultimately will approve the commercial for airing.

Every Storyboard Has a Price Tag

The cost of a commercial is clearly evidenced in the storyboard. Each storyboard needs to be scrutinized carefully to determine if all the cost elements displayed therein are really necessary to the creative product. Is the storyboard efficiently and effectively communicating with your target audience or is it designed to win creative awards?

Demand Estimated Costs

Never look at a storyboard unless the agency provides you with an estimated cost to produce it and an estimated cost to air it.

Time Is Money

Allow for enough time to carefully plan, bid and produce your commercial. Under normal circumstances, a typical cycle for planning and producing a television commercial is 12 to 16 weeks, depending upon the technical and artistic complexity.

Always Get Competitive Bids

The day you decide you have to have a certain director and a certain production company is the day you have lost all leverage to control costs. Invest maximum effort in preproduction meetings so that all issues, questions, and problems can be anticipated and resolved without an expensive crew waiting on the set for the arguments to subside. Don't necessarily limit production company considerations to New York and Los Angeles.

Examine Bids Critically

When reviewing production company bids, do not indulge your director. It is your money, not his, being spent.

Stay Involved

Do not make the mistake of treating your television production as on-the-job training. It is too important and too expensive to approach in that fashion. The professional who makes the decision to air (product manager, marketing manager, advertising director, vice president of marketing, president, or whoever) *has* to be the person involved from start to finish.

Editing Excesses

Beware of post-production editing. It is rapidly becoming an increasingly significant portion of commercial production expense. While most commercials are shot on film, the spot is transferred to videotape for editing or what is commonly called video finishing. This allows for the insertion of opticals and computer-generated graphics, while allowing for experimentation with many variations of the spot. The idea is not to shoot loads of footage and create the commercial in the editing suite. Better to decide in advance what the commercial is to be, shoot it that way and then expeditiously edit it under carefully controlled conditions.

Many believe that the cost of technological advances will eventually level off and perhaps decrease, but there's no indication of that happening. This technology is expensive; electronic effects can cost more than $1,500 per hour, and some animation can add $60,000-$70,000 to a spot.[20] In 1995, commercials with animation averaged $236,000 per 30 seconds, and special effects spots averaged $290,000.[21]

Call to Action

It is obvious that a serious commitment from advertisers, agencies, and production companies must be made to keep production costs from spiraling out of sight. Each party needs to be more sensitive to costs and whose money is really being spent in the process. Each one needs to communicate openly about creative, budget, and time constraints. Each one needs to learn from past experiences about what worked and what didn't. But each has individual responsibilities as well:

- Advertisers: Take the advice of the ANA and make the commitment to control your money. Communicate with your agency and production company about budgets and planning. But don't back them into a corner with no money and no time.
- Agencies: Remember whose money you are spending. Does every creative idea have to be expensive? If your creativity is hurt by budget limits, explain why. Prove that higher costs correlate with a more effective advertisement. In the long run will this director, or this location, or this piece of technology sell more cars or shampoo? And when the production company comes through for you, reward them with more work.
- Production companies: Make certain you are involved in all the planning. Remind agencies and advertisers that last-minute changes, extra hours of editing, and experimenting with new technologies during the shoot all cost money. Help the agencies make the job work creatively with alternatives that might not be so expensive. And if the production markup is what is of concern, communicate. Be explicit about what expenses the markup covers. After all, your markup is your profit.

Will the problem ever be solved? Who's to say? What is certain, however, is that if costs are not controlled, fewer commercials will be made. Nobody wins in that situation. Therefore, it benefits the players and their industry associations to work together to solve this much-debated problem. The solution to controlling production costs is in the hands of those who make the commercials.

Notes

1. George R. Bonner, Jr., "Costly TV Ads Get Double Take From Concerned Execs," *Christian Science Monitor,* October 6, 1983, 17.

2. Ira Teinowitz, "Bud Plans a Blitz," *Advertising Age,* December 26, 1988, 3.

3. Quoted in Anthony Vagnoni, "Production Execs Unite," *Back Stage,* January 18, 1985, 1.

4. Bonner, "Costly TV Ads Get Double Take."

5. James P. Forkan, "Spot Production Costs Drop 4%," *Advertising Age,* October 26, 1987, 46.

6. Ibid.

7. Ibid.

8. Ibid.

9. Gary Levin, "Cost of TV Spot Pegged at $145,600," *Advertising Age,* March 6, 1989, 68.

10. Ibid.

11. Richard Miller, "Four A's Study Shows National Spot Costs Rose 12% in 1988," *Back Stage,* August 4, 1989, 1.

12. Arden Dale, "1989 Production Costs Rise," *Back Stage,* May 11, 1990, 1.

13. Randall Rothenberg, "The Media Business: Advertising," *New York Times,* May 4, 1990, 17.

14. Joe Mandese, "Costs to Make TV Ad Near Quarter-Million," *Advertising Age,* July 4, 1994, 3. See also Joe Mandese, "Study Shows Cost of TV Spots," *Advertising Age,* August 1, 1994, 32.

15. Carolyn Giardina, "Spot Production Costs Dropped in '95 per Latest Four A's Survey," *Shoot,* May 24, 1996, 1; Laura Petrecca, "Four A's: Production Costs for TV Spots Up by 6%," *Advertising Age,* August 18, 1997, 30.

16. In Mandese, "Costs to Make TV Ad."

17. Walter Pidkameny, "Costs Versus Creativity," *Back Stage,* October 16, 1987, 25B.

18. Quoted in Brian McFarland, "ANA Task Group Formulates Spot Production Considerations," *Back Stage,* October 16, 1987, 10B.

19. Quoted in ibid.

20. J. Thomas Russell and W. Ronald Lane, *Kleppner's Advertising Procedure* (Englewood Cliffs, NJ: Prentice Hall), 539; Peter Caranicas, "Four A's Survey Shows Double-Digit Hike in Spot Production Costs," *Shoot,* July 15, 1994, 1.

21. Michael Clark, "Animation Community Sees Demand Pump Up Costs," *Shoot,* May 31, 1996, 8.

Part III

Media Aspects

Media-Medium-Mediorum

Media Definitions

Stephen P. Phelps

Having made the transition from a senior position in the professional world to a university faculty member, I can readily attest to the importance of continuing to grow in knowledge of the field of advertising, or chance to suffer the ignoble fate of becoming professionally obsolete (and probably acutely embarrassed by my students!).

This point was brought home to me early in my university career, when I taught an advertising course covering the field in which I had spent a lifetime of practice, "Advertising Media and Management." Despite the fact that I was able initially to "dazzle" my undergraduates with my repartee, which included my caution that the word *mediums* should be used in my class only when referring to the spirit world, I still experienced a slight case of an unidentifiable malaise.

And to this point, it wasn't until the second class meeting, when I directed the students to open their texts and draw a line through the word *mass,* used as a modifier for the word *media* in the definition of advertising, that I began to suspect that what I was experiencing was nothing less than an advanced case of "definitional wear-out."

My discovery was that, although I knew and was confident that media cover a wider field today than what the classical "mass" definition suggested, I was no longer certain that the elimination of the adjective helped to improve my students' ability to cope with the myriad media choices with which they would soon be faced.

Coincident with this revelation, I also happened to read an article by Erwin Ephron in *Inside Media* that suggested that the concept of "targeting" should be adopted as the organizing principle of media planning. As he concluded, "I would argue what a consumer is doing and thinking about, when exposed to the message, is the most important environment for an ad, and that it can be targeted."

Realizing, then, that it may be better to set forth a new media definition, rather than to suggest simply that we discard the old *mass media* term, and attempting to do this from the point of view of the consumer's involvement with the media, I offer the following.

First, I propose that we define the term *media,* as it relates to advertising, as "*any* paid-for means of transmitting the advertising message to the target audience." Second, I recommend that we employ a three-dimensional model to illustrate the various *dimensions* of media as viewed by the consumer. I would suggest that it be dubbed the *media-dimensional model,* the dimensions to include the following:

1. Whether or not the media carrier includes information/entertainment independent of the advertising message

That is, does the medium alone, without the advertisement, have any communication value to the consumer (e.g., a television program), or does the medium act solely as a carrier for the advertising (e.g., a billboard)?

2. The degree to which the target can interact with the media in order to access information

This dimension addresses the current trend toward empowering the media user to seek information or entertainment on demand, rather than relying on the media to preselect the correct "fit" for everyone.

3. Whether the media are edited to appeal directly to the consumer in a narrow-interest context, or if the information/entertainment is general in nature and, as a result, appeals to the masses

This dimension is intended to replace the single media adjective *mass* with a secondary consideration that encompasses those media that are more selective in their editorial focus. For our purposes, various media could be identified as *non-mass media* when they cover 1% or less of the general population.

So, other than a classroom exercise, you may ask, what have we accomplished? In this regard, I believe that insofar as we are able to group the media options categorically—if not exactly as outlined above, at least in an agreed-upon way—the benefits would be manifold to the student and beginner in the field as well as to the advertising industry. These include, among others, the ability (a) to define more readily areas of responsibility for planning/buying of each element, (b) to establish clearly where the budget for the vehicle properly belongs (e.g., advertising/promotion/other), and (c) to ensure that appropriate comparison bases are employed in the examination of alternative media options.

If adopted, the media-dimensional model would serve as a framework for today and yet be sufficiently flexible to fit our industry (and classroom) needs of tomorrow.

Television Advertising

Continuity Scheduling
(Advertising Without Gaps)

Erwin Ephron

I t is curious. Television advertisers spend their money the same way they have spent it every year for the past 20 years. They target younger consumers (the "18 to 49" or "25 to 54" age group demographics—demos for short) and concentrate their dollars into flights of heavy advertising. Never mind that the population has grown older, people are far too busy to "learn" advertising messages, network ratings are down by a third, and Gerald Ford is no longer president. When a media buying strategy endures 20 years of change in consumer markets, either it is Eternal Truth or someone is not paying attention.

This chapter discusses two better approaches to the use of television for advertising. The first is a *weekly reach* strategy that applies to all brands, large and small. The second is an unconventional *guerrilla media* strategy for smaller brands being outspent in the marketplace.

A Weekly Reach Strategy

Although advertisers may not give it much thought, they concentrate their television advertising to teach consumers brand messages. The tools they use are familiar: demographic targeting, concentration of gross rating points (GRPs), chasing cost-efficiency, and "flighting" (bursts of concentration with gaps in between). Planning for weekly reach to influence weekly purchases is a better strategy. Its tools are dispersion (not targeting), moderate GRPs (not GRP concentration), cost per reach point (not cost per thousand audience), and continuous advertising (not flighting).

Weekly reach planning builds on the ideas that advertising continuously at lower levels is better than advertising heavily for brief periods and that highest affordable average weekly reach, not 4-week frequency, should be the scheduling goal of a continuous advertising program. It is a choice between opposites: "effective" frequency, which concentrates messages to teach consumers, or weekly reach, which spreads out messages to intercept purchases.

In the following pages, I make an argument for weekly reach. I show how a weekly reach goal affects targeting, GRP level, and flighting, which is the current planning profile. Finally, I discuss how to buy weekly reach, which is different from how advertisers buy television today.

The case for weekly reach is built on two reasonable assumptions. First, *brand advertising's usual purpose is to remind the consumer.* Consumers know most brands. Unless an advertiser is introducing a new brand, or a new campaign, usually there is no learning involved. Most advertising messages correspond to Krugman's stage 3, the reminder. Not "What is it?" or "What of it?" but "It's that commercial again." [1]

Second, *advertising is most effective close to the purchase, and close to the purchase a single exposure appears to account for most of advertising's total effect.* This is based on the (unpublished) analyses of Nielsen data conducted by Walter Reichel of A:S Link; the original insights of Colin McDonald, as reported in Michael Naples's edited volume *Effective Frequency*; and information, again based on Nielsen panel data, published by John Philip Jones of the Newhouse School at Syracuse University.[2]

Advertising close to the purchase is common sense. Retailers have no problem deciding when to schedule advertising. If sales are highest on weekends, they advertise in the Friday papers. Movie companies use television on Thursday, Friday, and Saturday to fill the theaters Friday night, Saturday, and Sunday. Political candidates advertise heavily close to elections. The rule is simple: If you reach the consumer close to a purchase, you're more likely to influence that purchase. Sometimes advertising creates the purchase, but usually it is an unconnected stimulus, like summer and a new swimsuit, or the empty box and breakfast cereal. Most of the time, advertising tries to influence brand selection. Outside influences determine whether a consumer will buy a product in the category; advertising is concerned with the brand he or she will buy.

The Jones data also show that in the week preceding purchase, the first exposure produces most of advertising's total effect. For the 142 brands Jones studied, one exposure showed an average share increase of 11%. Additional exposures added only 3 percentage points.

Because purchase intervals vary and are not coordinated, we do not know which consumers are "close to purchase." All we know for sure is that there are some consumers purchasing each week. This directs us to get our message to as many target consumers each week as we can afford, *not worry about frequency,* and advertise for as many weeks as possible.

This sounds reasonable, but it is heresy. The first objection is, Why 1 week when we have always used 4 weeks for planning? Products that have a purchase interval longer than a week should use the week. Products that have a purchase interval shorter than a week, like soft drinks, beers, and fast foods, should probably plan by the day.

Another question is, Is one exposure enough? The answer is no, not in all cases—but it appears to be the most cost-effective use of the money. More frequency is always better, except if you have to reduce weeks of advertising to pay for it. Television budgets are set, so the scheduling decision is not how much to spend, but how best to spend it.

It is possible to sum up the case for the weekly reach strategy with a quotation from *The Naturalist,* an ancient bird book: "When the sea tern fishes he skims the water, looking for an easy meal. The deep-diving booby is not as clever." A cost-effective advertising program is like the sea tern. It skims the market to find ready-to-buy consumers first. Weekly reach is a skimming strategy.

The problems a weekly reach strategy presents to traditional media thinking do not end with frequency. Weekly reach and targeting do not get along either. Reach requires dispersion across different programs and dayparts. Targeting results in concentration in fewer programs and dayparts. It might seem unreasonable to give up targeting for reach, but targeting is not an especially effective television strategy. Most TV brands are mass products, selling to a mass market, through a mass medium.

The ideal targeting medium is print. For example, an upscale auto brand targets "men with household incomes of $75,000 or more" in selective magazines. The auto indexes at 225 in this demographic group (i.e., the readers of such magazines are more than twice as likely as the general population to buy expensive cars). The numbers do not work as well for television. A pain reliever brand targets "adults 25-54." It indexes 110 in that group (i.e., viewers of those ages are only 10% more likely than the general population to use pain relievers). Television cannot index much higher because adults 25-54 are 60% of the adult population. The group is too large to accommodate large increases above the average.

Targeting does not have leverage, and the demographics we target on television are too young for both our brands and the medium. But the biggest problem is that the networks see you coming. They charge high prices for young demos. In a typical Nielsen network cost per thousand (CPM) report, prime time shows this demographic pricing pattern: On CPM women 18-34, ABC is 76% of CBS, NBC is 82%, Fox is 70%; on total women, ABC is 110% of CBS, NBC is 117%, and Fox is 164%. When advertisers target young viewers, they pay more for all viewers. The premiums advertisers pay for targeting young are 10%, 17%, and 64%. The popularity of younger demo targets has led the TV networks to price high for young demos, so there is little gain for advertisers in demo targeting.

Geography is a far better way to target television, because most brands have very good and very bad markets. Pasta sauce, for example, sells better in Italian-heritage northeastern markets like Boston than it does in southern markets like Raleigh-Durham. It would make marketing sense to advertise more in Boston and less in Raleigh-Durham, but network television cannot do that—only spot television can.

It is typical for a television brand to have a third of the country account for more than 40% of sales. That is a consumption index of 133, far higher than for any age demographic. Taking dollars from national television and redirecting them to "best" market spot means the brand can influence 33% more purchases for the same dollars.

GRPs and Flighting

What about how weekly reach relates to GRP levels and flighting? Weekly reach planning turns them on their heads. The lower GRP levels encouraged by weekly reach planning result in longer periods of advertising and less flighting. The familiar decreasing slope of the reach curve shows why. Reach build slows as GRPs are added, so piling on GRPs and flighting the schedule is not a cost-effective way to build weekly reach.

As an example, the first 25 GRPs cost $2,000 and deliver a 20 reach; that is $100 per reach point. The next 25 GRPs also cost $2,000 and add 15 reach points; that is $133 per reach point. The next 25 GRPs add 7 reach points; that is $285 per reach point—and so on. Because additional GRPs produce less and less additional reach, moderate GRP levels and more weeks will produce more weekly reach points across 52 weeks.

A hypothetical Schedule A uses high GRPs and flighting: 100 target points per week in six flights covering 26 weeks. It has a weekly reach of 50% when the advertising is running. A hypothetical Schedule B uses moderate GRPs: 67 targeted GRPs per week over 39 weeks. It has a weekly reach of 40% when the advertising is running. The cost of the two schedules is identical. Because Schedule B, with 67% of the weekly GRP weight (67/100), achieves 80% of the weekly reach (40/50) and has 50% more weeks (39/26), it delivers 20% more weekly reach points over the year—1,560 compared with 1,300.

If we focus on the goal of influencing weekly purchases, the comparison has more point. Assume the product category is purchased evenly across the year. To intercept all potential purchases with a brand message, we would need a weekly reach of 100 for each of 52 weeks. That is a total of 5,200 weekly reach points, which is the theoretical (and unattainable) ceiling for a weekly reach plan. The flighted plan covers 25% of potential purchases (1,300/5,200). The continuity plan covers 30% (1,560/5,200).

But 30% still seems inadequate. We can, and usually do, increase our intercept rate by using 15-second commercials. Although the mix of 30- and 15-second commercials is not a media decision, our weekly reach model encourages 15s, because it assumes most brand messages are reminders. A 50/50 mix of 30s and 15s will give us 33% more weight. We can now schedule 52 weeks at 67 GRPs and increase our intercept rate to 40%. We are now covering 40% of the entire year's weekly purchases with a message.

Weekly Reach and Mixing Media

Now the weekly reach model quickly pushes the planner away from network TV and toward other media: first spot television, then media such as monthly magazines and network radio. Spot television has two strengths: It disperses the schedule into dayparts not used by the networks, which is a cost-effective way to buy additional reach; and, as we saw in the discussion of targeting, it concentrates advertising in markets with the highest purchase rates (remember, the job of brand advertising is to influence the next purchase). If consumers in a spot market purchase a third more of the product than the average, and the spot/network CPMs are similar, spot television can increase the brand's coverage of annual purchases without increasing the budget. In our example, 10% of the dollars shifted to spot will increase annual coverage of weekly purchases to about 44%.

If we move another 10% of the television budget to a different mix of media—monthly magazines and network radio, for example—we can nearly double the target rating points the dollars will purchase, because the CPMs are lower, and our coverage of weekly purchases will increase to about 48%, because of the extra targeted GRPs and because television "duplicates" other media audiences less than it duplicates its own.

Monthly magazines and network radio have uniquely valuable reach-building characteristics for weekly planning. The larger monthly magazines have high per issue "ratings" that are delivered, unduplicated, across several weeks, and network radio's typical run-of-station (i.e., unselective) scheduling builds significant reach across weeks.

How Do You Buy Weekly Reach?

The challenge in executing a weekly reach strategy in television is getting past the heavy viewer. The heavy viewer is the black hole of television. High GRP schedules get past the heavy viewer. Moderate GRP schedules can disappear—and reach many of the same heavy viewers each week. Weekly reach plans have to include a higher monthly and quarterly reach goal to make sure the message is getting past the heavy-viewer group. The goals should look like this: a 35-40 reach in the average week, a 65-75 reach in the average 4 weeks, an 80-85 reach in the average quarter, all against the target demo.

The way to accomplish these goals is to use cost per reach point (CPRP) (as well as CPMs), cross-networking (which is a crude form of "roadblocking"—buying time on all the networks at specific periods), and dispersion of the schedules to the point of buying each week differently.

Cost per Reach Point

We know that prime time is high reach and daytime is low reach, but each daypart also has a different reach pattern for different demo targets. The cost of a 35 reach against "women 18+" ranges from $273,000 in daytime network programming to $932,000 in late night.

Using CPRP changes the cost relationships of the TV dayparts. It makes prime time more affordable compared with daytime. Prime-time CPMs are 300% of daytime CPMs; prime-time CPRPs are 167% of daytime CPRPs. And CPRP substantially reduces the CPM advantage of cable.

The way to use CPRP is to start with the most reach-efficient daypart and add the next most efficient daypart when the reach build slows, and so on. With a buying strategy driven by cost per reach point, higher-CPM television becomes more affordable, but lower-CPM dayparts still get most of the weight. As noted earlier, weekly reach planning also encourages shifting the marginal dollars to spot and other media. CPRP analysis is also the tool for doing this.

Cross-Networking

Cross-networking—scheduling a brand's message in the same half hour on all networks—is an effective way to buy reach on television. Here are Nielsen tabulations comparing the weekly reach of a traditional three-network buy and a widely dispersed cross-network buy, both at 65 household GRPs a week over 4 weeks.

Cross-networking produces an average weekly reach increase of 10%: 4 points above the 40 level. That is a large difference. Traditional scheduling would require 15 additional GRPs, or 23% more dollars. Over 4 weeks (or 260 rating points), the cross-network spots that run in different time periods on different evenings reach 82% of households compared with 76% for the traditional schedule. Cross-networking is a very cost-effective way to build weekly reach—and, if dispersed, monthly and quarterly reach also.

Buying Off-Target

Dispersion is the traditional way to buy reach. We know that mixing dayparts increases reach and lowers cost per reach point. Comparing late evening, early evening, and late and early combined, at constant GRPs, the reach for the combination is significantly higher at all GRP levels. But there's also "hyperdispersion"—the trick of buying some of the schedule "off-target." This works because off-target programs add new viewers, and if the target is younger, buying off-target usually lowers cost.

Consider two schedules directed at women aged 25-54. The first is targeted the usual way: *Cosby, Roseanne,* and Teleplex (a movie package). The second is off-targeted: *Rush Limbaugh, Montel Williams, People's Court,* and again *Roseanne.* Both have the same number of weekly target rating points. Here are the Nielsen reach tabulations. The off-targeted schedule delivers a higher weekly reach (a 34 compared with a 31) for 84% of the dollars. Mixing dayparts, cross-networking, and buying off-target can deliver high weekly, monthly, and quarterly reach at moderate weekly GRP levels.

A weekly reach strategy goes for reach (not frequency) and uses dispersion (not targeting), moderate (not high) GRP levels, continuity (not flighting), and cost per reach point (not CPM). If the job of brand advertising is to influence purchases and produce sales, this makes more sense than what advertisers have been doing.

John Wanamaker, the old-time expert who is remembered for saying, "Half my advertising dollars are wasted, but I don't know which half," also said, "The successful merchant sells to everyone." He understood the value of weekly reach.

A Guerrilla Media Strategy

Weekly reach planning makes sense, but smaller brands need more. Media strategy is not solitaire. It is a battle plan in the fight for the life of a brand. Smaller brands have a chance of winning only if they ignore the rules. General Cornwallis blew the battle of Yorktown because he was a set-piece soldier and a gentleman. His idea of war was to line up the men in rows and blast away until luncheon. By Cornwallis's rules, even if the colonists were equal in weapons, discipline, and marksmanship, his bigger army would win. Cornwallis lost the war because Washington's army was a rabble and did not fight fair. They refused to line up, wouldn't wear bright colors, hid behind trees, and attacked on Christmas Day. Advertising is that kind of battle. Big brands have the firepower: higher awareness, better distribution, and larger budgets. Small brands have the freedom to ignore the rules and, with luck, to change them. Listerine's battle plan won't work for Lavoris. But if Lavoris is successful, Listerine's battle plan will not work for Listerine either.

Napoleon was the consummate underdog. He recommended, "Audacity, audacity. Always the audacity," which sounds less spastic in French. General Schwarzkopf preached "concentration and surprise." These are the small brand's best weapons, and their code name is *spot television*. Spot is the basic guerrilla medium for smaller brands. It targets effectively and "goes where they are not," placing messages in dayparts where there is less direct competition.

A small brand can *opportunity target* with spot television and surprise the bigger brands. Scanner data provide the *intelligence* on market-by-market sales, almost as they happen. A small brand can target markets where it is growing, or where its share is high, where the category is growing or where the competition is weak. The small brand can mix strategies, strike, withdraw, and read the results.

Big brands can also use an *audacious* spot strategy to good effect, but usually they will not because of ego. They are proud, like Cornwallis, and think that using spot is like hiding behind trees.

Another rule for guerrilla brands to ignore is "effective" frequency. Let the big brands pile up messages to blanket consumers. Smaller brands cannot afford that silliness. Consumers do not learn advertising by repetition; they screen it for relevance and respond to messages that are useful. A cornflakes commercial can be useful to a consumer who has run out of breakfast cereal that morning; otherwise the advertisement will be like wallpaper—present but unnoticed.

There are good counterstrategies for the megabrand. For example, category leaders should celebrate competitive clutter, because it is their most important ally. Research on competitive clutter done by Dr. Robert Kent of the University of Delaware has shown that competing commercials reduce recall by more than 25%. The loss is greater for the less familiar brand. This research shows that the consumer's ability to remember a "product claim" in such situations relates to familiarity with the brand.

At the height of the Cold War, the U.S. Navy assigned less costly "hunter-killer" submarines to follow the Soviet's missile-firing subs, to cancel their strategic value. Category leaders can assign hunter-killer "brand name" 15-second commercials to follow the competition's 30-second commercials in programs and dayparts where the competition advertises. By sowing confusion, hunter-killer 15-second ads cancel the competition's more expensive 30-second messages, and, if a competitor's claim is memorable, take credit for it. Often when a smaller brand's claim is remembered, it is attributed to the category leader. Leading brands can use this human frailty as part of their antiguerrilla strategy. It is not sportsmanlike, but this is war.

Because most competing brands have similar consumer targets and there is almost no competitive separation in media today, the hunter-killer effect is already at work. As early as 1991, *Advertising Age* found that 42% of prime-time commercials ran within an hour of an ad for a competing brand on the same network. Was that Mazda or Ford on the NBA playoffs? Coors or Miller Lite on NFL football? American Express or Visa on the Olympics? Dynamo or Tide on *As the World Turns*?

The counterstrategy for smaller brands is, in Schwarzkopf's words, to "go where they are not." Smaller brands have fewer individual advertisements running, so it is important for them to avoid being neutralized by competing messages. In media terms, this involves eccentric targeting. If the category targets the 18-49 age group, the smaller brand should concentrate its advertising in somewhat older-profile programs, where it is not as likely to be ambushed. Because many major brands use network time—they do not use much spot television—spot dayparts such as local news, fringe, and prime access may be safer choices for small brands.

What is remarkable about an eccentric targeting strategy is that the smaller brand will not lose anything by trying it. As I pointed out earlier, demo targeting is not very powerful, and older-profile programs, because they cost less, have competitive younger-profile CPMs.

This chapter has looked at a few examples of breaking the rules in media. There are many others. This is what makes media planning stimulating, demanding, and even fun. But if you really care about winning, you should remember the words of another general and say that *media is hell.*

Notes

1. Herbert E. Krugman, "Why Three Exposures May Be Enough," *Journal of Advertising Research,* December 1972, 11-14.

2. Colin McDonald, "What Is the Short-Term Effect of Advertising?" in Michael J. Naples (ed.), *Effective Frequency: The Relationship Between Frequency and Advertising Effectiveness* (New York: Association of National Advertisers, 1979); John Philip Jones, *When Ads Work: New Proof That Advertising Triggers Sales* (New York: Simon & Schuster-Lexington, 1995).

What Does Effective
Frequency Mean Today?

John Philip Jones

The words *effective frequency* imply more than they directly convey. In literal terms, effective frequency can mean that a single advertising exposure is able to influence the purchase of a brand. However, as all experienced advertising people know, the phrase was really coined to communicate the idea that there must be enough concentration of media weight to cross a threshold. Repetition was considered necessary, and there had to be enough of it within the period before a consumer buys a product to influence his or her choice of brand.

NOTE: An earlier version of this chapter appeared in the *Journal of Advertising Research,* July/August 1997. © 1997 by the Advertising Research Foundation. Reprinted by permission.

Did It All Begin in 1979?

The idea of effective frequency is rooted not so much in research as in common sense: the instinct to use advertising to knock consumers repeatedly over the head. Concentration—spending money in "flights" or "bursts"—is a policy as old as television advertising itself. I have personally seen it in practice for four decades. As far as operational policy is concerned, there was therefore nothing new in the strategy advocated by Michael Naples in the edited volume he published in 1979, *Effective Frequency: The Relationship Between Frequency and Advertising Effectiveness.*[1] This work did, however, provide an imprimatur: a stamp of academic respectability for a virtually universal practice within the advertising industry.

In Naples's terms, effective frequency means three "opportunities to see" within the purchase interval. Hard data do not exist to demonstrate how widely this policy has actually been followed since 1979, or at least had been followed during the 15 years after Naples's book came out, at which time a new notion, *continuity scheduling,* began to be propagated. But anecdotal evidence and my own personal observations both suggest that the effective frequency strategy was being implemented by 90% of packaged goods advertisers in the United States. Few doctrines have influenced professional practice in the advertising field to such an extent, although we must of course remember that most advertisers were planning for effective frequency before the Naples book came along to tell them that they were doing the right thing. It is in fact continuity scheduling that represents the real innovation, and that is the main subject of this chapter.

Naples's volume provided a valuable service in that it presented in succinct form the most salient evidence bearing on the issue of effective frequency. Nevertheless, three parts of the book eventually generated rather serious debate, although it was some time before any doubts were raised.

The first of these parts concerned Colin McDonald's research.[2] Much reliance was placed on McDonald's important pioneer experiment using consumer diaries and employing a type of single-source research that I have described elsewhere as the pure single-source method (see the brief glossary at the end of this chapter).[3] McDonald's work provided the strongest empirical underpinning in Naples's book, but it was too easily forgotten that this research was, despite its originality and virtuosity, merely a small-scale experiment carried out a number of years previously in a foreign country.

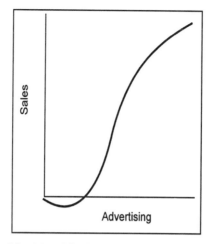

Figure 28.1. McDonald's Advertising Response Function

The most striking—and disturbing—finding of McDonald's investigation was that his advertising response function appeared to have the shape of the curve shown here in Figure 28.1. What McDonald was saying was that one advertising exposure actually *depressed* sales. If this conclusion could be properly supported, it is difficult to think of anything more likely to alarm advertisers who might have been considering deploying their budgets with a subthreshold degree of concentration.

What is now perfectly clear is that this remarkable response function is an artifact of McDonald's statistical method. He relied on brand switching to the exclusion of repeat purchase as his criterion of effectiveness. Brand switching of course tells only half the story. Moreover, the data from all his brands were aggregated: He had to lump together the ineffective campaigns with the effective ones, because he was working with too small a sample to analyze them separately. These two factors together managed to mask the positive effect of one exposure and to turn a sales increase into an apparent sales reduction.[4] When he recomputed his data to measure a straightforward change in share of market, pre- and postadvertising, McDonald produced a curve of diminishing returns (see Figure 28.2).[5] This showed that it was after all viable—indeed economic—to expose a single advertisement; there was no threshold before advertising began to work. This of course had serious implications for the effective frequency doctrine.

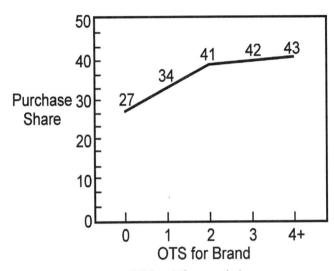

Figure 28.2. STAS Calculation, JWT Panel (9 categories)

The second controversial part of Naples's book was the extent to which he relied on Herbert Krugman's cognitive theory. Krugman plausibly hypothesized a hierarchy of effects from three sequential advertising exposures: (a) to prompt "What is it?"; (b) to prompt "What of it?"; and (c) to remind.[6] Consumers have to move through all three stages for a campaign to influence them.

However, the central point about Krugman's doctrine is that it applies only to unfamiliar advertising campaigns. It therefore operates in exceptional and not normal circumstances. Krugman makes it totally clear that, with established and familiar campaigns, any isolated repeat exposure acts as a reminder of the second—which may have been perceived by the viewer at an earlier time. In other words, a single exposure can operate effectively as part of an ongoing campaign because it triggers a recollection of advertisements exposed when the campaign was first introduced and when viewers were being educated about its meaning. This again cast a serious shadow on the effective frequency doctrine.

The third disputable point about Naples's book is its discussion of the purchase cycle. McDonald's research examined the effect of incremental advertising stimuli within this cycle—the period between last purchase and next—a methodologically sound procedure. However, the purchase cycle interval was badly misapplied to the process of media planning. Media planners appreciated that the cycle is more or less uniform between different buyers of any brand. However, they unconsciously assumed the same timing for these intervals. In planning the flights in an advertising schedule over 4 weekly periods with gaps between flights, planners assumed that consumers were all buying the brand during the flight—or more precisely toward the end of it, if the effective frequency theory was to be believed. This application of the theory ignored the possibility of some consumers buying during the early part of the flight and in the intervals between flights. There was therefore a large loss of potential business.

Although consumers do indeed buy at relatively uniform purchase intervals, the actual day of purchase will be different for different buyers. There are some buyers of a brand who are making their purchases today, others tomorrow, others the day after. There are buyers every single day—indeed, every hour of the day and perhaps every minute. It follows from this unquestionable fact that if we wish to expose our advertising to all these purchasers, we have to advertise continuously—or at least as continuously as our budget will allow. The germ of this notion is contained within Krugman's writings, and it has more recently been expressed elegantly and trenchantly by Erwin Ephron.[7] This is the basic idea behind the strategy of continuity scheduling.

The reinterpretation of the data in Naples's *Effective Frequency* that I have summarized, together with additional research carried out since 1979, is leading to a narrowing of the circumstances in which advertisers should plan to run their messages according to the original pattern of three exposures before purchase. I shall return to this matter at the end of this chapter.

The Prevalence of Diminishing Returns

The two best-known shapes that have been hypothesized for the advertising response function are very familiar and do not need much discussion. Figure 28.3 illustrates diminishing returns, in which the first "dose" of advertising boosts sales and additional doses have a progressively diminishing effect. Figure 28.4—the S-shaped curve—shows the "threshold" effect predicated by the effective frequency doctrine. In this, the first dose has little effect on sales, the second has more than the first, and the sales effect peaks at three; thereafter

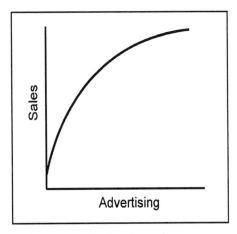

Figure 28.3. Response Function of Diminishing Returns

it declines in a pattern of diminishing returns. McDonald's response function (Figure 28.1) represents a very extreme form of the S-shaped curve.

The results of the pure single-source research into 78 American brands that I published in 1995 demonstrate that the prevailing pattern of response for repeat-purchase packaged goods follows a pattern of diminishing returns, as in Figure 28.3.[8] This work, which was reinforced by additional research I carried out in Germany,[9] shows quite clearly that a single advertisement can be effective—often highly effective. This conclusion has also been confirmed by other American data, from, inter alia, Lawrence Gibson, and by British data from both Andrew Roberts and Colin McDonald.[10] McDonald makes an important point by emphasizing propinquity. The greatest sales effect comes from advertising 1 day before purchase. Fewer sales come from advertising 2 days before, and fewer still from 3 days before.

My count of published response functions shows more than 200 brands whose campaigns show diminishing returns, and slightly more than 10 (mainly new brands) whose campaigns show S-shaped thresholds. The preponderance of diminishing returns is by now widely accepted by the research community, and the facts do not need to be discussed further here.

There is, however, a special point that is worth making about the difference between my findings from the United States and those from Germany. This illustrates dramatically the waste involved in concentrating advertising money

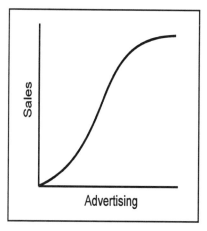

Figure 28.4. S-Shaped Response Function—Threshold Effect

in ignorance of the vicious effect of diminishing returns. The normal reduction in advertising efficiency caused by diminishing returns will have a long-range effect by causing a large drop between any immediate sales lift and the net sales increase at the end of a year. It is common to find a positive immediate effect ending up in a year-end sales *reduction.*

In the United States, I found a very sharp pattern of diminishing returns in my advertising response functions. In the period before purchase, an average of 73% of sales came from households exposed to one advertisement, with the remaining 27% coming from those seeing more than one. Media concentration—which swallows large amounts of money—causes the average advertising budget to be run down very fast, and the loss of potential sales caused by the diminishing returns means that short-term sales gains simply cannot be maintained across a year. This decay in sales can be measured by the difference between the short-term sales effect (STAS) and the year-end sales change (see the glossary at the end of this chapter). Table 28.1 shows all the brands from my American study in deciles, ranked from the campaigns with the strongest STAS (first decile) to the weakest (tenth decile). The inefficiency of concentrated scheduling is amply illustrated by the consistent dissipation of the short-term effects.

The situation in Germany is different. Here the rate of diminishing returns is much less sharp than in the United States, with a sales effect from the first

TABLE 28.1 STAS Minus Year-End Sales Change

Decile	United States (High Falloff) %	Germany (Low Falloff) %
First	–54	–16
Second	–43	–7
Third	–26	–1
Fourth	–12	—^a
Fifth	–13	—^a
Sixth	–10	—^a
Seventh	–9	–4
Eighth	–7	–5
Ninth	–5	–3
Tenth	–4	–1

a. No difference.

exposure compared with additional exposures in the ratio of 46:54. In Germany, therefore, concentrated pressure leads to less falloff in sales and less decay of the short-term effect than in the United States.

The difference in the rate of falloff between the two countries is startling, and it emphasizes the terrible loss of potential sales in the United States that concentrated advertising schedules will bring about. The data reported in my book *When Ads Work* point up this loss in very simple terms.[11] I found that 70% of campaigns generate short-term sales increases (measured by a positive STAS Differential). Of these, 46% maintained higher sales at the end of the year, although the effect was always less than the original STAS. But 24% (i.e., 70 minus 46) totally lost their positive effect on sales, for reasons connected with media weight and scheduling.

As Figure 28.5 shows, I believe that campaigns must surmount three hurdles before they can be fully effective:

1. They must be creatively strong enough to generate a positive STAS Differential. A higher rate of success here depends on the ability to produce stronger creative ideas as well as the ability to use reliably predictive pretesting to identify what is likely to work and what is not.[12]
2. The STAS effect must be repeated often enough to produce a net sales gain at the end of a year. This is determined by the brand's budget and its media plan (media strategy is discussed in the next section).

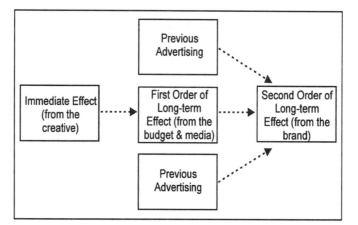

Figure 28.5. Jones Model of How Advertising Works

3. All elements of the brand, including the current advertising, must work in harmony to drive repeated repeat purchase—what I call a brand's *internal momentum*. (Previous advertising is also likely to influence this to some degree, although the effect will gradually decay if current advertising does not provide effective and fresh advertising stimuli.)

Internal momentum can be demonstrated objectively with certain robust measures of the brand's dynamics. Measuring advertising effects in isolation is inadequate. Advertising works in the long term in conjunction with consumers' satisfaction with the functional properties of the brand. There is a process of mutual reinforcement, and there are three explanatory/predictive measures (which are described in the glossary); if these are all positive, the brand's internal momentum becomes an important driving force.[13]

Diminishing Returns and Continuity Scheduling

I believe emphatically that *a media strategy of three exposures before purchase should be used only in the most exceptional circumstances.* Not only do flighting patterns cause a profligate loss of sales, as I have just demonstrated, but there is also a significant opportunity cost—a sacrifice of alternatives. This sacrifice is of course manifested in loss of continuity, which means the brand is deprived of the permanent advertising presence it so badly needs to contact and influence the constant body of potential purchasers.

The most effective media strategy for a brand can be described simply. However, it is not necessarily easy to implement such a strategy, because of the complexities of the media marketplace:

1. Aim to cover a substantial proportion of the brand's target group once every week with as little duplication as possible ("substantial proportion" is a judgment call).
2. To achieve this, determine the optimum number of weekly gross rating points (GRPs) and establish the best types of dayparts and television programs to use in order to minimize audience duplication. (These procedures are again judgmental, and they require expert knowledge of the television audience and of the fast-changing field of programming. During recent years, Erwin Ephron has done more than any other analyst to put flesh on these theoretical bones.)
3. Run the weekly advertising pattern for as many weeks as the budget will allow. Any inevitable gaps in the schedule should occur during the low season.

My recommendations call for redeploying advertising budgets to achieve a greater continuity than many schedules achieve at present, and of course this means less short-term concentration—an economically favorable outcome because of the avoidance or reduction of diminishing returns. I also recommend regional test programs so long as these can be carried out efficiently and economically.

These thoughts, which would at one time have been considered highly unorthodox, are not falling on deaf ears, in either the United States or Europe. (Perhaps the Europeans have always been more open-minded about marketplace experimentation.)

In the late 1970s, when I was working at J. Walter Thompson, London, the client and agency commissioned an econometric study of the advertising response function for Andrex, a very powerful brand and market leader in the bathroom tissue category. This response function—although it came in the form of a rather weak regression—seemed to show a pattern of diminishing returns. This was nevertheless good enough to persuade the client and agency to plan and run a pattern of continuous advertising in a single self-contained and relatively typical television area. A careful analysis of sales at the end of a year showed significantly stronger sales in the test area than in the rest of Britain (which acted as the statistical control).

As a result of this test, the national advertising was changed to a pattern of continuous advertising. This was a very unusual thing for an important national brand. However, it has been acknowledged by both client and agency to have benefited the brand enormously over the years. It did this by maintaining the brand's already high penetration and purchase frequency, and indeed by preserving Andrex's comfortable market leadership:

> [J. Walter Thompson] believe[s] that this high level of carry-over and behavior maintenance is in some measure attributable to the disposition of advertising weight within and between sales periods. Andrex has, for many years, disposed advertising weight continuously. It is not clustered in bursts.[14]

Such an unprejudiced, experimental mind-set has also been adopted by many American advertisers—an attitude that must be welcomed and applauded by the research community. During the course of 1996, I gradually learned about eight major advertisers, with an aggregate national billing of more than $4 billion, who were seriously experimenting with continuity scheduling on an area basis, and in some cases were producing demonstrably positive results.

I possess full details of the media experiments carried out by one of these organizations—an extremely prominent advertiser and a company with nine major marketing divisions whose brands are all household names. In 1995, the average number of weeks of advertising across all these divisions was 16, at an average weekly advertising weight of 97 GRPs. As a result of successful experimentation during the course of 1996, eight of the nine divisions adjusted the distribution of their advertising funds. In 1997, the average number of advertised weeks in all nine operating divisions had increased to 22, and the average weekly GRP level had been decreased to 84.[15] The company has taken—after good research and careful deliberation—a measurable step toward continuity scheduling. The plans also accommodated a good deal of detailed media innovation aimed at stretching the net reach of the schedules and reducing wasteful duplication.

During the course of 1996, the pace of interest in continuity scheduling increased. By December, 53% of major clients and 70% of senior media executives in agencies were aware of the research into single-exposure effectiveness and the value of continuous advertising. Similar numbers also claimed to be either implementing or considering implementing plans to advertise more continuously than before. Interest was particularly strong among packaged goods and automotive advertisers. In other fields, a larger proportion of executives were still sitting on the fence.[16]

It is a source of modest satisfaction for an academic to have had some influence, no matter how small and indirect, on business decisions in the real world. As we were once reminded by John Kenneth Galbraith—one of the less inarticulate members of the American university establishment—it is very rare indeed for the world of action to listen to the world of academe and to modify its behavior accordingly. But it has sometimes happened.

Is Effective Frequency Still Relevant?

Has the pendulum totally swung away from the direction in which it was moving in 1979? Does the argument in this chapter mean that advertisers should now turn totally away from the doctrine of effective frequency? Frankly, no. But, as I explained in the early part of this chapter, an effective frequency strategy should now be applied in exceptional and not normal circumstances. Here are three examples (and there may be others).

The first is new brands and new campaigns for existing brands. With both of these, there must still be a Krugmanesque buildup of exposures to get the message across cognitively if the campaign is to achieve any initial success. This buildup should be only a temporary necessity, however. It should not become a permanent strategy. The length of the period depends on the size of the brand and the total size of its advertising budget, but as a rule of thumb I would suggest a period of 3 months at most. After this time, one can generally assume that the advertising has made an impact and that additional exposures will act as reminders.

The second exceptional case is that of advertising for highly seasonal goods and services, such as toys, some retailers, and a few food and drink products (e.g., cranberries). The advertising period here is extremely curtailed, and advertisers are forced to accept the inefficiencies of diminishing returns for competitive reasons. All advertisers have to compress their expenditures and accept similar degrees of inefficiency if they are to make their presence felt in a competitive marketplace.

The third case is not dissimilar from the first. It is when advertising has to be piled into short periods to build with great rapidity a consumer base that will generate long-term purchase frequency. A typical example is advertising to generate publication subscriptions. With these, the need for a speedy growth of the subscriber base counterbalances the cost of the diminishing returns that the advertising will soon hit. But the size of this subscriber base governs the future profitability of the enterprise because of the repeat business that will result if the publication does its basic job of satisfying its readers.

Glossary

First order of long-term effect: The cumulative result of STAS effects over the course of a year. This is measured through comparison of a brand's share of market during the last 9 months of a year and its share during the first 3 months. The second share figure is indexed on the first.

Second order of long-term effect: A *long* long-term effect derived from consumers' satisfaction with the functional properties of a brand, reinforced by the added values nurtured by the advertising. It is measurable through (a) price analyses (strong brands are generally higher priced—that is, they rely less on sales promotions—than weaker brands), (b) analyses of purchase frequency (average purchase frequency—that is, consumer loyalty—tends to be higher for larger, stronger brands than for smaller ones), and (c) analyses of advertising share of voice (this tends to be smaller for larger brands—this is a quantifiable expression of advertising-related scale economies).

Single-source research: A technique that collects multiple data from each individual household; this is most commonly information about brand purchasing and advertising exposure. The pure technique isolates the effect of advertising by measuring (a) purchases of an identified brand in the households that had been exposed to advertising for that same brand during a defined period (normally 7 days) before the purchase and (b) purchases of the brand in the households not exposed to the advertising. Other things are normally equal between the two groups of households, and the latter figure is deducted from the former to calculate the advertising effect.

STAS (Short-Term Advertising Strength): The specific measure of immediate advertising effect measured by pure single-source research. A brand's market share in the households that had not received advertising for it in the period before purchase is the Baseline STAS. Its share of market in the households that had received advertising is the Stimulated STAS. Stimulated STAS minus Baseline STAS is the brand's STAS Differential; this is indexed on the Baseline, and it represents the net immediate effect of advertising on market share.

Notes

1. Michael J. Naples (ed.), *Effective Frequency: The Relationship Between Frequency and Advertising Effectiveness* (New York: Association of National Advertisers, 1979).

2. Colin McDonald, "What Is the Short-Term Effect of Advertising?" in Naples, *Effective Frequency.*

3. John Philip Jones, *When Ads Work: New Proof That Advertising Triggers Sales* (New York: Simon & Schuster-Lexington, 1995), 5-10.

4. John Philip Jones, "Single-Source Research Begins to Fulfill Its Promise," *Journal of Advertising Research,* May/June 1995, 9-15.

5. Colin McDonald, "Effective Frequency: The Relationship Between Frequency and Advertising Effectiveness," in *Conference Proceedings of Effective Frequency Research Day* (New York: Advertising Research Foundation, 1994).

6. Herbert E. Krugman, "Why Three Exposures May Be Enough," *Journal of Advertising Research,* December 1972, 11-14.

7. Naples, *Effective Frequency,* 26; see also, for example, Erwin Ephron, "More Weeks, Less Weight: The Shelf-Space Model of Advertising," *Journal of Advertising Research,* May/June 1995, 18-23; also Ephron, Chapter 27, this volume.

8. Jones, *When Ads Work,* 35-49.

9. John Philip Jones, *When Ads Work: The German Version* (Frankfurt am Main: Gesamtverband Werbeagenturen, 1995), 21-24.

10. Lawrence D. Gibson, "What Can One TV Exposure Do?" in *Conference Proceedings of Copy Research Workshop* (New York: Advertising Research Foundation, 1994), 16; Andrew Roberts, "What Do We Know About Advertising's Short-Term Effects?" *Admap,* February 1996, 42-45; Colin McDonald, "How Frequently Should You Advertise?" *Admap,* July/August 1996, 22-25.

11. Jones, *When Ads Work.*

12. See, for instance, John Philip Jones, *Getting It Right the First Time: Can We Eliminate Ineffective Advertising Before It Is Run?* (Henley-on-Thames, UK: Admap Publications, 1996); see also John Philip Jones, "Look Before You Leap," *Admap,* November 1996, 16-22.

13. Jones, *When Ads Work,* 61-64.

14. Evelyn Jenkins and Christopher Timms, "The Andrex Story: A Soft, Strong and Very Long-Term Success," in *Advertising Works 4: Papers From the Institute of Practitioners in Advertising (IPA) Advertising Effectiveness Awards* (London: Cassell, 1987), 185. This case study is one of two devoted to Andrex published by the IPA. The second came out in 1993.

15. Private information.

16. *Myers Report* (New York: Myers Report Industry Research, December 16, 1996). The data came from surveys of 711 and 300 executives in advertiser companies and advertising agencies.

29

Barter Syndication

Brian Philip Webster

The term *barter syndication* refers to a type of contract between broadcasters (television networks, network affiliates, independent stations, and cable stations) and television syndicators (the owners of the syndication rights to television programs). The commodity being bartered is advertising time within television programs. The basic issues of the barter revolve around the control of the advertising time: how much "available advertising time" there will be and who will sell that time. This is a deceptively simple summary, as barter syndication is no simple transaction. It is a powerful tool in the syndication business, which is still growing rapidly and possesses far-reaching benefits and consequences for the syndication, broadcasting, and advertising industries.

What Is Syndication?

As the Advertiser Syndicated Television Association has noted, "Syndication is simply a way of placing programs on TV stations—one that has been around since the start of television as a complement, and is now a competitor to, the network distribution system." [1] The main idea is that the owners of the rights to particular programs (syndicators) can try to negotiate broadcasting agreements with any broadcasters they wish.

Syndication is conducted by advertisers, independent program producers, independent broadcast stations, cable channels, network-affiliated stations, and the networks themselves. Television syndication gained tremendous strength as a result of the Financial Interest and Syndication Rule made by the Federal Communications Commission (FCC), which banned networks from producing programs. Because networks had to buy programming from outside producers and become middlemen—adding a layer of overhead in the process—this stimulated demand among stations for cheaper sources of programming. The syndicators met this demand. But because of the demise of this FCC rule, networks are now allowed to produce and own television programming, which they had not been able to do for a quarter century after 1970.

The networks (a) charge affiliates for the right to retransmit the network feed by selling some of each program's advertising time before they feed it and (b) levy a cash charge for each network program aired by each affiliate. This arrangement reduces affiliate revenues, pushing the affiliates to seek more efficient means of program acquisition. Additionally, the affiliates have had to address the networks' inability to maintain a feed appealing to every market at all times all across the country. Affiliates have needed a way to tailor their broadcasts to their individual marketplaces, because of the differences in audiences and the affiliates' competitive situations in various local broadcast areas.

Syndication grew because the syndicators began to bypass the networks, going directly to the stations, both affiliated and independent, and it continues to grow because of the vast sea of cable channels looking for programming and revenue. Avoiding the networks allows syndicators to sell directly from the studios to the affiliates, reducing the costs to the affiliates because of reduced reliance on their respective network feeds. Better programming also became available to independent stations as syndicators realized that negotiating/bartering syndication deals on a market-by-market basis was a profitable way to do business. This effectively provided affiliated broadcasting stations with more centrally originated feeds, as they could shop the syndicated offerings of Warner Bros., Paramount, King World, and so on in their search for high-rated programs that increase revenues by increasing audience share.

Broadcasting stations of course make their revenue by selling advertising time; the value of the advertising time is positively correlated with the program rating, or the measurement of the number of people viewing the program. The highest-rated program airing at any given time will attract the most viewers at that time, and will attract more advertising dollars than competing programs.

Barter Syndication

Barter syndication is a type of contract made between program producers/owners (syndicators) and program broadcasters. The term is generally used to refer to television, but radio also has barter syndication, because the businesses are similar. A program that originates as a first-run network television program, produced specifically for the network and aired exclusively on that network for a certain period of time, will often go into syndication as reruns (*M*A*S*H* is an example of such a program). Syndicators (perhaps networks) may also produce their own television series that are syndicated (Paramount's *Star Trek: The Next Generation* is an example). When such syndication takes place, the programs have a certain amount of advertising time built into them. Commercial programs run shorter than their time block, to leave room for advertisements to be inserted. And the advertisements inserted in syndicated programming can be changed. (If you watched *It's a Wonderful Life* last Christmas and watch it again next Christmas, you will see different advertisements.) These insertions can be tailored regionally, seasonally, and in combination with other media in highly coordinated media blitzes.

Who sells this advertising time? That question is answered in one of three basic ways in the contract drawn up between the syndicator and the broadcaster: (a) In full station compensation, the syndicator pays the broadcaster for airtime and the syndicator then sells all the advertising time; (b) in a partial-barter agreement, the broadcaster pays the syndicator partly in cash and partly in advertising time; and (c) in a cash-only agreement, the broad-caster pays the syndicator in cash.

Full Station Compensation

Full station compensation occurs when a broadcaster is paid in full for a program-length time slot by a syndicator. The syndicator purchases what it believes to be an opportune time slot to reach a target audience. The syndicator is responsible for selling all the advertising time in that program. This method gives the syndicator the greatest possible control; the syndicator can treat the program as sponsored and feature only one product line or company. To advertising agencies that own syndication rights or that want to purchase them, full station compensation means the ability to feature clients in the most controlled atmosphere possible. Total program content is known, including what will be advertised during the show. The sponsor can eliminate competing companies and their products from the purchased time slot and therefore from the program. Sponsored programs can be meticulously designed to fit the image and advertising message the sponsor is trying to achieve when the campaign is conceived and created before the program is produced.

Full station compensation contracts and the potential sponsorship allowed by them were commonplace before the 1980s, when they all but disappeared. Recently, however, they have experienced some new stirrings. One of the first revivals of the genre took the form of Exxon's sponsoring nature specials after the *Valdez* oil spill, in an attempt to improve the company's shattered environ-mental image. This is parallel to the corporate sponsorship of Public Broad-casting Service specials.

Partial-Barter Agreements

The second—and most common—type of barter syndication is partial barter. Under this kind of contract, the ownership of advertising time is split between the syndicator and the station. The syndicator sells some of the advertising time and leaves some for the broadcaster to sell. The broadcaster then accepts a reduced cash payment from the syndicator and sells the remaining advertising inventory (time) at its discretion. The exact ratio of the advertising "time split" is negotiated station by station. For example, if a half-hour program has 6 minutes of advertising time built into it, the syndicator might sell 3 of those minutes and the broadcaster the other 3 minutes. The more time the syndicator gives up, the lower the cash payment will be, because the broadcaster sells that time and takes that revenue.

Advertising sales are the lifeblood of broadcasters. In negotiations over the time split, they try to keep as much advertising time as possible for themselves. So why would they give any up? The "cash-only" price of the program can be too high for the broadcaster to afford. The cash cost to the station can be reduced with the concession that some, usually half, of the program's advertising time will be sold by the syndicator. The amount of advertising time that syndicators want to keep for themselves is increasing with time, upsetting many broadcasters, who are left with less to sell and less revenue to earn.

Partial-barter deals enable broadcast stations to afford higher-rated programs, "shifting eyeballs" away from the competition and onto their own broadcasts. Broadcasters are always trying to balance the need for high ratings and high market share against the limited financial resources available to purchase higher-rated programs. Barter syndication is a major element in the maintenance of this balance as stations use it to get what they otherwise could not afford. Stations forgo ad revenue in the interest of obtaining popular programs, which maintain an edge in the competition for viewership; and syndicators are compensated when they sell their share of the advertising up front.

An example of the syndication process in action comes from Resort Sports Network, whose national programs are distributed to all affiliated stations in various ways. The shows are sent first to the network with syndicator/production house-sold ads; the network sells national airtime, and then spaces are left open for the local affiliates to sell. The syndication can therefore go through a number of levels, ending with the local affiliates. As explained, the exact ratio of national to local advertising and the cash payment to the syndicator are negotiated station by station; the negotiation is a point of concern for broadcasters.

Cash-Only Agreements

Before barter syndication became popular in the early 1980s, networks and broadcast stations generally paid lump sums for the rights to air syndicated programs or series of programs. This payment gave them the right to air certain program episodes for certain periods of time. This type of agreement leaves the bulk of control and decision making to the broadcaster's discretion: the determination of when the show should air (yearpart, weekpart, daypart), the decision to stop airing the show if ratings fall, and, most important, the right to sell all the advertising time. After the initial purchase, profitability becomes a function of program ratings and the station's sales department.

Barter Syndication's Bad Reputation

Under the barter system, advertising rates are opened up fully to negotiation. The value of advertising time is a function of how well the negotiators can perform. There is no single neat price tag for everyone. The same program might be sold to several different stations for widely ranging prices during the same time period. Because it is not easy to place an objective dollar value on the time bartered, the business of barter syndication has acquired a bad reputation. There are inherently many ways in which the system can be abused.

The J. Walter Thompson/Marie Luisi "time banking" scandal in 1982, which involved $30 million worth of false barter syndication revenues reported as profits, is a key example of how the system can be manipulated. Time banking is the practice of selling time credits. Time credits are given by broadcasters to advertising agencies as compensation for paid spots that did not air because of technical difficulties or other reasons. These credits are accumulated and can be sold, with broadcasting station approval, to other agency clients for the amount they were worth at the time the spots did not appear on air. A major abuse of the system is a kickback scheme in which the original advertiser charges the client (the new advertiser) more than the spot was worth (when it failed to air) and splits the difference with the station.[2] Other known abuses include double billing for the same item and overcharging clients for payment of media broadcasting costs.

In response to these problems, "check and balance" schemes have been implemented by advertising agencies to prevent this type of activity from occurring. Despite its tarnished reputation, barter syndication is still growing rapidly.

Advertising expenditures on syndication have risen dramatically—by 170% over the decade 1988-1997. The level of spending on all television advertising during this period grew at less than half this rate. To put this figure in perspective, syndication still accounts for little more than 5% of all television advertising expenditure.

There has been an erosion of cash-only syndication deals. National advertisers more often purchase their airtime directly from production syndication houses, which have already made partial- and full-compensation deals with networks and/or individual stations, who then sell the remaining time.

Barter Syndication Effects

Barter syndication entered the picture in the early 1980s, when broadcasting stations began to lack the cash needed to purchase programs on a cash-only basis. An important effect of this type of deal is that programs are supported by both the syndicator's advertisers and the broadcast station's advertisers, not just the broadcast station's advertisers alone. Syndicators began to resemble stations in that they were selling advertising time in television programs. The syndicators' profits became tied up in the ratings success of the shows, just like the local stations' profits. Because syndicators are now dealing with advertisers, the advertisers have come to possess more direct control over program content. Advertiser concerns are no longer mediated back through the affiliates to the networks, to the syndicators, to the producers. Now, in many cases, advertisers are dealing directly with syndicators who are also the producers of the programming they sell.

Sharing a common interest in the success of syndicated programming with the syndicator is a boon for the broadcaster. Because the syndicator, who may be affiliated with an advertising agency or may *be* an advertising agency, is selling advertising for its shows, it must guarantee certain ratings to clients if it is to get the expected payment. The overall effect has been an improvement in the quality (i.e., popularity) of syndicated programming, but this higher quality has been achieved at the expense of the broadcast station's control over its own broadcast signal.

The syndicator's stake places many new issues on the bargaining table to be worked out between the stations and syndicators. If the syndicator has promised that the barter advertisements will be run in a 9:00 p.m.-11:00 p.m. window, then the syndicator must ensure the station will run the program and the advertisements it carries during the agreed-upon time slot. This means that a contract will be drawn up requiring the station to run the show for a certain period of days, weeks, or months in a time window to the exclusion of all the other available programs, even if the show has low ratings. The power of the station diminishes.

The stations are giving up control over the "what" and "when" of their broadcasting schedules, and this limits their profitability through a possible sacrifice of ad revenue. The station gets less revenue each time it barters, so the next time it must barter some more, which gets it into deeper trouble. Finally it will lose all strategic control, pinned to the ground by its inventory of barter syndication deals, which specify what runs when, *to the exclusion of all other possibilities.*

The television industry experiences many failures in its quest for successful programs. It is vital that stations be able to recognize and drop failed projects and to try something different as quickly as possible. When a station becomes weighted down with many barter syndication contracts, it loses the potential to dump unprofitable programs and switch to better ones. The big problem is how to forecast which shows will be popular when they are offered for syndication. Stations are pressed to search for good shows in order to beat their competition.

> "Of course, if TV stations don't want to put up with producers getting more of their time, the stations can just stop doing these deals, right?" "God, no," says one station group head. "I'm scared to buy *Robocop,* and I'm scared not to buy it. What if it's the biggest thing out there in nine months?" [3]

The Future

Barter syndication will not diminish unless stations begin making substantial gains in revenue. Many stations are unhappy with barter syndication and the perceived greed of the syndicators. New media vehicles are being created constantly, and barter syndication will undoubtedly find its way into these as stations begin making deals to secure programming. Syndication, which began quietly in the fringe markets, has slowly risen to an important place in those markets, and is now growing into prime-time programming as the competition for superior programming among the broadcasters rages on.

Barter syndication is likely to be a driving force in the syndicators' penetration of prime time because it is a proven generator of advertisers' money.

Glossary

Affiliate: A broadcast station that is part of a major network (i.e., a local NBC, ABC, CBS, or Fox broadcaster).

Barter syndication: An umbrella term referring to the type of airing agreement reached between syndicators and broadcasters. Specific kinds of barter agreements include full station compensation, partial barter, and cash only.

Cash-only syndication: A lump sum of money paid by a broadcaster to a syndicator for the right to air specific programs for a specific period of time.

Financial Interest and Syndication Rule: An FCC regulation (now lapsed) that prevented networks from producing, owning, and syndicating television programs.

First-run network television program: A program that airs exclusively on a particular network for its first run. Reruns of such a program may be found on other stations.

Full station compensation: When a broadcaster is paid in full for a program-length time slot by a syndicator. Parallels sponsorship, as the syndicator/advertiser has control over the time slot.

Network: A group of stations that air programs from a common programming source.

Partial barter: A negotiated split of a syndicated program's advertising time between a syndicator and a broadcaster for the purpose of reducing the cash charge to the broadcaster. The syndicator sells some of the advertising time in exchange for receiving a reduced cash payment from the broadcaster. The arrangement makes expensive syndicated programs available to cash-starved broadcasters.

Syndication: The selling of program airing rights to broadcasters by program owners (syndicators).

Notes

1. Advertiser Syndicated Television Association, *1994 Guide to Advertiser-Supported Syndication. Syndication: The Fifth Network* (Chicago: Crain), a6.

2. See Christy Marshall, "JWT Slates Audit of Auditors," *Advertising Age,* May 24, 1982, 3, 79; Christy Marshall, "Another JWT Money Flap," *Advertising Age,* February 8, 1982, 1, 76; Christy Marshall, "Sales Faked, JWT Says of Unit Shortfall," *Advertising Age,* February 22, 1982, 1, 84; Christy Marshall, "JWT Will Quit Time Banking," *Advertising Age,* March 8, 1982, 1, 22, 24, 66.

3. Quoted in Cheryl Heuton, "Broadcasters Balk at Barter Deals," *Adweek,* February 14, 1994, 12. See also Cheryl Heuton, "Barter Bites Back," *Mediaweek,* February 14, 1994, 14.

30

Cable Television

Jeremiah L. Rosen
Laura A. York
Aileen (Shih-I) Ku

The Definition of Cable Television

According to the Federal Communications Commission (FCC), cable television is defined as a nonbroadcast facility consisting of a set of transmission parts and associated signal generation, reception, and control equipment that distributes to subscribers the signals of one or more television broadcast stations. This definition does not include (a) any such facility that serves fewer than 50 subscribers or (b) such a facility that serves only subscribers in one or more multiple dwelling units under common ownership control or management.

In other words, cable television is a system of coaxial cable and associated electronic equipment operating from a central receiving point or tower. Television and radio broadcast signals are delivered directly off the air or by other indirect means, for a fee, to a subscriber's premises.

The Evolution of Cable Television

Cable television emerged in the United States in 1949 in Lansford, Pennsylvania. Although Lansford is only 65 miles from Philadelphia, the Allegheny Mountains interrupted Philadelphia's television signals to Lansford. In an effort to combat poor broadcast reception, Robert Tarlton, an entrepreneur, founded Panther Valley. Under his direction, the company built a master antenna at the mountain summit and delivered what was called Community Antenna Television, or CATV, to households downhill via coaxial cable hung on poles. Like this first one, early cable systems were used primarily to facilitate the reception of television broadcasts in isolated communities.

In 1961, a cable company in San Diego realized other capabilities of this new invention. It was able to pick up the broadcasts of stations from Los Angeles that were more than a hundred miles away and deliver them to its audience. Not only could a subscriber receive more stations, but cable also provided a higher-quality picture, and its unlimited channel capacity overcame the problems of the limited broadcast spectrum. Viewers in the San Diego area were willing to pay more for these additional channels, so television broadcasters started to view cable as competition. They feared that cable might adversely affect local television by fragmenting the audience.

The FCC began regulating cable television in 1962, when importing distant signals became widespread. The FCC argued that because cable companies were not paying for retransmitting other stations' broadcasts, they were at a competitive advantage. Among other regulations, the FCC banned cable operators from importing signals from different market areas into a top-100 market. It also required cable systems to distribute the signals of all television stations in their areas. However, in the early 1970s, the FCC found little economic evidence to support the restriction on importing distant channels. As a result, most FCC regulations were removed.

After a period of relative stagnation, the cable industry boomed.[1] In 1965, 3% of U.S. television households were cable subscribers. By 1972, the proportion rose to 11%. In 1975, the Satcom 1 communications satellite was launched, making it possible to distribute multiple programming options to cable systems across the country. Pay channels such as Home Box Office (HBO) developed, which in turn started a small trend toward relying for finances on subscription fees instead of advertising.[2]

Cable grew even more powerful throughout the 1980s and into the 1990s, until the 1992 Cable Act shook the industry. This act allowed all broadcasters to be carried on the cable systems in their areas of dominant influence for no payment, or to get a cash payment for cable's use of their broadcasts. Known as "must carry" rules, these laws were created to protect broadcasters from what Congress determined to be unfair competition by cable. The Cable Act guaranteed station placement on a cable, which was normally a difficult feat for local programmers.

In October 1992, Congress enacted legislation that rolled back the rates of basic cable by 10%. This, added to a 7% rollback from the Cable Act, brought down basic cable rates a total of 17% in a single year. The FCC then went on to reject the National Cable Television Association's programming incentive plan, which would have allowed operators to increase subscription fees by 25 cents a month for each new channel added.[3] The FCC argued that these rules were designed to protect consumers and that the inevitable increase in competition would soon force cable prices down.[4]

Penetration of Cable Television

Cable was once home to such snake-oil treatments as pills that allegedly caused weight loss while users slept. However, it now has sponsors (i.e., organizations that take on the rights for broadcasts) that are the cream of the country's advertising crop. In 1970, the numbers of sponsors of and subscribers to cable television in the United States were 2.5 million and 4.5 million, respectively. By the early 1990s, the medium had established its national presence. In 1993, the number of sponsors had risen to 11.1 million and the number of subscribers had reached 55 million: a 12-fold increase.[5] Among all television households, 73% of the prime-time viewing during November 1992 was to network affiliates, compared with 22% to cable networks. But within pay-cable homes, only 64% of all viewing was to network affiliates; cable channels garnered 35% of the viewing audience.[6]

Cable penetration in households grew quickly, but not deeply. In 1993, according to Nielsen Media Research, 98% of total households had access to at least one television set; 61% subscribed to cable television.[7] Thereafter, the rate of increase decelerated. However, currently more than 65% of households subscribe to cable, and on average they have access to more than 50 stations. Although cable television as a medium has wide market reach, individual cable channels lack substantial penetration. Nonetheless, advertisers remain optimistic regarding the effectiveness of cable advertising.

Advertising revenues have continued to rise steadily on cable networks. According to Competitive Media Reporting, Inc., overall cable advertising increased by 7.5% in 1993, and this rate of increase has been maintained subsequently (as described at the end of this chapter). These increases have most likely been a result of cable's high ratings. Cable networks averaged a 15.3% rating in total U.S. households in June 1994, which was a gain of almost 2 percentage points over June 1993. Even during prime time, cable channels have stolen audience shares from the four major networks. Cable averaged a prime-time rating of 21.8% in June 1994, which increased from 20.4% in June 1993. The networks lost 1.4 percentage points during the same period.[8]

The Advantages of Cable Television for Advertisers

Technical factors limit the number of broadcast networks to four. These four networks tend to air "lowest-common-denominator" programs in order to attract the majority of viewers. Lowest-common-denominator programs are those that contain elements least offensive to the greatest number of viewers. The networks, following this strategy and imitating each other's successes, have turned into virtual clones of one another. Viewers who do not conform to the interests of the mass audience are left out completely.

Cable television took advantage of the networks' shortcomings by offering an unlimited number of channels. Unlike the networks, cable permits advertisers to pinpoint target groups that are currently impossible to locate on network television. This distinction is described as *verticality*. A vertical network is one that focuses on a single type of audience (e.g., the Nashville Network, which caters to country music lovers). This allows advertisers to target homogeneous demographic groups with maximum effectiveness. With lower subscription rates (resulting from the 1992 Cable Act), higher advertising revenues have become an increasingly important resource for vertical networks that previously relied heavily upon subscription fees. In contrast, horizontal networks, such as NBC and USA, show a broad spectrum of programming. The original networks were defined by their horizontality, because of their diverse programming and broad audience appeal.

Cable advertising grew rapidly during the early 1990s, increasing by 11.6% from 1990 to 1991, whereas program revenues and installation fees grew by only 7.8% and 7.1%, respectively.[9] Advertisers realized not only that cable viewership was increasing, but also that it (a) had a low absolute cost per advertising spot, (b) could reach highly targeted audiences, and (c) was able to provide a high frequency of exposure to viewers. Because cable advertising can be extremely localized, advertisers are also able to pinpoint the exact areas where the advertisements are being delivered.[10] In addition, the incomes of households subscribing to cable are on average 39% higher than the median national income, which makes these audiences even more attractive to advertisers.[11]

The Disadvantages of Cable Television for Advertisers

Before the introduction of remote control television and multiple cable channels, it was sufficient for advertisers to treat program viewership as a direct indicator of audience size for commercials. In other words, networks assumed that viewership during commercials was equal to viewership during programming. This was primarily because viewers had no alternatives other than to watch the broadcast networks. With the advent of cable, viewers gained the option of zapping to noncommercial programming on cable during network commercial breaks. Research conducted by the J. Walter Thompson Company defined three television viewing behaviors: zapping, flipping, and zipping. *Zapping* refers to a viewer's changing channels when a commercial comes on, *flipping* is changing channels to some degree rather than watching a show from beginning to end, and *zipping* is fast-forwarding past commercials while watching recorded programs on a videocassette. Cable drove the trend toward zapping and flipping, because it gave viewers so many channels to watch while commercials were airing on other stations.[12]

Although cable operators boast of the possibility of future channels devoted solely to such topics as sewing, entomology, and high-fidelity, the trend of some of the larger cable networks is toward diversification. There has been a shift among cable networks from strict vertical programming to a broader emphasis on each channel's featured format—a trend toward horizontality. For instance, CNN has introduced a number of talk shows to augment its news and news-related format. One such show, *Real Personal,* features viewer calls to experts regarding matters of a personal nature.

The problem with the growth of these types of format is that viewers will lose station loyalty if, for instance, they cannot rely on CNN to give them 24-hour news anymore. Increasingly, as cable networks move toward horizontality, they place themselves in the awkward position of jack of all trades, master of none. Turner Broadcasting System (TBS), for example, airs programs that appeal to a diverse cross section of the population. Catering to larger audiences means diminished specialization, and without a regular schedule of special interest programming, horizontal cable networks eliminate the basic advertising lure of cable television—the ability to pinpoint target groups. These networks are something of a curiosity; they run network-like programming—sitcoms, game shows, and evening dramas—without broadcast network quality (compare ABC's *NYPD Blue* with USA's *Charlie's Angels* reruns).

Perhaps the greatest disadvantage of cable is its high subscription fees. Although currently 65% of TV households in the United States subscribe to cable, 35% do not. As a result, cable's penetration is unlikely ever to be as great as that of the networks, which carry no cost to the viewer.

The Future of Cable Television

Niche Marketing

Advertising is a vital part of cable television, and with the cable industry constantly changing, advertising must accommodate itself to those changes. One of the recent changes in cable television is the increase in competition from within the industry. Newly arrived channels (or channels rumored to appear imminently) include a golf channel, an outdoor life channel, a game show channel, a crime channel, a parents' channel, and a history channel. Mark Gjovik of D'Arcy Masius Benton & Bowles has observed, "If a special niche can be spoken through micro opportunities, the niche cablers will prosper." [13]

Advertisers look for television programs that attract audiences who will be interested in their products. In today's market, numbers are not as important as the audience's responses to the advertisements. Cable advertisers theorize that it is better to reach a few thousand people who are interested in a product than to reach hundreds of thousands of people who don't need or even care for it. For instance, advertising golf clubs on one of the major networks is wasteful, because only a small proportion of the audience plays golf. However, a cable channel devoted to golf would be an ideal place to reach prospective customers. The low absolute prices for spots on these niche channels also attract advertisers. The Military Channel charges $75 for a 30-second commercial; compare that with ESPN, which charges $2,700 for a 30-second spot.

Some experts disagree about the future of niche cable channels. Mass marketers need large audiences for their products in order to be profitable, and niche channels cannot provide high numbers of viewers. Harvey Ganot, who runs advertising sales at MTV, firmly believes that "advertisers want to put their money with the best prospects and will shy away from smaller channels." [14] On the other hand, magazines have gone through a similar experience. The arrival of television basically destroyed the mass-circulation general-interest magazines, such as *Life.* However, magazines devoted to specialized interests such as computers and skiing have flourished, as television cannot cater to all consumers' individual tastes. Today's society is increasingly defined more by hobbies and professions than by basic social classes, so niche marketing could be a prosperous business.

Interactive Cable Television

Interactive cable, which is currently being tested in many markets, could also have a major impact on the future of advertising. Hearst Corporation has invested $20 million in a new cable system that will offer interactive television to approximately 34,000 Canadian homes. In addition to financial services, e-mail, and lotteries, there are classified ads and business directories that will enable companies to advertise on the interactive system.

Ford Motor Company has been a front-runner in interactive advertising. It was the sole interactive sponsor of Quebec's telecast of the 1994 Olympic Games. By paying a 10% premium over regular sponsors, Ford was able to run interactive advertisements during Olympic coverage. When it was time for a Ford commercial, viewers could select their interests, so the appropriate Ford messages would be shown in their homes. After watching the commercials, viewers could use their remotes to answer questions on the screen about Ford and win prizes for correct answers. Unfortunately for Ford, and much to the dismay of interactive television proponents, only 25% of the viewers who watched the Olympics used their remotes interactively to choose commercials.[15] On a more optimistic note, advertisers do not have to reach many homes with interactive advertising in order to be effective, because audiences will represent a more concentrated group of potential customers.

Other companies have also taken the plunge into interactive cable advertising. Chrysler has tested advertisements that allow viewers to request a longer video with more information on Chrysler cars after a regular Chrysler advertisement. These "mini-infomercials" are usually selected by consumers who are interested in purchasing a car.[16]

Zing Systems, an interactive cable-television service, is taking the process even further. It has created the "Zing Blaster," which uses part of a cable network's television signal, called the vertical blanking interval, to transmit data to a handheld device in the home. There is great potential for direct-response advertising here, because a consumer will be able to purchase products on the device immediately after seeing an ad.[17]

Although interactive television and advertising seem to be the wave of the future, extensive testing still needs to be executed to see if consumers will use this technology. David McGlade of Telecom Inc. states, "Digital technology will soon make cable the spot medium of choice among advertisers."[18] For the time being, companies are more concerned with testing consumer response than with calculating advertising's role in the interactive systems.

The Crystal Ball

As for the immediate future, the Cable Advertising Bureau predicts that local spot cable will grow faster than any other cable advertising division. David Martin, president of Penta Communication, asserts that "spot cable advertising will be the fastest growing marketing tool in the U.S. for at least the next five years."[19]

Alvin Eichoff, president of A. Eichoff and Co., foresees that longer advertisements will be available on cable. Most products could benefit from more detailed advertisements, because this additional airtime would enable advertisers to focus on several of the product's features instead of simply trying to get a viewer's attention in 30 or 60 seconds.

Cable systems will need to start adding attractive features and promoting themselves more in order to have an edge over competition from the networks.

As competition increases and technology gets more expensive, cable will have to rely more heavily on advertising revenues than on subscription fees. This makes advertising a crucial part of the cable business and will be one of the most important determining factors for cable's survival in the future.

In 1997, advertising on cable accounted for $7.6 billion out of the total $44.5 billion spent on television advertising.[20] Not only does cable represent a sizable chunk of the television total, but its current rate of growth—12% per annum, compared with 7% for all advertising, in measured media plus other types—suggests that the more buoyant prognoses in this chapter have every chance of being fulfilled.

Notes

1. T. Barton Carter, Marc A. Franklin, and Jay B. Wright, *The First Amendment and the Fifth Estate* (Westbury, NY: Foundation, 1989).

2. Timothy Hollins, *Beyond Broadcasting Into the Cable Age* (London: British Film Institute, 1984).

3. Jim Cooper, "FCC Rate Rollbacks," *Broadcasting and Cable,* April 18, 1994, 37.

4. Gary Levin and Joe Mandese, "Cable Execs Moan About FCC Action," *Mediaweek,* April 18, 1994.

5. Warren Publishing, Inc., Staff, *Television and Cable Factbook* (Washington, DC: Warren, 1993).

6. Nielsen Media Research, *1992-1993 Report on Television* (New York: Nielsen Media Research, 1993).

7. Ibid.

8. Rich Brown, "Cable Boosts Record Rating Average," *Broadcasting and Cable,* July 11, 1994, 17.

9. Warren Publishing, Inc., Staff, *Television and Cable Factbook.*

10. Ronald B. Kaatz, *Cable* (Chicago: Crain, 1982).

11. Hollins, *Beyond Broadcasting.*

12. Carrie Heeter and Bradley S. Greenberg, *Cableviewing* (Norwood, NJ: Ablex, 1988), 1-5.

13. Quoted in Nikhil Hutheesing, "Looking Forward to 500 Channels," *Forbes,* September 13, 1993, 84.

14. Quoted in ibid.

15. Debra Ano, "Ford Hits Canada's Interactive Road," *Advertising Age,* April 18, 1994, 18.

16. Barry Frankel, "Coming Soon to a Set Near You," *Advertising Age,* December 13, 1993, 28.

17. Ibid.

18. Quoted in Joe Mandese, "Reinventing Cable to Find Place on Converging Super Highway," *Advertising Age,* April 11, 1994, 94.

19. Quoted in Cooper, "FCC Rate Rollbacks."

20. "U.S. Advertising Volume," *Advertising Age,* May 18, 1998.

Part IV

Sales Promotions and Specialist Media

31

Trends in Promotions

John Philip Jones

The most significant development in the marketing of repeat-purchase packaged goods during the past two decades has probably been a budgeting change—and a very important one. There has been an internal reallocation of funds within the total budgets that manufacturers devote to advertising plus sales promotions (A&P). The proportion devoted to advertising is now much smaller than it was two decades ago, and the proportion devoted to promotions has greatly increased.

The annual data displayed in Table 31.1 start in 1976; these represent the data collected in the Annual Surveys of Promotional Practices published by the organization now known as Cox Direct. The fact that the information is collected and presented annually makes this series of surveys particularly valuable for revealing trends. Indeed, the data show some remarkable changes.

Media advertising expenditure is often referred to as *above the line* and promotions as *below the line*. Table 31.1 shows that the ratio of expenditure above the line to that below the line changed from 42:58 in 1976 to 24:76 in

TABLE 31.1 Allocation of Advertising and Promotional Budgets (in percentages)

Year	Media Advertising	Trade Promotions	Consumer Promotions
1976	42	39	19
1977	42	38	20
1978	42	36	22
1979	42	36	22
1980	43	34	23
1981	43	34	23
1982	40	36	24
1983	38	37	26
1984	35	37	28
1985	35	38	27
1986	34	40	26
1987	33	41	26
1988	32	42	25
1989	31	44	26
1990	28	47	25
1991	25	48	27
1992	25	48	27
1993	24	49	27
1994	25	49	26
1995	24	51	25
1996	24	50	26

1996. This change in relative shares accounts for increases and decreases in budgets for these two activities that amount to tens of billions of dollars.

In Chapter 1 of this volume, I describe the trends in aggregate advertising expenditure in the United States. The relatively modest changes that are seen in that introductory chapter should be considered alongside the huge increases in sales promotional dollars. Sales promotions—especially trade promotions—accounted for the major growth in A&P dollars from the late 1970s until the early 1990s. The importance of sales promotions, both in their absolute size and in their share of total A&P, is even greater than is indicated by the dollar figures alone. Promotions have a seriously negative influence on manufacturers' profitability, the reasons for which I discuss in Chapter 37 of this volume. They therefore have ill effects on those manufacturers who indulge in them to an extreme degree.

Table 31.1 shows that manufacturers' relative allocations to media advertising, trade promotions, and consumer promotions have been stabilizing during the past 6 years. The main shifts from advertising to promotions had taken place during the period 1978 through 1991. There were four reasons for these shifts:

1. The inflation of the 1970s left a legacy in manufacturers' pricing policies. Manufacturers got into the habit of boosting their list prices and at the same time making deep tactical price reductions by boosting substantially both their trade and consumer promotions.[1] These are in effect a sacrifice of income rather than a positive expenditure aimed at building brands; it is not surprising therefore that they have no long-term positive effect on the strength of brands.
2. The growing muscle and bargaining power of regional retail chains in the food and drug trades have forced manufacturers to discount increasingly heavily.[2]
3. Throughout all types of business there has been a continuous emphasis on short-term management performance—for example, by measuring quarterly profitability. This is again a legacy of inflationary market conditions. The sales volume generated by sales promotions is invariably easier to measure than the volume generated by advertising, and this has naturally stimulated a siphoning of funds from above the line to below the line.
4. There has been increasing competitive pressure in all product categories, and this has forced manufacturers to follow their competitors in all types of marketing activity. As soon as a leading manufacturer increases promotions, this begins a trend that spreads like a forest fire.

The overall split of funds, which is almost three to one in favor of promotions, seriously depresses brand profitability. This is why most marketing companies probably welcomed the arresting of the trend from above to below the line that took place after 1991. The strategy of *everyday low pricing* (EDLP), pioneered by Procter & Gamble, influenced this. EDLP, which has been partially although not totally successful, is based on a reduction in a manufacturer's list prices. This is accompanied by a significant pulling back in its promotions of all types, together with a costly effort funded by the manufacturer to reduce the size of retailers' stocks of the manufacturer's product lines, to save the retailers the capital tied up in large inventories.

The most recent report from Cox Direct is the 19th in the series.[3] It is based on data from 30 major manufacturing companies, almost half of them with a sales volume in excess of $1 billion, plus data from 35 major grocery retailers and 761 consumers.

The Cox Direct 19th Annual Survey of Promotional Practices contains a large amount of data, and the Cox reports publish information in most cases on a uniform basis year after year. The following is a summary of the most important additional information about promotional activity relating to 1996:

1. Manufacturers are on balance optimistic that media advertising will increase in the medium term. They are less optimistic about growth of consumer promotions and a good deal less optimistic about increases in trade promotions.

2. The fact that 39% of manufacturers' media weight is designed to support consumer and/or trade promotional objectives as well as brand equity emphasizes the growing importance of integrated marketing communications.

3. Some 87% of consumers used a grocery or health and beauty care (HBC) coupon during the previous 6 months. Sunday newspaper freestanding inserts and direct mail are the coupon sources most preferred by consumers—by 65% and 56%, respectively.

4. Most product samples (80%) were received in the mail. Among consumers, 47% strongly agreed that "they would consider switching brands if they like the free sample," and 42% strongly agreed that "they often become aware of new or improved products through samples or coupons."

5. Most consumers (76%) received the majority of their information about new grocery/ HBC products, product usage, or recipes from the mail or newspapers. These media are also the leading sources of product information preferred by 6 out of 10 consumers.

6. The most popular feature of consumers' favorite supermarkets remains product pricing, with "specials on different items each week" (82%) the most popular feature, followed by "low prices on all items every day" (55%).

7. Almost two-thirds of the manufacturers responding have a Web page, and the rest are considering establishing one. Four-fifths of the manufacturers involved in the World Wide Web/Internet use on-line marketing to provide company/product information.

8. Two-thirds of consumers belong to supermarket savings clubs, and more than half rank their experience with these programs beneficial.

Notes

1. T. W. Wilson, Jr., *Achieving a Sustainable Competitive Advantage* (New York: Association of National Advertisers, 1982). See also Nancy Koch, *The Changing Marketplace Ahead and Implications for Advertisers* (New York: Association of National Advertisers, 1983).

2. Don E. Schultz and Robert D. Dewar, "Retailers in Control: The Impact of Retail Trade Concentration," *Journal of Consumer Marketing,* vol. 1, no. 2, 1983-1984, 81-89.

3. Cox Direct, *Navigate the Promotional Universe: Cox Direct 19th Annual Survey of Promotional Practices* (Largo, FL: Cox Direct, 1997).

Integrated Marketing Communications and How It Relates to Traditional Media Advertising

Don E. Schultz

O ver the past several years, a new concept in persuasive communications has developed. In North and South America, Asia, and Australia, it is called *integrated marketing communications* (or *IMC*). In Europe, it is often referred to as *through-the-line*. Depending on one's view, IMC can be described as (a) the natural evolution of mass-market media advertising, (b) a concept that has always been practiced by some advertisers and their agencies, (c) a major threat to traditional mass-market media advertising, (d) all of the above, or (e) none of the above. In this chapter, I describe the concept of integrated marketing communications and explain how it differs from traditional mass-market advertising as practiced by some major marketing organizations and their agencies. I then discuss some of the impacts IMC will likely have on established advertising and media institutions. Finally, I offer some speculation about how IMC might develop in the next few years.

Just What Is Integrated Marketing Communications?

As I will explain in the following sections, integrated marketing communications is a different communications development process from the one traditionally used by major media advertisers. It is a planning approach that attempts to coordinate, consolidate, and bring together all the communications messages, programs, and vehicles that affect customers, consumers, or prospects for a manufacturer or service organization's brands. When viewed in this way, IMC might seem somewhat silly. Why would any marketer consciously try not to coordinate or consolidate or integrate his or her marketing messages? Why would the marketer want to have consumers or customers or prospects confused by a barrage of unrelated or uncoordinated messages about the product or service? Therefore, why all the fuss about IMC?

The reason is simple. For the most part, advertising, which once was the dominant form of communication between the marketer and the consumer, is rapidly being diffused into a variety of subcategories, such as sales promotion, public relations, direct marketing, events, and packaging. As these specialties have developed and grown in importance in the marketer's communication mix over the past few years, there has been a natural inclination for the functional specialists—that is, those who are in charge of developing and implementing these programs and activities—to focus on their individual communication specialties, often to the overall detriment of the brand or organization's communication program. So, whereas there has been no conscious disintegration of the organization's marketing communications messages, there has been a natural drift to less integrated, less coordinated, and less concentrated messages and programs. This has been particularly true in the consumer product areas as marketers have moved their funds from brand-only media advertising, to various forms of communication in support of or in combination with local retailers and distributors.

In addition, as technology has been introduced in the marketplace, more and more media and message delivery channels and alternatives have become available to the marketer. So, rather than having access to only 3 television networks and perhaps 5 or 6 television stations in a market, today the advertiser can select from among 40 to 50 cable channels, 20 to 30 radio stations, and myriad newspapers, magazines, and other print media vehicles. So, from the point of view of the marketer, as funds become more scarce, competitors more aggressive, media alternatives more plentiful, and the new products and new distribution channels more available, the need to integrate the various forms of marketing communication used to reach the consumer has become greater.

The problem is that developing integrated marketing communications programs is not that easy. In many cases, the concept of IMC is in direct conflict with the way marketing, marketing communications, and, indeed, traditional media advertising have generally been practiced over the past 50 years or so. It is useful therefore to look at how advertising has traditionally been developed and how that contrasts with the newer concepts of integrated marketing communications.

How Advertising Is Planned and Implemented

For the most part, today's advertising is the result of an economic system that was based on mass production, mass marketing, mass communication, and, indeed, mass advertising. How the business of advertising is generally practiced today is illustrated as "historical marketing" in the bottom left quadrant of Figure 32.1.

As shown, historical marketing, which made substantial use of mass-media advertising, relied on a single message being delivered through mass-media vehicles to an undifferentiated audience. Because the advertiser knew so little about the consumer and relied primarily on the mass media, undifferentiated investments were made in media and marketing activities—that is, the marketer generally spent as much trying to reach nonprospects as true prospects for the product or service. The problem was, the media could not differentiate a good prospect from a nonprospect for the advertiser, so they delivered everyone who was available. The marketer talked to all of them at the same time and in the same way. Thus the advertiser assumed most of the consumers in the marketplace were a homogeneous mass or at least had enough common interests, wants, and needs that marketing could be done on the averages. That

Figure 32.1. New Marketing

has been the marketing approach and the advertising method of choice for most organizations since World War II.

The other reason marketers used this mass approach to advertising was that, historically, they have known more about their products and media delivery systems than they have about their actual customers. The advertiser, therefore, gained some level of confidence in purchasing network television time that supposedly reached 50%+ of the total population of the country even though little was known about who was in the audience and whether or not they were logical or legitimate prospects for the product or service being advertised. Even today, advertisers have only the grossest knowledge of the media audience, relying primarily on such identifiers as demographics (age, sex, education, income, and the like) and where, geographically, the audience resides. As a result, a tradition of advertising development evolved that always sought to find the common denominator that would appeal to the greatest potential audience at the lowest possible cost. The focus of traditional advertising, because so little was known about customers and prospects, was on message delivery efficiency rather than on communication effectiveness. And because so little was known, or for that matter is known today, about how advertising really works, the emphasis has been on delivering a sales message (which the advertiser believed to be persuasive) at the lowest possible cost.

Technology, however, has changed in the marketplace. Today, most retailers and a growing number of advertisers have a great deal of information on who buys their products, where they buy them, the prices paid, how often particular products are purchased, and the like. So, as information on the customer and consumer has grown, the emphasis has shifted from mass marketing and mass advertising to individualized or customized marketing and specific or targeted advertising and communication. This is shown in the box in the upper right-hand quadrant of Figure 32.1, which is labeled "new marketing." As the need for more targeted and more directly related and relatable advertising messages has grown, this has naturally had an impact on the demand for traditional mass-media advertising.

As the ability of the advertiser to identify customers and their purchases has increased, so has the desire on the part of the advertiser to send specific messages to selected groups of customers rather than to the mass. This has led to the concept of differentiated marketing communications investments, or marketing on the differences rather than marketing on the averages. Thus the advertiser wants to spend more money against good customers and prospects than on those who are unknown or may be less important. All this has dictated a change from traditional mass-market and mass-media advertising to the more strategic, targeted approach known as IMC. For many organizations, targeting means developing a new method of creating and delivering persuasive messages and incentives to customers and prospects. Integrated marketing communications is one way to move from mass to targeted communications programs.

Enter Integrated Marketing Communications

The major difference between traditional advertising and integrated marketing communications is the conceptual methodology that is used in the initial planning process. In traditional advertising development, because so little was known about the customer or the prospect, the focus naturally fell on the product or the service to be advertised. Tell the product story well enough, to enough people, enough times, and there would be some buyers. That was the philosophy of the old-line, traditional advertiser. It remains the approach used by many mass marketers today.

Advertisers who use this approach plan and execute their advertising programs "from the inside out." That is, as marketing organizations, they determine what products or services they want to make and sell. They do the financial calculations that are necessary to provide a profit to the organization, then they set the sales objectives and go to market. Advertising is used to "sell" the products the company has made, it is hoped at a profit. The goal is to find prospects in the maze of markets and audiences through the use of broadscale message distribution or mass advertising.

With the additional information now available to the marketing organization as a result of research—individual- and scanner-based purchasing information and the like—the marketer now truly knows who the customer is or who the prospects might be. Given this type of information, the need for traditional, mass-media, mass-market advertising to prospect for or influence a limited number of prospects in a very large media audience pool is no longer very relevant or very cost-effective. Today, there is a better way. That better way comes in various forms of database marketing, which provides the platform for the IMC approach.

Enter the Database

Many marketing organizations have developed or are in the process of developing databases containing information on their customers and prospects. These electronic storage systems provide marketers with the opportunity to identify, often at the household level, who buys what products or services, when they buy, how much they buy, where they purchase, and the like. Thus, where once the advertiser had to advertise in mass media and simply hope to reach some customers or prospects, today many organizations know who their customers are. They want to speak directly with them to reinforce their conviction to keep purchasing their products, or to influence those who don't purchase to switch from another brand. With the knowledge of customers and prospects that the database provides, the advertiser can move from "inside-out" or product-driven advertising to "outside-in" or customer-driven communications programs. Where traditionally advertising was used to speak to everyone at the same time with the same message, today integrated forms of marketing communications are used to influence specific groups of people about specific products or services, with specific marketing communications activities and programs, including tactics such as sales promotion, direct marketing, public relations, events and activities, and even in-store merchandising. The IMC approach is, therefore, the more targeted, accountable, generally measurable approach for delivering persuasive messages and incentives to customers. This is what is really changing the face of traditional mass-media advertising.

How Does IMC Work?

There are many approaches to integrated marketing communications. The one described below, which is the most public and well-developed concept of IMC, has been developed by the faculty at the Medill School of Journalism at Northwestern University. It has been accepted and is being implemented by a number of marketing organizations, agencies, and media organizations around the world.

The basic element in the Northwestern approach to IMC is the database. This approach assumes that the marketing organization has some level of knowledge about its customers, prospects, or potential prospects stored in some kind of electronic, accessible system. Increasingly this is the case. For example, many organizations have proprietary information about their customers that they have gathered over time. In addition, there are a number of research and service organizations that are developing information about each household in the United States, in some cases down to the level of brand purchased in a product category. Extensive internal databases are just now being developed by some organizations, but almost all marketers in North America and Europe can increasingly make use of some type of external database.

With the availability of a database, the IMC process starts first with an understanding of the customers or prospects for the marketing organization's products or services. Where traditional advertising development relied on consumer attitudes for market identification and segmentation, the IMC approach relies primarily on actual consumer behavior, generally in the form of proven purchases of various products or services. In the IMC approach, what consumers do in the marketplace is more important and more valuable than how they feel or say they feel. Traditional mass-media advertising development has been based on the premise that attitudes lead to behavior. Therefore, if advertising can influence attitudes, then behavior or sales should follow. Although this "attitude-to-behavior" process may occur in some instances, there is little research evidence that it is widespread enough to support current advertising development approaches. In contrast, in the IMC process, the focus is on the behavior consumers have exhibited in the past. The IMC process is designed to help the marketer understand and explain that behavior. This then leads the IMC planner to develop communications approaches that will either confirm or alter that behavior in the future. These three basic elements really differentiate IMC from traditional advertising development approaches:

1. A segmented or individualized understanding of customer groups available through a database rather than a mass-market, mass-communication, mass-advertising approach
2. An outside-in view of the consumer marketplace rather than the traditional inside-out, product-oriented approach to advertising development
3. A focus on explanation of past behavior rather than on the assumption that changing attitudes can lead to changing behavior

Figure 32.2 illustrates the Northwestern University IMC process. Because my goal in this chapter is to provide an understanding of IMC, and not necessarily an explanation of how to practice the process, my description of this figure will be brief. It should, however, indicate what IMC is all about. As noted earlier, the IMC process starts with a database. Using that database of customer and prospect information, the IMC planner develops some type of behavioral segmentation scheme. In this illustration, the behavior used is past brand purchases. Knowing the past behavior, the planner then has the goal of understanding that behavior. Knowledge of how the consumer thinks about the brand or product and what contact the consumer has had with the brand in terms of advertising, sales promotion, public relations, and the like helps the planner to gain that understanding.

By understanding what supports the consumer's purchase behavior, the IMC planner can then develop specific marketing objectives. For example, in the case of the loyal brand purchaser, only two alternatives are possible: (a) to maintain current use of the product or service or (b) to increase usage. Once that decision is made, the IMC planner then determines how the consumer's

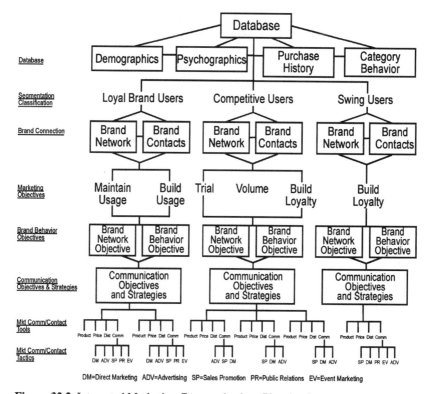

Figure 32.2. Integrated Marketing Communications Planning Process
NOTE: DM = direct marketing; ADV = advertising; SP = sales promotion; PR = public relations; EV = event marketing.

consideration of the brand must be either changed or reinforced to achieve that goal. Thus specific behavioral objectives are set. That leads to the communication objectives and strategies that will be used to generate those mental considerations and influence actual consumer behavior.

From this point, the IMC process is fairly traditional. Marketing elements are then determined that will help achieve the behavioral objectives, and the actual communication techniques (advertising, public relations, events, sales promotions, and the like) are selected to deliver those messages and incentives to the consumer.

As can be seen from this process, the IMC approach focuses first on the consumers. The IMC planner then tries to understand why consumers are behaving as they do and develops communication plans designed to influence or change that behavior. It is this outside-in planning that really differentiates IMC from the traditional mass-media advertising approaches in use today.

The Impact of IMC on
Traditional Advertising Activities

If IMC is so dramatically different from traditional forms of mass-media advertising, what impact will the acceptance of these concepts have on the traditional advertising business? Four major groups that are likely to be affected are marketing organizations, advertising agencies, advertising media organizations, and advertising support organizations.

Marketing Organizations

The chief group that will be affected by the acceptance of the IMC approach will be marketing organizations and those who develop the present mass-media advertising programs. For the most part, consumer product companies are organized along brand management lines. Everything is based on the products or the brands the organizations sell. That is what creates the inside-out planning process that most consumer product organizations use.

If, indeed, the consumer or customer or prospect becomes the focal point of the organization, this changes not only the internal organization of the marketing company but the way it does business as well. An IMC approach moves the objectives of the marketer from the number of units sold and share of market achieved, to considering what share of customer requirements are being fulfilled and the income flow from those customers that results from those purchases. In other words, it turns the marketing organization upside down. The organizational focus is now on customers, customer relationships, customer retention, and customer satisfaction as the key elements of success rather than focus on the product, economies of scale, channel logistics, number of units of the product sold, and share of market achieved. Thus the growth and acceptance of IMC will have and is having a dramatic impact on marketing organizations.

Advertising Agencies

Traditionally, advertising agencies have provided most of the outside guidance and counsel to marketing organizations. As the focus has shifted from advertising to other forms of marketing communications, such as sales promotions, direct marketing, and public relations, advertising agencies have become a less important factor in the planning and implementation of the overall communications of marketing organizations—and they will continue to become less and less important, unless they are able to change dramatically.

For advertising agencies to succeed in the future, they must move from being primarily developers and placers of mass-media advertising to being providers of counsel and guidance to marketing organizations in the whole realm of communication alternatives. By focusing only on media advertising, advertising agencies relegate themselves to the role of minor player in IMC programs of the future.

Advertising Media Organizations

Traditional advertising media in the United States have been developed primarily to provide mass marketers with mass-message distribution vehicles. As advertisers learn more about their customers through the use of databases and other research techniques, there will be declining interest in using these broadscale media, which have such inherent waste in their coverage. It is likely that the traditional mass media, such as television, newspapers, and national magazines, will be the ones hurt most by the move to IMC. More targeted methods and vehicles, such as cable television, direct mail, in-store merchandising, telemarketing, and targeted magazines, will likely grow in importance.

Advertising Support Organizations

All those organizations that have been created to assist and support the use of mass media and mass advertising will feel the impacts of the growth of IMC as well. For example, advertising research organizations, production houses, and audience and market measurement groups will be affected. The move to IMC, with its focus on measurable results among identified persons and households, will take its toll on organizations that give only estimates and guesses of audiences, advertising results, and the like.

With this overview of IMC, we can now move to discussion of the development of IMC programs—that is, how they are likely to develop in the next few years.

The Development of Integrated Marketing Communications

Although IMC has been discussed in some detail over the past several years, few organizations are practicing it as it has been described above. The reason is simple: IMC represents a major change in an established industry, and such systemic changes take time. There is great resistance to change in most marketing organizations. They have been too successful in the past. But they must change, and when they do, advertising agencies, the media, and the supporting organizations will change as well.

Who is likely to adopt IMC most rapidly? For the most part, that question has already been answered. IMC, like all major changes, is adopted by those organizations that face the greatest dislocations unless they are able to change. Today, that means, for the most part, those organizations that find themselves in declining-margin businesses with major, global competition, severe price pressure, and in industries or categories where there is an excess of supply compared with demand. That is already evident in such industries as airlines, computers, and consumer electronics; automobile manufacture; some areas of retailing; the hospitality industry, which includes hotels, resorts, and conference centers; and many other product categories that have increasingly become commoditized.

How will IMC programs develop? They will start initially with organizations developing databases of some type. From there, organizational planning will change from determining attitudes to identifying behaviors. That will provide new forms of market segmentation, which in turn will encourage the consideration of new types of media and message delivery systems that customers use or attend to. At this point, integration will usually become a well-accepted concept, and one that is easily and quickly adopted. We already see this sort of diffusion of the integrated approach occurring in organizations such as American and United Airlines; Hyatt, Sheraton, and Hilton Hotels; Dell and Gateway 2000 computers; Talbots, Nordstrom, and Toys "R" Us in

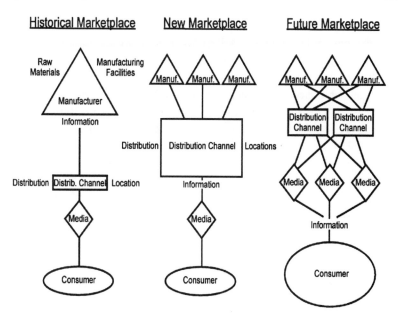

Figure 32.3. The New Information Power Paradigm

retailing; and Philip Morris and R. J. Reynolds in tobacco marketing. Others cannot be far behind.

Conclusion

Just what is integrated marketing communications? From the descriptions and explanation just offered, it appears to be the natural evolution of traditional mass-media advertising, which has been changed, adjusted, and refined as a result of new technology. It is hard to dispute that view. If advertisers had access to information about customer purchases 50 years ago, it is unlikely that mass-media advertising would have developed as it did. Technology has made IMC possible and has made more traditional advertising less viable and certainly less supportable from the view of marketing organizations.

More broadly speaking, what impacts will the advent of IMC have on the rest of us? There seems to be little question that it will change the direction of persuasive information. Where traditionally advertising messages have flowed from the marketer to the consumer or prospect, with the advent of two-way communications technology (such as is illustrated in Figure 32.3) and an integrated approach to marketing and marketing communications, traditional advertising media vehicles will come under tremendous pressure. The "free or almost free" mass media, such as newspapers, over-the-air broadcast, and even magazines, will find themselves with declining advertising revenues, which likely will have to be made up by the subscriber or reader or listener or viewer.

As advertisers become more sophisticated in their knowledge of their customers and prospects, they will become less interested in large circulations or ratings and more interested in quality and identification of the audience. This will dramatically change the way communication takes place around the world and how information is distributed. Will this be a problem? It could and likely will be.

So, as seen here, integrated marketing communications is a two-edged sword. It provides substantial marketing efficiencies to the marketing organization, but it will very possibly reduce the availability of subsidized or free mass media to the general population. Is that good or bad? Only time will tell. But IMC is not just coming—it is here. The changes it will bring will most likely be significant.

Integrated Marketing
Communications
in Practice

John Deighton

A well-integrated marketing communications campaign might be compared to a swan gliding across a lake: The observable grace gives little hint of the furious activity beneath the surface. In this chapter, I address integration both above and beneath the surface, using examples of integration in practice to show, on one hand, the fluid appearance that a well-integrated communications campaign presents to the observer and, on the other hand, the subsurface mechanics that sustain the illusion of fluidity. My emphasis here is on practice, and I draw on cases that illustrate how a number of communication tools have been made to work together to achieve some overarching communication mission. In selecting these cases for depiction and discussion, I had, of course, a more theoretical, less merely descriptive, underlying conception of the nature of integration; this needs to be stated at the outset so that readers can decide whether they share with me the same sense of what is meant by *integration.*

In any field of endeavor, the need for integration arises whenever cooperation must occur across boundaries. The need is most pressing when the boundaries are most robust, marking out areas of specialization that the actors want to preserve. In such cases it is naive to wish the boundaries away; indeed, the boundaries may be doing useful work, helping the specialists to focus their energies on tasks of manageable proportions. Instead of eliminating boundaries, the strategy of integration is to create cross-border communication conduits and incentives to use them. The specialists are given methods and incentives to make design trade-offs between the goals of the specialists' bounded regions of expertise and the goals of the larger system. What are the relevant boundaries in marketing communications, and how are the boundaries transcended by integration?

The first relevant boundary is that between one communication specialty and another. Most marketing problems are solved with a combination of tools, even if the blending is no more complex than synchronizing advertising with consumer promotion schedules. Thus integration can be defined, minimally, as integration across communication tools. The second boundary is the line that separates one target audience from another. It is organizationally easy to plan for an end consumer target market separate from, for example, a distribution channel market, yet each is an element in the system to be optimized. Integration means, therefore, integration of messages to distinct audiences. Third, a boundary exists between a target audience at one time and that same audience at another. It is organizationally attractive to mount a communication program to create awareness, separate from one to create trial, yet the communicator's bottom line is to move audiences all the way through the adoption process. In this sense, integrated campaigns can be defined as campaigns that stay with their audiences over time, explicitly moving them across the temporal boundaries that separate one stage from another.

Three stories of integration follow. One is long and the other two brief, serving to illustrate how these three features—integration across tools, audiences, and time—have been achieved in practice. In the conclusion to this chapter I repeat these themes and list the defining features of good integration.

The Tylenol Poisoning Recovery

On September 30, 1982, news media announced an apparent link between Tylenol and the deaths of several people in suburbs of Chicago. Within days it became clear that seven people had died, killed by capsules of Tylenol that had been contaminated with cyanide. Immediately the brand's share of the U.S. analgesic market fell, from 37% to almost zero. Many observers felt the brand was damaged beyond repair. Jerry Della Femina, chairman of a prominent advertising agency, commented, "You'll not see the name Tylenol in any form within a year." Within 4 months, however, the brand was almost fully recovered. The product had been relaunched and sales were within 80% of their level before the poisonings.

Here, then, is a compelling example of a communication program integrated across tools, across audiences, and, most impressively, across time. With respect to tools, the brand had been saved by a blend of advertising, public relations, couponing, sampling, trade promotion, and channel management. With respect to audiences, the program addressed users, the retail trade, medical practitioners, and hospitals. Precise integration across time was needed to manage the pattern of consumer concerns that unfolded over the 4 months of the crisis. So effective was this temporal integration that no competitor had time to secure any advantage from Tylenol's misfortune before the window of vulnerability had been closed. Over the 4 months of the crisis, consumer involvement moved from low to very high and back to relatively low. Consumer attitudes moved from bewilderment and fear to an informed aversion to the brand, and ultimately to a return to confidence and trust. Trade attitudes also moved sharply. Marketing tools were employed in a particular sequence. It can be speculated that the sequence was in part a response to and in part a cause of the patterns of involvement and attitude change, and the pattern was crucial to the brand's recovery.

Figure 33.1 indicates how Tylenol's market share moved during this 4-month period and highlights the important management actions. The period in which the recovery process took place can be divided into seven stages (as shown in Figure 33.2). Each episode had its own constellation of beliefs, feelings, and behavior on the part of consumers and the distribution channels. Each posed a discrete set of communication problems, and each transition also had to be managed.[1]

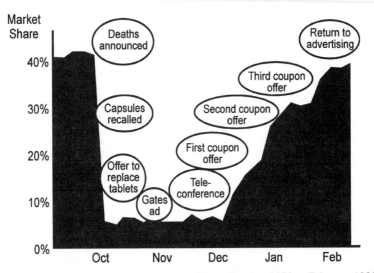

Figure 33.1. Movement in Tylenol's Market Share, October 1982 to February 1983

Stage 1: Habit

In 1982, Tylenol, manufactured by Johnson & Johnson (J&J), was the largest single brand in the U.S. health and beauty category. It was to be found in the homes and offices of 100 million Americans. Worldwide ex-factory sales approached $500 million. Advertising support in the United States ran at $40 million that year, some 30% of all analgesic advertising. The brand's image rested on two claims: trust ("Trust Tylenol—hospitals do") and potency ("The most potent pain reliever you can buy without a prescription"). Perhaps the most important feature of consumers' beliefs was what they did not know—that the active ingredient in Tylenol is acetaminophen, which is available from competing brands and often available at lower cost. The name Tylenol was the only name consumers knew for nonaspirin pain relief. They bought it routinely, the trade stocked it routinely, and no one had a strong incentive to behave differently.

Stage 2: Turmoil

The week that followed the September 30 press reports of cyanide poisonings was a period of confusion and fear for consumers. Reports (later proved false) implicated Tylenol in deaths in Texas, Pennsylvania, California, Tennessee, and Kansas. Eyedrops contaminated with sulfuric acid were reported in California. Many towns and suburbs called off Halloween celebrations for fear of copycat poisonings of "trick-or-treat" candy.

Johnson & Johnson was active on many fronts in the first week. The company issued a worldwide alert to the medical community, set up a 24-hour toll-free telephone service, recalled and analyzed sample batches of the product from around the country, briefed the Food and Drug Administration, and publicized a $100,000 reward offer. All broadcast advertising was immediately pulled, and all print advertising not already in production was withdrawn. All Tylenol products were off the shelves of Chicago stores by October 4, and on October 6 a telex message announced a nationwide recall of capsules to 11,000 retailers and distributors. Senior company officers made themselves available to the media to explain what they knew of the disaster and what they were planning to do. The company hired Burke Marketing Research to track attitudes among consumers of analgesics. The firm interviewed 1,000 people weekly, and in addition A. C. Nielsen's Scantrack monitored supermarket sales in four U.S. markets.

During the first week, in summary, the company's communication goals were to reduce the visibility of the Tylenol brand and increase the visibility of the firm. It mobilized many tools—public relations, the sales force, telemarketing, market research, and advertising media services—to transform a low-involvement, brand-based media presence into a high-involvement personalized corporate presence.

Stage 3: Reinterpretation

By the second week, research was showing that consumers understood the facts of the crisis relatively clearly, and a migration to the next stage of the communication cycle was possible. The challenge to Johnson & Johnson for the next 6 weeks would be to manage how consumers and the retail trade interpreted the hiatus that would result from Tylenol's withdrawal from the market. Burke's research showed that awareness of the poisonings was almost universal, that consumers understood that the problem was confined to capsules, and that they attached no blame to the maker. In terms of consumer beliefs and emotions, therefore, recovery of the brand seemed worth attempting (see Table 33.1).

TABLE 33.1 Public Knowledge of the Tylenol Tragedy (in percentages)

Knowledge of Tylenol tragedy	95
Problem involves Tylenol capsules exclusively	90
Problem could occur for any capsules	93
Maker not to blame	90

The first concern management faced was behavioral. Many capsule users had disposed of their capsules in the week of the poisoning, and Tylenol users had begun to buy competitors' brands. Branded and unbranded aspirin accounted for most of the replacement purchases, with Bayer the main beneficiary. Unit sales of analgesics in Chicago rose 20% above normal for the 3 weeks following the poisoning, in response to home inventory replenishment.

There was concern, too, about consumers' emotional interpretation of the events. Although consumers had accepted as a matter of fact that Johnson & Johnson was innocent of culpability in the disaster, the company could not be sure that the belief would inevitably evolve into a feeling of sympathy and an appreciation of the company as a victim. There was concern, too, about how consumers would interpret their own actions in abandoning the Tylenol brand. Where a purchase of a competitive brand had occurred, the consumer could choose to interpret it as a stopgap action or as the start of a new pattern of loyalty. Would consumers start to look for nonaspirin brands and decide that Tylenol was not materially different from its acetaminophen competitors?

Management's communication goals during this stage were to discourage consideration of competitive brands, to encourage use of Tylenol in tablet form, and to defend the Tylenol brand equity by convincing consumers they could continue to trust Tylenol. Management therefore mounted several initiatives. The first element was a capsule exchange offer. On October 12, half-page press announcements appeared in 150 major markets, stating: "We want you to replace your Tylenol capsules with Tylenol tablets. And we'll help you do it at our expense." They invited the public to mail in bottles of capsules and receive tablets in exchange.

The second component was a brief but intensive television announcement. It ran from October 24 to October 28 and reached 85% of the market four times in that period. It featured Dr. Thomas N. Gates, the company's medical director, as spokesperson, because he rated well on credibility in pretesting. The form of this advertising was quite different from the two campaigns that had built the brand's reputation, but the theme of trust was reinforced. His message read:

> You're all aware of recent tragic events in which Extra Strength Tylenol capsules were criminally tampered with in limited areas after they left our factory. This act damages all of us. . . . We have voluntarily withdrawn all Tylenol Capsules. . . . we urge all Tylenol capsule users to use the tablet form. . . . Tylenol has had the trust of the medical profession and 100 million Americans for over 20 years. We value that trust too much to let any individual tamper with it.

Burke's tracking studies indicated that "intention to purchase" Tylenol rose from 62% on October 22 to 74% on October 28. Although actual sales continued to languish, the company was reassured that the recovery was proceeding satisfactorily. In a third component of the interim campaign, the company intensified the visibility of senior management on television. Chairman James Burke appeared on *Donahue, Good Morning America,* and other television interview shows, and was interviewed on radio and by newspapers.

The fourth part of the campaign targeted the trade. Withdrawal of all capsule products had imperiled the brand's ability to command shelf space. The company used its sales force to keep the retail trade informed of developments and to maintain and if possible increase displays of its tablet form.

Competition, by this time, had begun to pursue share aggressively. Analgesic advertising expenditure rose 50% above normal in the final quarter of 1982 despite Tylenol's withdrawal. Acetaminophen brands increased unit sales from a 5% share to an 11% share in this period, although more of the share given up by Tylenol went to aspirin brands. Bayer sales rose 50% in October. American Home Products announced "unprecedented demand" for Anacin-3 and reported that production had increased from two shifts to three. The company's advertising copy emphasized the product's likeness to Tylenol: "Like Tylenol, Anacin-3 is aspirin-free." Bristol-Myers began to recommend: "Ask your doctor about Datril." Aspirin pain relievers used copy that stressed safety. Bayer's television commercials said, "At Bayer, we take care. . . . and we've been doing that for over 25 years." The product was given a slick coating to make it as easy to swallow as a capsule.

Stage 4: Preannouncement

Six weeks after the poisonings, the J&J management was ready to commit to a plan for relaunching. The communication strategy shifted from managing a period of inactivity to building a climate of anticipation.

Although it needed 4 more weeks to complete manufacture and trade stocking, Johnson & Johnson chose an early preannouncement. On November 11, the company chairman spoke live at a satellite-linked teleconference to 600 news reporters across the United States. His announcement of the triple-sealed capsule pack was carried prominently in news media throughout the country. Burke monitored the effect of this announcement carefully. A telephone survey over the next 5 days found that 79% of Tylenol users were aware of the new packaging and that 72% could name one or more specific elements of that packaging. Among former users, 95% expressed an intention to return to capsules in tamper-resistant packaging. Encouraged by these data, management called off plans to use a second commercial featuring Dr. Gates to announce the new tamper-proof packaging on television. The sales force carried this information to the retail trade and secured advance commitments to purchase capsules in the new pack.

Stage 5: Trial

By the end of November stocks of the new pack were in stores. The communication goal now was to induce consumers to try it. Management debated several methods of building trial: sampling in homes, sampling in stores, and couponing by mail or in magazines or newspapers. Coupons redeemable in stores were considerably more expensive than home-delivered samples, because a full retail margin was paid on each redemption. They did, however, ensure that retailers would carry shelf stocks, and consumers would have to make some act of commitment to the brand to secure their samples.

Management therefore launched on November 28 the largest program of couponing in commercial history. The first wave used Sunday newspapers nationwide to distribute 60 million coupons for a free Tylenol product to a limit of $2.50 each. Another 20 million coupons were offered the following Sunday. Samples distributed in this way began to appear in the company's audits of retail sales in four test cities. Share at retail rose by more than 10 share points, to within 6 points of predisaster levels. Management knew, however, that this performance needed support if it was to survive the end of couponing.

Stage 6: Restoration of Preexisting Attitudes

At the end of December 1982, sales promotion had worked well to return previous users of Tylenol to the brand, but it was extremely expensive.

Redemption by December stood at 30% of all coupons issued, which generated a charge of $45 million to the brand's budget. A less expensive communications tool was needed to consolidate the recovery.

Although couponing had reestablished consumer purchase patterns, there was a need to restore consumer attitudes and emotions. Consumers could interpret their own behavior in buying the brand with a full-value coupon either as a return to loyalty or as mere opportunism. Here, as in stage 3, management sought to support the interpretation most favorable to the brand. This task of influencing interpretations was one appropriate to advertising. The only television advertising for Tylenol in the 3 months since the poisonings had been the 4-day announcement featuring Dr. Gates. While the coupon effort had been supported with newspaper feature advertising by retailers, management had suspended the low-involvement advertising themes that had been part of Tylenol's marketing program in the past, for the obvious reason that Tylenol had ceased to be a low-involvement issue. An implied message in the return to advertising would be that the situation had returned to normal.

In this phase, therefore, advertising was exposed with the look and feel of precrisis advertising. The themes of trust and potency were reintroduced. To encourage repurchase, coupons were distributed with face values first of a dollar and later 50 cents. Trade promotions were mounted with the objective of rebuilding stock levels and store displays. The character of marketing communications was almost indistinguishable from the precrisis blend.

Stage 7: Habit

By the start of February 1983, 4 months after the first report of the poisonings, Johnson & Johnson's management had effectively disposed of the threat to the brand. Tylenol's share of analgesic market revenues was 35%, two share points below precrisis levels. Sales of the capsule form were at 85%, and the tablet at 105% of previous levels. No competitive product had made any permanent share gain. Whereas the absolute level of marketing expenditures was higher than for the same period a year before, the marketing mix was not materially different.

The Tylenol story has been told here as a story of a multiplicity of actions achieving an integrated impact that carried the consumer through six transitions in behavior, belief, and emotion, all within 4 months. Figure 33.2 presents the sequence as it might have been experienced by a hypothetical consumer. It shows that the consumer moves through successive stages tracked by market research, and that at each transition, management antici-

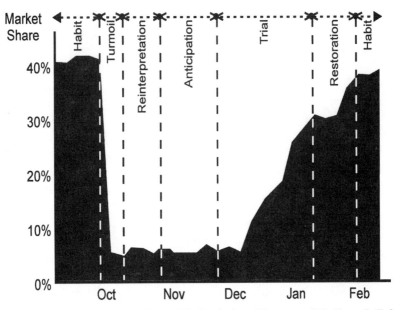

Figure 33.2. Tylenol Recovery Stages: The Evolution of Consumers' Feelings, Beliefs, and Behavior

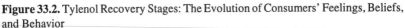

pates problems and limits options by deploying the appropriate marketing tools.

The total Tylenol plan is summarized in Figure 33.3. The various communications disciplines are seen to be coordinated and phased as part of a single integrated plan.

The Launch of Acuvue Disposable Contact Lenses

The launch of Acuvue disposable contact lenses by Johnson & Johnson, like the Tylenol recovery, illustrates communications integration as the phased deployment of multiple communication tools. Unlike the first case, coordination is achieved here with the use of an electronic customer database.

J&J anticipated that the window of opportunity within which to establish its foothold in the contact lens market would be narrow. The firm had no prior

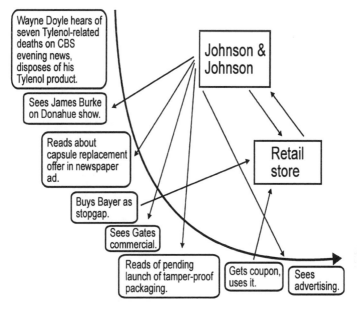

Figure 33.3. Management of the Tylenol Recovery as an Integrated Program

stake in the eye-care industry. In particular, it had no relationship with optometrists and opticians, and it knew that users of contact lenses would not switch to disposable lenses without the encouragement of an eye-care professional. As a newcomer to the industry, it would find it difficult to champion the diffusion of disposable lens technology. Competitors like Bausch & Lomb would be quick to follow if Acuvue had any success at all. Its strategy had to pioneer the market and dominate it in less time than its competitors could react and imitate.

The plan J&J chose to achieve this "blitzkrieg" launch involved a tightly coordinated program of advertising, personal selling, and database marketing. The latter depended on two linked databases: one a list of registered eye-care professionals who had responded positively to a sales call promoting Acuvue, and the other the names of contact lens wearers. The second database was constructed from responses to Acuvue's broadcast advertising, which described the benefits of disposable lenses and offered a toll-free telephone number for further information. Prospects identified in this way were sent the name and address of an eye-care specialist in their own zip code area, together with a voucher entitling them to a first pair of lenses at no cost if the eye

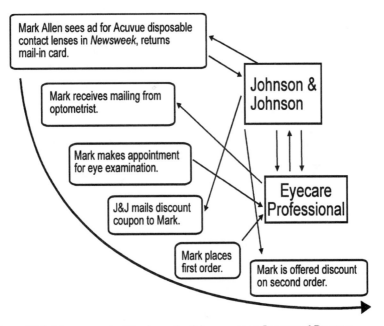

Figure 33.4. Management of the Launch of Acuvue as an Integrated Program

examination identified that they were likely to benefit from disposable lenses. Thus these prospective customers were individually tracked as they moved from expressions of initial interest, through a first appointment with an optometrist, to successive purchases of lenses.

Each step of the process of customer conversion was coordinated by the Johnson & Johnson computer: appointment making, delivery of collateral sales material, and delivery of purchase incentive coupons. What appeared to the customer as a seamlessly integrated flow of timely and pertinent communications was, in fact, the product of a number of quite distinct communication disciplines—print advertising, direct mail, telemarketing, and sales promotion. Figure 33.4 presents the management of the consumer adoption process from a similar perspective to that used to describe the Tylenol recovery in Figure 33.3.

The program achieved its objective of penetrating and dominating the disposable lens market so rapidly and comprehensively that other contact lens manufacturers were discouraged from direct competition. Integration between the consumer and eye-care specialist audiences, between direct mail and the supporting tools, and across stages in the adoption cycle was seamless.

Integration in the Agricultural Chemicals Market

Rhone-Poulenc, manufacturer of agricultural herbicides and insecticides, faced windows of opportunity quite similar to those we have seen in the cases of Tylenol and Acuvue. In its case, however, the windows arose from the rhythms of farming, not the actions of competitors. One of its herbicides, for example, must be applied in a 3-week period after plowing if it is to be superior to competitive products. Other products face other moments of peak performance, and coordinating a communications program across the entire product portfolio, the seasons, and the multitude of farming specialties that make up the agricultural market is a complex task. The job was made more difficult by the fact that the company's channels of distribution were, until the late 1980s, difficult for management to trace.

As Figure 33.5 illustrates, the company knew that it called on 100 distributors, but found it difficult to trace what happened to its products after they left the distributors' hands. It depended on advertising to deliver to end users its complex messages about timing and methods of crop treatment, with no strong evidence as to whether the messages were being received or acted on during the brief times when these messages were most relevant to the decision making of farmers.

Starting in 1989, Rhone-Poulenc began to build a database of its users and prospects in the agricultural community, linked through the dealerships that served them, and back to the distributors that served the dealers. As it did so, the channels of distribution became clearer, as did the boundaries across which integration would have to be forged.

It became apparent that the company faced multiple audiences. Principally, there were distributors, dealers, and end users (farmers), as shown in Figure 33.6. The farmers could be thought of as migrating through three stages of commitment to Rhone-Poulenc: an unknown number of prospects not yet identified by name and address, the identified prospects, and the committed users. These categories marked the stages in the adoption cycle through which the communication program would have to migrate customers. With this

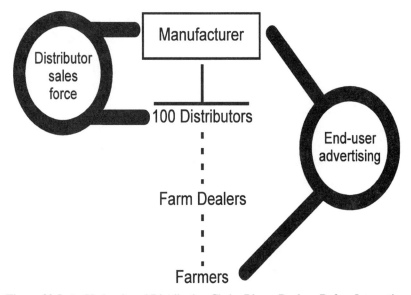

Figure 33.5. An Undeveloped Distribution Chain: Rhone-Poulenc Before Integration

improved picture of its communication targets, several new communication tools suggested themselves. The distributor sales force was supplemented by a sales force calling on dealers. Advertising planning could distinguish among a program to generate prospects, one to convert prospects into users, and a continuity program to ensure that buyers used the products that were right for them and used them in ways that would yield the best results and the highest satisfaction.

Generalizations

The cases discussed above let us approach a definition of integration inductively. Four features occur in all cases:

- *Multiple tools:* All three of the communications programs used more than one of the traditional communication tools, and used them to reinforce each other. This harmony among multiple modes of communication is integration in the most basic sense. The tools might span, for example, advertising, database marketing,

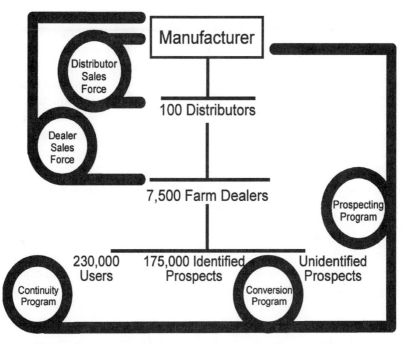

Figure 33.6. A Developed Distribution Chain: Rhone-Poulenc After Integration

sales promotion, sales force deployment, telemarketing, public relations, publishing, event marketing, and direct marketing.

- *Multiple audiences:* The communications program in each case targeted more than one audience. Consumer segments and members of the distribution channel were the audiences in these cases, but other targets, including opinion formers, could have been included.

- *Multiple stages:* The audiences in each case were moved through several psychological and behavioral stages. When, as in the Acuvue case, the target was new customers, the stages corresponded to a sequence of awareness, to interest, to desire, to action. As the Tylenol case illustrates, however, the stages can be idiosyncratic to the particular problem.

- *A coordinating mechanism:* In all cases, actions by the audience triggered the transition from one stage of the campaign to the next, using an explicit coordinating mechanism. In the Acuvue and Rhone-Poulenc cases, the mechanism was a database. Individual-level coordination is not mandatory, however; in the Tylenol case aggregate market research results supplied the evidence that it was time for a transition to occur. As databases become more widely available, so integration at the individual consumer level will become more common, but in the meantime aggregate measures can be quite informative.

Three of these elements, multiple audiences, multiple communication tools, and tools to coordinate the system, are not very revolutionary features of a communication project. They pose fairly traditional managerial problems for communication managers, and when one sees these problems overcome with finesse, as they were in these three cases, one is impressed but not startled. What may be startling, in the sense of solving a problem that does not usually get posed at all, is the fact that all of these projects carried their consumers through multiple stages. The revolutionary aspect of integrated marketing communications, then, is its ambitiousness. Traditional communication planning is really quite humble, setting for itself a relatively modest goal of, for example, a repositioning, the transmission of some information, or the generation of a list of prospects. The ambitious claim of integration is that it can take the customer all the way to the sale. Communication investments can then be held responsible for results that generate revenue.

This chapter has been concerned with defining integration as an outcome. A more important practical problem is to identify what it takes to achieve integration as a process. As a process, integration involves the harmonious cooperation of bureaucratic specialties to solve a communications problem. On one hand we have specialists in a variety of communications disciplines, such as copywriters, art directors, media planners, database technicians, and event marketing designers. On the other hand we have specialized management, such as sales force managers, sales promotion managers, advertising managers, and brand managers. These disparate interests must be made to work together.

To construct this partnership, it is necessary to forge a culture in which integration is understood and valued. That requires two kinds of learning: to come to know what an integrated product looks like, and to come to know what it can accomplish. On the first of these points, integration is recognized by four features: multiple tools, multiple audiences, multiple stages, and a coordinating mechanism. The second point, the question of what good integration is capable of accomplishing, is a matter for stories. Accounts of integration that has achieved an astonishing objective, such as the all-but-miraculous recovery of the Tylenol brand, inspire us with a sense of what is possible. New technologies, such as low-cost databases and new ways to communicate directly with individual consumers via on-line services, will supply ever more powerful means, but it is stories of success that feed our imagination with a sense of the ends that are now possible.[2]

Note

1. Robert C. Blattberg and Kenneth J. Wisniewski, *Product Tampering's Effects on Sales of Analgesics in the Chicagoland Market,* working paper (Chicago: University of Chicago, Center for Marketing Strategy Research, Graduate School of Business, 1982); John Deighton, *McNeil Consumer Products Company: Tylenol,* case study, unpublished manuscript; Stephen A. Greyser, *Johnson & Johnson: The Tylenol Tragedy* (Boston: Harvard Business School, 1982); Ian I. Mitroff and Ralph H. Kilmann, *Corporate Tragedies: Product Tampering, Sabotage and Other Catastrophes* (New York: Praeger, 1984), 3-16.

2. For more on integrated marketing communications, see Schultz, Chapter 32, this volume.

A Road Map to On-Line
Marketing Strategy

Rex Briggs

"Accountable media" has become the battle cry of advertisers. In 1995, when the first Web banners were sold on the on-line magazine *HotWired,* Rick Boyce, a former media planner who became *HotWired*'s cybersalesman, observed, "We have the first truly accountable advertising medium! We can literally count each consumer that responds to the ad banner with a clickthrough to the advertiser's Web site." Many marketers were captivated by the banner's powerful ability to allow direct and instantaneous response to its offer. "Clickthrough"—a direct marketing manifestation—quickly became the standard for evaluating the effectiveness of Web ad banners.

In 1996, Millward Brown conducted for *HotWired* the first advertising effectiveness study and discovered that clickthrough may not account for the brand enhancement that results from exposure to ad banners.[1] More than a

NOTE: This chapter is adapted from an article that appeared in *Admap,* March 1998. Used by permission.

year and several rigorous research studies later, we can be much more definitive: Clickthrough is the wrong metric to account for brand enhancement. The Web excels at direct marketing, but it does much more. Even as advertisers come to grips with what clickthrough does and does not measure, brand managers struggle to redefine on-line marketing strategy. In this chapter, I encourage potential users to think about how on-line advertising works, by putting clickthrough in proper context. From a perspective on how on-line advertising works, I am aiming here to provide a road map to on-line marketing strategy.

What Is the Value of Clickthrough?

The clickthrough metric (the percentage of those exposed to the ad banner who click on the banner to connect to the advertiser's Web site) is important in measuring how banners work in terms of direct marketing. However, when it is used to measure the effectiveness of advertising communication, clickthrough fails grotesquely. Why is this so? After all, many have argued that if someone is genuinely influenced by an advertisement, he or she will click through the banner and go directly to the advertiser's Web site for more advertising information. The point of view that Web ad banners are really little "ads" for a bigger ad that is delivered only when users click through is not completely unreasonable. It is generally true that a user who takes the time to transfer over to the advertiser's Web site will take away a heightened level of information about the advertiser. However, there is a flaw in the logic that Web ad banners have little value. This stems from a handful of incorrect assumptions:

- Brand enhancement can happen only on the advertiser's Web site.
- Brands have far more to say than could ever be conveyed in a Web ad banner.
- Clickthrough should be sought by all advertisers.
- The level of clickthrough determines the level of brand enhancement.

We at Millward Brown Interactive believe and can demonstrate that these assumptions are both incorrect and counterproductive. For the brand manager to make the most of Web investment, he or she must put clickthrough in its proper context and try to develop a superior on-line marketing strategy.

Brand Enhancement Can Happen as a Result of Exposure to an Ad Banner Alone

Although additional powerful communication may await the consumer on the other side of an ad banner, the ad banner itself does a significant amount of brand enhancement. In fact, among the 12 ad banners Millward Brown tested as part of the 1997 IAB on-line Advertising Effectiveness Study, the value of the ad exposure was found to be significantly greater on average than the value of the clickthrough.[2]

To put the clickthrough metric in proper context, consider that "recall of the advertisement" (ad awareness) was boosted by four-tenths of one percentage point (from 43.7% to 44.1%) as a result of those who clicked on the ad banners. That is an increase of less than 1%. Comparatively, the banner exposure itself boosted ad awareness by 9.7 percentage points, from 34.0% to 43.7%. 96% of awareness increase comes from its banner; 4% was caused by the clickthrough. This pattern is consistent across the various brand enhancement metrics examined (see Figure 34.1).

The model that assumes the user is passively exposed to Web pages and then, upon exposure to the right Web advertisement, miraculously shifts to an engaged mode upon clicking through is not supported by the data. Rather, the effectiveness of Web advertising seems to stem from the fact that Web usage is an actively engaging exercise, similar to reading magazines. Users are fairly attentive to the media environment—including the advertisements. Clearly, the belief that the ad banner is really a small ad for the "real" ad that waits on the other side of a clickthrough can be rejected on the basis of this analysis.

Many Brands Have Straightforward Messages That Can Be Conveyed in a Web Ad Banner

Many advertisers have developed clear and concise brand messages or themes that consumers have heard any number of times, such as "Behind every healthy smile is a Crest kid," "Ford trucks—built tough," and "Amazon.com: Earth's biggest bookstore." A clear and concise brand message is important if the advertiser is to lock that message into consumers' long-term memory and have it recalled in the appropriate circumstances. In general, such messages can be communicated within a Web ad banner and do not require the consumer to transfer over to a Web site for additional elucidation. These messages set up expectations for brands such that the consumer is more willing to try them

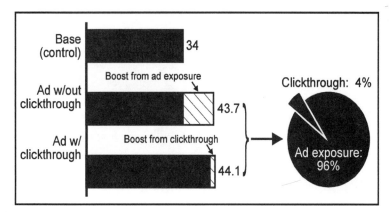

Figure 34.1. Impact of Clickthrough Versus Ad Exposure on Ad Awareness

when in an experimental mood (packaged goods) or is more likely to investigate the products further (considered purchase categories). If clickthrough works by presenting a compelling reason for the consumer to take action immediately and on-line, then what would a brand like Schick razors have to do to get a high level of clickthrough—short of changing its product? Consider the case of Schick razors, tested in the 1997 IAB Advertising Effectiveness Study. The banner exposure alone boosted Schick's brand-linked impression 26% and increased the perception of "meets your needs for a razor" by 31% and "is an acceptable price" by 28% (all statistically significant increases at the 90% confidence level).

Every level of the BrandDynamics Pyramid (see Figure 34.3), which measures the relationship consumers have with the brand, is enhanced. And the Consumer Loyalty Score, an accurate measure of the likelihood a consumer will purchase the product next, increased by 4%. Yet the clickthrough is only 0.5%.[3] Does the low clickthrough rate imply that the Schick ad was a failure? Focusing solely on the clickthrough rate might lead the advertiser to conclude that this ad was not a success—which is contrary to the evidence from multiple brand enhancement and ad effectiveness measures. Certainly there are applications of direct marketing and promotion that can create and fulfill an immediate need on-line. This capability is one of the tremendous assets of on-line. In these circumstances, clickthrough has meaning; however, when it comes to communicating a straightforward branding message, clickthrough has little or no relevance. The exposure alone has value.

Some analysts have suggested that a banner may be able to communicate a brand message, but a Web site can communicate much more. In an attempt to drive more eyeballs to the Web site, a few advertisers have experimented with a nonbranded ad banner, because it has been found that such ads generate higher clickthrough rates. The research design of the IAB study conducted by Millward Brown Interactive allows us to calculate the trade-off between using a nonbranded banner to generate high levels of clickthrough and using exposure to generate brand enhancement. An advertiser who sacrifices the brand message on initial exposure in hopes of achieving better brand enhancement by bringing more people to a dedicated Web site would need to achieve unattainably high 26.4% clickthrough rates to do as well as a branded ad banner with zero clickthrough to the dedicated Web site.

But what about using clickthrough as a surrogate measure (or predictor) of brand enhancement generated from the exposure? We certainly have heard of cases where an advertiser has said, "Ad A must be better than Ad B because it received higher clickthrough." *Beware.* We found an almost nonexistent .02 correlation between clickthrough and ad recall, suggesting that clickthrough does a very poor job of predicting the level of brand enhancement. Why does clickthrough fail to measure the brand enhancement value of an on-line ad banner? Our analysis indicates that consumers click on an ad banner not only because the ad is relevant and engaging, but because they perceive an immediate need (stimulated by the banner) that they can fulfill only by clicking through to a Web site where the "promise" made in the banner is delivered. There are many instances of effective advertising where the brand communication is relevant and engaging yet there is no credible reason to require a consumer to take immediate action—on-line is no exception to this principle. This is illustrated in Figure 34.2 which explains why clickthrough does not predict brand enhancement. Clickthrough measures a direct marketing phenomenon, not a brand one (Route B). Although the Web's direct marketing capabilities are exceptional, there are many brands for which the model does not apply. These brands should focus on the branding benefits of on-line (Route A).

Clickthrough Should Not Be Sought by All Advertisers

There are some situations in which clickthrough is directly relevant to marketing objectives. Few would argue against the idea that clickthrough is important for Web-based products and e-commerce services fulfilled via the

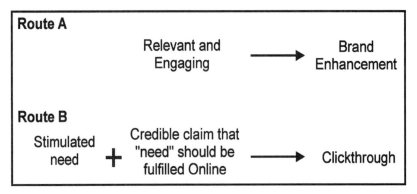

Figure 34.2. Brand Enhancement Versus Clickthrough

Web. Millward Brown Interactive does a significant amount of research for companies competing in this arena, and we advise our clients that clickthrough is often the beginning of a critical sales- and relationship-building process. For products that are not Web-bound, there is certainly a legitimate question as to whether or not clickthrough should be the goal of the advertisement.

Consider this scenario: Millward Brown Interactive's tracking of Web behavior through our nationally representative panel has demonstrated that a significant amount of Web usage occurs at work during work hours. Consider the opportunity for a snack brand to communicate to hungry working computer users. Perhaps the ad might show a candy bar package and ask, "Is hunger making it hard for you to concentrate?" The advertiser should not necessarily encourage users to click through; rather, the advertiser should aim to move the worker to the vending machine, where he or she can purchase the advertised brand. Maybe the ad copy should read, "Don't click here! Devouring a Web page won't satisfy your hunger. This will—[product illustration]. Now where is that vending machine?"

Undoubtedly, some people will click on the banner; however, the ad's goal is to reinforce top-of-mind consideration of the product and, perhaps, generate an immediate behavioral response (i.e., purchase) rather than clickthrough. Given this objective, measuring the success of the campaign by the number of clicks would be inappropriate. In fact, a brand pursuing this strategy should ask, What need are we accidentally tapping into that would cause someone to take an undesired action like clicking through?

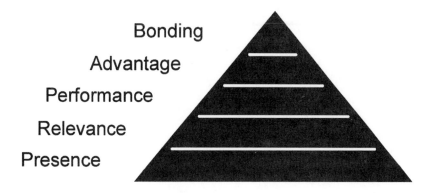

Figure 34.3. The BrandDynamics Pyramid

What About High-Consideration Categories?

What about high-consideration categories, such as automobiles? Should clickthrough be the critical metric used to evaluate the success of an automobile Web banner campaign? We believe the practice of evaluating automotive Web advertising on the basis of clickthrough could be compared to assessing television ads for automobiles on the basis of how many people visit the relevant showroom the next day. It is an ideal response, but not the most common one. So how should a brand like Volvo think about clickthrough?

We suggest that Volvo and other brands in high-consideration categories should think about Web advertising as a combination of traditional advertising and face-to-face selling. In an interpersonal, face-to-face selling situation, it would be extremely efficient if an automotive salesperson could simply present a prospect with the contract and ask the prospect to "buy right now"—efficient, but unlikely.

Consumers generally require a dialogue that evolves from establishing the relevance of the brand to demonstrating performance to discussing its advantage vis-à-vis competitors before they will become bonded with what is being sold. This evolution of the interpersonal selling dialogue is substantially similar to the hierarchy we use in our BrandDynamics Pyramid (Figure 34.3). We believe that Web advertising can be used to drive consumers through this relationship enhancement process. It is only in the later stages of this that it is important for the user to become directly engaged with the brand at the advertiser's Web site or, in the physical world, the dealer's showroom. An actual Volvo ad we studied demonstrates this point succinctly. The ad banner yielded less than .5% clickthrough, yet the Volvo ad banner generated a statistically significant increase on key metrics of product "relevance," "performance," and "advantage vis-à-vis competitors." [4] Given the low clickthrough, was the Volvo ad banner a success? We think so.

Clickthrough has its place—but it is the wrong metric for measuring brand enhancement. Indeed, there are many approaches to enhancing brands and driving sales among on-line users. On-line marketing is much more than building and supporting a corporate Web site.

Road Map to Marketing On-Line

Leading Web advertisers have come to grips with the new insight that the Web can work as both a direct marketing and a brand enhancement vehicle, but many others are struggling to form coherent Web marketing strategies. Although the direct marketing model is a legitimate and effective use of the Web, Millward Brown Interactive has come to the conclusion that those who are leveraging the Web only as a direct marketing vehicle may be significantly underutilizing on-line and leaving themselves vulnerable to their competitors.

The proven capability to enhance brands with exposure to on-line advertising creates a new landscape of possibilities for marketers. But this landscape is fraught with both opportunities and threats: opportunities to use exposure to on-line advertising messages to make consumers aware of products, to change consumer perceptions of brands, and to take market share from the competition, but also threats that competitors will figure it out first—or be more effective in their execution of on-line advertising. How can brand managers successfully navigate this new landscape? The brand manager is faced with two critical questions: Should my brand include on-line in the marketing mix? And if so, how?

What do brand managers really want to know when deciding to invest on-line? They want (and need) to know that the people they are reaching have economic value and that reaching them on-line is an effective use of their marketing dollars.

Should My Brand Include
On-Line in the Marketing Mix?

Answering this question is relatively straightforward. The brand manager must start by measuring the economic value to his or her category that on-line users represent. Take the example of an automotive manufacturer: 23% of the manufacturer's target market is on-line, and, because of the Web's fairly affluent demographics, these Web users are more likely to purchase higher-margin luxury automobiles—and therefore account for 40% of the company's profits. Garth Hallberg of Ogilvy & Mather suggests in his book *All Consumers Are Not Created Equal* that a marketer should spend marketing dollars in proportion to the segment's profitability.[5] Thus, in this example, the brand manager should spend 40% of the budget reaching these on-line consumers.

Should the brand manager spend the full 40% of the budget on-line? The answer is no. After all, on-line consumers are exposed to other media as well. But spending all of the marketing budget off-line to reach on-line users as they consume other media is not wise either. We know from extensive research that each medium can work in a unique manner to enhance the brand. Indeed, advertising across media can have synergistic results (as we observed in the Electronic Telegraph/Ogilvy & Mather Online Advertising Effectiveness Study).[6] We suggest that brand managers consider "Surround Sound marketing." They need to find the ways in which they can leverage each medium their consumers use to present and enhance the brand.

If brand communication in each medium has an equal impact on the bottom line, we would suggest that the brand manager examine the share of media time these users spend on-line. To continue the example, if the automobile manufacturer's consumers represent 40% of profits and spend 15% of their media time on-line, then it would be reasonable to earmark 6% (40% × 15% = 6%) of total media dollars for reaching and communicating with these consumers on-line (see Figure 34.4).

Unfortunately, all media do not make equal contributions to a brand. And there are many variables at play that make it dangerous to develop blanket generalizations regarding the relative effectiveness and the proper mix of media. Brand managers should determine their budget allocations using the "share of profit/share of media" time analysis (Figure 34.4) combined with good research measuring the relative effectiveness and synergy of each medium in building every specific brand. Finding the right balance will take

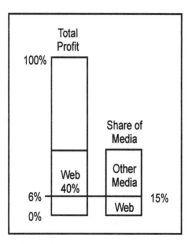

Figure 34.4. Economic Value and Media Usage of Prospects

experimentation and focused research. There is grave danger in complacency. If on-line has an impact and a brand manager chooses not to exploit it, but the competition does, he or she may be sacrificing brand equity in the long run and jeopardizing sales in the short run. As many on-line marketers have experienced, there are many approaches to marketing on-line. Some are well worth the brand manager's hard-earned marketing dollars; other on-line marketing strategies may be a waste of resources.

Which On-Line Strategies Are Right for My Brand?

It is constructive for marketers to think of the Internet as nothing more than a technology that enables information transfer. Because of the unique characteristics of the technology, communication can be fashioned along two key dimensions. The first dimension is a continuum that ranges from proactive to reactive communication; the second dimension ranges from broadcast communication to personal dialogue. Figure 34.5 illustrates these dimensions and provides examples associated with communication types.

What does this way of thinking imply for marketers? It means that they can reach and communicate with their on-line targets in a multitude of ways—from broadcast advertisements that proactively reach target audiences on mass-reach Web sites to personalized e-mail delivered in reaction to individual

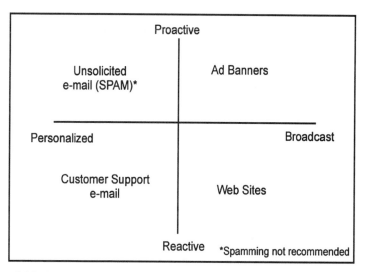

Figure 34.5. Two Continua

customers' queries. It means that on-line is not monolithic. It is multifaceted and requires an on-line communication mix appropriate to a given brand's marketing strategy. The effectiveness of an on-line strategy depends on the achievement of the right mix for the brand.

With the many options available and an evolving technology that seems to be expanding the list of options on a daily basis, how is a marketer to develop a coherent strategy and effective tactics? The task of such development requires that the marketer first define business objectives and then assess how the technology can be used to achieve these objectives. The marketer must not let the technology define the strategy. Some objectives are best achieved with a broadcast message, whereas others are best achieved with personal communication. Some objectives require waiting for consumers to initiate the dialogue, so that the brand can react to their perceived needs; other objectives are best achieved with the brand proactively communicating with the consumer. The development of realistic objectives should begin with the marketer's evaluation of the following:

- The nature of the product or service
- The current level of Web site category use by the target population
- Perceived legitimacy of personalized communication related to the product in the minds of consumers

Exploring these areas will help the marketer develop the appropriate objectives and optimize the on-line marketing mix of communication options.

Nature of the Product or Service

Certainly the nature of the product should have a dramatic impact on the types of on-line communication the marketer employs. Brands requiring (a) higher levels of support and customer service, (b) higher consideration prior to purchase, or (c) on-line acquisition of the product, are among the categories that will benefit from a comprehensive Web site that reacts to consumers and prospects. But even brands that enjoy a high degree of active consumer investigation should communicate proactively—not just to inform the consumer that a corporate Web site can be accessed with a "click here," but also to carry the brand message directly to the consumer, communicating the unique brand proposition. Brands that can be purchased only off-line, that have lower levels of formal information gathering prior to purchase, or that do not require significant customer support do not require a huge Web site to satisfy a consumer's need. Although brands finding themselves in this category may attempt to create content appealing enough to entice users to their Web sites, they run the risk of confusing the consumer regarding the focus of the brands. These brands will often achieve a greater impact on their bottom line, with advertising and exclusive content sponsorships on ad-supported content Web sites than with colossal corporate Web sites.

Consumers' Level of Web Site Category Use

How many consumers are seeking out the brand on their own accord? As Jeremy Bullmore, director of WPP and former chairman of the London office of J. Walter Thompson, has observed, there are some categories where consumers actively seek out product messages (such as automobiles) and other categories where the advertiser must seek out the consumer (such as packaged goods). This is as true on-line as it is in traditional media.

Based on Millward Brown Interactive's nationally representative "Interactive Consumer Network" panel of Web users, we have found that categories with higher information complexity and categories that can be purchased on-line have, predictably, higher levels of Web site category use. Categories with lower information complexity and those that cannot be purchased on-line, such as packaged goods, have lower levels of Web site use. What if a brand category has low Web site use, but a profitable segment of the market is on-line? Lower Web site usage categories, such as packaged goods, can reap significant value from on-line marketing communication without significant Web site investment. They can create value by focusing their on-line communication mix almost exclusively on Web advertising, exclusive long-term sponsorships, and similar brand communication strategies that leverage the power of the medium to reach consumers proactively and enhance the brand through advertising messages. A tightly focused micro Web site combined with extensive brand advertising may be the most effective communication mix in such a case.

Can brands "reinvent" the consumer's relationship with the category? Perhaps. The Web can help change product information gathering, purchase, distribution, fulfillment, and customer support profoundly. However, building a Web site with attractive content and a novel approach to obtaining the product is not enough. The service has to provide real value, let consumers know the service exists, and provide a compelling reason to use it. Some have assumed that the Web is a level playing field (with each Web site only a click away), and that consumers will seek out their brands. But the Web is not a level playing field. Usage is determined at least by awareness, and often by both a perceived need for a brand and preference for a given service over competitive offerings.

A direct marketing approach may not be sufficient to achieve marketing objectives. E*Trade's "Someday we'll all invest this way" advertising campaign provides a good example of Web advertising that communicates a brand message. Some users may click on the banner so that they can "invest this way today" through on-line financial services, but the ad's primary effect is likely to be enhancement of brand presence and perceived relevance in the minds of the consumers—thereby creating long-term brand health. Finding the right mix between a Web site that reacts to a consumer's needs and proactive banner advertising is key to a brand's on-line marketing success.

Legitimacy of Personalized Communication With the Target

The nature of the product and how much consumers use the Web site in the category help marketers determine the proper mix between proactive and reactive on-line marketing elements. But what about the dimension of person-alized versus broadcast communication? When considering this dimension it is important to bear in mind that consumers have limited time and can manage a finite number of relationships. Marketers should ask themselves, Why would a consumer want to have a relationship with my brand? Some marketers have sidestepped this question and answered, We will require consumers to give us their contact information—then we will have a relationship. But a relationship is more than an e-mail or postal address in a database.

Some brands lend themselves to relationships with consumers. Personal dialogue between a brand representative and the consumer is welcome and provides advantages in some categories. For other brands, consumers have no perceived need for a relationship, and personal dialogue lacks credibility with members of the target market—and may even annoy them. This principle is captured in the direct marketing riddle that asks: What is the difference between junk mail and personal mail? Answer: personal interest. Some basic questions marketers should ask are the following:

- What is the real personal interest for the consumer?
- What will the brand do for the consumer to justify the relationship?
- Can this relationship be maintained profitably?

Brands can communicate with different degrees of personalization, ranging from pure personal communication (such as Auto-by-tel's personal e-mail response from a broker regarding the price and availability of an automobile that suits a consumer's request), to segmented communication (such as CNN's custom news service), to undifferentiated broadcast communication (the approach used by the majority of Web sites). Unless the marketer will be creating genuine value for the consumer—and can do so profitably—the returns from sophisticated database and dynamic delivery tools may not justify the investment. The return on investment can and should be tested against the economic objectives. Auto-by-tel can measure the profit from selling cars with personalized response. CNN can measure the value from incremental exposure to advertising it sells as a result of the custom news offering.

These are powerful tools that enable mass customization of communication. The central questions related to the deployment of these tools are: What value can be created for the customer? And what is the return on investment for the brand?

The Next Steps

Once the marketer has identified the economic value of Web users and formed an appropriate on-line communication mix strategy for the brand, he or she must make sure that a strategy is in place to measure performance and to gain the knowledge needed to evolve the marketing strategy. It should not come as a surprise to the reader that the marketer must be certain to employ the right metrics in evaluating performance accountability. Measuring the wrong dimensions is bound to lead the marketer astray. Even more important than accounting for the investment of marketing capital, however, is incorporating the lessons of experience that will advance and evolve the marketer's understanding of the effective use of this burgeoning medium. These are what I call the "Two A's" of research: accountability and actionability.

What is the key to the Two A's? The marketer's measuring, to the best of his or her ability, consumers' responses to the marketing activities and then diagnosing how these activities can be improved. In traditional media, we accomplish these objectives by constantly tracking brand performance with regularly repeated surveys that measure and monitor consumers' attitudinal and behavioral responses to the brand. Marketers use this powerful brand-tracking tool to diagnose and enhance brand performance. For example, marketers can readily measure the impacts of a TV ad on the following:

- Relationship between advertising exposure and effect on specific dimensions, including ad awareness, brand imagery, purchase intent
- Cost-efficiency of the communication
- Impact of flighting and media weight on the brand

By talking directly with consumers through structured surveys, marketers have the ability to link the timing of key marketing events with changes in measurements of a brand's performance according to consumers' attitudes, brand perceptions, and purchase behavior (see Figure 34.6). Millward Brown pioneered this research approach more than two decades ago for traditional media. The approach is used by leading advertisers such as Kraft, GM, Hewlett-Packard, Disney, and Levi's. These advertisers use this information to help them make crucial decisions related to brand management and communication.

Recently, Web advertisers have gained the ability to gather the same feedback and learning from on-line brand communication. These new re-

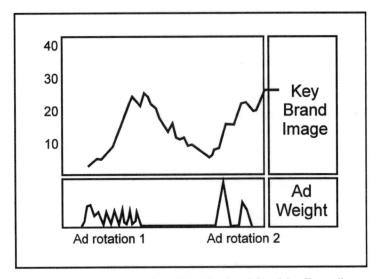

Figure 34.6. Tracking Consumer Perceptions Against Advertising Expenditure

search capabilities allow the measurement of all major on-line marketing activity—ranging from ad banners to targeted Web site communication. The power of the insight is substantial. Brands that had previously relied on impressions, clickthrough, and faith that their Web advertising works—conclusions that have been validated in general terms—now have the type of information that allows them to measure specifically the value of everything from discrete elements of their Web sites to the differential performance of specific ad banner executions. This new research system works by matching the marketing activities with consumer responses gathered through surveys of a brand's on-line target audience. In fact, brands that currently have the brand-tracking research program in place for traditional media can compare the value of key elements of the on-line marketing to traditional marketing communication, such as television and print advertising. This "across media" insight allows brand managers to understand how they can improve the return on investment from their communication mix both on- and off-line. This new type of Web research insight answers difficult questions such as these:

- How does the target market perceive the brand versus competitive brands?
- What creative approach is likely to work best against specific target markets?
- What Web sites are most efficient at reaching the target audience?

- What is the audience profile behind the ad impressions and clickthroughs?
- How have advertising and marketing activities affected the target audience?

To date, marketers operating on-line have lacked the information provided by rigorous research focused on these questions. Yet these questions are central to a brand's success. Marketers now have research tools within their reach that provide accurate measurement of the impacts of their communication—from mass-reach television to targeted Web advertising to narrowcast Web sites. These tools empower marketers to determine how each of their brand communications affects consumers, as well as how all the components interact to ensure they are achieving their objectives. This feedback loop helps marketers make even more effective use of the on-line marketing vehicle.

As a result of well-developed on-line strategy and new on-line market feedback tools, brand managers can confidently address the complex questions concerning what is—and is not—working for their brands. Applying these tools makes marketers more effective and efficient—ensuring that they have an accurate measurement of results and actionable learning to help build their brands into the future.

Notes

1. Millward Brown Interactive, *HotWired Advertising Effectiveness Study* (San Francisco: Millward Brown Interactive, December 1996), 37-38.

2. Millward Brown Interactive, *IAB Online Advertising Effectiveness Study* (San Francisco: Millward Brown Interactive, November 1997).

3. Ibid.

4. Ibid.

5. Garth Hallberg, *All Consumers Are Not Created Equal: The Differential Marketing Strategy for Brand Loyalty and Profits* (New York: John Wiley, 1995).

6. Millward Brown Interactive, *Electronic Telegraph/Ogilvy & Mather Online Advertising Effectiveness Study* (San Francisco: Millward Brown Interactive, May 1997).

Direct Marketing

Sidney C. Liebenson

D irect marketing has been one of the fastest-growing areas of the advertising business over the past two decades. Once associated strictly with mail order, direct marketing is now used by a broad spectrum of companies. The ability to measure the results of an advertising effort, the opportunity to communicate directly with prospects and customers, and the diminishing efficiency of mass media due to fragmentation of a mass market have led an increasing number of marketers to embrace direct marketing as a component of their overall marketing mix.

What Is Direct Marketing?

Direct marketing is a distinct marketing discipline that is more than just advertising. Adapting a definition put forth in the book *The Concept of Direct Marketing* by Vin Jenkins, *direct marketing is a marketing system in which the marketer establishes a direct relationship with the consumer through interactive communications.*[1] Characteristics that are unique to this system include direct-response marketing, measurement and analysis of response, a marketing database, media selection geared to target markets, and financial accountability.

Direct-Response Marketing

Direct-response marketing is advertising that leads to measurable action. This includes coupons, order forms, and reply cards to be mailed to the marketer; phone numbers (often toll-free) that allow consumers to call the marketer; certificates or coupons that can be redeemed at retail establishments; and other devices that can generate direct consumer action.

Direct-response advertising can be in any medium—direct mail, television, radio, magazines, newspapers, even point-of-purchase materials. Telemarketing and interactive media, including on-line computer services, the Internet, and interactive cable systems, are ideal for direct-response advertising because the ability to respond is so convenient and immediate.

Direct response is an advertising technique. Creatively, direct-response advertising is designed to generate action. It must do more than just communicate a brand image or create awareness—it must also sell. Direct-response advertising makes use of strong calls to action, urging consumers to do what the marketer wants them to do. There are clear benefits for taking the desired action. In addition, there are distinct offers, letting consumers know what they will get in exchange for their response.

Measurement and Analysis of Response

The results of direct-response advertising are tracked back to the source of response. This allows direct marketers to measure the effectiveness of each advertising medium and media vehicle, each audience segment, each creative execution, each offer configuration, and so on.

It is not enough just to generate response. Direct marketers must measure the response against response goals to determine the relative success of the advertising. They must also measure response against costs to determine the relative efficiency of the advertising.

Direct marketers measure and analyze response using various criteria, depending on the goals of the response advertisement. For example, if a product is being sold, response might be measured in terms of profit versus advertising costs, or dollars of revenue per 1,000 exposures, or advertising cost per unit sold.

Direct marketers analyze results in various ways to help them make decisions regarding future advertising activities. The job of measurement and analysis goes beyond the results of the initial advertising. Marketers track customers over time to help determine the sources of the best-quality customers and how to maintain their levels of purchase activity.

Marketing Database

Advertising results are maintained in a marketing database that includes the most relevant information about each prospect or customer, usually name, address, phone number, source of name, and response or purchase history. It might also include demographic information, product usage data, and other pieces of information to help the marketer reach the target audience more effectively.

The marketing database lets the marketer recontact prospects and customers with additional offers or information. The overriding goal is to reach the right people with the right message at the right time. The presence of a database is essential for developing a relationship with consumers through interactive communications. Stronger relationships lead to greater customer loyalty and greater profitability.

Of course, maintaining customer data has its responsibilities. Marketers must be careful to use the data they maintain for marketing purposes only, and in a responsible and ethical manner. Consumers place implicit trust in the companies with whom they do business, and betraying that trust can cost a company important customer relationships.

Media Selection Geared to Target Markets

Direct marketers choose media vehicles based on how efficiently they deliver the targeted audience. Mass reach is not as important as targeted reach. With data-based media, such as direct mail and telemarketing, direct marketers can often select segments of the audience that provide the most-qualified market. Carefully targeted media selections help improve response rates and thus profitability for direct marketers.

Financial Accountability

Because direct marketing is measurable, it is possible to relate sales to advertising costs and determine the overall profitability of an advertising program. Direct marketing programs are scrutinized in depth to make sure they are producing an optimal return on investment. Financial accountability is a very important aspect of direct marketing, and one that is very attractive to companies that want to understand the value of their advertising.

Front-End and Back-End Advertising

The direct marketing system begins with direct-response advertising, but a lot of the activity that goes into a direct marketing program takes place after the initial response comes in. The advertising designed to generate the initial response from consumers is called *front-end advertising*. The communications that go to identified customers or prospects constitute *back-end advertising*. In addition, response analysis and database maintenance are back-end activities.

In a typical direct marketing program, front-end efforts might include direct-mail, print, and broadcast advertising. If a consumer responds by phone, an inbound telemarketing operation must be set up to handle calls. Then, back-end activities will go into effect. Response (in any form) must be tracked, and a fulfillment operation must be in place to send the consumer the product ordered or the information requested. Follow-up mailings—to convert inquiries to orders, to sell additional items or services, or to build stronger customer relationships—will be sent out on a periodic basis. Further down the line, additional contacts will be made, depending on the consumer's past activities or demographic characteristics.

As is obvious from such a program, the advertising material that goes into direct marketing can include direct-response advertising, telemarketing scripts, fulfillment materials, follow-up mailings, telemarketing campaigns, and more. The back end of the business is usually more complex than the front end—but much more profitable. Customers typically respond at rates of four to six times better than prospects, and they are usually less expensive to reach than prospects because the list of their names is already owned. Many direct marketers do not make money on their front-end advertising. They invest in name generation and count on subsequent communications to build sales and profits.

Methods of Response and Tracking

Responses to direct marketing messages can come through mail, phone, electronic media, and personal action (in the case of traffic-building efforts). The important thing is that the results are tracked so the advertiser knows who responded from what source.

Direct-mail and print advertisements generally include codes on the reply devices that let the advertiser know the source of response. Many catalogs and direct-mail packages are designed so that the order form includes the addressing device (often a mailing label) that contains the consumer's code. This code can indicate list source, customer status, creative execution, date of mailing, and/or other information that can be analyzed when response is received.

Tracking can also be accomplished through the coding of the reply address. Different ads or mailings can carry small variations in the return address— usually a box or department code—that identify the respondents with particular advertising efforts.

Telephone response is rather harder to track. It is often difficult to assign unique telephone numbers to every ad or commercial in a campaign. Instead, advertisers might assign a different number for each publication or broadcast station and assign response based on time and date of the call. It also is possible to ask some qualifying questions on the inbound call to help allocate response properly. For example, catalog companies often ask phone respondents to read off the codes on their mailing labels.

When response requires consumers to go somewhere physically, they often are given coupons or invitations (or some other devices that can carry codes) to redeem the offer at the desired location. When people show up, they might be asked to complete a form designed to gather further data about the advertising source that prompted the visit.

Tracking response makes it possible for marketers to test a wide variety of variables to determine the most productive marketing methods. Different media vehicles can be tested as well as different creative approaches, different ad formats, different offers and prices, different timing, and so on. It is advisable for marketers to avoid testing multiple variables at the same time.

Each test cell should involve a single variable to help the advertiser isolate that factor for any change in response.

Direct marketers typically conduct tests on a "beat the control" principle. The most successful ad, mailing, or commercial is called the *control.* New efforts are tested against the control, but to reduce overall risk, the control is given the bulk of circulation. When creative alternatives or offers are tested, it is vital that the marketer ensure that all tests are done at the same time against the same audience, and that every test cell has a large enough audience to generate readable, reliable results. When a new approach beats the control by a significant margin, it becomes the new control.

Most direct marketers test regularly, because there are always new things to learn about how to be more efficient and productive in advertising. Continual testing helps keep messages current and relevant. Nevertheless, many advertisers have developed control ads that have gone many years before being replaced. In direct marketing, it is often the target audience that determines when it is time to change a campaign—and what the new campaign will be—because consumers vote with their response.

Relationship/Database Marketing

The existence of a marketing database allows advertisers to treat customers on an individualized basis. Messages can be personalized with references to consumers' past purchases, lifestyles, or known preferences. In this way marketers can provide a high level of customer service, adding value to the marketing relationship.

Data can be added to a company's customer list through internal and external sources. Purchase history and account activity can come from sales records. Customer surveys—including questions on product warranty cards— can generate lifestyle and product usage data. Information from census files and other public databases can be used to enhance customer files further.

Relevant customer contacts help to strengthen customer relationships. The advent of marketing databases has led to the growth of *relationship marketing.* Relationship marketing concerns itself with building stronger ties with customers as a way to increase their lifetime value to the marketer. The kinds of organizations involved in relationship marketing include airlines, telephone companies, hotels, credit card companies, financial services companies, packaged goods companies, retailers, and automakers. Often, the products they promote are not available on a "direct to consumer" basis. These advertisers use direct marketing to support other channels of distribution.

Frequency programs, such as the frequent-flyer clubs sponsored by airlines, are familiar examples of relationship marketing programs. Customers get added value from points or "mileage" for choosing a certain company to do business with. The more frequently the customer chooses the company, the greater the rewards. The most frequent customers get special recognition and privileges.

Relationship programs do not necessarily have to feature rewards to involve customers. Newsletters, catalogs, special offers, and friendly letters are other ways to provide welcome contact to customers and enhance customer loyalty. Relationship marketers understand that it is less expensive and more profitable to retain current customers than to generate new ones. They understand, through analysis of their customer databases, which customers are most valuable and which are most vulnerable, and they concentrate their efforts on maintaining the loyalty of these people.

The key to relationship marketing is the concept of customer lifetime value. When a company understands how much a customer is worth, it can determine how much it can afford to invest in acquiring new customers and extending the activity of current ones. By applying segmentation strategies to the customer database, a marketer can give different treatment to various groups, all to establish their closer relationships with the marketer.

Applications of Consumer Direct Marketing

There are several ways in which direct marketing can be employed in marketing to consumers. These include direct sales, lead generation, traffic building, fund-raising, sales support, and loyalty.

Direct Sales

Marketers can sell products or services directly to consumers through mail, telephone, print, broadcast, and electronic advertising. In such cases, the advertisement must provide all the information necessary for the consumer to make a buying decision—price, method of payment, method of delivery, guarantees, and more.

Direct sales efforts are examples of advertising and selling combined. Messages must not only create awareness and excitement, they must also move consumers to reach a purchase decision. Products ordered from direct sale advertising, whether by phone or mail, are often delivered by mail or courier service, and therefore are commonly referred to as mail-order items. Mail order is a distribution channel. Many times, mail-order advertising features products not available through retail or other distribution channels. In these cases, it can be said that "the medium is the marketplace," because the only way consumers can find these exclusive items is in the media in which they are advertised.

Lead Generation

Direct marketing can be used to identify prospects for a product or service through lead generation. Advertising is designed to elicit inquiries from consumers who want more information as a first step in a two-step inquiry and conversion process. The second step might be an information packet from which the consumer can make a purchase, a personal sales call or demonstration, or a phone call from a sales representative. There can be additional conversion efforts if the lead does not convert to a sale.

Lead-generation advertising differs from direct sales advertising because the marketer is actually selling the offer of more information. Many of the nuts-and-bolts details necessary to make the purchase decision can be left to the second stage of the selling process, thus ad messages can be shorter.

It should be remembered, however, that a two-step inquiry and conversion process is more expensive than a direct sales effort because of the additional contact. Products and services must have adequate margins per sale for a two-step approach to pay off.

Traffic Building

Direct marketing can be used to build traffic for retail establishments, cultural institutions, automobile dealerships, restaurants, seminars, and more. Advertising will invite consumers to visit the desired location and, often, include a special offer or money-saving coupon that can be redeemed at the location. Sometimes consumers are asked to call and make an appointment or reservation. Coupons or calls can be tracked to measure response by advertising source.

As part of a traffic-building program, marketers might hold sweepstakes or contests and send targeted consumers entry forms that they must bring to a retail location. Such forms might ask for information beyond name and address that can help identify the source of advertising or provide useful database information. It should be noted, however, that in the case of sweepstakes, response quantity will be much stronger than response quality.

Fund-Raising

It has been estimated that about 30% of all charitable donations are derived through direct marketing efforts. Fund-raisers can use direct sales or lead-and-conversion strategies. There is no tangible product being sold, but donors are tracked, recontacted, segmented, and given the same careful attention that would go to catalog buyers or customers of any mail-order product or service.

Sales Support

Direct marketing can be used effectively to support sales of products or services sold through non-mail-order channels. Take packaged goods, for example. Through surveys, promotional offer response, coupons that ask for name and address, and other methods, packaged goods marketers can identify their customers (or their competitors' customers) and start to build a database. Direct contact with consumers allows marketers a chance to build stronger relationships—and to learn even more about their customers. They can send consumers useful information (product use tips, recipes, lifestyle articles, and the like) that can enhance brand image, plus retail coupons to stimulate trial or repurchase. Identified heavy users can be given treatment different from that given to less frequent users or nonusers of the product.

Loyalty

Contact with known customers can keep them loyal to a marketer or brand. Sometimes incentives are built into loyalty programs to reward consumers for their frequent patronage. Frequent-flyer programs and similar schemes that reward consumers for greater usage are good examples. Shopping clubs, "privilege" cards, and long-distance discount plans are other common loyalty programs. Less elaborate loyalty efforts include customer-only mailings, such as newsletters or other informational materials. In all cases, customers are identified, recontacted, tracked, and measured in terms of continued sales activity.

Applications of Business-to-Business Direct Marketing

There are a number of common applications of direct marketing for business-to-business marketers. These include direct sales, lead generation, and sales support.

Direct Sales

Certain products and services can be sold directly to a business audience—references, directories and publications, office products and supplies, and courier or communications services. Sales to businesses tend to have a higher value than sales to consumers. Thus direct marketers often can be more elaborate in their efforts. Three-dimensional mailings in boxes or tubes, or mailings that incorporate computer disks, videotapes, or overnight courier packs might be employed—all of which have a better chance of reaching a corporate decision maker than conventional standard advertising (formerly third-class) direct mail. However, depending on the product, catalogs, standard-format mailings, and self-mailers also can work.

Direct marketing is often used to sell "aftermarket" accessories and supplies to businesses that purchase certain equipment or machinery. Rather than devote the time of expensive salespeople to selling aftermarket items, companies can send mailings and catalogs or make periodic phone calls to sell these additional items efficiently.

Lead Generation

With the average cost of a corporate sales call continually climbing, it makes sense for business-to-business marketers to deploy their salespeople in the most productive manner. Through a lead-generation program, marketers can identify interested prospects for sales calls. Sometimes initial leads are followed up by phone or with a mailing in advance of the sales call. These steps can further qualify the prospect and better prepare the sales representative.

Direct mail, telemarketing, trade and business magazines, and business card packs are the most commonly used media for business lead generation. Response information might include qualifying data and confirmation of the name and title of the person making the business decision.

Sales Support

Direct marketing can be used to support sales efforts made through a sales force or other channel. Two common techniques are preapproach campaigns and postsale efforts.

Preapproach campaigns typically involve mailings to business prospects designed to predispose them to a sales call. These might take the form of ingenious multiple mailings that involve the prospect (such as a set of three items, the first two of which are mailed with promotional information and the third delivered by a salesperson), a mailing series, or an informational newsletter. The primary objective is to get the prospect to agree to see a salesperson.

Postsale efforts are designed to maintain contact with customers and inspire loyalty. Such efforts often take the place of a follow-up sales call. Postsale efforts might include satisfaction surveys, mailings or newsletters about product usage and innovations, or business-related information. (For more on business-to-business advertising, see Barnes, Chapter 41, this volume.)

Direct Marketing Measurability

Because all efforts are measurable, direct marketing is very numbers-oriented. It is important to understand certain basic computations and terms when dealing with direct marketing programs.

Results are commonly analyzed on a "cost per" basis. This can be cost per lead, cost per customer, cost per unit sale, cost per subscriber, cost per donor, or some other measure. Advertising costs, including media costs and response-handling costs, are applied against the results of the direct marketing effort to determine a gross "cost per" figure. Product costs, fulfillment costs, and so on can be included to get to a net cost per response. This "cost per" figure can be used to compare results from advertisements across different media, among different vehicles within the same medium, or between different creative approaches or offers.

With a two-step approach, it is vital to measure the conversion percentage of leads to sales. The cost per lead indicates only initial response. The conversion percentage shows how many leads become sales and allows for the determination of actual cost per sale. It is possible for one ad or medium to generate a very attractive cost per lead, but convert so poorly that the effort is ultimately unprofitable. On the other hand, a certain ad or audience might convert so well that the marketer can accept higher lead costs. Understanding conversion by ad, medium, audience segment, and so on helps direct marketers maintain cost-efficiency.

Some direct marketers prefer to analyze results on the basis of return on investment (ROI). Advertising costs are compared to revenue generated by sales. This approach also allows for comparisons across media, ads, offers, and so on. Often, a marketer has ROI standards for each direct marketing effort. However, many advertisers apply *lifetime customer value* to the sales figures, thus allowing for a look at estimated long-term revenue generated by the direct marketing effort.

Lifetime value is typically calculated by taking a random sample of customers who first became customers at the same time, and determining their average value in net revenue based on sales over a period of time (chosen to represent an average customer lifetime), minus the cost of advertising to the market over that period. Through further analysis, it is possible to assign different lifetime values to customers from various audience segments.

Direct Marketing Trends, Today and Tomorrow

Like all areas of advertising, direct marketing is undergoing constant evolution, adapting to changes in the market and the media environment. The growth of cable television led to greater availability of affordable broadcast time, making television a more attractive medium for direct-response advertising. The proliferation of credit cards and the acceptance of toll-free telephone numbers helped facilitate ordering from TV. Thus it is easy to understand why direct marketers capitalized on broadcast deregulation in the 1980s to create the long-form advertisements known as infomercials.

Increased use of broadcast media also has led direct marketers to a greater understanding of multimedia campaigns. In many cases, the presence of direct-response advertising in multiple media in a market enhances response to individual media. For example, in markets with mail and broadcast advertising, mail response is often stronger than in markets with mail alone.

At the same time, direct marketers are learning more about how to combine media messages. A campaign might start in one medium, phase into another, and close with yet another. Moreover, the message might be different from medium to medium. Telemarketing, for example, has worked effectively as a follow-up to direct mail solicitations.

Today, direct-response advertising is finding a place in the overall advertising plans of mass marketers. Separate response campaigns might be spun off from an awareness campaign, to identify customers or stimulate sales. Such campaigns must be fully integrated with the awareness advertising to present a consistent brand message. In other cases, direct marketing might combine with sales promotion efforts to build ongoing relationships with people identified as brand users through response to promotional offers. As such, direct marketing extends the value of sales promotion activities.

Even those advertisers who use direct marketing exclusively are becoming increasingly aware of the value of branding. Research methods borrowed from the field of repeat-purchase packaged goods help determine brand personality and assess how well direct marketing efforts meet brand communication efforts. Traditional direct marketers, such as book clubs, music clubs, and catalogers, are now concerned with building and enhancing their brand images as well as building sales and enhancing customer relationships. As further research is done on the connection between image and response, we might see increasing similarities between awareness and direct-response advertising, bringing about greater integration of the two disciplines.

Another trend that is important to direct marketers is the emergence of interactive media. Direct marketers, who already know how to target messages to market segments, involve an audience, work with response data, and build customer relationships, are among the best positioned to pioneer one-on-one marketing. As interactive media become an increasingly important component of client marketing plans, all advertisers will have to understand the use of direct marketing.

Note

1. Vin Jenkins, *The Concept of Direct Marketing* (Sydney: Australia Post, 1984).

Direct-Response Advertising

Creative Principles

Emily Soell

D irect-response creative is different from other advertising creative. It
serves a different master. It has different objectives. It operates under a
different time frame. Its success is measured in a different way. It uses a
different vocabulary. And although direct-response creative is an art like other
advertising creative, it is also a science.

Direct-Response Creative
Serves a Different Master

Before you can understand direct-response advertising, you have to understand the marketing discipline it serves. Direct-response creative is the com-

389

munication vehicle for direct marketing, and direct marketing is more than a way of advertising a product or service. It is a *distribution channel*—because it sells those goods and services directly, with no middleman.

Consequently, the direct-response creative product operates as the salesman, because there is no other salesman. It is the store—often the only store. And when you think about it, direct marketing creative is the product, because the only way for a prospect to see, touch, feel, try on, try out the product is through the words and pictures in the advertising piece.

Direct-Response Creative Has a Different Objective

The primary purpose of communication in direct marketing is to provoke a discrete, concrete *action*—to get a prospect to buy, try, join, donate, subscribe, request additional information—respond to the message (hence "direct response"). This differs from general advertising, in which action is a consequential, rather than primary, aim. General advertising creative is mostly about making an impression, forging a position, expressing a strategy, building a brand or carving out a niche for it in memory. Of course a sale is the eventual objective of general advertising, but general advertising is not a place of purchase. It is not the "store" in the way that direct-response advertising is.

Time Frame Is Different in Direct-Response Creative

Like a retail environment, direct-response advertising must elicit an instant, impulsive purchase, inquiry, or demonstration of interest from customers before they leave "the store." It has to interrupt people, rivet their attention, and find a way to touch them so profoundly with what it has to say and sell that they immediately stop what they are doing to

> get a pen,
> fill out an order card,
> write a check,
> insert it all in an envelope,

find a stamp, and
put the order in the mail;

or, alternatively,

call the toll-free phone number and reveal a credit card number,
or fax a reply,
or take a coupon to a retail store,
or seek out a Web site.

And immediately! Because if prospects put the communication aside for a moment—to consider it later—chances are the direct marketer has lost them for good.

Direct-response creative, therefore, needs the stopping power of a bad accident and the magnetism of a solar eclipse. It must have the seduction of a siren, the promise of baking bread, the logic of a pyramid, the urgency of a smoke alarm, and the perseverance of a dog with a bone. It has to build an airtight case for the intellect, but at the same time achieve a dead-center hit on that sweet spot of desire and dreams.

Conversely, general advertising assumes (in fact benefits from) the built-in time lapse between receipt of the message and the actual purchase. The mission of general advertising creative is to implant and replant a reason to purchase that prospects carry with them—often at a subconscious level. Then, when a need or buying opportunity presents itself, customers will reach for the advertised product, for reasons they may not even be aware of at the time.

The mission of response advertising is to get prospects to take the action *now*—for reasons that are identifiable, essential, and of the moment.

The Merciless Measurement of Direct-Response Success

Because the action channel is provided by the direct-response communication, the effectiveness of direct-response creative is always *instantly measurable* based on whether the actions are taken or not. Think about the pressure this imposes on direct-response creative practitioners. They must constantly ask themselves, *What* will impel this instant action? What look, what line, what pledge, what lead phrase, what proof of the product's value, what kind of arguments can they advance, and what sort of rhetoric should they employ, to accomplish this feat?

Direct-Response Creative Needs a Different Vocabulary

Direct-response advertising does not operate on puns and plays on words, jingles or jokes. With very few exceptions, these are land mines for direct response. If a joke falls flat—if, in pursuit of a deft turn of phrase, an advertisement confuses prospects about what is offered, what is good about it, and what the marketer wants them to do about it—the chances of getting a response are nil. That is why so few successful direct-response creative headlines or television commercials make use of the kind of humor that often marks general advertising and makes it so entertaining. Direct-response advertising can succeed without being clever—but it can't succeed without being *clear.*

Moreover, the voice of a direct-response communication must ring unassailably true. It must be precisely relevant to the prospect's needs, dreams, desires—and problems and disappointments, too. It must be totally credible—it must make the prospect feel that the advertiser understands and can help. It must use arguments that are understandable, typefaces that are readable. It must have simple, straightforward statements of what the advertiser believes are the prospect's wishes and what the advertiser proposes to do to help the prospect realize them. It must appeal to drives as basic as the desire for love, sex, money, comfort, good looks, good health, personal popularity, and professional success; or, conversely, it must show how to avoid criticism, effort, humiliation, and pain.

And because direct response is a dialogue (I not only talk to you in a piece of direct marketing, but I ask you to respond), its communication must have the characteristics of personal communication. It needs to sound like a human voice.

General advertising lives in a land where cookie dough can talk, and disembodied voices in the washing machine discuss the cleanliness of your shirts. Direct marketing land is real life, where one customer tells another,

"You really should try this product. It has a new ingredient that gets shirts unbelievably clean."

Direct-Response Creative Is an Art and a Science

Because of the response-driven nature of the direct marketing discipline, the direct-response creative person must develop a secondary skill. We are not just artists or salespeople or apt communicators. We are scientists and researchers, constantly observing, analyzing, computing, and capturing those elements of the creative that cause telephone numbers to be called or coupons to come back to us. So if you ever find direct-response creative to sound disturbingly familiar—if you think of it as being obvious, redundant, simplistic, or trite—know this: Decades and decades of hard-won experience have gone into our collection of "motivates." We use them in our battle for response as soldiers use their most trusted and reliable weapons.

The Direct-Response "Motivates": A Changing Lexicon

"ANNOUNCING!" "FREE!" "YOURS" "YOU" "NEW" "NOW" "NEVER BEFORE" "AT LAST"

Up until some 20 years ago, the paint was still fresh on the rules for creating response-generating advertising. In fact, it was common for practitioners to reel off a list of words the simple use of which would go three-quarters of the way to getting the desired action. Those of us who joined this burgeoning industry were dutifully taught those selling ideas, those sharply-honed phrases, those tactical triggers that had worked again and again in the past and were certain to work into the boundless future. Although today these words might seem tired, trite, and overused, the concepts behind them are as powerful as ever.

The concept of *free* is still an invincible incentive. Scratch even the most jaded, cynical, and sophisticated among us and you will still find someone who harbors the dream of the unexpected windfall.

The *announcement* of something *new* is intrinsically intriguing. It takes on an added dimension if the new item—dearly wished for—has arrived *at last,* or is something that has *never* been seen *before.*

The notion of consumer benefit—what a product will do for *you*—what will happen as a result of its being *yours*—is still far more motivating than company philosophy, details of product production, size of headquarters, and number of 25-year employees.

What changes and can profoundly alter the effectiveness of a direct-response advertisement are the nuances of how these concepts are articulated. How relevant, how credible, how involving are they to the particular prospect and his or her view of the world?

The Six Ps: A Focusing Exercise

Here is an exercise I find helpful when I am creating direct-response advertising. It is a way to "lay out the tools" at your disposal in order to write an effective direct-response piece. It consists of a series of questions to ask yourself before you start the actual creative work. As the operative words in these questions all start with the letter *P*, they have come to be known around our agency as "the Six Ps of direct response."

- Who is my prospect?
- What is his or her problem?
- What is my product?
- What is its promise?
- What is my proposition? (your offer)
- What is my proof? (that the product can fulfill the promises you make)

Don't answer these questions in your head. Write your answers down, so that you can refer back to them. Don't answer in generalities. Don't tell me your prospect is women, ages 18 to 34. Put flesh on the bones. Be specific. Define prospects in terms of your product or product category.

(Incidentally, the Six Ps do not have a definitive order. It doesn't matter where you start. Start where you have the most information—perhaps with your product and its promise if that's where you feel the most comfortable.)

Who Is My Prospect? What Is His or Her Problem?

It does, however, matter a great deal where you start when you begin to craft the actual direct-response advertisement. And here is an ironclad rule: *Start where the prospect is!* What does the prospect already know, what does he or she already think or already want, where is the prospect attitudinally as relates to the product or service you have to sell? What problems does he or she face that your product can solve? What wishes does the prospect have that your product can satisfy?

Many a great direct-response advertisement has succeeded simply by identifying the prospect in relationship to the product. For example, this envelope line appeared on a direct-mail package that sold subscriptions to a new travel magazine:

AT LAST, A MAGAZINE FOR PEOPLE WHO LOVE TO TRAVEL BUT DON'T CARE MUCH FOR TRAVEL MAGAZINES.

This headline appeared on an ad offering hosiery for large women:

DON'T LARGER WOMEN HAVE A RIGHT TO COMFORTABLE PANTY-HOSE TOO?

This one appeared on an ad for clothing for large men:

BIG MEN, TALL MEN . . . 287 SHIRTS THAT FIT.

An ad for a new hair-weaving technique began:

IMPORTANT NEWS FOR WOMEN WITH FLAT OR THINNING HAIR.

Or consider the small space ad with a one-word headline:

CORNS?

Who's going to read an ad with a headline like that? No one—except a person with corns.

This relevance of the ad to prospect and problem should not be restricted to the headline. It must pervade the piece. For example, when a major shaving product manufacturer launched a new razor, it decided to use a very personal mailing piece to target young men who were just beginning to shave. "A GIFT FOR YOU ON YOUR 18th BIRTHDAY," announced a handsome box that arrived as close as possible to the actual day. And inside was a sample of the razor, coded coupons for blades (so that responses could be tabulated) and a personalized letter that began:

> Dear John:
>
> Turning 18 is a real milestone. A time when looking good is really important. A great way to look good is with a great shave. We want to start you out with the best.

In this way the new razor became part of this young man's step into manhood.

Sometimes, the direct marketing challenge is compounded by the fact that the prospect is unaware that he or she has a problem. The prospect for disability insurance is a perfect example. First of all, no one likes insurance. But more important, no one likes to pay for insurance for something they don't think will ever happen. And no one believes that they could have a terrible accident or illness that would lay them up so long and so totally that they couldn't earn a living.

So although we know who the prospect is, it is up to the advertising piece to convince the prospect that the problem exists. In a mailing about disability coverage from a major insurance company, this was accomplished with a poker hand. The envelope promised:

> ENCLOSED: A FIVE CARD STUD POKER HAND AND A GIFT CERTIFI-CATE THAT BRINGS YOU THE REST OF THE PACK.

Inside, tucked into a slot on the reply card, there was a poker hand, randomly dealt, sealed in plastic so the prospect could see only the top card. "Before you look," announced the reply card, "How much would you gamble on this hand?"

> Dear Mr. Buxton:
>
> Before you look at the five-card poker hand above, tell me—how much would you gamble it's a winner and not a dud? Fifty cents? A dollar? Five dollars? Maybe.

> How about your home? Your car? Your kid's education? Of course not! Gambling vital things like that is out of the question, isn't it?
>
> Yet I would be willing to wager a full deck of cards that right now you are gambling your lifestyle on a chance you have as little control over as the poker hand enclosed.

Sometimes an objection to the product has turned the customer away from the product category altogether. In cases like these, the direct-response creative person has to find a way to turn these negative feelings around. This was the situation confronted by a well-known by-mail book club. So an ad and direct-mail campaign geared to attracting new members sported a headline that proclaimed, "BOOK CLUBS CAN BE HELL!" Having thus bonded with the reader, the mailing went on to explain that the sponsoring service had taken all the "hell" out of membership by doing away with the onerous commitments usually associated with such clubs.

What Is My Product? What Is Its Promise?

Conventional wisdom, and certainly direct marketing conventional wisdom, has always said that if you're trying to sell a product, you show the product. People need to see what it is they're expected to buy. Today, showing the product is not enough. What we have to show is the promise of the product. We have to show not so much what it looks like as what it will do for the prospect.

For example: Propane is the fuel of choice in France, with 69% of home owners preferring it over electricity—preferring it so strongly that they are willing to put up with the choice between an ugly gas tank in the yard or an underground tank that has to be dug up and replaced every several years. One company, however, managed to design the first propane tank that can be buried for life. It was direct marketing's job to bring this breakthrough to the attention of top home builders in France.

The marketers sent an envelope with a full-bleed, close-up photograph of a grassy lawn. What's on the grass? Nothing. On the cover of the brochure—more lawn. Not a word of copy—no interruption of any kind. Open the brochure, and the lawn stretches across the spread, now interrupted by a few choice words on the right-hand page: "Life is more beautiful when 'it' is invisible." When *what* is invisible, that's the puzzle! But the puzzle is solved easily, because the left-hand page of the spread is a jigsaw puzzle. Remove the pieces and underneath the "lawn" you find a picture of the tank and the news about the invention of a propane tank that can be buried for life. Here, too, is information on how to prepare, install, and service the tank. This is one dramatic way to demonstrate the promise of the product.

A specialty store that based its appeal on the unique and unusual character of its merchandise prepared a catalog especially for Father's Day. It promised a collection of gifts Dad was sure to appreciate. And the name of the catalog supplied proof of the promise—it was titled "NOT A TIE."

A magazine that positioned itself as an indispensable resource for women interested in beauty sent out a direct-mail package with a headline on the envelope that asked, "IS IT WORTH IT? THE $72 FACE CREAM? OR THE ONE FOR $6. THE $200 HAIRCUT? OR A CUT FOR $22.50. THE $18.00 MASCARA? OR ONE PRICED AT $2.95." Point made! That kind of information *is* indispensable to women in the target group.

At its very best, the brilliance of a direct-response piece—in and of itself—can bring home the promise of a product. One that accomplished this was created to promote the city of Memphis to meeting planners as a convention site. The marketers sent each planner prospect a box that arrived wrapped in crumpled, creased, plain brown paper—apparently hand-addressed. It looked completely genuine, as if somebody had hastily wrapped and mailed it. And scrawled in the same writing as the address were the words, "We found your wallet in Memphis." When the box was opened, there was indeed a wallet inside and a suggestion, "Next time why not come with it?"

"We know this isn't your wallet," said the copy. "We're using it to make a point: Thousands of meeting planners are finding out that Memphis is one of the most cost-effective convention cities in the U.S." The wallet was loaded with imitation credit cards, each one used to tell a different story about a benefit of Memphis as a meeting place. The back of a Diners Club look-alike, called "The Dining Club" card, listed the top Memphis restaurants; "The Accommodation Express Card" noted the names and numbers of good Memphis hotels.

Clearly, no prospects will have the opportunity to understand a product or its promise if they fail to open the advertisement—if, sight unseen, they throw it in the trash. But there was no way for prospects *not* to open this piece and read it and thus open the avenue to be convinced that Memphis might be worth a shot as a meeting site.

What Is My Proposition? What Is My Proof?

I have left what is perhaps the most critical piece for last. This is where you have to get the prospect to agree to give your product a try.

There are multitudinous offers that have been successful in direct marketing. Jim Kobs, in his book *Profitable Direct Marketing,* provides a list of 99.[1] Basically they break out into free trials, free gifts, free information or analysis, free samples, free previews, risk-free inquiries, discounts, sales, time-limited opportunities, special privileges, limited editions, contests, sweepstakes, and exclusive memberships.

Today, more than ever, your offer needs another supporting piece, which I call "proof." Today's consumers are squint-eyed, cynical, and savvy. They know that if something seems too good to be true, it probably is. Their response to such offers is likely to be "Why are you being so good to me?" That is why you need to provide prospects with incontrovertible proof that you're on the level—proof that your product is all that you claim, your price is more than fair, and your offer is honorable.

What would constitute that sort of proof? Money-back guarantees, for one. Credible testimonials from recognized experts, celebrities, and other public personalities, or positive personal experiences with the product from ordinary folks—people prospects can identify with as "like me." Newspaper articles. Research figures. Price or quality comparisons with a well-known competitor. At-home tests that prospects can perform to "see for themselves." The "borrowed landscape" of a respected institution—a government agency, nonprofit association, hospital, university, successful and trusted corporation, and so on.

Which are the most powerful offers? Which are the most convincing pieces of proof? How I wish I could tell you. But the answer to those questions varies with each direct marketing challenge. Add to that the vicissitudes of an inconstant world, shifting consumer attitudes, fluctuating economic climate, and the basic burnout factor of the familiar—it is like trying to play and win a game in which somebody keeps changing the rules.

But here's the good news. Direct marketers have at their disposal a built-in barometer to those changes, as well as a fail-safe way to predetermine which proposition will perform. We can *test in the marketplace* the validity of our assumptions on the very customers we wish to sell. And because direct-response advertising is accountable advertising, we can get honest answers—in a matter of mere weeks.

Let me share a test we recently did for a major gasoline company credit card. The card, like most gas credit cards, is free for the asking. But a customer has to ask—the company cannot send the card unsolicited.

We created four direct-mail packages, each with a different offer or positioning, in order to determine which would do best at pulling requests. As I describe them to you, see if you can spot the winning concept.

In the first package we enclosed $10 in credit vouchers good for gas and services at the company's stations. These were usable only if the bearer had a credit card. "The $10 enclosed," said the letter, "is cash in your pocket pure and simple. Granted, you can't use it to buy groceries or clothes for your family. But you can use it on feeding and caring for your car at any of our service stations. As long as you have our Credit Card."

One of the most widely admired products this particular company produces—one you used to get free and now have to pay for—is the road map. Our second package offered one free. Moreover, the free map was personalized to the respondent's state: "Our new map of Illinois is ready. And we've got one with your name on it. All you have to do is say yes to a credit card."

In the third package, the local service station owner was the cosponsor of the credit card invitation. "Sam Smith over at our service station on 1063 Worcester asked us to send you the attached Credit Card Request," says the letter. "We were happy to oblige. Sam is a valued dealer for us . . . ."

The strategy of the fourth package was to position the decision as a "no-brainer." The envelope said, "THE QUESTION ISN'T 'WHY,' MR. NAMEHERE. THE QUESTION IS 'WHY NOT'?" There was a one-page letter with big headlines at the start of each paragraph that told Mr. Namehere, "IT'S FREE." "IT'S EASY." "IT'S EQUAL." "IT'S LOCAL." To make the point that the card was available at no cost, the application was virtually completed for the prospect; the letter also mentioned equal pricing for cash or credit purchases and a convenient station in the prospect's neighborhood (for proof, we put in a little computerized map so that he or she could see where the station is).

Which of our packages do you think won? To be honest, I thought it would be the package with the $10. These people owned cars, and $10 worth of premium gas is a powerful incentive just to accept a free credit card. Of course, the map package was also great for many of the same reasons. The local dealer concept was possibly a dark horse. But the "no-brainer," the last package, won hands down.

I can hypothesize (and I have) as to why. But regardless of whether I might be intuitive enough or experienced enough to understand the reason, this test gave me the answer I needed. "No-brainer" pulls more orders than three other contenders. That's the kind of information that can go straight to the bottom line.

Last question: Do the results of this test mean that "no-brainer" is more *creative* than the other concepts? In the world of direct-response advertising, *yes, it does.*

Note

1. Jim Kobs, *Profitable Direct Marketing,* 2nd ed. (Lincolnwood, IL: NTC Contemporary, 1994).

37

Promotions and Advertising

Comparison of Effectiveness

John Philip Jones

The Productivity of Sales Promotions

Sales promotions are often described as *below-the-line activity,* to distinguish them from media (theme) advertising, described as *above-the-line activity.* These are both funded by manufacturers' advertising and promotional (A&P) budgets. A promotion is a device that enables a manufacturer to make tonnage sales on a once-and-for-all basis. Repeat purchase is only rarely stimulated. And although a promotion does normally have a measurable short-term effect on sales, the downside is that in the great majority of cases, manufacturers pay a very high price in terms of profit forgone.

During the 1970s and 1980s, manufacturers progressively increased the proportion of their A&P budgets that they spent below the line. The reasons were complex, but they were related to several factors:

1. Inflation encouraged manufacturers to boost list prices and make deep price cuts to stimulate retailer interest in their brands.[1]
2. Stagnation occurred in the sales of most consumer goods categories, and manufacturers discovered that they could more easily seize market share with promotions than with media advertising (although they could do this only temporarily and unprofitably).
3. Marketing management concentrated on short-term rather than long-term performance—again, an inflation-related phenomenon.
4. Sales generated by promotions can be measured with relative ease, in contrast to the measurement of advertising effects. This is the topic addressed in this chapter.

What promotions mean in the majority of circumstances is price reductions. This procedure is disguised by manufacturers' own terminology. Promotions are often described as "investments", when they are in reality income sacrificed; they should appear on the income side of the ledger (as a reduction, a negative item), and not on the expenditure side (as money invested to achieve a productive return). For manufacturers of repeat-purchase packaged goods and marketers of services, trade promotions in 1996 accounted for 50% of total A&P budgets. Trade promotions virtually always mean price reductions, even when described by such names as slotting allowances, advertising rebates, and display incentives. Of consumer promotions (26% of A&P expenditure), the most important are coupons and various types of temporary price reductions (TPRs): price rebates printed on the label, banded packs, free samples, and so on. These devices, both those directed at the trade and those directed at the consumer, are mostly variations on the theme of price cutting. As I note in Chapter 31 in this volume, the fact that in 1996 76% of A&P funds went into promotions means that the share accounted for by main media advertising for packaged goods and services was only 24%.

The sales effect of price cutting can be quantified—with a good deal of trouble and given enough data to allow the calculation of a coefficient of price elasticity. This is a number, and it means simply the percentage by which the sales of a brand will increase immediately as a result of a 1% reduction in price. The number is preceded by a minus sign, demonstrating that lower prices cause sales to go up, and vice versa. The calculation is made from a laborious examination of historical price and sales data that establish an average sales change associated with a price change, and this should be arrived at from a range of prices. Exogenous variables (i.e., those unconnected with price) have to be accounted for, as well as time lags between price change and sales change. The data on prices must also be corrected for inflation.

The elasticity can of course be calculated for sales to the retail trade and also for sales to the consumer, and there are some interesting differences between the two. However, these are not the concern of this chapter. The main focus here is on the consumer, but it should be remembered that trade and consumer promotions can be connected. In particular, the profit from a trade promotion is not always retained by the retailer, but is sometimes passed to the customer (for example, by doubling the value of manufacturers' coupons). Incidentally, consumer promotions are all, to some extent, also directed at the retail trade insofar as they are intended to encourage retailers to display the merchandise promoted. Display is an important sales stimulus in its own right, and it can also reinforce other stimuli.

Price elasticity is essentially a measure of how easily the consumer will accept the brand being promoted as a substitute for other brands he or she may be tempted to buy. Low price elasticity means that substitution is difficult and that a change in price will not affect the demand for the brand very greatly. The opposite also holds: If elasticity is high, price change greatly affects demand as the buyer reduces or increases purchases of alternatives. As the number of competitors grows (something that tends to happen over time even though markets do not grow much in absolute size), we would logically expect price elasticities to rise.

Calculations of price elasticity are not simple, and manufacturers only rarely have in their marketing departments statisticians capable of making the estimates. However, they have been made in hundreds of cases. They are almost invariably based on a relatively narrow range of price variations, so that they should not be extrapolated too far outside this range. They can nevertheless be used for sales optimization and profit maximization.

A number of estimates have been published of the average price elasticity of groups of brands. In the most substantial study, Gerard J. Tellis of the University of Southern California has reviewed and summarized the figures for 367 different brands that appeared in the academic literature between 1961 and 1985.[2] The most striking feature of Tellis's survey is the high level of the average price elasticity, −1.76. This means that, for an average brand, a 1%

TABLE 37.1 Effect of a 10% Price Reduction

Variable Cost as Percentage of NSV	Price Elasticity	Effect on Sales (%)	Effect on Net Profit If 5% of NSV (%)	Effect on Net Profit If 10% of NSV (%)
40	−2.2	+22	+20	+10
50	−2.2	+22	−24	−12
60	−2.2	+22	−67	−34
40	−2.0	+20	—[a]	—[a]
50	−2.0	+20	−40	−20
60	−2.0	+20	−80	−40
40	−1.8	+18	−20	−10
50	−1.8	+18	−56	−28
60	−1.8	+18	−92	−46
40	−1.6	+16	−40	−20
50	−1.6	+16	−72	−36
60	−1.6	+16	−104	−52

a. No change.

reduction in price would boost sales by 1.76%. Of course, manufacturers do not vary their prices in 1% increments; a more realistic 10% price reduction would lift sales by 17.6%—an impressive figure. However, this sales increase alone provides an extremely incomplete picture of the effect of the price reduction, a point that I will demonstrate and discuss later.

Table 37.1 shows a number of calculations of the sales effects of a 10% price reduction based on price elasticities of −1.6, −1.8, −2.0, and −2.2. Tellis has argued that typical marketplace elasticities may be much higher than the −1.76 average he worked out from his 367 cases. However, the empirical support for this hypothesis is much more tenuous than that for his −1.76 average. Estimates based on European experience suggest that even Tellis's average of −1.76 may be too high. I have therefore limited the calculations here to the range of coefficients listed above, which cover not only Tellis's average, but also elasticities on both sides of it.

If we look solely at the sales projections in the third column of Table 37.1, these provide ample support for the view that promotions can shift merchandise. It is therefore perfectly easy to understand the attraction they hold for a brand manager, particularly one who finds him- or herself in the uncomfortable situation of running a brand whose shipments during the year have been slower than planned and whose sales target has to be met by December 31.

But the attractive volume figures are not the whole story. We must look at how costs have been affected. In order to do this, we have to make certain assumptions about the cost structure of the brand that is being examined. In Table 37.1, alternatives have been worked out on the basis of ratios that are reasonably typical for real brands: variable cost representing 40%, 50%, and 60% of net sales value (NSV), or the manufacturer's net receipts; and net profit representing 5% and 10% of NSV. As I have already noted, the table displays four different levels of price elasticity and a single price reduction, of 10%.

The most obvious feature of the profit calculations is that most of the sales increases provided by the price reductions yield a lower profit than before the sales rise. Indeed, some of the resulting profit reductions are disastrously large. The reasons for this unappealing outcome are (a) an increase in variable costs (raw materials, packaging, labor, and so on) required by the extra sales volume, in conjunction with (b) a deflation in the NSV, which applies to all sales resulting from the lower consumer price (i.e., all sales of the brand offered on the promotional terms; unpromoted merchandise will be sold at list price, on which it will earn normal profit).

A certain amount of promotion is undertaken for defensive reasons—for example, to maintain high distribution and display for brands in an increasingly concentrated retail trade. This approach is understandable, although manufacturers also should be able to provide a countervailing force to retailers' strength, by the obvious method of ensuring that their consumer advertising will pull the merchandise through the retail pipeline and, perhaps equally important, by ensuring that retail buyers will be aware of this process.

Although promotional actions are conducted from a mixture of offensive and defensive motives that cannot often be separated from one another, the former are generally the more important. Indeed, it seems clear that in the majority of circumstances, manufacturers who promote heavily are deliberately exchanging profit for volume; in other words, they are making less profit on greater sales, or, to make the point more crudely, slicing into their own margins in order to dump their merchandise.

Longer-Term Considerations

There are three worrying long-term legacies of promotions, and they are all in fact related to one another. First, there is overwhelming marketplace evidence that the majority of promotions have only limited long-term effects. A price-off promotion causes sales to rise, but they then return to their original level once the promotion stops. The blip on the consumer purchases graph looks like the silhouette of a stovepipe hat. The reason is that the strategy for such a promotion aims to move merchandise by bribing the retailer and the consumer. When the bribe stops, the extra sales also stop, and sales return to normal or even below. The danger that the postpromotional sales level will be below normal comes from what Nielsen calls a "mortgaging" effect. Promotions bring sales forward from a later period; thus full-price sales in the period following the promotion may be even less than they would otherwise have been. Mortgaging thus prolongs the period during which the manufacturer is paying a heavy promotional subsidy to the consumer.

Some commentators have argued that a proportion of promotional money has a long-term franchise-building effect. There is a limited degree of truth in this argument when it relates to promotions that encourage repeat purchase. However, all trade promotions and the most important consumer promotions (TPRs and coupons) have the smallest long-term effects of any below-the-line activity. With TPRs in particular, there is no stress on building a consumer franchise by emphasizing the competitive benefits of the brand or building warm, nonrational associations with it—activities that might encourage the public to buy the goods on a continuous basis. As a consequence, such promotions lead to volatile demand, in contrast to franchise building (for instance, by consumer advertising), which leads to relatively stable demand.

This all leads to a not insignificant weakening of the brand. A parallel point for which there is some evidence is that brands that are supported more by advertising than by promotions often carry a higher-than-average list price and tend therefore to be more profitable. The consumer pays the premium price because the advertised brands have more psychological added values than do heavily promoted brands. This point is related to the third legacy, to be discussed later.

The second long-term disadvantage is that promotions fuel the flames of competitive retaliation to a far greater degree than do other marketing activities. As a result, diminishing returns set in with frightening rapidity. When the competition is drawn into the promotional war, it can cause the sharp sales increases predicted by the original price elasticity coefficients to be significantly reduced—with an even more disastrous effect on the profit outcome of the promotions. The long-term result of such retaliation has sometimes been that all profit has been eliminated from total market categories. There are a number of examples of this self-destructive effect; it has happened in various countries in promotions of airlines, packaged detergents, and soft drink mixes, and it could be beginning now in the fast-food business in the United States.

The third long-term legacy of promotions is the one that is most talked about. Promotions are said to devalue the image of the promoted brand in the eyes of the consumer. This theory accords with common sense, although the argument may not be quite as powerful as it appears, because once a brand has established a consumer franchise and a brand image, it takes a long time for these to decay, as the image is maintained more by people's personal familiarity with and usage of the brand than by external marketing stimuli. However, promotions have occasionally had a demonstrably unfavorable influence on consumers' brand perceptions, as happened during the "hamburger war" between McDonald's and Burger King in the 1980s.

As a general rule, the image of a brand can never be improved by promotions—a matter directly related to the stability of the consumer franchise. There is a vicious circle sometimes described as *promotion–commotion–demotion*.

On the other hand, the image of a brand is very often strengthened by consumer advertising. This reinforcement represents a long-term effect in addition to short-term sales generation, and it leads to an increasing perceived differentiation of the advertised brand from rival brands. This differentiation in turn reduces consumers' willingness to substitute for it, thus leading to greater stability—less elasticity—of consumer demand for the advertised brand. In effect, this means that strongly advertised brands can justify and command a premium price (i.e., they need to be promoted less than is the case with weaker brands). This is a powerful and often measurable long-term effect of successful advertising.

The Return on Advertising Investments

If promotions involve such massive short-term costs and bring about such worrisome long-term problems, can advertising investments promise anything better? Setting to one side the potentially favorable *long-term* effect of advertising, which provides something like an added bonus, we can on occasion quantify advertising's strictly short-term effect. This is based on a calculation of the advertising elasticity of a brand. This calculation is also a number, and it represents the percentage increase in sales that can be expected from a 1% increase in advertising weight. The coefficient is preceded by a plus sign rather than a minus sign, because (it is hoped!) an increase in advertising will result in an increase in sales.

Estimating advertising elasticity involves complex regression analysis, but (as for price elasticity) the computation has been carried out in hundreds of cases. The most important examination of advertising elasticity undertaken to date is a study based on 128 cases published by Gert Assmus, John Farlet, and Donald Lehmann.[3] This study provided an average short-term advertising elasticity of +0.22, a figure that agrees well with earlier published studies. The reader will be struck by the large difference between the advertising elasticity coefficient of +0.22 and the average price elasticity of –1.76. It is, however, extremely dangerous to draw conclusions about the apparently much greater effectiveness of promotions. The key difference between promotions and advertising is that promotional price reductions cost the manufacturer much more money than advertising increases, so it is misleading to evaluate their relative effectiveness by their sales effects alone.

Table 37.2 displays the sales and profit outcomes of a 50% advertising uplift. This table (like Table 37.1) is concerned solely with the sort of operational changes in marketing variables that a manufacturer is accustomed to making. Business does not operate with 1% advertising variations any more than it does with 1% price changes; 50% is the minimum uplift in the advertising appropriation that will get the needle to swing. The profitability estimates in Table 37.2 are based on the following reasonably typical figures:

- Variable costs of 40%, 50%, and 60% of NSV
- Advertising-to-sales (A:S) ratios of 4%, 6%, and 8% of NSV
- Advertising elasticity coefficients of +0.1, +0.2, and + 0.3
- Net profit representing 5% and 10% of NSV

What is strikingly obvious in Table 37.2 is that, despite the relatively small sales effects of the extra advertising, these sales produce profit increases in the majority of cases. This outcome is quite different from the effect of the price reductions analyzed in Table 37.1, where the sales increases are all substantial, but nearly all of them are accompanied by serious reductions in profit.

TABLE 37.2 Effect of a 50% Advertising Increase

Variable Cost as Percentage of NSV	A:S Ratio (%)	Advertising Elasticity	Effect on Sales (%)	Effect on Net Profit If 5% of NSV (%)	Effect on Net Profit If 10% of NSV (%)
40	4	+0.1	+5	+20	+10
50	4	+0.1	+5	+10	+5
60	4	+0.1	+5	—[a]	—[a]
40	4	+0.2	+10	+80	+40
50	4	+0.2	+10	+60	+30
60	4	+0.2	+10	+40	+20
40	4	+0.3	+15	+140	+70
50	4	+0.3	+15	+110	+55
60	4	+0.3	+15	+80	+40
40	6	+0.1	+5	—[a]	—[a]
50	6	+0.1	+5	−10	−5
60	6	+0.1	+5	−20	−10
40	6	+0.2	+10	+60	+30
50	6	+0.2	+10	+40	+20
60	6	+0.2	+10	+20	+10
40	6	+0.3	+15	+120	+60
50	6	+0.3	+15	+90	+45
60	6	+0.3	+15	+60	+30
40	8	+0.1	+5	−20	−10
50	8	+0.1	+5	−30	−15
60	8	+0.1	+5	−40	−20
40	8	+0.2	+10	+40	+20
50	8	+0.2	+10	+20	+10
60	8	+0.2	+10	—[a]	—[a]
40	8	+0.3	+15	+100	+50
50	8	+0.3	+15	+70	+35
60	8	+0.3	+15	+40	+20

a. No change.

From Theory to Practice: Three Operational Recommendations

The basic discipline described in this chapter, the use of mathematical techniques to help project the sales volume and profits that are likely to follow specific marketing actions, is intended to sharpen the efficiency of marketing practice. This discipline is currently rather rarely applied, mainly because few manufacturers are prepared to go to the considerable trouble to develop the tools—that is, estimating the price elasticity and advertising elasticity for their brands. This estimation is more than a once-and-for-all process, because the actual outcome of promotional and advertising activities may differ slightly from predictions, so that manufacturers must expect to have to monitor their price and advertising elasticities continuously and to adjust them as necessary.

It will be obvious to readers that the first basic task is to carry out a good deal of homework to produce the tools, the elasticity coefficients. Everything said in this concluding section is predicated on the assumption that this work will be done. We come now to three operational recommendations.[4]

Price Elasticity and List Price

The first possibility a manufacturer should consider is a permanent price increase for its brand. At the lower levels of price elasticity, the loss of sales that would result from a 5% or 10% price boost is so small and the increased revenue from the higher price so significant that the price rise will often lead to a net increase in the profit earned by the brand. Indeed, this is a realistic possibility for brands with elasticities of -1.0 and less. If the elasticity is below -0.5, the chance of a profit increase is very good indeed.

Price Elasticity and Promotional Planning

The second recommendation is that manufacturers should do everything possible to evaluate the sales and profit results of each specific promotional action, and accumulate (and eventually use in promotional planning) a battery of data on results.

It is not necessary to repeat the lessons contained in this chapter about the danger of overpromoting and sacrificing profit for volume—lessons that point to the danger of implementing promotions in anything but a carefully planned and well-disciplined fashion. In order to test the tightness of the planning for each brand's promotional program, manufacturers should estimate how much promotional activity is necessary for strictly defensive purposes: (a) to maintain competitive levels of display in supermarkets, and (b) to counter the more aggressive promotional actions of the largest and most direct competition.

Promotional expenditure in excess of what is needed for these defensive purposes should be scrutinized with great rigor. This is a judgment call. However, the projections of sales and profit from specific price reductions provide the best available data on which an evaluation of the probable results of the manufacturer's own actions can and should be based.

Advertising Elasticity and Advertising Planning

The third recommendation to manufacturers is that they use the best available professional talent to compute the advertising elasticity of each brand they market. A common problem, however, is that the mathematics, no matter how skillfully executed, may show a complete absence of sales effect attributable to the advertising. There could be two reasons: continued mathematical insensitivity and inadequacy and/or (against the manufacturer's own judgment) an absence of any sales effect to be discovered.

It is difficult not to be disheartened by the discovery that a well-loved campaign has no effect on sales in the marketplace. Yet although the lack of success may be disappointing, the accurate intelligence of the failure should in fact be welcomed.

The absence of any evidence of effectiveness does, however, put the manufacturer in a difficult position. If the manufacturer is forced reluctantly to conclude that the emperor has no clothes, the most pressing task to be addressed is what must be done to achieve some measurable effect that can then be evaluated for its financial implications. This means embarking on an energetic program of experimentation, covering alternative advertising campaigns, budgets, media, and phasing, and this testing should go on until the manufacturer and its agency manage to achieve some perceptible results (or are forced to give up in despair). There will be a high research cost, because market testing must be used to evaluate both the campaign's short-term sales-generating effects and the long-term job that it may be doing.

A long-term effect of advertising may involve something that can be monitored by surrogate measures (e.g., the advertising may be slowly modifying consumers' perceptions of brand attributes), but what the advertising is doing may possibly be well below the surface. For instance, it may be doing a protective job for the brand in a competitive environment, and this may be measurable only when a cutback causes an erosion in market share—a very serious outcome that may take a long time to manifest itself. This possibility means that experimentation, particularly if it involves downweighting, must be evaluated over an extended period.

But what should be done if, after advertising has been given every chance, there is no perceptible short-term or long-term effect? Quite simply, the manufacturer should cut its losses. It is by no means unknown for a brand to be maintained in effective distribution by a minimal level of promotional support and with only enough media advertising to keep the brand name intermittently in front of the sales force and the retail trade—sometimes even with no media advertising at all. It is too much to expect growth from brands that are only modestly supported in this way, but they may be quite capable of maintaining a low level of profitable sales, in some cases for decades. Lux toilet soap still sells in the United States, and it has not been advertised since 1967.

A final but rather important point is a restatement of something I have already noted. This relates to brands for which advertising does have a demonstrable marketplace effect. In this effect, it will probably influence the consumer by strengthening the image attributes of the brand and hence its perceived differences from the competition. The process, which is stimulated by image-building advertising and nourished by repeat purchase, is likely to result in a reduction in the price elasticity of demand for the brand, by the process of making it less easy to substitute competitors for it. The result is that a strengthening of image attributes will make the demand for the brand less responsive to promotional price cutting. In the last analysis, this is the reason larger and stronger brands have the balance of their promotional effort tipped more toward media advertising than is the case with smaller and weaker brands.

Notes

1. Nancy Koch, *The Changing Marketplace Ahead and Implications for Advertisers* (New York: Association of National Advertisers, 1983), 5.

2. Gerard J. Tellis, "Point of View: Interpreting Advertising and Price Elasticities," *Journal of Advertising Research,* August/September 1989, 40-43.

3. Gert Assmus, John U. Farlet, and Donald R. Lehmann, "How Advertising Affects Sales: Meta-Analysis of Econometric Results," *Journal of Marketing Research,* February 1984, 65-74.

4. John Philip Jones, "The Double Jeopardy of Sales Promotions," *Harvard Business Review,* September/October 1990, 145-152.

Specialty Advertising

William H. Bolen

Calendars, matchbooks, pens, pencils, and memo pads, along with an estimated 30,000 other items, can all be used as specialty advertising items. By definition, specialty advertising is an advertising, sales promotion, and motivational communications medium that employs useful articles of merchandise that are usually imprinted with an advertiser's name or logo and are distributed without obligation to the recipient. A careful examination of this definition will reveal the true nature of this advertising medium.

The Purpose of Specialty Advertising

Specialty advertising items can be used for various purposes: to thank a customer, to introduce a new product and/or service, to develop sales leads, to motivate employees, to recruit new employees, to promote an established product—the list is endless. What the advertiser must do is determine the purpose of the promotion and then select a specialty advertising item or items to match that purpose.

Consumer Value

The idea behind good specialty advertising is to give something that people will use. Then, when people use the item, they will see the ad. For example, a 20-match matchbook has the potential for 20 ad impressions inside the matchbook cover and at least that many for the outside cover ad. Of course, to get it used, the specialty must be useful in the eyes of the recipient. If a person has no use for a 20-match matchbook, then the potential ad impressions of that specialty item will not be realized.

The uniqueness of the specialty advertising item as viewed by the target market also influences its perceived usefulness. Consumers who already have received numerous calendars will have little use for another calendar. But what if the calendar to be given is unique in some way? Perhaps the calendar begins with August and contains information about a particular school's academic year. Such a calendar would probably be used by people associated with that school, who would also likely discard other promotional calendars they receive. There is no doubt that uniqueness promotes use and, consequently, the number and quality of the ad impressions obtained.

Identification

All specialty advertising items are identified physically with the advertiser in some way. Although most will have the name and address of the firm as part of the imprint, others may identify the advertiser in a more creative way for particular promotions. Special colors or the company logo may be used to identify the organization providing the specialty item. A special green may be used to promote John Deere tractors, for instance, or pink may be the color used on specialty items for selling a particular brand of insulation in the do-it-yourself home improvement market. The advertising imprint may include words, but it doesn't have to—symbols, colors, illustrations, pictures, and so forth can all be used either separately or in combination as the means to identify the advertiser.

Free Gift With No Strings

By definition, the customer has to do nothing to obtain specialty advertising. In fact, if the customer is required to take a test drive or make a purchase or do anything of substance to obtain the imprinted ice scraper or piggy bank, then the item is being used as a premium instead of as a specialty advertising item. Note that the same physical item can be used as a specialty advertising item or as a premium. How the item is presented to the prospective customer is the determining factor. A specialty is free in every way to the recipient—in the same manner as a television ad or an outdoor poster is free to the viewer of these ad forms. A premium is not free; an individual must purchase something or otherwise meet some requirement to obtain a premium.

Types of Specialty Advertising

Specialty advertising can be classified into three groups: advertising specialties, advertising calendars, and business gifts. Before discussing these three categories, I should note that many people refer to the whole specialty advertising field as *advertising specialties.* Others refer to the field as the *novelty industry.* In the former case, the choice of term may be just a matter of preference. In the latter case, the term may reflect the way a person views the specialty advertising industry. I believe that anyone who understands specialty advertising must realize that it encompasses much more than simply the advertiser's use of novelty items or gimmicks to reach a target customer or prospect.

As mentioned, there are an estimated 30,000 specialty advertising items commonly available through the specialty industry. Some of the most popular product categories include wearables, desk/office/business accessories, glassware/ceramics, writing instruments, and calendars. Other categories include sporting goods/leisure products, food gifts, automotive accessories, housewares/tools, buttons/badges/ribbons/stickers/magnets, and games/toys/inflatables.

Advertising Specialties

Items that are useful, insignificant in dollar value, and bear the advertiser's identity are known as advertising specialties. Examples include ballpoint pens, ice scrapers, litter bags, pot holders, and key chains. Because of their very small dollar value, such items are usually well suited for general distribution to both customers and prospects; most specialty advertising items are included in this category.

Advertising Calendars

Although some calendars would be included under the category of advertising specialties, many calendars are not insignificant in dollar value. Many are also given as gifts rather than used strictly for advertising purposes. In either case, calendars offer the advertiser the potential of 365 days of advertising exposure—even more in the case of a perpetual calendar. One significant aspect of a calendar promotion is that many customers get in the habit of using particular calendars from particular firms year after year, and they learn to expect to receive the calendars on an annual basis. This can be good, but it can also be bad if a firm wishes to change to a different type of promotion. If the calendars they have come to expect are suddenly no longer available, some customers will be upset. What the advertiser must decide is the level of effectiveness of the calendar from a promotional standpoint.

Business Gifts

By their nature, business gifts are not usually trivial in value. Normally, they are also limited as to the advertising on the items. In addition, personalization is quite popular, especially in the business-to-business market. One factor of significance concerning business gifts is the Revenue Act of 1962, which limits tax-deductible gifts to $25 per year per person but excludes from the deductible amount imprinted advertising specialties costing $4 or less. Therefore, it is very attractive for business firms to give business gifts (e.g., lighters, coffee cups, rulers, pens) costing less than $4 each. Many such gifts are given as a way of thanking firms for their orders or as a goodwill gesture. Of course, the law also encourages other types of gifts that cost less than $25. It is important to note that the money spent on a gift is not as important in many cases as the uniqueness of the gift. By giving a unique nutcracker or a special pen to a client, the advertiser can make a lasting impression that has the potential to turn into a sale—the ultimate goal of most advertising.

Advantages of Specialty Advertising

The advantages of specialty advertising include longevity, flexibility, limited clutter, and selectivity. The relative advantages will vary with the specialty items in use.

Longevity

The standard 20-match matchbook already mentioned has an expected life span equal to at least 20 ad impressions. An imprinted ballpoint pen may be used for 3 months to 3 years. The desk set with a perpetual calendar can have virtually endless use. No one knows how long the yard thermometer or rain gauge may be used. If the specialty item is used by the recipient over time, the life of the specialty ad message can easily exceed the life expectancy of almost any other advertising media.

Flexibility

Specialty advertising is not limited by page size or minutes on the clock. Both small items and large items can be used as advertising vehicles. The advertiser can choose the one thing that is best for a particular promotion. Flexibility may also involve giving a series of items to a prospect over time. If a long message is needed, there are specialty items that can carry it. The same is true for a short message.

Limited Clutter

Much is said about the problem of advertising clutter in newspapers, television, and other major media. There is no doubt that individuals are exposed to numerous ad messages—probably more than a thousand—in any given day. But with specialty advertising, the ad vehicle is not usually surrounded by other advertising at the time of the initial advertising impression on the customer. This is especially the case when the specialty advertising item is distributed to the prospect in a personal manner. Compare this situation with the running of several ads back-to-back on television or all the newspaper ads placed side by side on a page. In almost all situations, specialty advertising will not be faced with similar clutter problems.

Selectivity

Depending on the needs of the advertiser, specialty advertising can be presented to the masses or to a select group. By careful distribution, 400 pen sets can be delivered to 400 prime prospects. At the same time, imprinted yardsticks may be made available to anyone who wants one. The degree of selectivity is up to the advertiser. Naturally, the more expensive business gift will be aimed more at existing customers or top prospects than at cold prospects. But like all advertising, all specialty items should be selected in relation to the target market of the product or company.

Disadvantages of Specialty Advertising

Limited copy space and relatively high cost are problems that are inherent in the specialty advertising medium. The proper use of specialty advertising can aid in minimizing these disadvantages.

Limited Space

Advertising copy must be brief on most specialty items because of their size. Many specialties are found to be limited in terms of ad copy to name, address, and telephone number of the advertiser, but more copy may be possible. Users of specialty advertising must be quite creative in making use of the small amount of space available on most specialty items.

Advertising Costs

Like direct mail, the cost per reader or recipient of specialty advertising is quite high. An item such as a watchband calendar may cost 25 to 50 cents per piece. It also costs something to get it to the customer. In most cases, these costs will be higher on a per person basis than would mass-media advertising. However, proper distribution virtually eliminates waste circulation, thereby making the cost picture much more favorable in comparison with the mass media.

Audience Measurements

What do consumers think of specialty advertising? Do businesspeople regard specialty advertising favorably? Given the fact that almost everyone has been the recipient of a specialty item, the answers to these two questions should provide insight into the audience for advertising specialties, advertising calendars, and business gifts.

Consumer Audience

In one study, consumers were found to favor specialty advertising. More than half of all recipients of specialties read the ad messages on the specialties. More than half of the specialty recipients felt more favorably toward a firm when they had received a specialty item from that firm. More than half of those consumers taking part in the study indicated that they would tend to act more favorably, at least sometimes, toward the firm that provided them with a specialty item.[1] In another study conducted by the leading market research company, A. C. Nielsen, the procedure went a step further. The researchers ascertained that, among respondents who received one or more specialty advertising items during a 12-month period, 70% purchased products and/or services from the specialty giver, whereas 49% purchased products and/or services from similar organizations not giving specialty advertising items.[2]

Business Audience

Consumers appear to view specialty advertising in a favorable manner. But what about business firms? Creative Research Associates found that more than half of all business executives and proprietors surveyed had positive feelings toward specialty advertising. In addition, almost 60% of the firms in this sample did business with the specialty giver within a year of the time that the specialty item was received.[3] Although it is very difficult to say that the specialty item was the direct cause of the sale, more than two-thirds of the business firms could associate the specialty received with the advertiser's name. In the companion report to the consumer study cited previously, A. C. Nielsen found even more favorable results than those noted by Creative Research Associates. In Nielsen's study, 74% purchased products and/or services from firms that had earlier given specialties to the business. Even though this is quite favorable, Nielsen also found that these same firms bought from nonspecialty givers in the same business categories in 64% of the cases.[4] The data thus tend to indicate that business advertisers should consider the possible use of specialty advertising in their media mixes, but should not expect a massive shift in buying behavior as a result of the use of specialty advertising.

General Audience

In a study conducted by Schreiber & Associates, almost 4 out of every 10 persons receiving specialties could recall the names of the advertisers as long as 6 months after they received the items.[5] Other studies indicate that specialty advertising items work effectively in conjunction with other media, that they can enhance incentive programs for both customers and employees, and that they can assist the advertiser in building customer relationships by means of ongoing specialty promotions such as yearly calendars or almanacs.

Advertising Costs

The cost of specialty advertising is figured in terms of fixed and variable components. The cost of artwork and special work of any kind is a one-time charge, whereas the per unit cost of the specialty item normally goes down as the quantity purchased rises. The advertiser should also be aware that most contracts include the feature of a 5% over/under provision. Under such a contract, the advertiser agrees to accept between 950 and 1,050 pens for an order of 1,000 pens, and to pay for the number of pens delivered. This feature of specialty advertising has been an unwelcome surprise to inexperienced businesses with tight advertising budgets when orders are delivered with a 5% overage. Of course, as in all advertising, the actual costs of specialty advertising are subject to negotiation with the advertising counselor, the specialty salesperson who is in many instances an independent distributor for many specialty advertising lines.

Advertising Uses

Specialty items are used by businesses of any size, from General Electric to the neighborhood appliance store. Given this broad range of applications, specialty advertising may be viewed either as a primary medium or as a support. A firm with a heavy concentration on personal selling may use specialties as its only advertising. Most firms will, however, use specialty advertising in conjunction with other media, so that each form of advertising serves to complement the other forms in use. As in point-of-purchase advertising, the use of specialty advertising is usually enhanced if it is developed as part of a synergistic advertising package. If developed and implemented properly, the whole effect can be greater than the sum of the parts.[6]

Notes

1. William H. Bolen, "Speciality Advertising," in *Advertising*, 2nd ed. (New York: John Wiley, 1984), 415-419.

2. Cited in ibid., 418.

3. Cited in ibid.

4. Cited in ibid.

5. Cited in ibid.

6. For the most current information on speciality advertising, contact the Promotional Products Association International, 3125 Skyway Circle North, Irving, TX 75038; telephone (972) 258-3043; fax (972) 258-3092; Web site at http://www.ppa.org.

Event Marketing

Shirley F. Taylor
Peggy H. Cunningham

E*vent marketing* is a term used to describe the integration of an event sponsorship with a mix of marketing activities around the event theme. As a commercial activity, it is a relative newcomer. It is only since the 1980s that the use of events as promotional vehicles has become widespread. Yet event marketing's growth rate exceeds that of any other promotional vehicle. The International Events Group (IEG), a Chicago-based event trade association, has estimated that in 1998 firms around the world would spend $17.4 billion sponsoring sports, arts, entertainment, and fund-raising events.

Despite event marketing's increasing popularity, many companies are still not aware of the potential benefits of leveraging an event sponsorship. They are not sure how event marketing fits into their corporate or marketing strategies; they do not see the benefits of using events to provide an integrating theme to their marketing and promotional efforts. Thus event sponsorships are often not effectively utilized. One industry expert has estimated that at least

50% of the companies supporting events have underdeveloped programs that are not well planned, leveraged, or integrated with their overall marketing strategy. Thus it is important that companies sponsoring events understand their potential as a strategic marketing tool that can provide an integrating force for all of the marketing mix elements.

What Is Event Marketing?

Event marketing is an extension of event sponsorship. It includes sponsorship, but it also involves the process, planned by a sponsoring organization, of integrating a variety of marketing mix elements (product, pricing, promotion, and distribution) behind a sponsored event's theme. It comprises strategic planning, careful event selection, and integration of the sponsorship into the organization's overall marketing mix. An event sponsorship is chosen because it represents an effective and efficient way of reaching a target market with a particular message. It fulfills specific marketing objectives, and its effectiveness is evaluated against those objectives.

It is important to note that event marketing is done for strategic, not altruistic, reasons, as has often been the case with sponsorship. Consumer segments are targeted and events are selected because of their ability to reach those targeted segments. Events should not be chosen based on a top executive's personal involvement with the activity, a common situation in sponsorship. Careful attention must be paid to matching the event audience with that of the firm's target consumer segment. Because event marketing is a strategic marketing tool, funds for event marketing are sourced from the marketing budget. An important distinction between event marketing and pure sponsorship is that other marketing mix elements are integrated around the event theme, a clear distinction from traditional sponsorship. For example, when Iceberg (an Italian clothing company) sponsored the Rainforest Foundation benefit concert at Carnegie Hall, many marketing mix elements were integrated around the event theme. Iceberg commemorative T-shirts were sold in the company's retail outlets (integrating product and distribution), with some of the proceeds going to the Rainforest Foundation (integrating pricing). In addition, the Rainforest Foundation theme was prevalent in Iceberg's catalogs and in-store promotions (integrating promotion). Table 39.1 provides a number of examples of event marketing campaigns, illustrating how sponsorships can be leveraged.

The Event Marketing Process

Marketing Strategy

The starting point for any event marketing decision is whether the sponsorship is consistent with the company's marketing strategy and whether it will help the firm accomplish its marketing objectives. All strategic decisions involve choices about how to allocate a firm's scarce resources among the marketing mix elements to create and enhance its competitive advantage. Because event marketing is a vehicle through which a firm can align all the marketing mix elements around an event, it is a particularly effective strategic communication tool. Investments in event sponsorship should be compared with other promotional investments to see which offers the most effective and efficient means of reaching a particular target segment and achieving marketing objectives.

For any marketing strategy, a target segment and marketing objectives must be determined. Certain questions must be answered, such as, Whom does the firm want to reach? and What effect does the firm want to have on them? Only then can specific, measurable event marketing objectives be established. These objectives can usually be classified into two broad categories: communication objectives and sales objectives. For events, communication objectives usually are couched in terms of image enhancement, increasing awareness, building goodwill, improving relations, changing positioning, enhancing corporate relations, generating sales prospects, or good public relations. Sales objectives, on the other hand, are discussed in terms of increasing sales, market share, or distribution. These two categories of objectives parallel the types of objectives set for other elements of the promotional mix, such as advertising or sales promotion.

Once objectives are set, proposals for event sponsorship are screened using policies that outline the criteria necessary to achieve the event marketing objectives. The cost of the sponsorship (which encompasses the sponsorship fees plus the cost of the marketing program needed to leverage the sponsorship) is compared with the potential benefits derived from achieving the

TABLE 39.1 Examples of Event Marketing

Year	Company	Event Sponsored	Integration
1993	Parts Plus	B.A.S.S. Inc., all of the organization's programs	*Package:* official auto parts store; ID in mailings; inserts and ads in B.A.S.S.'s 4 consumer magazines; credit in TNN's *The Bassmaster* series *Leverage:* purchased 30 ads; considering product discounts for B.A.S.S. members; cross-promotion with cosponsors; separate contract with a pro B.A.S.S. fisherman
1993	Pepsi-Cola Co., New England Regional Office (Mountain Dew and Diet Mountain Dew)	Mountain Dew Vertical Ski Challenge	*Leverage:* use "Get Vertical" as slogan for the brand at POP; on-pack ski-area discount coupons; ski-themed cans and 2-liter bottles carrying a number for toll-free ski conditions
1993	Iceberg (Italian clothing manufacturer and retailer)	Rainforest Foundation (benefit concert at Carnegie Hall)	*Package:* ID in ads, programs, tickets, and venue's marquee; entertain retailers and media on-site *Leverage:* designing commemorative T-shirts in which the proceeds go to the cause; fall catalog featuring clothing with "Rainforest-inspired" prints; promotions in-store
1993	Mennen Co. (Speed Stick deodorant)	Speed Stick Rollerblade America Tour (10-city series)	*Package:* local and national media packages and ID in all printed material, signage, and sampling *Leverage:* POS cross-promotion opportunities at retailers selling Rollerblade brand skates
1993	U.S. Bancorp (U.S. Bank of Washington)	Seattle's NorthWest Flower and Garden Show	*Leverage:* on-site booth to give a half-point discount on the home-improvement loan rate and fax credit applications to a local branch; selling discounted show tickets; program in the *Seattle Times Sunday Magazine*; entertain clients at 4 show previews
1993	Procter & Gamble (Tide)	RC Cola Unlimited Hydroplane Series; NASCAR's Winston Cup circuit Other: The Fiesta Musical "Keep America Beautiful" "Give Kids the World"	*Leverage:* 8 NASCARs and 2 powerboats visit grocery stores, mass merchandisers, and warehouse clubs; retailers—in-store signage or features; sell Tide in parking lot and display POP materials; in-store offers of racing premiums for proof of purchase

TABLE 39.1 *Continued*

Year	Company	Event Sponsored	Integration
1993	Toyota Motor Sales, USA, and Toyota Dealers Assn. of Greater New York	Toyota Comedy Fest (25 events)	*Package:* signage and ID on tickets and venue marquee and the event's print & broadcast ads, radio promotions, and collateral *Leverage:* additional 50% to monthly $1M print, radio, and TV ad; whole program of ways for dealers to tie in (e.g., support local talent shows or fund groups to go to comedy club)
1993	Eastman Kodak Co.	*San Francisco Chronicle* Chinese New Year parade and festival (23-day festival)	*Leverage:* taking photos from its booth and providing tickets for a free 5 x 7 print when the subject visits a participating Chinatown dealer; dealers give additional discounts (e.g., two-for-one coupons); first-time ads in a Chinese-language newspaper; use booth to demo its new Photo CD; concurrent sponsorship of a photo exhibit of local children at Chinatown's Chinese Cultural Center
1992	Jaguar Cars Inc.	United States Croquet Association (USCA)	*Package:* ads and editorials in USCA quarterly newsletter event programs and other publications; signage, hospitality; on-site vehicle display and test drives at USCA events *Leverage:* mailing USCA members a sponsorship-tagged invitation offering extended test drives plus a leather-bound history of the company and a contribution in test-driver's name to the World Wildlife Fund ("Project Jaguar")
1992	Coors Brewing Co. (Keystone/Keystone Light)	NASCAR (Wally Dallenbach Jr.)	*Leverage:* cans bearing Winston Cup schedule; racing-themed secondary packaging arranged in special displays; consumer sweepstakes; calendar; cosponsor with Planters LifeSavers Co., built joint displays

marketing objectives. Companies use a large number of screening criteria, but the following are some of the most common considerations:

- The event must have a theme that is consistent with the company's overall goals and strategies.
- The event must help the firm achieve its objectives.

- The event must "fit" with the interests or activities of the chosen target segment, the image of the company, and the image and positioning of the sponsoring product or service.
- The event should enhance the value of the product or service.

The event must also have the potential to be integrated with other elements of the marketing mix.

In viewing the options available for sponsorship, firms have a number of categories of events to choose from: sports, the arts, festivals, fairs, annual events, causes, music/entertainment tours. Subcategories within these are numerous (see Table 39.2). Sporting events have traditionally attracted the largest numbers of sponsors; they currently constitute 65% of the industry. Sponsorship of music/entertainment tours comes second in the spending race, followed by expenditures on festivals/fairs/annual events. The remaining expenditures are devoted to events to support charitable causes and the arts. Many people believe that sporting events are reaching the saturation point with regard to sponsorship opportunities, whereas arts and cultural opportunities have been largely underdeveloped; these latter sponsorship opportunities represent a large growth area. Sponsorship of causes has also experienced recent growth, as firms seek to achieve their marketing objectives while contributing to worthy causes.

In choosing events to sponsor, companies must decide whether the events and the corresponding event marketing efforts should be local, regional, or national. Although national events are more likely to draw broad mass-media exposure, demand for such events has intensified. As a result, many companies have turned their event marketing dollars toward the support of regional and local events in order to reach their targeted audiences more effectively. This is particularly the case for small and midsized firms that have just recently started using events as promotional vehicles. These grassroots sponsorships are valued for their potential to create emotional ties with consumers or to build personal relationships that enhance brand loyalty.

Another consideration in event selection is the size of the audience attending the event and the degree of customer participation in the event. Some events, such as the B.A.S.S. Inc. ProTournament sponsored by Parts Plus, are participant focused, whereas some involve very little, if any, customer participation. For example, Pepsi-Cola's Mountain Dew Vertical Ski Challenge has few participants, but still generates high levels of customer involvement and national media coverage. Some practitioners believe that one of the major growth areas in event marketing is in participatory events, because consumers are perceived to be more receptive to a firm's promotional message when they are personally involved in an activity.

In event selection, sponsors must also consider the number and type of other sponsors and the history of the event's sponsorships. The more sponsors, the more sponsorship "clutter," making it more difficult for each firm to communicate its message. This prompts firms to search for contracts that allow them to have "title" as the primary event sponsor. In addition, most firms will not sponsor events that have a direct competitor as a sponsor. In many cases, there are also "first mover" advantages for firms sponsoring events. A firm that is the first to sponsor an event forms a strong relationship or alliance with the event. Through this long-term arrangement, the firm becomes strongly associated with the event in consumers' minds, so that the image and energy associated with the event are transferred to the brand. In other words, the firm "owns" this position and creates an image for its product or service that its competitors cannot duplicate. These factors have led some firms to create their own events in attempts to avoid sponsorship clutter and to create perceived ownership of particular events. For example, in Canada, Molson Breweries not only sponsors the Molson Indy car race in Toronto, it also owns the race.

Other elements of event sponsorship also play a role in the achievement of the firm's objectives. These include the publicity and media exposure generated by the event, the length of the proposed sponsorship agreement, the ease of termination or renewal, the originality of the event, the reputation and professionalism of the event coordinators, opportunities for guest hospitality or for merchandising opportunities, and the tax benefits available.

Execution

Once an event has been chosen, decisions need to be made regarding the execution of the sponsorship. Sponsoring firms must examine what areas of expertise they can bring to the sponsorship relationship. Although most firms leave the actual management of events in the hands of event organizers, they may take over some of the responsibility for marketing their events. Often companies using event marketing are more experienced at the marketing task than are the organizations they sponsor. By using this expertise, they add value

TABLE 39.2 Event Sponsorship Opportunities

Acrobatics	Cowboy poetry	Scandinavian	Jai alai
Aerobics	festivals	Scottish	Jet skiing
Air shows	Croquet	Ukranian	Kart racing
Aquatics	Curling	West Indian	Kinetic sculpture
Archery	Cycling	Expo-arts	races
Arts festivals	Races	Auto	Kite festivals
Athletics	Rides	Children	Lacrosse
Auto racing	Dance companies	Design	Laser shows
Hill climbs	Dance festivals	Environment/	Lawn mower racing
Off road	Dance presenters	conservation	Luge
Rallies	Drum corps/drill	Fitness	Lumberjack/
Vintage	teams	Food	loggers
Badminton	Duathlons	Motor sports	competitions
Ballooning	Equine competitions	Music	Marbles
Baseball	Breed	Seniors	Martial arts
Basketball	Cutting horses	Fairs and expositions	Military
3-on-3	Dressage	Fencing	Military tattoos
Biathlons	Reining	Field hockey	Motorcycle racing
Billiards	Show jumping	Film festivals	Multisport events
Boardsailing	Steeplechase/	First-night	Museums
Bobsledding	hunting	celebrations	Music festivals
Bowling	Three-day	Fishing	Bluegrass
Boxing	eventing	Football	Blues
Broomball	Ethnic festivals	Frisbee/footbag	Classical/
Canoeing/kayaking	African American	Golf	chamber/opera
Charities/causes/arts	Basque	Government	Country
Education	Cajun	Gymnastics	Folk
Education, arts	Caribbean	Handball	Gospel
Environment/	Czech	Highland games	Jazz
conservation	Dutch	Historical	Marching band
Fund-raisers	French	reenactments	Reggae
Health	German	Hockey	Rock/pop
Social	Hispanic	Horse racing	Musical theater
Cheerleading	Irish	Horseshoe pitching	companies
Chess	Italian	Hurling and Gaelic	Off-the-wall events
Children's festivals	Japanese	football	Olympics/Olympic-
City/community	Jewish	Ice-skating	style competitions
celebrations	Multicultural	In-line skating	Opera companies
Climbing	Native American	Intercollegiate sports	Orienteering
	Polish	Interscholastic sports	Parades

TABLE 39.2 *Continued*

Parks	Alpine	Taste/food festivals	Fairgrounds
Pentathlons	Cross-country	Tennis	Malls/
Performing arts	Freestyle	Theater companies	developments
festivals	Nordic	Theater festivals	Racetracks/
Polo	Sled dog races	Touring attractions	speedways
Powerboating	Snowboarding	Bands	Ski areas
Promotion councils	Snowmobile races	Circuses	Sports facilities
Racquetball	Soccer	Million-dollar	Theme parks
Renaissance festivals	Softball	hole-in-one	Velodromes
Rodeos	Speed skating	Monster trucks	Volleyball
Roller-skating	Sporting clays	Pig races	Walking/striding
Rowing	Sports councils	Trapshooting	Weight lifting
Rugby	Squash	Triathlons	World's fairs
Sanctioning	Storytelling festivals	Truck competitions	Wrestling
bodies/sports	Surfing	and tractor pulls	Yacht racing
organizations	Symphonies/	Venues—arenas/	Zoos/aquariums
Shooting	orchestras	stadiums	
Skiing	Table tennis	Auditoriums/	
		theaters	

SOURCE: Lisa Ukman (ed.), *IEG Directory of Sponsorship Marketing* (Chicago: International Events Group, 1992), 259.

to their events both for themselves and for the event organizers. For example, for some of the cultural events it sponsors, American Express handles and pays for all the event advertising, including inserts that promote the event in customers' monthly billing statements. The direct-mail campaign, which uses American Express's database, plus the media advertising the company designs, increases awareness and demand for tickets for the event beyond what the event organizers could have accomplished using their own resources. Because American Express's cardholders purchase tickets with their AMEX cards, American Express's corporate sales objectives can also be reached.[1]

Thus firms must ask whether it is more efficient for them to pay sponsorship fees and take a hands-off approach to event execution or to negotiate to have the sponsorship fee reduced in consideration for such things as cooperative advertising with the event. One study suggests that less than half of sponsorship investments are in cash; the remainder are treated predominantly as either product or operational support.[2]

Integration With Other Marketing Mix Elements

Managers have come to realize that the payment of sponsorship fees is only part of the investment, and that simply sponsoring an event is not sufficient. Often using a ratio of 1:2 or 1:3, sponsorship fees are now matched with expenditures on sales promotions, public relations, and advertising in order to increase the return on sponsorship investment. Integration with the firm's overall marketing strategy as well as the other components of the marketing mix is key to the achievement of preset objectives and the firm's ability to speak to its target audience with one cohesive marketing campaign.

The sponsorship of the 1994 Olympic Games by John Hancock Financial Services is one example of event marketing by a firm that understands the power of an effectively integrated event program. Paying sponsorship fees to the Olympic Committee was only a small part of the firm's event marketing effort. Because John Hancock's sponsorship of the 1994 Olympics was designed to enhance awareness of the company and consideration of the brand, the firm's media advertising as well as its sales brochures were tied to Olympic themes. The company also created an internal marketing program called the "President's Cabinet" as part of its Olympic sponsorship program. It was designed to increase corporate morale as well as to motivate sales personnel. Although the insurance industry growth rate has been virtually flat at 5%, Hancock was able to increase its sales quotas by 20%, which resulted in $20 million in increased revenue under this program. None of the sales force complained about this steep quota increase, because achieving the new quota gave them a chance to attend the 1994 Olympics with their families.

Evaluation

Finally, event marketing efforts must be evaluated and return on investment assessed. Effectiveness should be defined as—and ultimately measured by—the degree to which objectives were met. Unfortunately, many companies undertake event marketing efforts with only a vague notion of what they are attempting to achieve. A lack of precise and quantifiable objectives will make the task of assessing effectiveness very difficult, if not impossible.

Some companies measure event marketing effectiveness by applying traditional promotional effectiveness measures. For example, companies may use audience research, attitude/image change studies, feedback from the trade, market share data, or sales data. Studies have reported that between 27% and 46% of companies use sales data to assess event marketing effectiveness; less than 20% use any type of event audience research.[3] This lack of measurement of effectiveness is partially due to the fact that event marketing is still relatively young, and thus research techniques specific to measuring its effects have not been developed. In other cases, firms neglect to budget for follow-up research. Furthermore, if only relatively small financial outlays are involved in the event marketing effort, researching the effects of such expenditures may cost more than the event marketing itself.

Because such research is costly, firms often resort to proxy measures, such as the amount of media coverage that the sponsoring company gets as a result of the sponsorship—the "measured media value." A survey of event sponsors found that 73% of respondents calculated effectiveness in this fashion.[4] Presumably, the greater the media coverage, the better able one might be to achieve communications objectives (e.g., increased awareness). However, this may not be the case. Although measured media value allows a company to compare directly the cost of exposure generated by a sponsorship to the cost of advertising in the same medium, this method neglects the differences in the quality of exposure and the unique effects that integrated event marketing programs can create compared with traditional advertising.

Perhaps one of the biggest challenges in measuring event marketing effectiveness lies in the fact that event marketing involves the simultaneous use of many different elements of the marketing mix; therefore, it is difficult to isolate the effects of any one component of the event marketing package. The converse is also true: Attempting to measure each element of the event marketing package may ignore the synergistic effects of the total package.

For the practitioner, a useful measure of effectiveness would allow one to compare the effectiveness of event marketing with the effectiveness of other promotional tools, because the key issue is not what works, but what works best. When sales objectives are set for event marketing programs, firms can track the increase in sales over a designated period. For companies that set communications objectives the task is more difficult, because these effects often take place over the longer term. Consumer attitude research often needs to be conducted to capture changes due to event marketing efforts.

Conclusion

With an increasingly competitive marketplace, tight economy, proliferation of products, and rising advertising costs, marketing executives have turned to events as an alternative promotional vehicle that can provide a cost-effective competitive edge for their products and services. Fully integrated event marketing programs can be an effective and efficient means to reach current and potential consumers with one voice. Too often firms use the various components of the marketing and promotional mixes as independent entities with different themes, objectives, and target markets. Instead of the creation of a consistent and powerful brand personality, confusion often results. Event marketing can provide a unified theme from a firm's marketing mix that can cut through existing promotional clutter, get target groups involved, increase the value of product and service offerings in the eyes of trade personnel as well as final consumers, establish emotional ties, and build relationships between a firm and its target markets. By picking the right events, companies can effectively reach specific geographic, demographic, or psychographic segments. Thorough event research, strategic planning, larger investments, and an integrated marketing mix characterize current event marketing efforts. Today's companies use increasingly creative ways to leverage their events in their attempt to get every penny's worth of value out of every sponsorship dollar.

Notes

1. Gina Mallet, "Let Me Entertain You," *Canadian Business,* December 1991, 60-64.

2. Robert Copeland, "Sport Sponsorship in Canada: A Study of Exchange Between Corporate Sponsors and Sport Groups," unpublished doctoral dissertation, University of Waterloo, Canada, 1991.

3. Ibid. See also Meryl Paula Gardner and Philip Joel Shuman, "Sponsorship: An Important Component of the Promotions Mix," *Journal of Advertising,* vol. 16, no. 1, 1987, 11-17.

4. Neil Wilson, "Why Does a Sponsor Renew?" *IEG Sponsorship Report,* October 5, 1992, 4-5.

Sports Marketing and the Super Bowl

Rick Burton

What is sports marketing? It is much more than just sponsorship of sports events. Ford, General Motors, Coca-Cola, Pepsi, Budweiser, Miller, Philip Morris (which also owns Miller), and R. J. Reynolds pay not only for name-in-title rights (e.g., the Coca-Cola 600 NASCAR auto race) but also for advertising using sports themes (on TV, radio, print, and giant billboards at the stadiums or tracks), corporate entertainment at the events, sales promotions taken to their full retail extensions, public relations, and athlete endorsements/appearances for sales meetings and key sales calls. In one way or another, all of these companies seek compelling "exposure" for their companies or key brands.

How early can we determine that sports marketing came to exist? Did the Romans promote chariot races? Did the Greeks wish to increase attendance from one Olympiad to the next? Although the complete answer may be difficult to determine, we can hypothesize that in ancient times excellence in sport was probably applauded and almost certainly rewarded. With those early rewards came recognition that competition created winners (those who lived or stood victorious over fallen foes) and also losers. Sports became the ultimate diversion from the rigors of daily life.

The Scope of Sports Marketing

As sporting events grew in popularity as forms of entertainment, we can logically gather that certain marketable elements emerged and created fertile breeding ground for early sports marketing areas. Key aspects came to include the competitors (and their sponsors), the venues, the deal makers, the equipment makers (including associated products), the vendors, the spectators, and the media (and their advertisers). Not surprisingly, these seven components exist more fully in modern sports, and the marketing derived from each frequently influences popular culture far beyond the outcomes of the games played. Let us look at these categories and identify some of the specific elements within each:

- *The competitors:* These include the athletes, the teams, and the leagues that govern the rules of each sport, the number of teams, and the game schedules. Almost every team has a marketing department whose job it is to increase awareness, attendance, and local viewership. Similarly, the leagues have significant properties departments, which have the task of bringing in corporate sponsors and national advertisers.
- *The venues:* These are the stadiums, fields, arenas, racetracks, and civic centers where sporting events take place. Many are owned by the primary tenant teams or largest spectator-drawing municipalities. All require operating staffs to maintain the facilities for team play, and they rely on frequent spectator attendance to remain financially healthy.
- *The deal makers:* These are the individuals who ultimately package the sports events and combine the competitors with the games they play. Included in this group are promoters, lawyers, sports marketing agencies, and event underwriters.
- *The equipment makers and associated products:* This group goes beyond ball, glove, pad, and backboard/goal suppliers. It includes the manufacturers of uniforms, footwear, and undergarments, and the producers of all licensed goods. In 1993, revenues from these products totaled $34 billion.

- *The vendors:* This group includes concessionaires (food, programs, parking, and the like); security; insurance representatives; legal representation for the teams, leagues, or venue tenants; and groups selling licensed products. Generally, this last function concentrates its efforts at the venue. Increasingly, however, the selling of licensed goods is expanding into new territories (e.g., shopping malls, mail-order catalogs).

- *The spectators:* Whether fans view in person or watch on TV, listen on the radio, or read Internet, newspaper, or magazine accounts, all sports played for a profit require fan involvement/participation. That involvement or interest creates a demographic base for marketers to target.

- *The media:* These comprise the broadcast and print media that either report on or carry games to the spectators. Recently, broadcast networks have paid significant fees for the rights to broadcast a league's or team's games. The networks attempt to recoup those fees by selling advertising to interested parties. Advertisers wishing to associate with "big" games or winning sports teams (which usually draw more spectator interest) often pay a premium.

Basic Facts/Important Users

Because of the competitive nature of sports, the seven parties described above have helped make sports marketing into a massive industry that continues to grow dramatically. According to the International Events Group's *Sponsorship Report,* by 1998, North American marketers were expected to spend $6 billion to sponsor sports events, up 10% from 1997.

When Quaker Oats laid out a reported $18 million for its Gatorade brand to woo basketball star Michael Jordan away from Coca-Cola, sports marketers were not surprised. Jordan is the ideal sports warrior. He is an articulate champion, as well as young, handsome, and congenial. He even has his own Nike-funded image: the brand Air Jordan. Not surprisingly, Jordan emerged as the leader among a rapidly growing number of modern athletes (Tiger Woods, Dale Earnhardt, Grant Hill, Andre Agassi) who found themselves able to make more money from commercial endorsements than from teams or leagues.[1]

By 1993, basketball star Shaquille O'Neal, borrowing wisely from Jordan's sports marketing trailblazing, created a new consumer concept called Team Shaq. Working closely with lawyer and agent Leonard Armato, O'Neal developed his own logo and fully copyrighted his nickname (Shaq) and pet phrase (Shaq Attack). His endorsement deals have been with Pepsi, Reebok, Spalding, Score Board, SkyBox, Kenner Toys, and Tiger Electronics. He has also worked as an actor (the movie *Blue Chips*) and rap star (his debut disc *Shaq Diesel* produced a top-10 rap single). Elevated by the sports media and companies hoping to associate with Shaq, this 21-year-old, 7-foot center was virtually everywhere, and reaping royalties every time his endorsed products moved off the shelf. As *Forbes* magazine saw it, Shaq was pro basketball's first prepackaged multimedia superstar.[2]

What can we make of these modern sports heroes? Are they worth more than the president of the United States or the CEO of a major company? Or are they overpaid jocks who just happen to hit home runs or three-point jumpers? Either way, they represent modern-day diversions, placed on towering pedestals by what Sal Randazzo calls our "collective dreams." Randazzo also says that "advertisers have learned they can make their sales pitch more effective if they wrap their products in our dreams and fantasies." [3] He further notes that brands, and the celebrity athletes representing them, are akin to ancient gods and mythical heroes. They are visualized images of our unspoken dreams.

Miller Lite apparently grasped this concept when the company created the award-winning Lite All-Star television commercials in 1975. For more than 15 years (an extremely lengthy period for any image-driven advertising campaign), Miller created a premise that viewers of sports on television (primarily men) could simulate the experience of having a cold beer with football heroes like Matt Snell, Dick Butkus, and Bubba Smith.

Ultimately, it did not matter that Miller Lite's sports stars were retired (following a beer industry agreement with the television networks and the federal government) or mediocre in terms of their athletic achievements (e.g., baseball players Bob Uecker, Marv Throneberry). What mattered was the creation of a memorable male camaraderie fantasy and the all-important image that men who are manly drink a low-calorie beer.

Thus when crowds in real stadiums shouted "Tastes Great" and "Less Filling" at each other, they simply mimicked the RSVP line of an invitation to dine with the modern gods of sport. Not surprisingly, Miller's advertising, which was hitched to the enormous appeal of sports figures in American society, helped rocket a new product from an unknown brand to the second-largest-selling beer in the United States.

By the early 1990s, other advertisers sent out invitations ranging from Nike's "Just do it" and Gatorade's "Be like Mike" to McDonald's "What you want, is what you get." This general slogan for America's number-one quick-serve restaurant was used to humorous effect when basketball superstars Jordan and Larry Bird (and later National Football League kickers Chip Lohmiller and Pete Stoyanovich) challenged each other to make impossible shots (kicks) in order to win a Quarter Pounder With Cheese.

The consumer, ordinary mortal that he or she is, did not need those athletic skills to win the product of choice. Instead, advertisers simply required an ongoing awareness among consumers that McDonald's, Coke, or Budweiser is associated with winners, is conveniently located everywhere, and is almost always available.

In terms of consumer reach (the number of people upon whom advertising impressions are made) and frequency (the number of times an advertised message is exposed to a target audience), it has been hard to top the sports marketing efforts of the automotive, soft drink, beer, and tobacco companies. This became evident in the late 1970s and early 1980s, when sports marketing at these companies exploded in importance and became a critical area for establishing competitive advantages.

At the time, those four product categories had large cash reserves available to market competitively similar products to consumers facing improving economic conditions. The marketers in these categories were also sustained by the knowledge that a desirable target demographic (usually men 21-34) was closely following auto racing, football, baseball, and basketball. Those were sports marketing's four biggest "annually contested products."

Frequently, competitors within a category (e.g., Pepsi and Coke) have battled ferociously for visibility that often overlapped. In 1993, Coke spent $14 million creating its successful "Monsters of the Gridiron" consumer promotion campaign. In this integrated promotion, Coke used television advertising featuring 28 professional football players, like Lawrence Taylor of the New York Giants and Randall Cunningham of the Philadelphia Eagles (dressed up as Halloween monsters), to alert consumers to look for in-store displays of Coke in order to enter a football-themed sweepstakes run interactively through a toll-free telephone number. More than 35 million calls were received. Coke would later update its NFL promotion by creating the "Red Zone," which thematically connected a football phrase with a key brand equity for Coke (the color red).

The Super Bowl

Almost any discussion of sports and its behavioral imprint on American society in the late 20th century eventually leads to a discussion of the National Football League's (NFL) annual Super Bowl championship. This single-day event (traditionally held on the last Sunday in January) has become so dominating in U.S. culture that 9 of the top 10 most-watched television programs of all time are Super Bowl broadcasts.

But is it a smart advertising buy? Does a 30-second unit aired in January 1999 (at a cost of $2 million per 30-second commercial) do the job? [4] Let's look at the facts. History would suggest that it does. In January 1994, despite featuring a rematch between the defending champion Dallas Cowboys and the Buffalo Bills, losers of the three previous NFL championships, Super Bowl XXVIII produced a 45.5 national rating (representing 45.5% of all homes with a television set being tuned in to the program) and a 66 share (the percentage calculated for the number of television sets in use). With more than 750 million viewers worldwide and 130 million in the United States, it was the most-watched television show in U.S. history.[5]

What generated this huge audience? More important, why did so many major advertisers agree to pay about $900,000 that year for one 30-second Super Bowl commercial, a price more than three times higher than the highest prime-time program unit during that week? After all, the Super Bowl, in any given year, is only one of more than 200 professional football games played.

Part of the answer lies in recognizing that Americans love sports. Advertising agency D'Arcy Masius Benton & Bowles noted in a comprehensive 1992 research study that approximately 70-75% of all Americans "participated in a sport, watched, listened, read about or attended at least one sporting event within the last year." The researchers also noted that "sports seem to define who we are, both socially and personally." Additionally, involvement with sports was considered a good way "to make friends and have fun with other people." [6]

In another study, "ample leisure" was found to be one of the major aspects of the "American Dream." In fact, the value of ample leisure was rated equal to or higher than "securing an enjoyable job," "developing a rewarding career and family life," or "procuring wealth." [7] It is not surprising, therefore, that Americans increase their interest and television viewing when sports championships (e.g., baseball's World Series, professional basketball's NBA Finals, or college basketball's NCAA Final Four) are decided. Long regular seasons and graduated playoff systems combine with huge preevent media coverage and significant corporate sponsorship investments to make the World Series, Super Bowl, hockey's Stanley Cup, and basketball's NBA Finals national forms of entertainment. But of these events, only professional football's Super Bowl is decided in a one-day, one-game, winner-take-all championship.

The Super Bowl is a major television viewing experience. It is infused with hype, game heroics, and halftime concerts. It causes American consumers, both male and female, to host and attend annual parties rivaling those traditionally held on New Year's Eve. One advertising agency research study found that more than 80% of the people who viewed the Super Bowl on television attended a Super Bowl party.

Advertisers with substantial marketing/advertising budgets also seem to throw a party. Many spend millions to create and produce commercials (some of them complex 1-minute movies) and then pay millions more to air their advertising masterworks. The Super Bowl's past ratings and share would appear to support this as sound business practice: big parties, big viewing numbers—high aided recall of brand messages.

Recently, however, different sources have challenged the Super Bowl's position as the ultimate advertising choice. Advertising agency N. W. Ayer showed in early 1994 that for $900,000, an advertiser could follow at least two alternative plans that would outperform the reach and ratings points generated by a commercial on the Super Bowl (the findings are summarized in Table 40.1). Granted, buying a block of advertising on prime-time programming may not sound as exciting as buying one commercial unit on the Super Bowl. And that prime-time buy will probably not include tickets to the game (provided by the selling network as a merchandising benefit). But greater numbers of ratings points and greater potential reach should speak loudly to the objective media buyer.

In addition, advertisers know that not every viewer of a program will see a particular commercial (viewers leave television rooms to visit kitchens, bathrooms, and so on) and that Super Bowl viewership can carry incremental distractions:

- The game can be lopsided (i.e., not offer an evenly matched contest) by as early as halftime, and viewers may turn off the game.
- Super Bowl party etiquette favors viewers' talking during the commercials and not during the game, so that visual awareness is high but overall message comprehension is low.

TABLE 40.1 Super Bowl Options

Scenario I ($891,000; one 30-second spot on one prime-time show each night of the week)	Scenario II ($895,000; a 30-second prime-time "roadblock" on Sunday and Monday nights)
Monday: *Murphy Brown* (CBS)	Sunday: *ABC Sunday Night Movie*
Tuesday: *Coach* (ABC)	*CBS Sunday Night Movie*
Wednesday: *48 Hours* (CBS)	*NBC Sunday Night Movie*
Thursday: *Wings* (NBC)	*Married . . . With Children* (Fox)
Friday: *Picket Fences* (CBS)	Monday: *Day One* (ABC)
Saturday: *The Commish* (ABC)	*Dave's World* (CBS)
Sunday: *CBS Sunday Night Movie*	*Blossom* (NBC)
	Fox Movie
Comparison with Super Bowl XXVIII	Comparison with Super Bowl XXVIII
Ratings points: +48%	Rating points: +64%
Reach: +6%	Reach: +25%

SOURCE: N. W. Ayer (1994).
NOTES: Ratings points/reach comparisons are based on adults 18-49. Reach is based on actual delivery of each schedule from the week of November 15, 1993. Nielsen's cumulative audience data were used for this analysis. Costs were based on October MediaWatch figures. A single Super Bowl commercial (30 seconds) cost $900,000 in 1994.

- Many Super Bowl commercials use similar themes (Nike, Reebok, Converse, and McDonald's all used basketball story lines for 1994 Super Bowl ads), making key selling messages/brand names harder to remember, which means lower recall.
- Many Super Bowl commercials utilize celebrity endorsers who may make sports memorable but reduce brand retention (Chevy Chase, Cindy Crawford, Bo Jackson, Larry Bird, and Michael Jordan were featured in four of the five top-rated advertisements during the 1994 game).[8]
- The absolute number of commercials during the game (56 national 30-second units were available for the January 1996 game) creates a great deal of advertising clutter.

Studies conducted by researchers at the University of Delaware found that one day after Super Bowl XX, consumers surveyed remembered an average of just three commercials. Although the methodology featured "a very strict measure of unaided recall," requiring consumers to identify correctly company, brand, and advertisement content, this finding is suggestive of the Super

Bowl's advertising overload. Despite some aided-recall measures in the 60% range, very few commercials are so intrusive on one viewing that they are memorable and brand beneficial the next day or the next week.

So why is there an annual rush to purchase Super Bowl spots at increasingly higher rates? Why do many advertisers debut entire advertising campaigns during the Super Bowl? Why do newspapers like *USA Today* dedicate entire pages to Super Bowl advertising coverage? (*USA Today*'s annual Super Bowl Ad Meter features a panel of volunteers convened specifically to rate commercials seen during the game.)

The reason, in part, is that the Super Bowl is an American celebration that annually combines the most-watched American sport with performances by giants in the American entertainment industry (e.g., Michael Jackson was featured as the halftime entertainment at the 1993 Super Bowl); further, it is heavily promoted via preevent advertising (e.g., Budweiser, Sprint, McDonald's). These high-profile ingredients, plus an unusually high female viewership—for a male-only sport—are not found annually as a mixture in other American media events.

A portion of the answer might also be found in what the University of Delaware researchers investigated in trying to determine if the Super Bowl creates a processing efficiency whereby information (i.e., advertising) is processed "more efficiently when viewers [are] feeling pleasure because pleasant states facilitate learning." Although this thinking was not completely supported, there are indications that viewers of the Super Bowl are unusually aware of the advertising.[9]

Cramer-Krasselt, a Milwaukee advertising agency that has annually conducted Super Bowl advertising research, found in 1992 that 94% of the Super Bowl viewers surveyed felt that if advertisers were paying the highest possible fees for airtime during the game, they would use their best commercials.[10] By inference, if almost half of America tunes in to see some portion of the game, and the new advertising has richer production values than commercials in pre-Super Bowl regular prime-time programming, then discussion of the advertising and the potential for retention will be elevated, because of the very quality of the messages.

Cramer-Krasselt's 1994 aided-recall work showed that 61% of the respondents recalled specific commercials when probed. This compares more than favorably with the 23% average aided recall for prime-time program advertising. In addition, although Super Bowl costs per thousand (CPM) are, on average, higher than a prime-time CPM, Cramer-Krasselt found 62% of viewers think Super Bowl commercials are "more interesting" than commercials shown during a regular television season.

A celebrated Super Bowl ad premiere was Budweiser's "Bud Bowl," now a commercial series that costs brewer Anheuser-Busch millions to produce yet runs only once each year. In fact, in 1991, Budweiser reportedly spent more than 3 months and $1.8 million to produce one 30-second Bud Bowl commercial. It was thought at the time to be the most expensive commercial ever produced.

Other memorable Super Bowl examples include Nike's debut pairing of Michael Jordan and Bugs Bunny, Pepsi's "Flying Geese," and American Express's pairing of comedian Jerry Seinfeld and Superman. Master Lock, which did not use celebrities, for many years reportedly invested more than one-third to one-half of its entire consumer advertising budget to show a slow-motion sequence of a bullet smashing into a steel padlock.

What creates this supercharged environment for the Super Bowl? Is it possible that advertising featuring celebrities and outlandish locations or exotic sets is a more memorable setting because extensive reach means more people see highly creative commercials and then talk as knowledgeably about the commercials the next day as they talk about the game?

Many advertising experts feel that advertising on the Super Bowl has become so highly publicized, it is akin to the Academy Awards of advertising. The best new commercials and advertising campaigns are presented, and the best of the best are remembered.

One of the most highly recalled (and interesting) commercials of all time is Apple Computer's famous 60-second commercial "1984," which *Advertising Age* has called "the most powerful TV advertisement of the 1980s" and a creative execution thought to have changed the advertising industry. Although it aired in 11 U.S. markets 2 weeks before the Super Bowl, it was premiered nationally on the 1984 Super Bowl. The reaction to and awareness of this commercial were substantial.

Some believe the development of the Super Bowl as an advertising "Super Event" was due, in large part, to the public relations success (and subsequent sales success) enjoyed by Apple Computers after the airing of "1984" during the third quarter of the 1984 Super Bowl. Apple's communications approach to the Super Bowl advertising platform was strategically distinctive. In gauging the advent of the computer/technology revolution, Apple and its advertising agency, Chiat/Day, used the 1984 Super Bowl as a forum for "teasing" the American public about the power of personal computing. More astutely, the agency and Apple executives determined that the new Apple advertising was news. All three network television news programs showed parts or all of the commercial as a major story following the game. Almost overnight, Apple's advertising was elevated from the role of nonpersonal, paid-for information to that of supplying endorsed social commentary and highly entertaining drama.

More recently, Reebok used the 1994 Super Bowl for an advertising first when it shot and edited a commercial during the game's fourth quarter. Airing a 30-second spot immediately following the game's 2-minute warning, Reebok took advantage of gains in technology to create, produce, and air an advertising-based presentation of the game's Most Valuable Player (Cowboy running back and Reebok spokesman Emmitt Smith). This was newsworthy, and, as with other notable commercials, the television media covered the advertising as news. In doing so, the media significantly increased reach and frequency for Reebok, the NFL, and the Super Bowl.

But did the advertising generate a sales increase? Was Reebok's investment returned in a quantifiable fashion? Although robust research on sales effectiveness was not conducted, the advertising trade press noted that Reebok was "pleased with the effort but not likely to revisit this expensive creative application." Perhaps the expense of creating and purchasing one shot was prohibitively high for a measurable return on investment (ROI).

But if 1998's Super Bowl was any indication, ROI uncertainty is not an overriding issue. Pepsi, Nike, McDonald's, Taco Bell, Ford, Visa, Toyota, and Pizza Hut all lined up quickly to buy units on 1999's Super Bowl. And despite paying about 9% more than the previous year for a 30-second spot, these advertising giants continued a recent tradition by producing commercials with celebrities like Deion Sanders, Michael Jordan, Shaquille O'Neal, and Andre Agassi. These advertisers knew there would be a large audience watching the NFL's championship game. How big was unknown, but history had shown they could expect at least a 55% share. So, to avoid being left out, they committed to participation months in advance and sought, where they could, category exclusivity arrangements.

The Future of Sports Marketing

Sports marketer Gordon Kane (of the U.S. Olympic Committee) believes the use of sports is in its infancy when viewed from the perspective of consumer marketing's overall tactical spending mix. Still, Kane sees a rapid growth spurt for a very healthy youngster. With 1998 sports sponsorship expenditures exceeding $15 billion worldwide, the sports marketing industry should continue to enjoy strong growth well into the 21st century.[11]

This is plausible when one considers the role of expanding technologies (the convergence of phones, computers, and televisions) and that broadcast networks like Rupert Murdoch's Fox Broadcasting, Disney's ABC and ESPN networks, and Westinghouse's CBS-Sports are willing to pay $17.6 billion for 8-year broadcast rights to NFL games. Projects like the World Cup, the Summer and Winter Olympics, and an expanding NFL and National Hockey League have put millions of dollars for rights fees and category exclusivity into play and will influence future corporate spending plans for years to come.

To put this in perspective, it has been reported that the Arizona business community took in more than $300 million from visitors and businesses for the 1996 Super Bowl.[12] Boston, meanwhile, had projected the total estimated economic impact of six 1994 World Cup games exceeded $250 million. By contrast, when the Olympics came to Atlanta in 1996, the economic impact was well over $1 billion.

Still more examples of the economics of sports are the $50 million investment moves by entertainment giants like Disney and Blockbuster, who purchased NHL hockey teams. Both companies made these moves to take advantage of "built-in audiences" that can bring sports-spending loyalties to movies, video stores, and theme parks. Of particular interest to these family-oriented organizations are the dynamic cross-marketing opportunities and significant revenues to be secured from licensing (selling the right to use team trademarks) and merchandising.

Like Mickey Mouse and Bugs Bunny, team mascots and logos can be gold mines. In the NHL, the logo of the San Jose Sharks expansion team, which shows a hockey stick-chewing shark, was designed to appeal to males, females, and young people alike. The calculated result: Within one year, the Sharks, despite a losing record in the mid-1990s, had the highest licensing revenues of any team in the NHL (more than $100 million) and were outselling 95% of all other sports teams in football, baseball, and basketball.

In optimizing the growth of licensing, the NFL, NBA, NHL, and Major League Baseball have been particularly aggressive; combined, the four generated more than $10 billion in licensing revenue in 1998. The NFL's arrangement with its member teams is interesting, in that it provides the league with ownership of every team trademark and logo.

Private NFL research carried out in 1990 and 1991 showed that the league has an extremely positive image, with 94% of U.S. women and men recognizing NFL symbols like the league's shield and team logos. Additionally, 64% of NFL fans indicated that "companies, products or services associated with the NFL are of high quality and superior to their competition."

Another growing aspect of sports marketing is cross-marketing. This takes advantage of the marketing strengths of multiple organizations and makes it possible for two or three companies (or broad-based conglomerates) to combine resources and grow distinctly different products. An example was when the NHL and ABC-TV tied in with Blockbuster Entertainment to promote the hockey playoffs in Blockbuster Video's 1,500 video stores. ABC promoted the upcoming NHL games and Blockbuster's NHL promotion via the airwaves. Blockbuster used its distribution capabilities to encourage its video renters to watch the ABC telecasts of the NHL via in-store point-of-purchase materials. The NHL, for its part, allowed the promotion to happen.

The NHL also allowed Disney to name its new team the Mighty Ducks of Anaheim. That might sound funny to the traditional sports fan, but any moviegoing child of the 1990s can tell you that *The Mighty Ducks* was a successful children's movie franchise for Disney. With Disney owning record labels, TV stations, cable channels, theme parks, and retail stores, it will come as no surprise that the Mighty Ducks licensing efforts and cross-marketed attendance programs have benefited hugely from nontraditional selling efforts that stretch across multiple boundaries.

These cross-promotions, whether engineered in-house across company-owned portfolios, or brokered with interested second and third parties, have the luxury of leveraged strengths. One company brings the distribution channel (stores on every corner), one brings the media visibility (national advertising or, in the case of a network broadcast partner, national promotional announcements), and another brings the team or league.

Planning for Success

All of the elements discussed above make sports marketing a very exciting field. It is growing, dynamic, highly visible, and always competitive. But does it work? Many marketers believe it does, but they are often hard-pressed to produce quantifiable evidence. Few companies realize that sports marketing

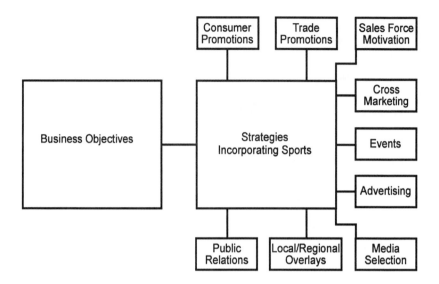

Figure 40.1. Sports Marketing Planning Procedures
SOURCE: Clarion Sports and Entertainment, Greenwich, Connecticut. Reprinted by permission.

is rarely a general strategy for business success; rather, it is an expensive tactic that must fit within a comprehensive business objective and plan, such as that illustrated in Figure 40.1.

Research often shows that fans love to be associated with a winner or a high-visibility property and believe, with varying degrees of confidence, that celebrity-endorsed products are more popular. Evidence gathered by the Roper organization suggests that 9 out of 10 people view corporate sponsorship of professional sports as a "good thing" or that they don't care one way or the other; 70% say that corporate sports sponsorship provides useful product information.

Success at the cash register, however, requires a sales and marketing relationship that stretches far beyond an image in a 30-second television commercial or a billboard at a racetrack. What most companies fail to create is a tightly designed sports marketing component in their overall marketing plan. Integration—the buzzword of the 1990s marketer—is a way to tie multiple elements of a sports investment together. Advertising, in-store materials, sales force incentives, public relations, event hospitality, and in-stadium giveaways can all tie together to reach target consumers with a determined and focused frequency.

The cost to integrate, however, will often represent a significant percentage of a brand or company's marketing investment. Results must be evaluated in a manner that allows an ROI analysis to take place. Additionally, companies and their managers must show a residual benefit over time. This is most frequently seen when other noncompetitive companies, teams, or leagues promote the sponsoring company's involvement at no charge to the sponsoring company.

A 1- or 2-year entry into a major sports property, followed by a sudden pullout, eliminates the ability to get a clear reading on ROI and to take advantage of potential residual benefits. In almost every case, start-up costs must be endured that, at first, make the sports marketing investment costly and inefficient. It is only over a period of time (usually 3-4 years) that a company can start to track consumer awareness of the sports investment and research can show a positive correlation.

Ideally, awareness of a sports association may change a consumer's perception of an existing company or introduce a new brand to a target consumer. If the awareness leads to trial, conversion, or most-often usage, the investment can be seen as beneficial to the corporation's goals. For most companies considering sports marketing in the 21st century, the decision process will come down to at least seven key questions:

- What will a particular sports investment cost?
- Is the event/sport consistent with corporate or specific brand objectives/strategies and can it create positive impressions with targeted demographic groups?
- Who will be influenced by this involvement and in what fashion will they react?
- How will this sports marketing investment affect sales over a defined time period?
- How will the investment be analyzed (i.e., what are the evaluative criteria)? Can it be seen as cost-efficient versus more traditional financial outlays (i.e., is the measurable outcome consistent with other available options)?
- How can the company leverage this investment across multiple internal and external publics (e.g., consumer, sales, corporate, retail)?
- Does this investment have the ability to create a distinct retail advantage?

Already, sports marketing programs are heavily scrutinized and evaluated by multiple departments within the corporate structure of many large organizations. Stringent criteria, with an increasing eye toward quantifying results, will replace the excitement company executives might feel at seeing their company logo on the stadium wall or the roof of a stock car.

Sports marketing into the next century will have to show more than a causal relationship with increased sales. In a global environment where the bottom line clearly shows stakeholders the results, the competitive nature of the business world is forcing marketing decision makers to select the right alternatives in a dynamic marketplace.

Notes

1. Randall Lane and Peter Spiegel, "The Year of the Michaels," *Forbes,* December 16, 1996, 244-259.

2. Randall Lane, "Prepackaged Celebrity," *Forbes,* December 20, 1993, 86-90.

3. Sal Randazzo, "Advertising as Myth-Maker: Brands as Gods and Heroes," *Advertising Age,* November 8, 1993. See also Sal Randazzo, *Mythmaking on Madison Avenue* (Chicago: Probus, 1993).

4. James B. Arndorfer and Chuck Ross, "A-B Shells Out Record Price for '99 Super Bowl," *Advertising Age,* April 13, 1998, 1, 40.

5. Rick Burton, "A Case Study on Sports Property Servicing Excellence: National Football League Properties," *Sport Marketing Quarterly,* vol. 5, no. 3, 1996, 23-30.

6. D'Arcy Masius Benton & Bowles, *Games, Gender and Generations: America's Passion for Sport* (St. Louis, MO: D'Arcy Masius Benton & Bowles, 1992).

7. Summary of *Roper Report* 94-1, May 1994, 4-5.

8. Martha T. Moore, "Super Bowl Ad Meter VI: Humor Is the Star in Bowl Ads," *USA Today,* January 31, 1994, 3B.

9. Mark A. Pavelchak, John H. Antil, and James M. Munch, "The Super Bowl: An Investigation Into the Relationship Among Program Context, Emotional Experience, and Ad Recall," *Journal of Consumer Research,* vol. 15, December 1988, 360-367.

10. Cramer-Krasselt, Milwaukee, as cited in "How People Watch," *Adweek's Marketing Week,* January 13, 1992, 24.

11. Gordon Kane, personal communication, 1995.

12. *Arizona Republic,* May 30, 1996, cited in *Sports Business Daily,* May 30, 1996.

Business-to-Business Advertising

Beth E. Barnes

What Is Business-to-Business Marketing?

Business-to-business marketing is a process in which one firm markets its product(s) or services(s) to another firm. Rather than focusing marketing activities on individual consumers, business-to-business firms deal with business customers, who purchase their products for one of three major reasons: (a) to use the products in the manufacture of other products (e.g., a bakery firm's purchase of eggs and flour or an automobile company's purchase of sheet metal), (b) to use the products to manufacture other products or to offer services (e.g., a construction firm's purchase of an excavator or an airline's purchase of aircraft), or (c) to use the products in the course of running businesses (e.g., a consulting firm's purchase of office supplies or a restaurant's purchase of a cash register).

Although business-to-business activities do not receive as much public attention as consumer marketing efforts, the business-to-business sector is quite large. According to a 1995 estimate, there are 1,700,000 U.S. business-to-business marketing firms.[1] This figure does not include the many companies that sell products or services to both consumer and business markets.

Business-to-Business Purchasing Decisions

Business-to-business purchasers generally follow one of three decision-making models. The first, and simplest, is the straight rebuy. In this situation, a firm buys a product or service it has purchased in the past from a supplier it has dealt with before. This is essentially a reordering situation and carries very little risk. If the company has been satisfied in its past purchase and use of the product, the straight rebuy greatly streamlines decision making. This is the equivalent of routinized response behavior in consumer decision making.

The second approach is the modified rebuy. Here, a company purchases a familiar product from a new supplier. For example, a bakery might shift its purchase of flour to a new flour mill. The modified rebuy carries some risk, as the buyer and seller will have to negotiate the terms of their new relationship. The decision to switch suppliers is usually based on such considerations as product quality, pricing, and delivery terms. The modified rebuy is the business-to-business equivalent of a consumer's limited problem solving.

The third and most complex approach is the new task decision. Here, a buyer purchases an unfamiliar product from a previously unknown supplier. If the hypothetical bakery decides to start making fruit pies in addition to bread and rolls, it will need to find a fruit supplier. The bakery will have to make decisions as to the necessary specifications for both the product (quality of fruit, quantity to be purchased, and so on) and the supplier (pricing terms, delivery system, guarantees, and so on). New-task decision making is similar to extensive problem solving in consumer product decision-making.

The Role of Advertising in Business-to-Business Marketing

Business-to-business marketers use advertising for a variety of reasons. In the straight rebuy situation, advertising acts as a reinforcement for the customer's purchasing decision. A consistent advertising presence ensures that the supplier's name is kept at the forefront of the customer's memory and signifies that the supplier is stable and reliable. It also acts as a defensive measure against potential competitors. In some situations, a strong advertising presence may even reduce the need for frequent personal sales calls to maintain the customer relationship.

Under modified rebuy conditions, advertising plays an important role in alerting prospective buyers to the existence and merits of alternative suppliers. Business-to-business advertising is often used to generate leads, or a list of prospects, for the company's sales force. A firm looking for a new supplier might start its search by looking through advertisements, using the information in the ads to compare the new supplier's offerings to those of the current supplier.

In new-task buying, personal selling is likely to be the dominant marketing communications technique. Advertising still has a role to play, however. Advertisements can be used to generate sales leads, as in the modified rebuy situation. The would-be supplier's advertising presence also acts in a presell role for the sales force, generating name recognition and increasing the chances that the prospective customer will agree to meet with a sales representative. In this case, advertising creates awareness for the supplier company and its products, lending an air of credibility.

Business-to-Business Advertising Media

Advertising media choices for business-to-business firms take into consideration two important characteristics of the business-to-business marketplace: Business target audiences are extremely specialized in their needs and are usually much smaller than consumer target audiences. As a result, business-to-business advertisers rely on more specialized versions of consumer mass media.

Direct marketing media, particularly direct mail and telemarketing, are widely used by business-to-business advertisers. In fact, spending by business-to-business firms accounts for the majority of direct marketing expenditures in the United States. These companies spent an estimated $77.4 billion on direct marketing in 1996.[2] Advances in mailing list compilation and management have resulted in a vast array of mailing lists being available to business-to-business advertisers. Lists are available for virtually any industry and can be further segmented by job title, number of employees in the firm, and geographic location, among other specifications. For an additional fee, many business-list brokers will also provide office telephone numbers, simplifying telemarketing efforts. Many business-to-business advertisers will use a combination of direct marketing media, beginning with a direct-mail effort to generate leads and then following up on those leads through telemarketing designed to assess just how interested the prospect is in the product.

Direct-mail advertisements range from simple postcards and one-page letters to glossy multipage brochures. In an effort to break through the clutter from other advertisements and grab prospects' attention, many business-to-business advertisers also use direct mail to distribute advertising specialties, useful items imprinted with the advertiser's name. For example, a printing company prospecting for new customers might mail out a race-car-shaped telephone packaged in a standard $8\frac{1}{2} \times 11$-inch paper box to highlight its fast pickup-and-delivery service. (For more on specialty advertising, see Bolen, Chapter 38, this volume.)

In addition to their ability to target likely prospects specifically, direct marketing media are appealing to business-to-business advertisers because the results of direct marketing campaigns are measurable. If the advertiser includes some sort of response device (a postage-paid reply card, a toll-free telephone number, an order form, or the like) in the direct-mail package, leads generated or orders placed as a result of the mailing can be tabulated and compared with similar counts from other mailings. Business-to-business advertisers tend to be particularly interested in advertising accountability, because the budgets of business-to-business firms are generally much smaller than those of their consumer counterparts.

Most business-to-business advertisers who use direct marketing media rely heavily on house lists—that is, lists of current or past customers and prospects. Because these people have previously indicated an interest in the product or service, they are particularly good prospects for future purchasing. The house lists are supplemented with lists obtained from brokers and other external sources as described above.

Business-to-business advertisers also make extensive use of magazine advertising, particularly focusing on trade publications—tightly targeted magazines that serve particular industries or, more often, specialized segments of given industries. For example, the construction field is served by such publications as *Concrete Construction, Better Roads, Masonry Repair Digest,* and *Construction Equipment.* There is even a magazine for those firms that market products to the construction industry, *Construction Marketing Today.* The specialized nature of such publications allows business-to-business advertisers to focus their communications and this results in little wasted circulation in trade publication media buys. Business-to-business advertisers spent more than $5 billion on trade publication advertising in 1994.[3]

Trade publications usually offer advertisers "controlled circulation." Rather than charge subscription fees, these publications identify "qualified" readers, that is, people working in the particular industry. These individuals complete a small survey (name, job title, type of industry, company size in terms of number of employees and dollar sales, and so on), and their answers "qualify" them to receive the publication at no charge. An independent organization, the Business Publications Audit of Circulation, verifies individual publications' circulation claims annually.

Trade publications typically provide several special services for advertisers. First, most trade publication advertisements carry a "reader service number," an identifying code number keyed to a postage-paid response card in the back of the publication. Readers who are interested in particular products or services advertised in the publication circle the corresponding numbers on this form, which looks like a bingo card, and then mail the form back to the publication. The magazine generates a monthly listing for each advertiser with the names and addresses of those readers who have indicated that they want more information.

A second service is the tying together of editorial and advertising material. Trade publication sales representatives routinely inform their advertiser customers about the editorial content of upcoming issues of the publication that might be particularly relevant for those advertisers. For example, an advertiser with a computer program that helps restaurants monitor their inventory would be especially interested in buying space in an issue of *Restaurants and Institutions* that focuses on computerization in the restaurant industry. The advertiser's sales representative would alert the customer and probably try to get the advertisement placed adjacent to an article on inventory control systems. Although consumer magazine sales representatives often provide a similar service to their customers, a relationship between editorial and advertising has traditionally been considered more acceptable in trade magazine publishing.

In recent years, many trade publications have also begun offering advertisers services that extend the magazines' reach. For example, magazines frequently sponsor trade shows, which gather their readers at central locations for in-person exposure to advertisers' products. Such a show might include workshops or seminar sessions that build from the magazine's editorial material, such as sessions led by the publication's regular columnists or editors. Or, if a magazine does not sponsor its own show, it might publish a special issue keyed to an industrywide meeting. The issue would attract trade show exhibitors, many of whom probably advertise in the publication during the rest of the year as well.

Another advertising vehicle sometimes offered through trade publications and other times as a stand-alone is the postcard pack. This is a deck of anywhere from 50 to 100 or more postcards, each carrying an advertisement for a different product. Typically, one side of the card carries the sales message and the other side has space for interested readers to fill in their names and addresses. The card is then mailed directly to the advertiser. Although the postcard format does not allow room for a particularly detailed selling message, the fact that leads go directly to the advertiser (as opposed to going through a trade publication) is viewed as an advantage. Also, advertisers with particularly limited budgets appreciate the reduced mailing costs associated with postcard packs, because the postage cost is spread over all the advertisers who participate in the mailing. In some cases it is possible for an advertiser to purchase category exclusivity, so that its message will not have to compete with those of direct competitors.

Business-to-business advertisers also make use of newspaper advertising, particularly when promoting business services such as financial products. Many newspapers in major markets carry a business section either daily or weekly, an ideal spot for a business-oriented advertisement. One of the best-known and most widely read sources of business information is the *Wall Street Journal,* which is published Monday through Friday. This entirely business-focused newspaper carries a great deal of business-to-business advertising, much of it purchased by the largest business marketers in the United States.

Business-to-business advertisers have recently begun experimenting with other advertising media. Many companies are putting introductory sales presentations on videotape and mailing the tapes to prospects on targeted mailing lists in an effort to increase effectiveness and pare down expensive personal sales calls. The business-to-business sector has also been quick to jump on the interactive advertising bandwagon, with many advertisers establishing sites on the World Wide Web. These sites frequently provide customers with the ability to place orders for product literature or products themselves, functioning as an additional distribution channel.

Similarly, other business-to-business advertisers have developed CD-ROM versions of their product catalogs. For example, an office furniture manufacturer's CD-ROM allows potential customers to view many different table, desk, and chair models in all available sizes, colors, and configurations, a quantity of information that would be prohibitively expensive in a traditional paper catalog. Because personal computer penetration is much higher in business than in home use, a business-to-business prospect is far more likely to be able to access computer-based advertising messages than would be the case in the consumer products market.

Business-to-Business Advertisements

Some important characteristics distinguish business-to-business advertisements from their consumer market counterparts. First, most business-to-business advertisements rely heavily on copy, which may often contain a great deal of detailed information about the product or service being offered. This is true even of smaller-space trade journal and newspaper advertisements and the postcard advertisements described earlier. Most business buying decisions are considered purchases, and potential buyers want and need product information to aid them in their choice of products and suppliers.

Second, although business-to-business advertisers sometimes experiment with emotional appeals, the vast majority of business-to-business advertising messages involve studied arguments and rational appeals for choosing a particular product or service. For example, testimonials from satisfied customers are a hallmark of many business-to-business advertisements. This approach reduces the perceived risk to a new customer; if someone in a similar firm has tried the advertiser's product and has been satisfied with it, the chances are it will also perform well for other purchasers. Testimonial ads often focus on improved performance and cost savings, important rational appeals for the business buyer.

Third, it is unusual for a business-to-business advertisement not to include some sort of response device. As mentioned earlier, the generation of sales leads is a primary objective of business-to-business advertising. Most advertisements carry the advertiser's mailing address, telephone number (which is often a toll-free number), fax number, and, increasingly, electronic mail address and/or World Wide Web site address. In trade publication advertisements, these response elements are in addition to the reader response number discussed earlier. It is common practice for business-to-business advertisers to evaluate their media choices on the basis of cost per lead generated as well as more traditional measures, such as cost per thousand prospects reached. And in addition to counting the number of leads produced by each advertisement, many business-to-business marketers also evaluate the quality of those leads. (Lead quality is determined by tracking how many leads result in completed sales calls and how many end up in completed sales.)

The Future of Business-to-Business Advertising

Business-to-business advertising expenditures are likely to remain stable, although the distribution of budgets across media types may shift. If the recent forays into computerized media prove profitable in terms of increased lead generation and/or increased sales, business-to-business advertisers are likely to move money out of trade publications and into increased computer investment. Computerized media offer the advantage of immediate response and immediate prospect identification, eliminating the time lag associated with leads generated through trade publication advertising. In addition, the virtually unlimited space available on a Web site allows the marketer room to include detailed product specifications and technical information. The current audience for the World Wide Web closely matches the profile of business-to-business prospects: predominantly male, professional/managerial, and well educated.[4] If this group continues to make use of the World Wide Web as a source of information on products and services, more business-to-business advertisers will be attracted to the medium.

Notes

1. Jonah Gitlitz, "Direct Marketing Boosts B-to-B Selling," *Business Marketing,* vol. 80, no. 8, 1995, 82, 84.

2. Direct Marketing Association, *DMA 1996 Statistical Fact Book: DM Advertising Expenditures by Medium and Market* (New York: Direct Marketing Association, 1996), 321.

3. Keith J. Kelly, "Business Ads Up 9%," *Business Marketing,* vol. 80, no. 6, 1995, 30.

4. Nielsen Media Research, *The Commercenet/Nielsen Internet Demographics Survey* (New York: A. C. Nielsen, 1995).

Product Packaging

The Silent Salesman

Jan S. Slater

I n the late 1800s, the local grocery store was filled with barrels that contained flour, sugar, coffee, pickles, crackers, and many other foods that were sold in bulk, unidentifiable and unpackaged. The idea of individually packaged products began late in the 19th century, primarily for protection and convenience in handling. The National Biscuit Company (now known as Nabisco), was one of the first manufacturers to begin packaging products, thus providing some differentiation. They replaced the crackers in the barrels with packaging that included an inner wax-paper wrapping, which kept the crackers dry and fresh.

Today, in the late 1900s, the local supermarket is stocked with more than 20,000 products, and product packaging has become a vital element in the success of the brand. The product package has exceeded its utilitarian use of containment, protection, and convenience. In today's marketplace, with supermarket shelves bulging, hundreds of new brands introduced each year, and advertising clutter reaching unprecedented proportions, the product package has indeed become the workhorse of the brand. Packaging has been referred to as "the silent salesman" by Dr. Ernest Dichter, one of the pioneers of consumer research and the founder of the Institute of Motivational Research. Dichter believed that consumers often bought certain products because of the package, instead of its contents.

Packaging the Product

The basic purpose of packaging is to hold and protect the product, and it must be easy to use. Therefore, the first feature of any package is functionality. The container must not only keep the product fresh, it must protect the contents from damage during shipping. Also, today's products require elements to protect against product tampering. In 1982, someone's tampering with Extra-Strength Tylenol capsules made safety and security an important consideration in package design.[1] Ever since, nonprescription drug companies have been required by the Food and Drug Administration to make their bottles tamper resistant.

Although tamper-resistant packaging overcomes safety concerns, many adults found the new Tylenol containers difficult to open. This was especially true of older adults, and Tylenol introduced the Fast Cap, recommended for households without children. Johnson & Johnson, the manufacturer of Tylenol, garnered the endorsement of the Arthritis Foundation for its Fast Cap package.

Convenience is an important feature of package design. Flip tops and twist tops relieved the mess associated with ketchup and mustard caps. Bacon, ice cream, and pizza manufacturers use a window technique to allow consumers to see the product through the packaging. Many lunch meats, cheeses, frozen foods, and potato chips come in resealable containers to make reuse easier and to keep the product fresh longer.

Retailers are also interested in the convenience factor, but for different reasons. They are responsible not only for displaying the products, but for storing inventory as well. With shelf space already at a premium, retailers are interested in packages that stack and don't take up much space.

Product identification is another important feature of packaging. The combination of trade name, trademark, and trade character—reinforced by the package design—can quickly identify the brand and differentiate it from competitors. In this sense, the packaging of a product becomes a communication device.

Package as the Message

In today's self-service retailing environment, the consumer is faced with endless aisles of products. In 1976, the average supermarket contained 9,000 products. Today, as I have noted, the average is well over 20,000, and in hypermarkets the total jumps to more than 30,000.[2] Research shows that more than 60% of all consumers' buying decisions are now made in the store.[3] Furthermore, the average shopper spends 20 minutes in the store, viewing 20 products a minute.[4] Indeed, it is the package that becomes the brand message in those few precious seconds. The package must do 100% of the selling at the point of purchase. And when the package works with the advertising—that is, when the package is featured in advertisements—it acts as a cue to consumers in the store, catching their attention and presenting that familiar brand image.

Acting as a medium of sorts, the package functions in two specific ways. First, at the point of purchase, it reminds, informs, and persuades the consumer.[5] When the consumer goes to the store with a brand in mind, the purpose of the packaging is to grab attention. However, today consumers are most often at the point of purchase without any particular brand selection in mind. The package not only has to grab their attention, it also has to convince them that it is great tasting or that it works.[6]

Second, at the point of use, packaging not only informs and reminds the consumer again, it acts as a reinforcement of the purchase decision.[7] Furthermore, many products are packaged in permanent containers, which act as constant reminders for repurchase. For example, Nabisco sells tins containing Fig Newtons. An empty tin acts as a powerful reminder to replace the brand. Procter & Gamble uses a similar technique with Downy fabric softener. Refills packaged in cardboard are used to replenish the large plastic bottle.

Like the name, packaging is a crucial element in establishing a brand presence in the marketplace, as well as in building and maintaining brand equity.[8] And amid the shelf clutter and proliferation of "me-too" brands, packaging can increase brand differentiation and brand identity. The package design must reflect the tone, image, and personality of the product concept. In fact, the package often reveals more about the product concept than about the product itself. A brand's packaging is loaded with psychological implications. The consumer visualizes the product through the package's shape, colors, symbols, and words, and forms an opinion about its value and performance.[9]

This is especially true of cosmetics and perfumes. With more than 700 brands of perfumes and colognes on the market, manufacturers use packaging to differentiate the products at the beauty counter.[10] More than any other category, the fragrance market is all about image, and in such a saturated market, if the package doesn't sell image, consumers will pass it over. The image that the bottle projects gives them an idea of what the fragrance smells like. The key, however, is for the fragrance package to be so unusual, so image laden, that consumers will stop to look at it and pick it up. Only then will they smell the fragrance.[11]

Package Redesign

Marketers are replacing old packages at an ever-increasing rate. As recently as 10 years ago, a new package design was considered to be usable for 8 or more years. Today, marketers review their packaging every year, when they review their marketing strategy.[12] Several trends explain why marketers redesign packages:

- *The growing importance of lifestyle purchasing:* Consumers are basing purchase decisions on the lifestyle communicated by a brand. As manufacturers tailor products to specialized and niche markets, package redesigns are used to reinforce brand equity and minimize consumer confusion.[13]
- *Eroding brand loyalty:* As couponing has grown and private-label products have improved in quality, consumers have been attracted to try different brands. Brand loyalty is turning into brand switching. To fight back, many companies are turning to redesigns to emphasize the brand identity that has been their power in the marketplace.[14]

- *Shelf information overload:* With the large increase in the number of products on supermarket shelves compared with 10 years ago, there is increased "noise" as all brands shout for shoppers' attention, with the in-store environment cluttered with competitive displays, shelf-talkers, branded and private-label deals, and now on-shelf coupon dispensers.[15] Marketers are learning that package redesigns cut through the clutter by giving a product a new visibility.

- *Replacement of new product introductions by line extensions:* Building new brands is expensive and risky, so many companies bring on new products as brand extensions, with package designs that keep the extended line unified.[16] In this way, the brand becomes recognizable throughout the store. Of the 15,879 new products introduced in 1990, two-thirds were different sizes, flavors, or varieties of existing products.[17] Is it any wonder that package redesign becomes a major factor in extending the brand?

- *Declining marketing budgets:* During the recession of the early 1990s, marketing budgets were slashed, and they took a long time to rebound. Packaging redesigns became a cost-efficient medium to communicate product benefits and added values at the point of purchase.[18]

Package redesign is indeed an efficient way to refresh the brand and give it new visibility.[19] Package design can be the most inexpensive tool in the marketing mix. As costs of ad campaigns escalate, package redesign seems a relatively inexpensive means of stretching valuable marketing dollars. The cost of package redesign with a new logo or label is relatively low, between $100,000 and $200,000 for a small brand, and seldom more than $500,000 for a market leader. In comparison, advertising budgets are $10 million to $20 million on average.[20] When Coca-Cola introduced Diet Coke, $50 million was spent on advertising and promotion; the package design cost $100,000.[21]

There is growing evidence that packaging has a strong impact on sales. It can yield the highest return on investment among all the communications elements in the marketing mix. Following are some examples of how marketers are using package redesign to benefit sales.

Rice-A-Roni, a well-established product with strong brand equity, was being battered by the proliferation of new competing products crowding the shelves. A revitalization of the package focused on the true personality of the brand, unified the line, and added a dimension of quality and appetite appeal. The updated Rice-A-Roni package has been credited with a 20% increase in sales.[22]

Rayovac, the number-three manufacturer of batteries, was facing the clutter problem as well. Brand loyalty for batteries is almost nonexistent; 70% of batteries are bought on impulse. Therefore, the packaging becomes vital. The redesign continued to emphasize the lightning bolt logo, but it became more vivid. The color scheme was changed from gold and black to neon blues and fire-engine reds. Rayovac's market share jumped from 12.7% to 17.8%, even though Duracell and Eveready outspent Rayovac in advertising dollars.[23]

Coca-Cola introduced its contour bottle design in 1899. Although it was changed slightly in 1916, the bottle was trademarked in 1960 and is undoubtedly the most recognizable product package in the world. Yet by 1990 Coca-Cola estimated that only about 1% of Coke was being sold in the glass bottles. The bottles were being phased out, and the focus changed to the popular aluminum cans and plastic bottles. But in order to stand out in the massive, crowded soft drink aisles, Coca-Cola returned the curvy fluted bottle to the shelves in 1994, adapting it from glass to plastic containers. Company officials attribute a 12% earnings increase to the reintroduction of the signature contour bottle.[24]

However, new packaging is not always the solution to increase sales. Following Revlon's repackaging of its popular Flex shampoos and conditioners in 1989, company revenues dropped 6% in 1990, largely due to a decline in Flex sales. The basic problem: The old bottles were clear, and the new bottles were tinted. Consumers liked the clear bottles precisely because they could see what was inside. Revlon is still trying to recover its market share, which dropped from 8% to 4%.[25] Clearly, the redesign of a package must always be considered in terms of its effect on package equity. Familiarity can be very reassuring to the consumer.[26]

Protecting the Package Design

Private-label products are creating havoc in stores as they clamor for shelf space, and comparable havoc among national brands because they are copycats. Usually, private-label producers copy not only the products but also the packaging of the national brands. Procter & Gamble filed 12 suits in 1994 for product infringement regarding packaging, trademarks, and patents.[27]

Distinctive packaging falls into a legal category known as "trade dress," the unique way in which a product is presented to the public.[28] Trade dress laws can protect the shape, color, and other nonfunctional elements of the package if they are distinct. In addition, copyright and design patent laws may be used for package protection as well.[29]

Trade Dress Protection

One court defined trade dress as "the total image of the product, including features such as size, shape, color or color combinations, texture, graphics, or even particular sales techniques." This definition includes a wide spectrum of nonfunctional design elements, from the instantly recognizable shape of a package (e.g., a Coke bottle) to the overall look and atmosphere of a place (e.g., a restaurant). The package distinction must be one of a nonfunctional nature to qualify for trade dress protection. A feature is considered functional if it contributes to the efficiency of or economy in manufacturing or handling, or if it contributes to durability.[30]

Design Patent Protection

The federal government will issue a design patent for a novel, ornamental packaging element that is neither functional nor obvious. Manufacturers often use both trade dress and patent protection for their packages. However, unlike trade dress protection, which lasts as long as the packaging is used, design patent protection is only for the life of the nonrenewable patent, which is currently 14 years from the date the patent is issued.[31]

Copyright Protection

Copyright laws protect original pictures and designs and sometimes slogans or phrases, regardless of whether they appear on packaging or in other media. To be copyrighted, packaging must contain at least a slight amount of original, creative text or pictorial material. For copyright infringement to take place, the alleged infringer must actually copy the package design, not merely come up with a similar package by coincidence.[32]

In our high-tech world, manufacturing and graphic design have become inexpensive and quick to produce, and the potential for copycat products is increasing. Therefore, more than ever before, companies need to protect their distinctive packaging legally. This reality also suggests that it might become increasingly difficult to develop distinctive package designs among all this competition.

Conclusion

The consumers of the 1990s are more value conscious and less brand-loyal than ever before. This makes it even more difficult to persuade consumers through advertising alone. Packaging becomes "the shelf medium." Dichter's "silent salesman" cues the shopper to recognize the quality of the brand and allows for differentiating among competing products all on the same shelf.[33]

Once considered a necessary evil, required only to contain and protect the product, packaging today has expanded into a powerful tool used to excite, motivate, differentiate, and communicate core product values and personality.[34] Although working hand in hand with advertising and sales promotion, packaging cuts through the clutter of "everyday low pricing," couponing, and trade promotions. Packaging becomes a viable competitive strategy that can overcome economic variables that are important in encouraging consumer loyalty.[35]

And, unlike its counterparts advertising and promotion, which often are seasonal or flighted, packaging is relatively permanent. A design may be in use for several years. Packaging designs for Ivory soap have often lasted 20 years or more.[36] The package functions on a daily basis, durably and believably communicating the brand message. It is a permanent advertisement, with a reach and frequency that no other medium can provide. The consumer sees the advertisement at the most crucial time of purchase decision—at the store, in the aisle, at the front of the shelf.

Notes

1. Roy Paul Nelson, *The Design of Advertising,* 7th ed. (Dubuque, IA: William C. Brown, 1994).

2. Eliot Schreiber, "Retail Trends Shorten Life of Package Design," *Marketing News,* December 5, 1994, 7.

3. Gretchen Morgenson, "Is Your Product Your Advocate?" *Forbes,* September 14, 1992, 468.

4. Schreiber, "Retail Trends Shorten Life."

5. Frank Tobolski, "Package Design Requires Research," *Marketing News,* June 6, 1994, 4.

6. Cyndee Miller, "The Shape of Things: Beverages Sport New Packaging to Stand Out From Crowd," *Marketing News,* August 15, 1994, 1.

7. Tobolski, "Package Design Requires Research."

8. David A. Aaker, *Managing Brand Equity* (New York: Free Press, 1991).

9. Murray J. Lubliner, "Brand Name Selection Is Critical Challenge for Global Marketers," *Marketing News,* August 2, 1993, 7.

10. Ian Murphy, "Perfume Bottles Make a Fashion Statement," *Marketing News,* December 5, 1994, 6.

11. Ibid.

12. Schreiber, "Retail Trends Shorten Life."

13. Ibid.

14. Ibid.

15. Michael Prone, "Package Design Has Stronger ROI Potential Than Many Believe," *Marketing News,* October 11, 1993, 13.

16. Schreiber, "Retail Trends Shorten Life."

17. John Blyth, "Designers Can Help Build Brand Equity," *Marketing News,* April 15, 1991, 23.

18. Schreiber, "Retail Trends Shorten Life."

19. Howard Alport, "Lesson of Recession: Make the Most of What You've Got," *Packaging,* October 1992, 92.

20. Morgenson, "Is Your Product Your Advocate?"

21. Nancy Giges, "After 150 Tries Comes a Winner Design," *Advertising Age,* October 18, 1982, M4-5.

22. Prone, "Package Design."

23. Morgenson, "Is Your Product Your Advocate?"

24. Miller, "The Shape of Things."

25. Morgenson, "Is Your Product Your Advocate?"

26. Thomas Pigeon, "Package Redesign: How Far Should You Go?" *Canadian Packaging,* May 1991, 28.

27. "Private-Label Package Designs: P&G Lawsuit with F&M," *Packaging,* October 1994, 3.

28. Pan Demetrakakes, "Private-Label Copycats Rankle Big Brands," *Packaging,* June 1993, 37.

29. Maxine Lans Retsky, "The ABCs of Protecting Your Package," *Marketing News,* October 9, 1995, 12.

30. Ibid.

31. Ibid.

32. Ibid.

33. Howard Schlossberg, "Packing Consultant Emphasizes Value of In-Store Promotion," *Marketing News,* November 8, 1993, 2.

34. Pigeon, "Package Redesign."

35. Katrina Carl, "Good Package Design Helps Increase Consumer Loyalty," *Marketing News,* June 19, 1995, 4; Melissa Larson, "What Do Food Retailers Really Want?" *Packaging,* December 1992, 28.

36. Cecelia Reed, "A Classic's Redesign," *Advertising Age,* August 20, 1987, 114.

Public Relations and Advertising

Ian R. Bruce

I f advertising decisions are most often founded on the question, Will this sell? then public relations decisions are often founded on the question, Will this help establish beneficial relationships? If advertisers are primarily interested in consumers, public relations professionals are interested in any group—consumers, investors, employees, or government regulators—that has an influence over, or some interest in, an organization's ability to function.

In 1955, the public relations pioneer Edward L. Bernays defined his vocation as "the attempt, by information, persuasion or adjustment, to engineer public support for an activity, cause or institution." [1] Others have characterized public relations as "enlightened self-interest." Public relations scholars Cutlip, Center, and Broom, after studying numerous descriptions of the field, selected the following succinct definition: "Public relations is the management function that establishes and maintains mutually beneficial relationships between an organization and the publics on whom its success or failure depends." [2]

This definition distinguishes public relations from other organizational functions in several ways. First, public relations is identified as a management function and not, as many assume, a marketing function. In many people's minds, public relations equates to "publicity," the task of attracting favorable media attention to an organization, its products, or its services. In reality, this is only a small part of good public relations practice. As the description above indicates, public relations recognizes that in a complex, pluralistic society, an organization's long-term well-being and optimal performance are contingent upon that organization's garnering the understanding and tacit approval of many groups and institutions, both private and public, not simply consumers. In fact, any group that is able to organize and exert influence upon an organization is relevant to public relations. So public relations includes aspects of publicity, the general functions of the press agent, and even advertising, but it also includes public affairs, community relations, investor relations, lobbying, issues management, employee relations, and consumer affairs. These different roles address diverse publics with often divergent needs, desires, and concerns. Good public relations recognizes and assimilates these needs and desires, and establishes an open dialogue between the organization and its various constituents.

An important function of public relations is to ensure that those in senior management are apprised of the climate of public opinion in which the organization exists. Indeed, good public relations involves being actively involved in the formation of organizational policy and strategy; it has been said that good public relations is born of the realization that public opinion can demand obedience. So whereas advertising is a communications tool, public relations is a management function: It is the deliberate, planned attempt to reconcile the goals and practices of an organization with those of its various publics. Like advertising, public relations involves communications. However, whereas advertising places an emphasis on the transmission of persuasive messages to large, relatively anonymous audiences, public relations is equally interested in receiving communications from publics. Whereas feedback in marketing and advertising is often reduced to aggregated counts of awareness or some similar variable, in public relations it is important to understand the substance of a group's opinions and attitudes, and, by a process involving management counsel, adjust an organization's practices or images so that there is an alignment of concerns and interests. This open, balanced dialogue between an organization and its publics (often referred to by public relations theorists as a *two-way symmetric flow of communications*) is a hallmark of excellent public relations practice. In this regard, public relations can be best thought of as the communications process by which an organization (a) surveys its publics, (b) ascertains those publics' salient attitudes and opinions, (c) develops and implements a management plan in response to these attitudes and opinions, (d) communicates back to the organization's publics, and finally (e) evaluates feedback.

Is public relations important? Ask representatives of the tuna industry about their reluctance to heed the advice of their public relations counsel and, in the face of public protest, adopt "dolphin-safe" fishing practices. Sales plummeted. Or ask the management of Perrier, who refused to address widespread public concern about the purity of their product. Or consider the tobacco industry's long refusal to listen to the concerns of nonconsumers, legislators, and the medical establishment regarding its marketing practices. Or ask the management of Johnson & Johnson, which largely credits the successful handing of the 1982 Tylenol disaster to a decisive program of action handled by the company's public relations department. In each case, the organization's ability to function was critically affected by the actions—or inaction—of the public relations department.

Aspects of Public Relations

Although the roots of public relations can be traced back over much of human history, the modern practice dates from the early 1900s. The growth of public relations in the United States parallels the rise in influence of the mass media, and early public relations practice was largely limited to the functions of press agents and publicity.

Although the goals of publicity are often similar to the goals of advertising, and the intended audience for both is often consumers, the two are different in several important ways. First and most obviously, advertising is a paid promotional message, whereas publicity involves the development of persuasive messages that are not directly paid for by the organization. Publicity works by attracting the attention of the mass media, who then report on the organization's message because it is deemed newsworthy or otherwise of interest to an audience. Although "PR hacks" are often chastised for their perceived ability to manipulate the media's news agenda through various gimmicks or "pseudoevents," in reality the relationship between public relations practitioners and journalists is complex and symbiotic.

Most journalists rely on outside sources for news stories, and the vast majority of such sources are trusted public relations professionals. In one study, researchers found that fully 58% of front-page stories for the *New York Times* and the *Washington Post* were taken directly from sources such as press releases, news conferences, and other public relations efforts, whereas less than 27% of stories were the proactive work of investigative journalism.[3] Public relations researchers have found that publicity programs are effective at influencing the news agenda only when they are well planned, well targeted, and newsworthy. Research has also shown that the most effective news sources are those whom journalists consider trustworthy (i.e., those who can be relied upon to supply factually correct, timely, and newsworthy information) and those considered expert (i.e., those in acknowledged possession of privileged information or insight on a topic).

Communications scholars have used the phrase "information subsidy" to describe the way public relations professionals and journalists work together to develop news stories.[4] Using arguments borrowed from economic theory and marketing, they suggest that there is an "information economy" in which some information is in surplus (an example is advertising) and some information is scarce and valuable. Public relations professionals supply valuable information to journalists (i.e., they subsidize the news) in exchange for favorable media exposure.

A second important distinction between public relations as publicity and public relations as advertising is that publicity is an essentially uncontrolled method of placing messages in the media. With advertising, all aspects of the persuasive message are within the creative control of the producer, whereas with public relations, control over the message content is given over to the journalist, who is free to edit or editorialize at will. This lack of control has an upside—increased credibility. Audiences that view advertising with increasingly jaded eyes often look upon news stories and other editorial material—even those stories that overtly promote organizations or products—as being more objective and as having the inferred endorsement of the journalist or medium. This enhanced source credibility is an important factor in gaining audience attention, especially in highly cluttered markets. Harman and Coney conducted a study on the perceived effects of source credibility in both buy and lease situations. In the buy situation (which they characterize as "high risk"), source credibility affected the attitudes of individuals, whereas in the lease situation (characterized as "low risk"), the effect of source credibility was negligible. These results suggest that the greatest benefit from publicity might be for higher-risk or higher-involvement products and services.[5]

Publicity is just one aspect of public relations. Public relations is practiced in business, education, government, and nonprofit organizations, with widely different publics. The strategies and tactics required in these different settings have led to a specialization. Consider the case of investor relations. Stockholders constitute a unique public with a special financial power over a corporation and the ability to express opinions regarding management decisions in binding votes. Maintaining a dialogue with investors involves open disclosure of all aspects of the company's finances and strategic plans. Often, as in the case of proxy conflicts or an aggressive takeover of one company by another, the public relations department will mount a campaign to attempt to garner support for management's position from the majority of stockholders. Such was the case in 1990 when Lockheed Corporation successfully prevented an attempt by the billionaire Harold Simmons to capture control of the board of directors by proxy. Solicitation of proxies involved letter-writing campaigns, a targeted campaign toward the many employees with stock, full-page advertisements in the *Wall Street Journal,* and even video news releases sent to institutional investors.[6] More recently, the information technology giant Computer Sciences Corporation mounted a concerted media campaign to fend off the $10 billion hostile takeover bid by software company Computer Associates. Interestingly, much of the PR work was conducted using the two companies' Web sites.

Another setting for public relations practice is trade associations, which typically represent the common interests of a group of organizations that produce similar products or services. In 1989, one group of trade associations representing the U.S. apple industry faced a crisis when a nonprofit activist group called the National Resources Defense Council (NRDC) gained considerable public attention for its claim that Alar, a chemical sprayed on apples, is a potential carcinogen. Senate hearings were called, and apple sales plummeted. In response, public relations counsel working for various apple-producing trade associations convinced three federal agencies, including the

Food and Drug Administration, to dispute the NRDC publicly. This was immediately followed by a public relations campaign extolling the health benefits of eating apples, and sales recovered.

Activist organizations such as the environmentalist Greenpeace and the gay rights group ACT UP often rely heavily on the strident use of public relations tactics to focus attention on their causes. Whole nations can also use public relations in attempts to influence public opinion favorably; for example, Colombia and Kuwait both hired public relations counsel to try to present favorable images of these countries to government agencies and the public at large.

Advertising as a
Tool of Public Relations

Advertising can be a tool of public relations. Most corporate or institutional advertising campaigns do not exclusively sell the organization's products or services, but are intended to generate goodwill, advocate organizational policies or positions, or enhance public opinion of the organization. The targets for such advertisements may include consumers or potential consumers, but will also involve other groups, such as employees, government agents, and the general public. Image advertising, which is intended to strengthen an organization's identity in the eyes of the public, is often used by large corporations operating in diverse markets to promote consistent, favorable images. Chevron and the nuclear fuel industry have both executed long-running image advertising campaigns to aid their public relations efforts and to counteract negative public opinion.

More controversial is advocacy advertising, in which an organization attempts to influence public opinion on a political or social issue. A company that has long practiced both image and advocacy advertising as part of a public relations effort is Mobil Oil. Mobil's advertising campaign has largely concentrated on print media, especially the *New York Times,* where it ran more than 1,000 nonproduct advertisements from 1970 through 1992, of which 37% were image advertisements and 63% issues- or advocacy-related.[7] Often these advertisements promote Mobil's sponsorship of quality entertainment or educational programs, such as Public Television's *Masterpiece Theater* and various museum exhibits. Often the message is remarkably forthright, as with the advertisements titled "Art, for the Sake of Business," which explained that the "arts can be your partner in the pursuit of excellence. They can help you meet your business objectives. And they can shape the public's view of your company." Mobil has consciously used advertising to help create an image of a corporation that is philanthropic, public-minded, and altruistic. It has also used advertising to expound the company's stance on numerous issues, including environmental concerns and the broad economic benefits of big business. These advocacy advertisements often chide the media for what Mobil sees as biased reporting of issues involving the petrochemical industry.

Advocacy advertising has three advantages over conventional public relations efforts to gain editorial exposure: certainty, consistency, and impact. Advocacy advertising can also keep a message in the public eye long after the initial novelty of a news story has faded. And if planned correctly, advocacy advertisements can generate secondary public relations effects and additional favorable media exposure. For example, advocacy advertising is frequently a tool of activist groups and cause-related organizations, and is often deliberately contentious.

In 1995, the organization Stop Teenage Addiction to Tobacco (STAT) ran a series of half-page advertisements that included mug-shot-like photos of prosperous media CEOs beneath which were shown their salaries. The ad copy bluntly accused the CEOs of taking "blood money" to help promote a product that the surgeon general had declared harmful and addictive (the campaign was timed for the eve of the publication of the surgeon general's annual report on tobacco products). As STAT had hoped, the campaign received considerable media attention when it was revealed that many newspapers, including the *New York Times* and *Los Angeles Times,* refused to run the advertisements. Ultimately, network news reports, wire stories, and front-page features were generated that drew attention to STAT and its cause. This example shows that when attention is paid to journalists' news values, and when executed properly, advocacy advertisements inevitably become part of the information stream and can themselves make news.

Sometimes, the generation of news stories from advocacy campaigns can come full circle. For example, when the tobacco giant R. J. Reynolds ran a series of full-page print advertisements gently suggesting that the dangers of secondhand smoke have been exaggerated, the story was picked up by the *Wall Street Journal.* The newspaper story was subsequently reprinted in its entirety in a second R. J. Reynolds advertising campaign that used the headline "If we said it, you might not believe us."

Public Relations and
Integrated Communications

Public relations should play a vital role in any organization, a role that is distinct from and complementary to advertising and marketing. However, the question of where marketing (and, often by extension, advertising) ends and public relations begins is hotly contested by practitioners and theorists alike. Turf wars are raging in corporate offices and in journal articles. Much of the recent debate about the roles of public relations, marketing, and advertising has arisen over the emerging concept of integrated marketing communications (IMC), which challenges many of the conventional ways in which organizations communicate (see Schultz, Chapter 32, and Deighton, Chapter 33, this volume).

Traditionally, the purpose of marketing was to "sense, serve and satisfy customer needs at a profit," whereas the purpose of public relations was to "engender goodwill among the company's publics so that these publics do not interfere in the firm's profit-making ability." [8] The two were seen as separate but equal. Today, marketing and public relations functions often overlap within an organization. The communications goals of the organization are likely to be strategically planned with input from all parties, and the result will be a single, integrated communications program. Responsibility for publicity and consumer affairs is likely to be shared. Advertising, although most often a tool of marketing used for promotions, can just as effectively be used as a tool of public relations to help garner public goodwill. In the same vein, some of the practices of public relations, especially publicity and focused media relations, can be used to great effect to achieve marketing goals. Public relations is seen as an essential part of the marketing communications mix. Often, IMC theory seems to subsume public relations completely into the marketing function. For example, when an organization addresses a public other than consumers, this is often referred to as "social marketing," and an emphasis is still placed on the marketing mission to sell at a profit. [9]

Many public relations experts disagree completely with IMC theory, believing that it reduces public relations to little more than a tool for generating sales. Broom, Lauzen, and Tucker argue that IMC assumes that the bottom line should be an organization's sole concern. They suggest that "belief in the sanctity of 'I sell, you buy' is simplistic and ignores the new reality of today's business climate. No organization can survive while ignoring the impact of social, political, technical and economic changes on its relationships." [10]

In part the vehemence of the IMC debate is a result of long-standing cultural differences associated with both parties. Marketing professionals are usually drawn from the ranks of business school graduates, where they are taught economics, finance, and quantitative analysis techniques. In contrast, public relations professionals are usually drawn from the ranks of communications graduates, where they are taught the skills of journalism and reporting. Inevitably, members of the two groups will have different perspectives. However, these cultural differences alone do not account for many of the fundamental and substantive differences of opinion that exist between the two fields.

The rise of IMC and the resultant pressure to integrate public relations into the marketing function has also been attributed to marked recent changes in the mass media in many markets and in consumer behavior. In their 1992 book *Integrated Marketing Communications,* Schultz, Tannenbaum, and Lauterborn argue that the era of mass markets and mass communications is drawing to a close. Markets are fractionating and the media are demassifying. These authors argue that the theories of mass marketing, in which a standardized product is promoted to an amorphous, undifferentiated public, are long outdated. Mass marketing is being replaced by niche marketing, with an increased emphasis placed on differentiating consumers from nonconsumers using relationship or database marketing. In addition, consumers are seen to be increasingly autonomous and increasingly sophisticated. In this splintered marketplace populated with diverse individuals, conventional advertising becomes less effective. Finally, Schultz et al. argue that the cost of advertising and the problem of market clutter are rising, and audiences are becoming increasingly skeptical of paid promotional announcements.[11]

With all this in mind, the IMC philosophy and the application of public relations (sometimes referred to as marketing public relations, or MPR) as a surrogate for advertising suggest a solution to many problems. After all, if audiences have a jaded view of advertising, then why not include promotional messages in the editorial content of the media, where they will have much greater credibility? And might not public relations programs be able to reach diverse and hard-to-reach audiences that elude advertisers in a fragmented marketplace? And if the cost of advertising in a cluttered environment is escalating, why not use public relations instead, the media costs of which are very favorable indeed? In many respects the concept of IMC can be seen as a logical reaction to the changed demands of the marketplace. Although it clearly makes good sense to integrate communications programs so that messages are consistent, this does not suggest that public relations should be reduced to being a lackey of marketing. Public relations should be independent.

Advertising and Public Relations Agencies

Many of the ideas of integrated marketing communications have been taken to heart by the advertising community and its clients, with the result that of the 20 largest public relations companies in the United States, 10 are now wholly owned subsidiaries of advertising agencies. Although advertising agencies have long offered public relations counsel (N. W. Ayer began a publicity service in 1920), the trend in recent years to offer "one-stop shopping" has been dramatic. At the time of this writing, the largest public relations firm, Hill and Knowlton, Inc., is owned by J. Walter Thompson Company/WPP Group. Burson-Marsteller is owned by Young & Rubicam, Inc., and Omnicom PR Network is owned by the Omnicom Group.

Advertising agencies argue that the integration of both functions allows for better cooperation between marketing and public relations. For example, they suggest that the more sophisticated research departments found in most large advertising agencies can better inform the development of public relations programs, and public relations agencies' greater experience in dealing with diverse publics can help create more sensitive advertising campaigns with broad appeal. Critics of integrated advertising-public relations firms argue that the public relations department inevitably loses independence because the advertising department will make the larger billings and have the greater economic clout. They suggest that much of the acquisition activity is financially motivated: The rate of growth of advertising agency billings during the late 1980s and early 1990s slowed significantly, while public relations agencies prospered at their expense.

Public relations firms can be full-service or specialized. Full-service firms are still dominant, but specialist public relations agencies are growing in popularity. For example, a firm in the Washington, D.C., area may concentrate exclusively on lobbying, public affairs, and legislative affairs. Which agency is preferable depends entirely on the strategic goals of the client. For example, to help launch its Windows 95 operating system software, Microsoft Corp. hired a public relations agency that specializes only in working with consumer products, because the firm felt that this is where its existing marketing and public relations expertise was weakest.

Many public relations agencies actually offer little more than publicity; they confuse public relations with unpaid advertising. In selecting an agency, the client must be sure of the nature of the services required. A good first step is for the client to prepare a white paper on the organization and its specific public relations goals. What are the target publics? What are the messages? How will success be measured? What public relations expertise is available within the organization? Will the agency be used for specific projects, or on a continuous basis? From this white paper, the criteria used to select an agency will become more apparent. Generally, four categories for evaluation will emerge: competence and reputation (years in business, size, examples of work); clients (existing client list, possible conflicts of interest, average length of client relationship); staff (qualifications of staff, staff turnover); and results and measurement (understanding of objectives, techniques to measure results, billing process).

Notes

1. E. L. Bernays, *The Engineering of Consent* (New York: Prentice Hall, 1955).

2. S. M. Cutlip, A. H. Center, and G. M. Broom, *Effective Public Relations* (Englewood Cliffs, NJ: Prentice Hall, 1994).

3. D. Nimmo & J. E. Combs, *Mediated Political Realities* (New York: Longman, 1983).

4. O. H. Gandy, *Beyond Agenda Setting: Information Subsidies and Public Policy* (Norwood, NJ: Ablex, 1982).

5. R. R. Harman and K. A. Coney, "The Persuasive Effects of Source Credibility on Buy and Lease Situations," *Journal of Marketing Research,* vol. 19, May 1992, 255-260.

6. D. L. Wilcox, P. L. Ault, and W. K. Agee, *Public Relations Strategies and Tactics,* 3rd ed. (New York: HarperCollins, 1992).

7. A. L. Page, "We're Good Guys: Image Propaganda From Mobil Oil," *Business and Society Review,* vol. 93, 1995, 33-37.

8. P. Kotler and W. Mindak, "Marketing and Public Relations," *Journal of Marketing,* vol. 42, no. 4, 1978, 13-21.

9. P. Kotler and E. Roberto, *Social Marketing: Strategies for Changing Public Behavior* (New York: Free Press, 1989).

10. G. M. Broom, M. M. Lauzen, and K. Tucker, "Public Relations and Marketing: Dividing the Conceptual Domain and Operational Turf," *Public Relations Review,* vol. 17, no. 3, 1991, 219-226.

11. D. E. Schultz, S. I. Tannenbaum, and R. F. Lauterborn, *Integrated Marketing Communications* (Chicago: NTC Business Books, 1992).

Part V

Legislation and Ethics

44

The Supreme Court of the United States and First Amendment Protection of Advertising

Jay B. Wright

"Congress shall make no law . . . abridging the freedom of . . . the press"—
these words of the First Amendment to the Constitution of the United
States that provide so much protection for freedom of expression were adopted
two centuries ago with relatively little analysis of their exact meaning. Does
the First Amendment protect advertising, or is such commercially motivated
expression so different from the political, religious, and social expression the
First Amendment was intended to protect that the First Amendment is inap-
plicable?

This question cannot be answered with a simple yes or no. The Supreme
Court of the United States has been faced with the question numerous times

since 1942, when the Court decided that advertising was not protected by the First Amendment. But in a series of cases beginning in the 1970s, the Court returned to this question, finding that some advertising in the United States is protected by the First Amendment, whereas other advertising is not. The Court created, then subsequently modified, a four-part test to determine whether advertising is protected.

The courts typically refer to advertising as "commercial speech," distinguishing it from journalism, political speech, religious speech, and so on. Despite the fact that some journalistic business enterprises make huge profits, they are not seen as commercial in this same sense. Commercial speech, as the courts use the term, includes both media advertising by for-profit companies selling products and services and advertisements by nonprofit organizations that buy space to print editorial messages.

For obvious reasons, it has consistently been important to the Supreme Court to recognize that truthful advertising is more deserving of protection than is false, misleading, or deceptive advertising. The latter is without First Amendment protection and can be regulated. The Federal Trade Commission, along with other federal and state regulatory agencies, typically does the regulating.

To understand the Supreme Court's views on advertising, it is essential to consider specific cases. The 1942 case referred to above involved truthful advertising for tours of a submarine—a classic test of protection for commercial speech. This case was *Valentine v. Chrestensen*. F. J. Chrestensen had bought a surplus submarine from the government with the intention of exhibiting it as a tourist attraction in the East River in New York City. The city's sanitary code prohibited the passing out of handbills to pedestrians because of the potential for littering. When police stopped Chrestensen from distributing handbills advertising his tours, Chrestensen sued. Chrestensen apparently reasoned that newspapers, to use one example, create litter too, but their distribution is not restricted by a sanitary code. The Supreme Court held that Chrestensen's motive was a commercial one, and therefore his messages were not entitled to First Amendment protection. In fact, as an interim step, Chrestensen had printed an editorial against the police on the back of his handbills—thus making them 50% editorial content and 50% advertising— but the Supreme Court thought his commercial intention was clear.

Although in today's world of multimillion-dollar advertising budgets Chrestensen's problem may seem minor, the Court's decision was anything but minor, because it set commercial speech law for three decades. It was cited, for example, to justify Congress's 1971 decision to ban millions of dollars of cigarette advertising on television.

In 1964, the Supreme Court decided the famous *New York Times v. Sullivan* libel case, which dramatically changed defamation law in the United States. The fact that the case involved a paid advertisement sometimes gets lost in discussions of the libel aspects. The *New York Times* had published, in 1960, a full-page advertisement by the "Committee to Defend Martin Luther King and the Struggle for Freedom in the South." The text was, in effect, an editorial. It described events in the South and protested the treatment of African Americans by "Southern violators of the Constitution." There were inaccuracies in the advertisement's description of events in Montgomery, Alabama, and the governor of Alabama and four county commissioners sued for libel. The suit by Commissioner L. B. Sullivan was tried first and resulted in a trial verdict for him in the amount of $500,000. An appeal eventually reached the Supreme Court of the United States. The Court held that, in the interest of free and open debate about their official conduct, public officials would henceforth have to prove "actual malice" (in addition to the other usual requisites for libel suits) in order to win. The decision in favor of Commissioner Sullivan was reversed, and the case was sent back to the state courts. Sullivan ultimately collected nothing.

Traditionally, newspapers were responsible under libel law for anything they printed, regardless of whether they wrote it themselves or were publishing something written by someone else. For that reason, relatively little of the Supreme Court's attention related to the fact that the editorial was in the form of a paid advertisement. Nevertheless, the fact that a case precipitated by a paid advertisement could result in such an important victory for freedom of expression is significant.

Valentine v. Chrestensen and *New York Times v. Sullivan* were distinctly different cases, separated by more than two decades. Advertising was clearly found not to be protected in *Valentine.* It would be wrong to generalize from the *Sullivan* decision to say that all advertisements were subsequently protected by the First Amendment, but the First Amendment grounds for the decision did amount to a recognition that, in some perhaps highly specialized instances, a message in a paid advertisement might deserve First Amendment protection.

Bigelow v. Commonwealth of Virginia (1975) provided an opportunity for the Supreme Court to return to the commercial speech questions. In a period when abortions were illegal in Virginia, activities to promote abortions were similarly illegal. Jeffrey C. Bigelow was the managing editor of a Virginia newspaper that published a paid advertisement for the Women's Pavilion, a New York City agency that arranged abortions. Bigelow was prosecuted by Virginia authorities and convicted, but his conviction was overturned on appeal to the Supreme Court. Because abortions were legal in New York, and the advertisements were truthful, the Supreme Court held that the advertisements were protected by the First Amendment. Obviously abortion has generated one of the century's greatest social-religious-political debates, and ads for abortion services are quite unlike the vast majority of product and service advertising. It is also important to note that the restriction against distributing handbills on the streets of New York City could be viewed as a *time, place, or manner* restriction that did not preclude Chrestensen's advertising his submarine tours in some other way. The Virginia statute at issue in *Bigelow,* however, would apparently have precluded all forms of expression about the New York abortion referral service.

An important principle was established in Bigelow: At least some advertising is protected by the First Amendment. It then remained for the Supreme Court to define more clearly which advertising is protected and which is not.

The Court had ample opportunity to do so in commercial speech cases in the 1970s. In *Virginia State Board of Pharmacy v. Virginia Citizens Consumer Council* (1976), the Court found that truthful price advertising for prescription drugs was protected by the First Amendment and could not be restricted by the Virginia State Board of Pharmacy. In *Linmark Associates v. the Township of Willingboro* (1977), the Court found that truthful "for sale" signs on residential properties were protected by the First Amendment. In *Carey v. Population Services International* (1977), the Court held that truthful advertising for birth control devices was protected by the First Amendment and could not be restricted by the state of New York despite the fact that some people might find such advertisements offensive. And in *Bates v. State Bar of Arizona* (1977), the Court held that truthful advertising by lawyers was protected by the First Amendment and could not be restricted by the State Bar of Arizona.

Although the Court stopped short of saying that all truthful advertising is protected by the First Amendment, it seemed headed in that direction until it decided *Central Hudson Gas & Electric Company v. Public Service Commission of New York* (1980). During the energy shortages of the 1970s, the agency that regulated New York State's public utilities had prohibited promotional advertising by the utilities. The utilities eventually challenged the restriction, because it prevented them from promoting the use of energy-saving devices in addition to preventing other promotional advertising. Supreme Court Justice Lewis Powell, writing for the Court, said that four questions must be considered in determining whether a restriction on commercial speech is constitutional:

- Does the expression concern lawful activity and is it not misleading?
- Is the asserted governmental interest substantial?
- Does the regulation directly advance the governmental interest asserted?
- Is the regulation "not more extensive than is necessary to serve that interest"?

Although this four-part test has since been modified, most of it is still intact, and it continues to be the basis for evaluating restrictions on commercial speech.

Just as some activities are illegal in some or all states, it can be illegal to run advertisements promoting such activities. An ad reading "Hit man needed to murder my business partner" would not be protected under the First Amendment. Similarly, if the purpose of the Supreme Court's recognition of First Amendment protection for advertising is to further the dissemination of information, then it would not make sense to protect false, misleading, or deceptive advertisements. But if the expression/advertisement is about a lawful activity and is not misleading, it is thought to deserve First Amendment protection. This is essentially the analysis in *Bigelow* that resulted in the Supreme Court's reversing Bigelow's conviction.

By adding, in the *Central Hudson* opinion, three more parts to the test, however, the Supreme Court was essentially saying that answers to the questions asked in the last three parts might outweigh the answers to the first part: Some governmental interests might be viewed as more important than the First Amendment. If legislators or regulators crafted the language of a restriction in such a way that it would further a substantial government interest and do so with enough precision that it could not be struck down on grounds of overbreadth, the regulation could stand.

But *Central Hudson* was not a case that would yield that result. Instead, when the Court used the four-part analysis, it found that

1. yes, the messages Central Hudson wanted to run were protected by the First Amendment;
2. yes, the governmental interest in conserving energy was substantial;

3. yes, the regulation would directly advance that governmental interest; but
4. the regulation failed because of overbreadth.

In other words, the Public Service Commission's regulation not only restricted what it might justifiably restrict, but it restricted other speech that it was not necessary to restrict. And so the Supreme Court of the United States reversed the decision of the New York Court of Appeals.

Because Central Hudson had won the case, it might look at first like just another case in the long string of victories for First Amendment protection for advertising. But the Supreme Court had clearly signaled that just because a government agency's attempt at regulation failed in this case, that did not mean that all such attempts at regulation would fail.

A turning point came when the court took up the case of *Posadas de Puerto Rico Associates v. Tourism Council of Puerto Rico* (1986). Puerto Rico had legalized casino gambling in 1948 in an effort to encourage tourism. The government did not want to encourage local residents to gamble, so legislation was passed that precluded casinos from advertising to the locals, even though they could advertise to tourists. The casinos challenged the restriction.

This time, when the Supreme Court applied the four-part *Central Hudson* test, it found that the restriction was acceptable. On the first prong of the test, the Court held that the advertising was about a lawful activity and was not misleading, so it was protected by the First Amendment. Turning to parts 2, 3, and 4 to assess whether the answers to those questions might outweigh the answer to part 1, the Court held that the governmental interest in not encouraging gambling by the locals was substantial. It also held that regulation would directly advance the governmental interest asserted. And when it examined that restriction for overbreadth, it found that the restriction was no broader than necessary to achieve that goal. So the Court upheld the restriction.

The decision in *Posadas* encouraged antismoking forces to call for a ban on all tobacco advertising. Such calls inevitably lead to assertions by tobacco companies that, as long as cigarettes are a lawful product and the ads are truthful, the companies should be as free to advertise as anyone else—despite the *Posadas* precedent.

Many observers were inclined to treat the fourth prong of the test, the one that said restrictions must be "not broader than necessary" to achieve their goals, as meaning that regulators must craft language so precisely as to regulate by the "least restrictive means." But the Court said not in *Board of*

Trustees of the State University of New York v. Fox (1989). The case involved a regulation prohibiting commercial demonstrations (in this instance a Tupperware party) in college dormitories at the State University of New York. Although the Court had said in *Central Hudson* that "if the governmental interest could be served as well by a more limited restriction on commercial speech, the excessive restrictions cannot survive," the Court in effect changed its mind in *Fox*. Justice Antonin Scalia, writing for the Court, said, "The reason of the matter requires something short of a least-restrictive-means standard." He thought such a standard would make it too difficult to justify restrictions on commercial speech. He wrote:

> What our decisions require is a "fit" between the legislature's ends and the means chosen to accomplish those ends, . . . a fit that is not necessarily perfect, but reasonable; that represents not necessarily the single best disposition but one whose scope is "in proportion to the interest served," . . . that employs not necessarily the least restrictive means but, as we have put it in the other contexts discussed above, a means narrowly tailored to achieve the desired objective.

The Supreme Court decided three commercial speech cases in 1993— yielding two victories for commercial speech and one defeat. In doing so, it provided more indications of what might constitute a "reasonable fit." *City of Cincinnati v. Discovery Network, Inc.* (1993) involved an attempt by the city of Cincinnati to maintain public safety and an attractive appearance by forbidding Discovery Network from using racks on public property to distribute its magazines promoting its "educational, recreational, and social programs" and Harmon Publishing Co. from doing the same with its publications showing homes for sale. The Supreme Court affirmed a lower court decision in favor of Discovery Network and Harmon. Writing for the Court, Justice Stevens said:

> [Cincinnati's] regulation is not a permissible regulation of commercial speech, for . . . it is clear that the interests that Cincinnati has asserted are unrelated to any distinction between "commercial handbills" and "newspapers." Moreover, because the ban is predicated on the content of the publication distributed by the subject newsracks, it is not a valid time, place, or manner restriction on prohibited speech. For these reasons, Cincinnati's categorical ban on the distribution, via newsrack, of "commercial handbills" cannot be squared with the dictates of the First Amendment.

In *Edenfield v. Fane* (1993), the Supreme Court struck down a Florida ban on in-person and telephone solicitation by certified public accountants. The Court distinguished the case from *Ohralik v. Ohio State Bar Association* (1978), in which the Court had held that in-person solicitations by lawyers could be barred, by arguing that CPAs (trained in "independence and objectivity, not advocacy") are different from lawyers and that CPAs' prospective clients are "sophisticated and experienced business clients" less susceptible to "manipulation than the young accident victim in *Ohralik.*"

In *United States v. Edge Broadcasting Company* (1993), the Supreme Court had to decide "whether federal statutes that prohibit the broadcast of lottery advertising by a broadcaster licensed to a State that does not allow lotteries, while allowing such broadcasting by a broadcaster licensed to a State that sponsors a lottery, are . . . consistent with the First Amendment." Edge Broadcasting is licensed in North Carolina but is near the Virginia border, and the majority of its listeners are in Virginia. Edge wanted to accept advertising for the Virginia State Lottery. The Supreme Court held that the statutes "regulate commercial speech in a manner that does not violate the First Amendment." In reaching that conclusion via the *Central Hudson* test, the Court found that

1. if allowed to, Edge would air nonmisleading advertisements about the Virginia lottery and that the Virginia lottery is a legal activity;
2. at least by implication, the governmental interest asserted (North Carolina's "antigambling" policy) was substantial;
3. the statutes directly advance the governmental interest asserted; and
4. the "fit" between what is necessary to serve that governmental interest and the statutes is a reasonable one.

On the last point, the Court said, "To prevent Virginia's lottery policy from dictating what stations in a neighboring State may air, it is reasonable to require Edge to comply with the restriction against carrying lottery advertising."

In *Ibanez v. Florida Department of Business and Professional Regulation, Board of Accountancy* (1994), Silvia Ibanez, a Florida lawyer/CPA, had referred to her credentials, including the fact that she was a "Certified Financial Planner," in her Yellow Pages listing and on her business cards and stationery. She had been reprimanded by the Board of Accountancy for engaging in "false, deceptive, and misleading" advertising—incorrectly, in the board's view, implying "state approval and recognition." The board pointed out that Ibanez was not practicing in an accounting firm and was not performing all the duties of an accountant. The Supreme Court found the board's position to be "insubstantial" and ruled in favor of Ibanez.

The next year the Supreme Court considered a case involving a dispute over a provision of the Federal Alcohol Administration Act prohibiting statements of alcohol content on malt beverage labels and in advertising unless such disclosures are required by state law. Adolph Coors Company had sought approval of the Bureau of Alcohol, Tobacco and Firearms for its labels and advertising disclosing alcohol content of its malt beverages. Finding that the regulation did not directly advance the government's asserted interest— preventing strength wars—"because of the overall irrationality of the Government's regulatory scheme," the Court struck down the provision of the statute. The Court also said that, even if the regulation had passed the part of the *Central Hudson* testing having to do with advancing the asserted interest, it would have failed on the part of the test requiring it to be not more extensive than necessary. The Court said that a number of alternatives, including limiting the alcohol content of beers, existed. The case was *Rubin v. Coors Brewing Co.* (1995).

The following year, the Court heard another challenge to alcoholic beverage advertising in *44 Liquormart, Inc. v. Rhode Island* (1996). Rhode Island state law had prohibited, since 1956, advertising the retail price of alcoholic beverages (except for price tags or signs with merchandise within the store and not visible from the street). Justice John Paul Stevens, writing for the Court, said that although a state might protect consumers from misleading or deceptive practices, "when a State entirely prohibits the dissemination of truthful, nonmisleading commercial messages for reasons unrelated to the preservation of a fair bargaining process, there is far less reason to depart from the rigorous review that the First Amendment generally demands." Applying the *Central Hudson* test, the Court held that the price advertising ban had not been proved to advance significantly the state's asserted interest in promoting temperance. Further, the Court found that Rhode Island had failed to establish a "reasonable fit" between the restriction and its goal of temperance. Thus Rhode Island's restrictions were struck down on First Amendment grounds.

The *44 Liquormart* decision was, in the view of many commentators, so different from the decision in *Posadas* that many concluded that the latter case was no longer good law—that is, that its result was no longer useful as guidance for future cases. The justices, however, were widely divided in their reasoning in the *44 Liquormart* case—thus leaving many questions hanging over commercial speech law.

The case law clearly demonstrates that commercial speech in the 1990s enjoys considerable protection from the First Amendment, but it is still apparently less protection than that enjoyed by noncommercial political, social, and religious expression. The Supreme Court put it this way in the *Fox* decision:

> Our jurisprudence has emphasized that "commercial speech [enjoys] a limited measure of protection, commensurate with its subordinate position in the scale of First Amendment values," and is subject to "modes of regulation that might be impermissible in the realm of noncommercial expression."

Some products and services—although they are perfectly legal—are less than socially desirable for a variety of reasons, including possible effects on public health, public welfare, public safety, and the environment if they are misused or used to excess. Although tobacco, alcohol, and gambling may be the most likely candidates for inclusion in such a list, all-terrain vehicles, disposable diapers, high-fat hamburgers, and even little red sports cars might make the list too. It is perhaps inevitable that government regulators will continue to test their authority to regulate advertising as a way of trying to minimize the sale of products and services that are seen as potentially hazardous or even just as less than socially desirable. However, so long as the Supreme Court follows its current course, regulators will have to be prepared to demonstrate that their regulations will serve a substantial public interest and will be effective and that the regulations are framed with sufficient precision to avoid unnecessary restrictions on other commercial speech that should be unfettered.

Cases Cited

Bates v. State Bar of Arizona, 433 U.S. 350 (1977).

Bigelow v. Commonwealth of Virginia, 421 U.S. 809, 1 Med.L.Rptr. 1919 (1975).

Board of Trustees of the State University of New York v. Fox, 492 U.S. 469 (1989).

Carey v. Population Services International, 431 U.S. 678 (1977).

Central Hudson Gas & Electric Company v. Public Service Commission of New York, 447 U.S. 557, 6 Med.L.Rptr. 1497 (1980).

City of Cincinnati v. Discovery Network, Inc., 507 U.S. 410, 21 Med.L.Rptr. 1161 (1993).

Edenfield v. Fane, 507 U.S. 761, 21 Med.L.Rptr. 1321 (1993).

44 Liquormart, Inc. v. Rhode Island, 517 U.S. 484, 24 Med.L.Rptr. 1673 (1996).

Ibanez v. Florida Department of Business and Professional Regulation, Board of Accountancy, 512 U.S. 136 (1994).

Linmark Associates, Inc. v. the Township of Willingboro, 431 U.S. 85 (1977).

New York Times v. Sullivan, 376 U.S. 254, 1 Med.L.Rptr. 1527 (1964).

Ohralik v. Ohio State Bar Association, 436 U.S. 447 (1978).

Posadas de Puerto Rico Associates v. Tourism Council of Puerto Rico, 478 U.S. 328, 13 Med.L.Rptr. 1033 (1986).

Rubin v. Coors Brewing Co., 514 U.S. 476, 23 Med.L.Rptr. 1545 (1995).

United States v. Edge Broadcasting Company, 509 U.S. 418, 21 Med.L.Rptr. 1577 (1993).

Valentine v. Chrestensen, 316 U.S. 52, 1 Med.L.Rptr. 1907 (1942).

Virginia State Board of Pharmacy v. Virginia Citizens Consumer Council Inc., 425 U.S. 748, 1 Med.L.Rptr. 1930 (1976).

Ethics of Advertising

Oxymoron or Good Business Practice?

Peggy H. Cunningham

An advertising agency, hoping to make an impression on a large corporate client, sent the client background research information and the creative it had developed for one of the corporation's smaller competitors.

A recent television advertising campaign for Armstrong flooring shows a man installing a floor and commenting on his wife's indecisiveness while she stands by, mop in hand, waiting to clean the floor.

A research study revealed that young children have higher recall rates for "Joe Camel" than they do for Mickey Mouse.

These brief vignettes all raise ethical issues related to advertising practice. Although none of the people responsible for what is described in these three examples overtly intended harm, they all have potentially detrimental outcomes.

In the first instance, the advertising agency breached a client's trust by revealing confidential information. Needless to say, the large corporation to which the agency sent this proprietary material refused to deal with the agency, because its lack of integrity was obvious. In the second case, stereotypes were perpetuated—women cannot make up their minds, and they are more focused on domestic chores than are men. In the final case, it cannot be denied that even though cigarette advertising is not directed toward children, they are affected by it.

This chapter deals with the topic of advertising ethics. It is not intended as a comprehensive review, but topical areas relevant to the practice of advertising are discussed. I first define ethics and its core concepts, and then review three different levels of ethical criticism in advertising (the societal level, the industry level, and the level of individual practice). This is followed by discussion of specific ethical issues pertaining to advertising and an overview of the ethical principles and codes that guide it. In the final section, I address the management of advertising, and I conclude that *advertising ethics* is not an oxymoron, but instead a sound business practice.

Ethics Defined

Advertising ethics can be defined as what is good or right in the conduct of the advertising function. It is concerned with questions of what *ought* to be done, not just with what legally must be done. Although ethical issues are implicit in most advertising decisions, few advertising textbooks mention the topic. The few texts that do contain some reference to ethical issues usually restrict their discussion to laws regulating advertising or to the codes of ethics governing advertising practice. Although good ethics takes compliance with the law as the base or minimal level of any ethical decision, ethical concerns go far beyond mere compliance with the law.

A number of concepts lie at the heart of ethical decision making. The first is the concept of *responsibility*. Both individuals and businesses form a complex set of relationships. These relationships have responsibilities, duties, and obligations associated with them. The advertising industry has a responsibility to serve the society in which it functions. Individual advertising practitioners have numerous obligations: the duty to comply with the law, the responsibility of helping their firms make a profit, the duty to serve their clients well, the obligation to treat suppliers fairly, responsibilities to their employees, obligations to the people toward whom their promotions are directed, duties to society in general, and obligations to themselves. Ethical dilemmas arise when these varying obligations conflict, when more than one group of stakeholders must be served, and when personal values are opposed to business needs.

The second concept forming the heart of ethical decision making is *accountability*. People making advertising-related decisions are accountable to a diverse group of stakeholders, both within their firms and among the general public. They must consider the concerns and perspectives of these publics when creating, designing, and executing advertising.

The final core concept is that of *intention*. For actions to be considered ethical, the decision maker must intend no harm to the parties affected by the decision. Some critics of advertising state that intention is an insufficient criterion for advertising decisions. Because advertising is so pervasive—almost environmental in nature—ethical advertisers must consider intended and possible unintended consequences of their activity. The third of my opening examples, which describes the effect on children of the "Joe Camel" campaign, is a case in point. Although the creators of the campaign did not have children in mind as a target of the advertisements, they should be aware of and concerned about the unintended consequences of the program.

Understanding Ethical Critiques of Advertising: The Different Levels of Ethical Criticism

Advertising, the most visible of all business functions, is a powerful tool that has a critical role to play in helping firms achieve their goals. This power and visibility have also caused it to be the function most often criticized for breaches of ethical conduct. Critics of advertising approach their subject from a wide variety of perspectives. This diversity has caused considerable confusion. In examining the ethical criticisms of advertising, it is helpful to understand that advertising has been judged on three quite different levels: (a) the macro or societal level, (b) the level of the advertising industry as a whole, and (c) the micro level of the individual advertising practitioner or campaign.

Societally based criticisms focus on the role that advertising plays in society as a whole. Ethical criticism of advertising at this level centers on the belief that advertising does not respond to needs in the marketplace, but works to create needs for unnecessary products and services. In other words, critics believe that advertising has been instrumental in creating a highly materialistic society in which the pursuit of possessions is valued above all other goals, where scarce business resources are wasted for no productive purpose, and through which environmental harm is done by the generation of large amounts of solid waste.

To counter the above ethical criticisms, the defenders of advertising point to its economic necessity. Advertising is an essential activity in a competitive marketplace because it helps inform the public of the features and characteristics of the numerous product offerings on the market so that consumers can make meaningful choices among them. It cannot be denied that advertising is a powerful force that shapes people's attitudes and preferences (if practitioners didn't believe this, they wouldn't be in advertising). However, due to this power, advertising has the potential to be used in inappropriate ways.[1]

The second level of ethical criticism comes from within the industry. Advertising is said to perform three core roles: to inform, to persuade, and to remind. It is the second function—persuasion—on which most critics of the advertising industry focus. Michael J. Philips, the author of *Ethics and Manipulation in Advertising,* claims that manipulative ads account for more than 50% of all advertising.[2] To understand why Philips makes such a provocative statement, one needs to appreciate how he classifies advertising practice. He clearly distinguishes between informational ads (those whose essence is rational persuasion that "induces change by convincing a person through the merits of the reasons put forward") and manipulative ads (all persuasive ads, especially associative advertising and "subliminal" ads that "foil the rational evaluation of a product by creating the illusion that it will satisfy conscious or unconscious desires that it may not, in fact, satisfy"). Those who criticize advertising on ethical grounds see persuasion as unfair manipulation of consumers that denies them their right of free choice. Those who defend advertising's right to persuade point to the fact that competitive firms strive to differentiate themselves through advertising and that this, in fact, increases consumers' knowledge and options.

Other industry-level criticisms center not on the advertising industry itself, but on the industries that advertise. Some people believe that certain products and services have the potential to harm the individuals who purchase, use, or consume them and, as such, no advertising should be allowed for these products. Well-known examples include products within the alcoholic beverage industry and the tobacco industry. However, the pharmaceutical industry is also open to this type of criticism. Although many drugs are lifesaving, misuse of them, overdependence on them, and using them in unauthorized ways is detrimental to people's health. Thus advertising that promotes their overuse or unauthorized use is seen as the main culprit creating this type of problem. Certain products, such as chlorofluorocarbons, are viewed as highly harmful to the environment. Critics believe that products containing these chemicals should not be promoted. Defenders of the right of these industries to advertise point to the principle of free speech and the right to conduct business within the legal framework of the country in which the corporation operates.

The third and final level of criticism rests on a more micro plane. Such ethical critiques center on the practices of individual firms and practitioners. At this level of criticism, advertising is accepted as an essential function that plays a valuable role in both business and society. However, critics want advertising to be carried out in a more ethical and socially responsible manner. They look at specific advertising practices deemed harmful, such as untruthful advertising and advertising aimed at disadvantaged groups.

Ethical Issues in Advertising Practice

There is such a wide range of advertising practices that have inherent ethical overtones that it is impossible to discuss all of them in one chapter. However, some issues have attracted considerably more attention than others; I address some of these in this section.

Truth in Advertising and Lack of Deception

One of the primary tenets of a free market society is that consumers have free, informed choice and that it is consumers, voting with their dollars, who govern business conduct. Advertising is the business function that brings this concept to life. Consumers cannot make informed choices without information, and it is advertising that brings this knowledge to them. Thus it is not surprising that truth in advertising is seen as one of the most central ethical principles guiding the business. This means that advertising claims must be accurate.

Although few people challenge this basic premise, problems sometimes arise with the manner with which advertising is created and executed. The question often centers on the limits that must be placed on such common advertising techniques as "puffery"—the inflation of advertising claims—and on metaphors and hyperbole. Although advertising slogans such as "East Side Mario's—the Best Italian/American Restaurant in the World" may not be literally true, advertisers expect that they are dealing with an advertising-literate audience (i.e., an audience that has no illusions about the sales objectives of advertising or the techniques used to accomplish those objectives). Such informed, rational audiences discount such puffery and exaggerated claims. Thus ethical advertising, like more intrinsically important types of communication, such as fiction and belles lettres, can use symbols, illustrations, similes, and metaphors to emphasize its claims.

An advertisement that is not literally true is not the chief issue. An advertisement designed to deceive or misinform a consumer is another question. Although placing untrue claims in advertisements is illegal as well as unethical, the possibility that an advertisement deceives or misinforms a consumer is a more troublesome question. Advertisements that provide only partial information on a topic may be deceptive, as are advertisements that have misleading price claims. Advertisements that display perhaps truthful information in a format that average consumers cannot understand are open to the same criticisms, as are advertisements designed to appear as part of the editorial content of a newspaper or magazine, or as part of a radio or television program.

Ethical Issues Related to Executional Techniques

There are a number of ethical issues associated with the techniques used to execute advertisements. For example, many consumers fear that they are bombarded with "subliminal" messages. Because such messages are, by definition, delivered at a level below conscious sensory perception, this type of advertising is often not only illegal but unethical, as it may have the power to manipulate consumer choice unfairly. Despite the fact that research has shown that such techniques are ineffective, the public suspects that their use is widespread.

When an advertising claim is delivered through a testimonial or an endorsement, ethical concerns also arise. The greatest level of concern is with endorsement: messages delivered by well-known celebrities. Famous sports figures and film stars have great power to influence the purchase decisions of various publics, thus special guidelines have been suggested and are used to govern this type of advertising and make it more ethical. The endorser must be a user of the product, and the endorser's statements must reflect his or her honest opinion of it. All claims made by the endorser must be able to be substantiated. Concern about such endorsements is so high that in some countries, such as Canada, they are forbidden for certain types of products, such as alcoholic beverages and items specifically directed toward children.

Certain executional techniques, such as fear appeals, have also drawn ethical criticism. Product claims such as some recently designed to promote certain bran- or oat-based cereals have used consumers' fear of getting cancer to advantage. Critics point out that these products have no more fiber than many other natural products, and that they may prevent only a single type of cancer, whereas the advertisements imply that they are a general cancer preventive. Such ads have been criticized as deceptive, exploitative, and manipulative.

Advertisements that use sweepstakes and contests have recently drawn scrutiny. Consumers may not understand special conditions associated with winning a prize, or, in other cases, the number of prizes actually offered. During the 1980s, the English Hoover vacuum cleaner company ran into problems with such a promotion. Hoover promised a free airline ticket to the United States for anyone purchasing a new vacuum cleaner within a certain promotional period. The company seriously underestimated the response to this advertisement and initially refused to honor all the claims for prizes. Only the threat of lawsuits made the firm fulfill its advertised promise.

The way the visual portion of advertisements is produced has drawn almost as much ethical criticism as the verbal text in advertisements. Because consumers tend to pay more attention to the visual elements of advertisements than they do to the accompanying text, they too are open to ethical scrutiny. There are ethical concerns around such issues as products that appear much larger in advertisements than they are in reality. This has drawn special criticism in the area of children's products. Many women's groups are concerned with the way models are portrayed. Special photographic techniques allow models to appear to be flawless, without blemishes or wrinkles. Critics say that such techniques establish ideals for people that cannot be reached. Attempts by consumers to emulate these perfect models have created much unhappiness and dissatisfaction, led to loss of self-esteem, and increased feelings of inadequacy and guilt. Models are tall and extremely thin. Although height is beyond anyone's control, advertising that influences women and young girls to starve themselves to the point of anorexia is being increasingly condemned.[3]

Creation of Detrimental Stereotypes

Advertising has been accused of fostering a number of demeaning or derogatory portrayals of various groups. Such stereotypes contribute to the way these groups are treated by the rest of society and to their position as underprivileged citizens. The portrayal of women, for example, remains one of the hottest ethical issues in advertising. Advertisements for household products have traditionally shown women as the primary performers of household tasks. When decisions concerning major purchases are depicted, women are often shown in supporting rather than decision-making roles. Voice-overs in commercials usually feature male voices, so even in this area of advertising practice, women are underrepresented.

An even more controversial issue is the objectification of men, women, and children. Women have long complained about portrayals of members of their gender as sex objects, and these criticisms can hardly be silenced simply because men are now being portrayed in a similar manner. Even more troubling is the use of very young children, posed alone or with adults, in sexually suggestive stances, heavily made-up, and only partially clothed. Adding fuel to this fire is the growing practice of showing only parts of human bodies as the central focal points in advertising. Many believe that such disembodiment denies the model a sense of humanity as well as heightens the focus on sexuality.

The elderly form another group that has been detrimentally treated in much advertising. Feeble, doddering, wrinkled old men and women are often the brunt of advertising humor, shown to be "amusingly" incapable of the most basic tasks. Their image in advertising is often a far cry from a reality in which elderly people are leading active and rewarding lives.

Exclusion From Advertising

Many advertisers argue that advertising does not create reality, but merely holds up a mirror reflecting society. If this were true, then one would expect many different groups to be portrayed in advertising. However, in the majority of advertisements in North America and Europe, models (both male and female) are young, white, and thin, or extremely muscular or athletic. Although some advertisers are beginning to realize the importance of targeting distinct cultural groups through the portrayal of ethnic personalities, much advertising still has a long way to go. Blacks are appearing in more commercials and print advertisements, but people of Asian and Latino origins are still relatively rare. Disabled individuals are almost universally excluded from advertising portrayals, and, as has been stingingly pointed out, elderly people are seen only in advertisements for dentures and Geritol.

Segmentation Issues and Advertising to Special Groups

The concept of segmentation—dividing the market for a product or a service into homogeneous groups that can be targeted with specialized campaigns—lies at the heart of all marketing, not just advertising. Despite the fact that this practice is essential for all advertising strategy and the effective allocation of resources, it too has ethical implications. Certain groups should be targeted with caution, because they may have limited abilities to process advertising information. This often goes beyond just reading the fine print in advertisements.

Certain segments of the population may take visual portrayals as reality, may not understand special conditions or warnings about appropriate product use, or may not comprehend the limits of an advertised warranty or the costs of responding to a promotional offer. In a society that includes increasing numbers of functionally illiterate individuals, this concern is becoming more important. Recent immigrants may have poor use of the English language and may not understand advertising claims. Some elderly consumers may no longer have the ability to decipher the information in advertisements. Children, particularly those from disadvantaged homes, may not have the sophistication to understand advertising. In a recent example of the kind of problem that can arise, children were targeted by advertisements for 900 telephone numbers that charged a fee to speak to Santa Claus. Many children—including latchkey children, who often watch television alone after school before their parents come home from work—called these 900 numbers without realizing the costs associated with such practices. They ran up bills for this service that their parents often had great difficulty paying.

Ethics and Advertising in the Technology Era

Advances in technology have enabled the growth of two practices: direct advertising and on-line advertising. A number of ethical concerns have been raised about these practices. In direct advertising, marketers use databases to target specific consumers and tailor their advertising messages to consumers' exact interests, needs, and wants. Although this can be highly beneficial to consumers, ethical concerns have been raised about invasion of privacy, the selling of mailing lists, and the use of consumers' personal information for advertising purposes. To avoid these criticisms, direct advertisers must protect the sanctity of their databases, fully inform consumers of the purposes for which they are gathering information, and respect consumers' wishes if they ask to be removed from a database.

Some analysts believe that there will be more than a billion Internet users by the year 2000. It is not surprising, therefore, that more firms are placing their advertising material on the World Wide Web. Paralleling the growth in the use of this medium has been growth in ethical concerns. Many of these concerns rest on the fact that currently there are no regulations in place to protect consumers who use the Web. Although many of the same ethical issues faced by advertisers who use conventional media must be avoided by Web advertisers, there are a number of special concerns. The first is truth in advertising, because the sources and accuracy of the information posted in Web advertisements are often obscure. The next is consumer protection. If consumers respond to Web advertisements and initiate purchases on-line, there is a small risk that unauthorized "hackers" may be able to access their credit card information and use it to make fraudulent purchases. New encryption technology is helping Web advertisers avoid this dilemma. Finally, because on-line marketers can track the people who visit their Web sites, concerns about consumer privacy and the use of this information have also been raised.

Guidelines to Ethical Practice

A number of ethical principles and codes of conduct guide advertising practice in North America. One of the first principles guiding advertising is that both individuals and businesses have a right to free speech. The free speech argument has been used by tobacco and alcohol manufacturers to defend their right to advertise. This principle is often pitted against a second principle, the duty of benefice. This principle states that business has a duty of care toward the members of society in which it operates and that more good than harm should result from business practice.

The principles of freedom of choice and freedom of action also guide advertising ethics. As discussed earlier, these principles are derived from belief in the benefits of a free market economy. Informed consumers who have freedom of action regulate business practice through their individual purchase decisions. Consumers' right of choice is paralleled by two other principles: freedom from coercion and freedom from harm. Advertising must not unfairly persuade or manipulate consumers into making poor choices. Truthful, information-based advertising is essential so that individuals can make informed decisions about the products and services they select.

In 1962, President John F. Kennedy gave a speech titled "A Special Message on Protecting Consumer Interest," which manifested the above principles. He stated that there are four basic consumer rights: the right to safety, the right to be informed, the right to choose, and the right to be heard. These principles are important to any consideration of whether or not advertisements are ethical. Ethical advertisements do not promote unsafe products. Instead, they provide consumers with accurate and truthful information, assist them in making informed choices, and provide them with an outlet to make their voices heard through public media.

Codes of Ethics

Both ethical and legal principles have been incorporated into the codes of ethics that guide advertising practice. Two of the most widely used codes in the United States are those produced by the American Marketing Association and the American Association of Advertising Agencies. The code of the American Marketing Association states that all marketers, advertisers included, must accept responsibility for the consequences of their activities and make every effort to ensure that their decisions, recommendations, and actions function to identify, serve, and satisfy all relevant publics—consumers, organizations, and society. All marketers must be guided by the basic rule of professional ethics: Do not knowingly do harm. In addition, all marketing practices must adhere to all applicable laws and regulations. Communications about products and services are not to be deceptive, and false or misleading advertising is to be avoided.

The American Association of Advertising Agencies's Creative Code includes similar dictates. Not only does it stress that false or misleading advertising, either visual or verbal, is a breach of ethical conduct, it also contains guidelines with regard to specific areas of advertising practice. For example, testimonials must reflect the real choice of the endorser. No misleading price claims should be made. No comparisons that unfairly disparage a competitive product or service should be featured. Claims made by professional or scientific authorities must not be misconstrued. And finally, no statements or visual cues offensive to public decency are to be used.

American legislators and persons concerned with advertising standards have recently been examining the Canadian regulations and ethical codes, which are stricter than their American counterparts. For example, Canadian law includes exacting provisions with regard to advertising to children. The code of the Canadian Advertising Foundation contains rules similar to those in the two codes discussed above. However, it also explicitly states that no advertisements shall be presented in a format or style that conceals their commercial intent. It forbids "bait and switch" advertising, stipulates that advertised guarantees and warranties must be fully explained, and prohibits the imitation or copying of another advertiser's copy, illustrations, or slogans. Furthermore, advertisers must not exploit persons with disabilities or consumers' superstitions or fears. The code also provides guidelines with regard to sex role stereotyping that include recommendations to display both men and women (of all ages and ethnic backgrounds) in authority and decision-making roles; to avoid exploiting sexuality; to portray males and females equally sharing household tasks; and to use gender-inclusive language.

Managing an Ethical Advertising Practice

Although the codes of ethics described above are useful for the creation of ethical advertising, they are not sufficient. The context in which advertising is created—that is, the moral atmosphere of the advertising agency itself—must also be considered. Although it is individuals who make and implement decisions, they work within organizations, and it is organizational norms, practices, and processes that influence ethical choice. In other words, factors within advertising organizations themselves must be managed so that ethical advertising practices are implemented.

Recent research has shown that one of the most significant factors in creating ethical behavior is individuals' perceptions of the organization's climate or culture. An ethical organizational culture helps members of the firm develop preconceived notions of what is correct behavior. This helps create an advertising ethic that can be used as a positive rather than a constraining force in the creation of effective advertising.

An organizational climate does not just happen—it is created by the people within the firm, and it can be managed. It has a great influence on the way problems are perceived and on the way ethical conflicts are handled. Managers influence culture by taking the time to think about what values are to be endorsed, about what goals and objectives are important, and about appropriate means by which those goals can be reached. Once core ethical values have been identified, managers must communicate them to all levels of the organization.

Managers also design and implement reward systems. Ethical behavior is often just expected and rarely explicitly rewarded. To draw the attention of employees to its importance, good ethical conduct should be rewarded just as much as poor conduct is punished. The process through which advertising tasks are undertaken is often as important as the end results of the process. Thus managers have to ensure that the daily activities of their firms are conducted in an ethical manner.

Individuals are strongly influenced by both their peers and management. Managers cannot just pay lip service to ethical codes. They have to "walk the talk" and lead by example. If a manager is unethical in his or her daily conduct, every individual in the advertising organization soon follows in that manager's footsteps. If an individual becomes aware that a member of a peer group has achieved success by following unethical practices, it is not long before the entire organization learns that such conduct is condoned and the entire organization starts down the slippery slope to unethical conduct.

Conflict is inherent in making decisions that have ethical components. Unresolved conflicts can lead to more serious types of unethical behavior. The viewpoints of many stakeholders have to be considered in the design of ethical advertising. Some ethicists have suggested that decision makers place themselves in the roles of the individuals most affected by their decisions, to help determine if their choices are ethical. For example, men designing advertising for women might want to think of themselves in the female role depicted in the advertising and ask themselves if they would be happy with the image they are creating. It is also important that the organization have a forum where ethical concerns and conflicts can be aired. Individuals who participate in decisions feel more responsible for their outcomes and are more likely to make ethical choices. Further, it is essential that formal procedures be in place for examining the ethics of advertising at the strategy formulation stage. The appointment of people to do audits of the firm's practices and to act as ombudsmen to encourage the expression of ethical concerns helps to convey the importance management places on these issues.

Ethics as Good Business Practice

Individuals who follow ethical advertising practices are not just endorsing "good" conduct; they are practicing good business. Many business and advertising managers are aware of the issues and concerns discussed in this chapter, but they still ask the question, Does ethics pay? Most managers and executives are "bottom-line" people, and this question is a bottom-line question. Although there is no direct evidence that indicates that ethical companies are more profitable companies, a recent survey by accountants Touche and Ross revealed that 65% of the corporate directors surveyed believe that ethical standards make a company a stronger competitor. Furthermore, many researchers believe that in the long run, ethical performance has a positive effect on profitability.

Following an unethical path in the pursuit of greater profit by its very nature increases risks to the organization, and such risks have costs associated with them. When conduct is illegal as well as unethical, these costs are in the form of fines and other legal penalties. Public concern with unethical advertising practices is growing. If the advertising industry does not respond to these concerns, it will be faced with increased government legislation and regulation. Not only may such legislation restrict the creative freedom of advertisers, there are also hidden costs of conforming to increased legislation; for example, firms will have to increase the size of their legal departments.

Advertisers, more than any other group, understand the importance of a good image. Unethical conduct results in the loss of a corporation's image and reputation. Considerable time and thousands of dollars must be spent to refurbish a tarnished reputation.

Trust is the glue that holds business relationships together. Client firms place considerable trust in their advertising agencies to serve their interests well. If clients perceive that an advertising agency is unethical in one respect, they may fear that this is an indication of how the agency generally does business. Clients who lose faith in the integrity of their agency will take their business elsewhere.

Good advertising breaks through promotional clutter, transmitting a unique and distinctive message about a product or service to prospective customers. Thus it is surprising that a minority of practitioners defend their use of unethical advertising practices with the reasoning that such practices are the standard in their industry and that all their competitors use such practices. If this were remotely true, unethical advertising would then lack the ability to differentiate itself from the throng. Advertising that breaks from unethical standards can be unique and can set the standard in the industry. It creates value for both clients and customers. Thus advertising ethics is not an oxymoron—it is definitely good business practice.

Notes

1. For a complete review of the unintended consequences of advertising, see Richard W. Pollay, "The Distorted Mirror: Reflections on the Unintended Consequences of Advertising," *Journal of Marketing,* vol. 50, April 1986, 18-36.

2. Michael J. Philips, *Ethics and Manipulation in Advertising; Answering a Flawed Indictment* (Westport, CT: Quorum, 1997), 16, 18.

3. For a complete presentation of the harm that may be caused by the inappropriate portrayal of women in advertising, see the film *Still Killing Me Softly* (Cambridge, MA: Harvard University, Graduate School of Business Administration).

Name Index

Tellis, G. J., 405-406
Termini, S., 197
Thorson, E., 209-216
Tinker, J., 11, 147
Travisano, R., 127
True North Communications, 10
Tryson, M., 205
Tucker, K., 480
Tyson, Mike, 193

Unilever, 118

W. B. Doner, 129
Wanamaker, J., 280
Warwick Baker & Fiore, 128, 129
Washington, R., 197
Wayne, John, 203
Weber, J., 91
Webster, B. P., 299, 301-307
Webster, J., 39

Wehling, R., 93
Weilbacher, W., 116, 123, 124
Weinstein, C., 222
Weinstein, S., 222
Weiss Whitten Stagliano, 45
Welles, Orson, 205
Wells, M., 11, 138, 147
Whelan, M., 92
White, R., 44
Wieden & Kennedy, 44, 129-130
Wolff-Olins, 134
Woods, Tiger, 439
Woolams Moira Gaskin O'Malley, 43
WPP Group, 10, 94, 482
Wright, J. B., 487-497

York, L. A., 309-317
Young & Rubican, 10, 11, 45, 482

Zielske, H., 167

Subject Index

ABC, 91, 276, 449
Abortion referral, 489-490
Above the line activity, 321, 403
Absolut Vodka, 64, 69-76
Account executive, 29-34
  briefing, 32
  "Four Ps" marketing tool, 30-31
  generalist versus specialist orientation, 31
  ideal skill set, 32-34
  salesmanship, 33-34
  See also Account planning
Account planning, 35-40, 41-49
  AAAA definition, 41-42
  account planner, 38-39, 41-42. *See also*
    Account executive
  agency structure, 36-39
  American versus European culture, 46
  award-winning campaigns, 43
  backlash against, 47
  British agencies, 37-40, 43
  creative philosophy, 42
  history of, 37, 43
  importance of client relationships, 36
  media planning and, 35
  scale considerations, 45-46

  significance of, 47-49
  training, 47
  U.S. agencies, 43-46
Account reviews, 121-131
  account switching data, 122
  client perceptions of excessive agency
    profits, 124-126
  compensation proposal, 129-130
  consultants and, 126-127
  cost of, 130
  creative work, 123, 127, 128-129
  credentials visit, 126-127
  final presentation, 130-131
  old-boy networking, 122-123
  politics, 131
  research, 128, 130
Accountability, 101
  agency remuneration systems, 119
  business-to-business advertisers, 456
  clickthrough metric for on-line media, 357
  direct marketing, 378
  ethical decision making, 501
  evaluating on-line marketing performance,
    371-373
  media buying, 94

About the Contributors

Beth E. Barnes is Associate Professor and Chair of the Advertising Department at the S. I. Newhouse School of Public Communications, Syracuse University. She has also taught at Northwestern University and Pennsylvania State University. She was educated at the College of William and Mary, and she received her Ph.D. from Northwestern University. Her professional background includes work at IBM, in product marketing in the field of consumer and industrial durables, and at DDB Needham, Chicago. She is coauthor, with Don E. Schultz, of *Strategic Advertising Campaigns,* and she has published a number of book chapters and articles.

William H. Bolen is Business Alumni Professor of Marketing and the Director of the Center for Retailing Studies at Georgia Southern University. A graduate of Georgia Southern (B.S., 1964) and the University of Arkansas (M.B.A., 1966; Ph.D., 1972), he joined the Georgia Southern faculty in 1966. He serves in leadership roles in various professional organizations, including the American Collegiate Retailing Association, where he holds the office of President, and Beta Gamma Sigma Business Honorary, where he serves as President of the Georgia Southern Chapter. He has written for numerous publications and serves on several editorial boards. In addition, he is the author of two books: *Contemporary Retailing* and *Advertising.* He is also active as a consultant to business organizations and provides seminars on various topics for the business community.

Rex Briggs is Vice President of Millward Brown Interactive and the leading authority on the study of on-line advertising. In 1997, he and his colleagues conducted the landmark IAB Advertising Effectiveness Study. Recently, Millward Brown Interactive won the 1997 Tenagra Award for Internet Marketing Excellence because of the company's methodology, providing advertisers with the right metrics to quantify the value of brand advertising on the Web. As a result of this groundbreaking work, he has been quoted extensively in the *New York Times, Time, Marketing Computers,* and *Advertising Age.* Formerly, he was research director of *HotWired* (Wired Ventures's family of Web sites), where he spearheaded the 1996 *HotWired* Advertising Effectiveness Study, the first of its kind. Before that, he spent several years at Yankelovich Partners, where he headed up major technology adoption studies, including the Cybercitizen Study.

Carri Brown, a graduate of the S. I. Newhouse School of Public Communications, Syracuse University (M.S. in advertising), is Associate Media Director at Ogilvy & Mather, Toronto. Previously, she worked as a media planner in New York City at Margeotes, Fertitta & Partners. She has worked on such accounts as Tylenol, Benckiser (Jet-Dry, Calgon, Electrasol), Godiva Chocolatier, MediaOne, and American Movie Classics.

Ian R. Bruce has had more than 12 years' experience in marketing communications and public relations in Europe and the United States, primarily in the high-technology area. His award-winning public relations campaigns have resulted in international media exposure, and one campaign was credited with raising the stock valuation of his client by more than 15%. He holds a B.Sc. in electrical engineering and an M.A. in communications, and is currently working on his Ph.D. at the S. I. Newhouse School of Public Communications, Syracuse University.

Jeremy Bullmore was educated at Harrow School and afterward served in the British army before going to Oxford University, where he spent 2 years not reading English. His first job, in 1954, was as a Trainee Copywriter with J. Walter Thompson in London, and he stayed with that agency until his retirement in 1987. He became, successively, Copywriter, Writer/Producer, Creative Group Head, and Head of Television; then, from 1964 to 1975, he was Head of the Creative Department, and from 1976 to 1987, Chairman of the London agency. He was a member of the J. Walter Thompson worldwide board and, from 1981 to 1987, Chairman of the (British) Advertising Association. In 1985 he received a decoration from the British government for his services to the advertising profession. Throughout his time in advertising he wrote and spoke frequently on the subject. Since 1988, he has remained active in the business as a nonexecutive director of the British newspaper organization the Guardian Media Group plc. and WPP Group plc. (the parent company of J. Walter Thompson and Ogilvy & Mather).

Rick Burton, a graduate of the S. I. Newhouse School of Public Communications, Syracuse University, is Director of the James H. Warsaw Sports Marketing Center and Woodard Family Instructor of Sports Marketing, Lundquist College of Business, University of Oregon. He received his M.B.A. from Marquette University, where he also taught promotional strategy. He spent more than 12 years at the Miller Brewing Company (Milwaukee) in sports public relations, advertising, and product management, and then served as Vice President of Sports and Entertainment Marketing for Performance Properties (Clarion Marketing and Communications). He has consulted for National Football League Properties, the National Hockey League, the Australian National Basketball League, Nike, Inc., and Universal Studios.

Peggy H. Cunningham is Associate Professor at Queen's University's School of Business in Kingston, Canada. She holds a B.A. from Queen's University, an M.B.A. from the University of Calgary, and a Ph.D. from Texas A&M University. She is an experienced instructor who has taught in Germany, the United Kingdom, and China, as well as in the United States and Canada. She has received a number of teaching awards, including the Frank Knox Award for Teaching Excellence. She is coauthor of the Canadian edition of *Principles of Marketing* (with Philip Kotler and Gary Armstrong). She is currently researching the advertising effects of cause-related marketing campaigns and the ethics of these campaigns. She also studies event marketing, marketing strategy, and international marketing. The results of her research have been published in a number of marketing journals.

John Deighton is Associate Professor of Business Administration at the Harvard Business School. He was formerly on the faculties of the University of Chicago and Dartmouth College. He has had extensive professional experience at Unilever, and his research specialty is in marketing communications and database marketing, with a particular interest in the strategic use of directly addressable communication technologies.

Erwin Ephron is a Partner at Ephron, Papazian & Ephron, Inc., a Manhattan-based consulting group, serving major advertisers, agencies, and the media. He is well-known for his pioneering work in recency planning, which has become the mainstream media planning model in the United States. He is also an unusual combination of researcher, media strategist, and entrepreneur. He has worked for Nielsen, held high-level media and marketing positions at major agencies, and owned and managed his own agency (Ephron Raboy and Tsao). He is the only person ever to have been elected president of both the Agency Media Research Directors Council and the Media Directors Council, and he is an elected member of the Market Research Council and an active member of the Advertising Research Foundation, having chaired several major ARF initiatives for improving television and print audience measurement. He is a founder of the Media School and a frequent speaker and writer on advertising matters. He is an honors graduate from Swarthmore College and holds an M.B.A. in economics from New York University.

Betzi-Lynn Hanc graduated summa cum laude from the University of Massachusetts at Amherst with dual bachelors' degrees. Upon completion of her M.B.A. at Syracuse University, where she did course work at the S. I. Newhouse School of Public Communications, she relocated to Boston, where she is a Services Marketing Program Manager in the high-tech industry.

John Philip Jones has been a Professor in the S. I. Newhouse School of Public Communications, Syracuse University, for 18 years; for 7 years, he served as Chairman of the Advertising Department. He is also Adjunct Professor at the Royal Melbourne Institute of Technology, Australia. He graduated in economics from Cambridge University (B.A. with honors and M.A.). He has 27 years' professional experience as an account director in advertising agencies in Europe (including 25 years with J. Walter Thompson), where he managed the advertising for major international brands of packaged goods. He currently works as a consultant to many leading manufacturing companies and advertising agencies worldwide, and he has published five books and more than 70 articles in all the important professional journals in the United States and other countries. In 1991, he was named Distinguished Advertising Educator of the Year by the American Advertising Federation. He is a member of the National Advertising Review Board. A specialist in the evaluation of advertising effects, he is the originator of the concepts of the advertising-intensiveness curve (AIC), the penetration supercharge, and Short-Term Advertising Strength (STAS).

Herbert E. Krugman started his career in the Psychological Branch, Office of the Air Surgeon, HQ, U.S. Army Air Force. He has been on the faculties of Yale, Princeton, and Columbia Universities. He became Research Vice President at Raymond Leowy Associates and at Marplan before becoming Manager of Public Opinion Research at the General Electric Corporation. It was at GE that he became a seminal contributor to the study of the psychological workings of advertising, and originator of the concepts of high and low involvement. He later became Principal of Herbert E. Krugman & Associates. He has been President of the American Association for Public Opinion Research, the American Psychological Association (Consumer Psychology), and the Market Research Council, and board member of several research organizations, including the Advertising Research Foundation, Marketing Science Institute, and Roper Institute. He has published 60 articles.

Aileen (Shih-I) Ku was born in Taiwan and was educated there as well as in Indonesia and the United States. She received her bachelor's degree in international business from Fu-jen Catholic University, Taipei, Taiwan, in 1994, and graduated with a master of science/advertising degree from the S. I. Newhouse School of Public Communications, Syracuse University, in 1995. She has been employed as a Senior Media Planner at Leo Burnett, Taipei, and as Account Coordinator at Investor's Business, Los Angeles. Currently, she is Media Director at Gauger & Silva, San Francisco.

Sidney C. Liebenson has been a direct marketing professional since 1974. He is now Executive Vice President, Director of Marketing, for DraftWorldwide, a global agency specializing in brand building, direct marketing, and promotional advertising. He supervises the Worldwide Marketing Resource Services for the agency, assisting in strategic planning and corporate training for all offices in the agency's worldwide network. He has worked with a wide variety of clients, including traditional and nontraditional direct marketers in various business categories, helping develop innovative, award-winning campaigns. A frequent speaker at industry functions, he has conducted direct marketing courses at Northwestern and DePaul Universities. He is a former Chairman of the Direct Marketing Association's Agency Leaders Group and served as President of the Chicago Association of Direct Marketing, 1995-1996.

Carla V. Lloyd is a tenured Associate Professor at the S. I. Newhouse School of Public Communications, Syracuse University, and former chair of the Advertising Department. She holds a B.A. from the University of Utah; an M.A. from the Medill School of Journalism, Northwestern University; and a Ph.D. in sociology from the Maxwell School of Citizenship and Public Affairs, Syracuse University. She is a widely recognized teacher who specializes in advertising media planning and has won a number of awards. She also has professional experience in publishing, retailing, and newspaper sales. Before she joined the Syracuse University faculty, she was an Instructor at the University of Miami in Oxford, Ohio. She has copublished articles with Dr. Dennis Martin (author of the widest-selling media workbook, *The Media Flight Plan*).

Abhilasha Mehta is Director of Research, Gallup & Robinson, Inc., Advertising & Marketing Research (G&R), in Pennington, New Jersey. Prior to joining G&R in 1993, she was Assistant Professor at the S. I. Newhouse School of Public Communications at Syracuse University. She has had more than 15 years' experience in advertising and marketing communications research, both in the industry and in academe. She received the 1998 ARF David Ogilvy Research Award for Outstanding Research Contributions to the Development of Successful Advertising Campaigns. She has published widely, including in the *Journal of Advertising Research*. She has also been an active presenter at the national conferences of the Advertising Research Foundation, American Academy of Advertising, and American Psychological Association. She holds a Ph.D. in social psychology from the Maxwell School of Citizenship and Public Affairs, Syracuse University.

Debra L. Merskin is Assistant Professor at the School of Journalism and Communication at the University of Oregon. She received her Ph.D. from the S. I. Newhouse School of Public Communications at Syracuse University in 1993. Her extensive experience includes working as an account executive and media planner at a number of small advertising agencies in Florida, as a broadcast media buyer for W. B. Doner & Company, and as media director for Bozell. Accounts she has handled include Heilman Breweries, American Airlines, Chrysler Corporation, De Laurentiis Films, and the Florida Lottery.

Her publications include articles in *Journalism & Mass Communication Quarterly, Journalism Educator,* and *Journal of Communication Inquiry.*

Eric Mower heads Eric Mower and Associates, the largest advertising and public relations agency in New York State outside Manhattan (the agency was ranked at number 87 on *Adweek*'s 1997 listing of America's Top 100 Agencies). Since 1968, he has guided his fully integrated marketing and communications agency in its growth to nearly 200 professionals, with offices in Buffalo, Rochester, Syracuse, and Albany, New York. Agency capitalized billing in 1997 approached $120 million. He graduated from Syracuse University with a bachelor's degree in the liberal arts and he holds a master's degree from the S. I. Newhouse School of Public Communications. He has served as Director-at-Large and Secretary-Treasurer of the American Association of Advertising Agencies, as Chair of the AAAA Eastern Region Board of Governors, and as Chair of the AAAA New York State Council. He currently serves on the National Advertising Review Board, the Coalition for Advertising Supported Information and Entertainment, and the New York State Governor's Task Force on New Media and the Internet.

David Ogilvy is a Scot born in England in 1911. Educated at Fettes College, Edinburgh, and Oxford University, he came to the United States in 1938. He had a variety of jobs between the time he left Oxford and his founding of Ogilvy & Mather in New York in 1948. By the time he had retired, Ogilvy & Mather had become one of the leading advertising agencies in the world. With a background in market research, he made his name as a creative thinker and writer of forceful and elegant advertising. Without any question, he is the most important figure in the advertising world since the 1950s. This series of volumes is dedicated to him.

Damian O'Malley is a Director of O'Malley and Hogan Ltd., a marketing company based in Dublin, Ireland, that provides fresh insights into consumer self-construction and new thinking on the definition and successful management of brands—international brand architecture. He launched the company with partner Declan Hogan in November 1997. They are working with domestic and international clients to develop and implement brand and communication programs based on rigorous strategic analysis and brilliant creativity. He has a unique breadth of account planning and marketing experience. In 1977 he began his career in the United Kingdom at the home of account planning, Boase Massimi Pollitt. He founded his own agency, Woollams

Moira Gaskin O'Malley, 10 years later; for 5 years, he was Executive Vice President and Strategic Planning Director of the New York Office of DDB Needham.

Nujchayada Pangsapa is an account executive at Grey (Thailand) Limited in Bangkok, where she handles Procter & Gamble's Pantene Pro-V hair-care account. She graduated with a master's degree in advertising from the S. I. Newhouse School of Public Communications, Syracuse University in 1996, having completed her undergraduate studies in marketing at the Lubin School of Business, Pace University, where she earned a bachelor's degree in business administration in 1994.

Stephen P. Phelps is a nationally recognized media professional, with a career spanning more than 20 years at Leo Burnett and D'Arcy Masius Benton & Bowles, ending as Senior Vice President and Media Director, with experience with major repeat-purchase packaged goods clients. A former Chair of the New Media Model Committee at the Advertising Research Foundation and Assistant Professor at Southern Illinois University at Carbondale, he is currently Executive Director of the Council of Lutheran Churches of Greater St. Louis.

Paula Pierce is Vice President, Director of Qualitative Services, for McCollum Spielman Worldwide (MSW). She holds a B.A. in psychology and sociology from Fairleigh Dickinson University, and has completed doctoral course work at the City University of New York Graduate Center. She is heavily involved in the development and direction of MSW's international, multicultural projects, qualitative, quantitative, and custom. With some 20 years in the business, her experience encompasses concept, strategy, copy, and product and packaging evaluation, as well as attitude/usage and customer satisfaction studies. She writes and edits MSW's newsletter, *Topline,* and has written many MSW white papers on topics such as celebrities in advertising, humor in advertising, emotional advertising, and multicultural advertising. She has had articles published in the *Journal of Advertising Research, Quirk's,* and other industry journals, and has recently contributed chapters to the marketing/advertising college textbooks edited by Larry Percy and Giep Franzen. She is a member of the Qualitative Research Consultant Association.

Jay Quinn was educated at the College of the Holy Cross, Worcester, Massachusetts, and has a master's degree in advertising from the S. I. Newhouse School of Public Communications, Syracuse University. He joined

Eric Mower and Associates, Syracuse, in 1974 as Account Executive. He was made Executive Vice President in 1987 and appointed Managing Partner of Eric Mower's Rochester office in 1994. He has extensive experience of a wide variety of advertising clients and is an active member of many professional organizations.

Jeremiah L. Rosen received his master's degree from the S. I. Newhouse School of Public Communications, Syracuse University, in 1996. That same year, he also graduated from the Syracuse University College of Law with a J.D. In August 1996 he moved to New York City to begin a career in advertising at N. W. Ayer & Partners. Since November 1997, he has been an Account Executive working on the Coca-Cola account at Wieden & Kennedy in Portland, Oregon. He is a member of the New York State Bar Association.

Randall Rothenberg, a graduate of Princeton University, is an author and journalist who has covered communications, technology, and culture for 20 years. He is the author of *Where the Suckers Moon: An Advertising Story* (1994), the chronicle of the birth, evolution, life, and death of a single advertising image. He is also author of *The Neoliberals: Creating the New American Politics* (1984), the first book to detail the rise of the "New Democratic Party." From 1986 to 1991, he worked at the *New York Times* as the science, technology, and food editor of its *Sunday Magazine,* and as a media reporter and the daily advertising columnist. Subsequently, he served as a senior consulting editor for *Bloomberg Business News* in Europe, and as a writer, columnist, and editorial director at *Esquire* magazine. He is currently a contributing editor to *Wired* magazine.

Rana S. Said is a graduate of Valparaiso University, Indiana, and received her M.S. in advertising from the S. I. Newhouse School of Public Communications, Syracuse University. An experienced traffic manager, she is currently an account manager in an advertising agency in Dubai, United Arab Emirates, handling a number of local and international accounts. In the early 1990s she held the position of Advertising Instructor at Syracuse University, teaching the principles of advertising, and has been teaching at the American University in Dubai, specializing in integrated marketing communications and the environmental/economic factors influencing buying behavior. In 1991, she participated in a research project devoted to this topic that was published in *Adweek.*

Don E. Schultz is Professor of Integrated Marketing Communication, Medill School of Journalism, Northwestern University. He is also President of the consulting firm Agora, Inc., in Evanston, Illinois, and Senior Partner of Targetbase Marketing International in Dallas, Texas. He holds a marketing/journalism degree from the University of Oklahoma, a master's in advertising, and a Ph.D. in mass media from Michigan State University. After 10 years with Tracy-Locke Advertising, where he resigned as Senior Vice President, he reentered academia and has been on the faculty of Northwestern since 1977. He has authored many books and articles, including *Integrated Marketing Communications,* the seminal text in the area, and *Measuring Brand Communication ROI.* He lectures, consults, and gives seminars all over the world, is a member of numerous professional and academic organizations, and has been recognized repeatedly for contributions in the area of marketing and communication.

John L. Sellers is Professor of Visual Communications at Syracuse University. He received an M.A. from the George Peabody College for Teachers in 1961. After an award-winning professional career in advertising and publishing, he began teaching advertising design at Syracuse University. He has advised 1,000-plus undergraduate and 300-plus graduate students, most of whom are now art directors, copywriters, creative directors, agency partners, and/or advertising faculty members, internationally.

Jan S. Slater is Assistant Professor of Advertising in the E. W. Scripps School of Journalism at Ohio University in Athens, Ohio. Prior to her appointment at Ohio University, she was Assistant Professor and coordinator of the advertising major at Xavier University in Cincinnati, Ohio, and an Instructor in Advertising at the S. I. Newhouse School of Public Communications at Syracuse University as well as at the University of Nebraska in Omaha. In addition to her 10 years of teaching experience, she has 20 years' experience in the advertising industry, having worked in both private industry and advertising agencies. Until 1990, she owned her own agency, J. Slater & Associates in Omaha, Nebraska. She earned her B.A. from Hastings College in Hastings, Nebraska; an M.S. in advertising from the University of Illinois, Champaign-Urbana; and a Ph.D. in mass communications from the S. I. Newhouse School of Public Communications at Syracuse University.

Emily Soell is Vice Chairman, Chief Creative Officer of DraftWorldwide, the world's second-largest direct marketing agency. She began her career at Rapp

Collins, training with Tom Collins and Stan Rapp—two of the industry's most respected practitioners—and rose from Copywriter to Executive Creative Director before joining Draft in 1996. She has created direct-acting advertising for such accounts as American Express, Avis, Chase Bank, Condé Nast, Delta Airlines, Gillette, Hyatt Hotels, IBM, Pharmacia & Upjohn, Philip Morris, and Mercedes Benz. She was named the 1995 Direct Marketer of the Year by Target Marketing. She has also won the Irving Wunderman Award for a lifetime body of creative work, and was named "Woman of the Year" by the Women's Direct Response Group. She has served on the Board of the Direct Marketing Association and helped create the direct marketing curriculum at New York University, where she has also taught.

Nicholas Staveley (1934-1994) was a British advertising practitioner and journalist. He spent his childhood in the United States, but attended Rugby School in Britain and graduated from Oxford University. He had extensive advertising agency experience in London at Ogilvy & Mather and J. Walter Thompson. From 1972 he held senior marketing positions at Unilever, the International Wool Secretariat, and British Telecom. He ran his own consulting business from 1988 to 1994, and served as Editor of *Admap* from 1990 to 1994. His chapter in this volume is his last piece of work.

Shirley F. Taylor is Associate Professor of Marketing in the School of Business at Queen's University in Kingston, Ontario. Her research revolves around three streams: event marketing, services marketing, and predicting the adoption of new behaviors.

Esther Thorson was educated at Macalester College and the University of Minnesota (Ph.D. in psychology). She has taught at Denison University and the University of Wisconsin–Madison. She is currently Associate Dean for Graduate Studies and Research at the School of Journalism, University of Missouri at Columbia, and Acting Director of the Center for Advanced Social Research. She has published many papers on perception, memory, and emotional processes, as well as on political advertising. She is coauthor of *Integrated Communications: The Synergy of Permissive Voices.*

Brian Philip Webster is Production Manager with Internet and travel and resort television provider, Resort Sports Network. He is also a production freelancer for such groups as E!, NBC Nightly News, Harpo Productions, and Lifetime. He received an M.S. in media administration from the S. I. Newhouse School of Public Communications, Syracuse University, and a B.S.

in communications, television field production, from Fredonia College. His career began with a 2-year stint as a mastercontrol operator/sports-news photographer for WTZA in Kingston, New York. He has since worked extensively in news production with NBC Syracuse on its number-one morning news program. He currently specializes in mountain sports and auto racing videography. He is involved in syndicated negotiations on a day-to-day basis.

Jay B. Wright is Professor at the S. I. Newhouse School of Public Communications, Syracuse University, where he teaches communications law. His bachelor's and master's degrees in advertising are from the Medill School of Journalism, Northwestern University, and his Ph.D. in mass communications is from Syracuse. He earned a master of studies in law degree from Yale Law School as a postdoctoral Ford Foundation Fellow. He has also taught at Northwestern University and at the College of Law, Syracuse University. He is the coauthor of three books on communications law: *The First Amendment and the Fourth Estate* (7th edition, 1997), *The First Amendment and the Fifth Estate* (4th edition, 1996), and *The Legal Handbook for New York State Journalists* (3rd edition, 1998). He is a former advertising agency copywriter and was Executive Director of the New York Fair Trial Free Press Conference.

Laura A. York graduated cum laude from Miami University, Oxford, Ohio, and received her M.S. in advertising from the S. I. Newhouse School of Public Communications, Syracuse University. She is currently an Account Executive at Arnold Communications in Boston, Massachusetts.